Edmund Spenser

Edited by Paul J. Alpers

Edmund Spenser

A critical anthology

edited by Paul J. Alpers

Penguin Books

15,145

Penguin Books Ltd, Harmondsworth,
Middlesex, England
Penguin Books Inc., 7110 Ambassador Road,
Baltimore, Md 21207, U.S.A.
Penguin Books Australia Ltd, Ringwood,
Victoria, Australia

First published 1969
This selection copyright © Penguin Books Ltd, 1969
Introduction and notes copyright © Penguin Books Ltd, 1969

Made and printed in Great Britain by
Hazell Watson & Viney
Set in Monotype Bembo

Contents

Part Two **Neoclassical and Romantic Criticism**

7 Contents

8 Contents

10 Contents

Preface

This anthology needs no special introduction, but I would like to pass on to the reader some words that appeared while the book was in the press which seem to me particularly relevant to its purposes and materials. The American poet Hayden Carruth – taught by the critics and poets he most admired to scorn *The Faerie Queene* – has recently written (*Hudson Review*, Spring 1969) of reading the poem seriously for the first time, and of his surprise and delight in finding it continually alive and interesting, fully engaged with truths and problems that still concern us today. He also read for the first time some Spenser criticism of past centuries, about which he says:

It is easy to say what the poem is not, much harder to say what it is; which explains the long critical labor that has attended it. From the beginning men of sensibility have tried to define the poem and their own responses to it. . . . Much of this work is brilliant. I do not see how anyone who looks into even a little of it . . . can fail to be struck by the human splendor of this love that only intelligence can display: so much warmth of heart engendered by great words on a printed page.

I hope the reader will find these words justified and that this book will assist his own discovery, or re-discovery, of Spenser's great work.

Otherwise I need only note some technical details. All quotations from Spenser have been made to conform to the Oxford texts edited by J. C. Smith and E. de Selincourt. The sixteenth, seventeenth and eighteenth century texts have been modernized. All translations and glosses are the work of the present editor unless otherwise stated; the glosses are based on the glossary in the Oxford Standard Authors edition. All other kinds of footnotes are the work of the individual authors, unless otherwise stated.

I should like to thank Kathryn Guberman for painstaking assistance of many kinds, and David Evett for the bibliographical help given by his Harvard dissertation on nineteenth-century Spenser criticism.

Table of Dates

1582   Grey recalled to England; Spenser leases New Abbey, Kilcullen (twenty-five miles south-west of Dublin).

?1584   Becomes deputy to his friend Lodowick Bryskett, clerk of the council at Munster.

1588   Becomes proprietor of the manor of Kilcolman, as part of a general English resettlement of Munster, which had been laid waste in combating the Desmond rebellion. A stanza of *The Faerie Queene* (II iv 35, identified as such) is quoted in Abraham Fraunce's *Arcadian Rhetorike* (i.e. parts of the poem were circulating in manuscript in London).

1589   Sir Walter Raleigh visits Spenser at Kilcolman, and Spenser returns with him to England.

1590   Publication of *The Faerie Queene*, Books I–III.

1591   Spenser granted an annual pension of fifty pounds. Returns to Ireland (he seems to have returned for a brief visit in 1590). Publication of *Daphnaida*, an elegy on the death of Lady Douglas Howard, wife of Sir Arthur Gorges. Publication of *Complaints*, a collection of poems written in the preceding decade. They are (in the order in which they appear in the volume) *The Ruines of Time, The Teares of the Muses, Virgils Gnat, Prosopopoia: or Mother Hubberds Tale, Ruines of Rome: by Bellay, Muiopotmos: or The Fate of the Butterflie, Visions of the Worlds Vanitie, The Visions of Bellay, The Visions of Petrarch.*

1594   Marries Elizabeth Boyle.

1595   Publication of *Amoretti and Epithalamion*, sonnets and a marriage song or hymn addressed to the poet's wife. Publication of *Colin Clouts Come Home Againe*, a long pastoral poem about Spenser's trip to England with Raleigh and about the court of Elizabeth I. This volume also includes elegies on Sidney by various hands, including Spenser's *Astrophel*. Comes to England, presumably to see the six books of *The Faerie Queene* through the press.

1596   Publication of *The Faerie Queene*, Books I–VI. There are minor corrections and changes in Books I–III, and

one major one: the original ending of Book III
(stanzas 43–7), in which Scudamour and Amoret are
reunited, is replaced by the present stanzas 43–5. This
edition is the textual basis of the standard modern
editions, J. C. Smith's (Oxford English Texts) and the
Johns Hopkins Variorum. Publication of *Fowre
Hymnes* (*Of Love*, *Beauty*, *Heavenly Love* and
Heavenly Beauty). This volume includes a second
edition of *Daphnaida*. Publication of *Prothalamion*, a
'spousall verse' in honour of the double marriage of
the eldest daughters of Edward Somerset, earl of
Worcester. Writes *A View of the Present State of
Ireland*, a treatise in the form of a dialogue. The
View was entered in the Stationers' Register in 1598
and several manuscript copies exist, but it was not
published until 1633 in Dublin. Returns to Ireland
(exact date unknown).

1598   Spenser and his wife flee Kilcolman when it is spoiled
            and burned by Irish rebels; return to London in
            December.

1599   Dies (13 January). There are several allusions in
            contemporary sources to his dying in want. He was
            buried in Westminster Abbey near Chaucer.

1609   First folio edition of *The Faerie Queene*, the first
            edition containing the *Cantos of Mutabilitie*.

1611, 1617 The first folio editions of Spenser's collected works.
            They are conventionally identified by these dates
            (which are those of the title pages to the volumes),
            but in fact the various parts were printed at various
            times and with various dates on the separate title
            pages.

1653   Edition of *The Shepheardes Calender*, with a facing
            Latin translation by Theodore Bathurst; the
            arguments and glosses are not included.

1679   Third folio edition of Spenser's collected works, the
            last seventeenth-century edition.

Part One Contemporaneous Criticism

Introduction

Bernard Shaw once said that he would gladly sacrifice half a
dozen of Shakespeare's plays (he did not say which ones) for one
of the prefaces he should have written. The remark smacks of
Shaw's irreverence for Shakespeare, but more important it
assumes that critical discourse and authors' explanations of their
own work were the same for Shakespeare and his contemporaries
as they were for Shaw and his. Shaw's age was one of great
prefaces – Wordsworth's and Arnold's to their poems, James' to his
novels, Shaw's to his plays – while much critical writing by
modern poets (one thinks of Yeats, Eliot, Pound, Stevens) has been
animated by their own concerns as writers and serves to comment
on or justify their own works. With such writings in mind, the
modern reader may be disappointed in Spenser's Letter to Raleigh
or the prefatory epistle to *The Shepheardes Calender*. Before
Dryden, critical prose in English is immature, and most works of
criticism are patchy, mediocre, and derivative. Even with work of
indubitable excellence, like Sir Philip Sidney's *Apology for Poetry*,
the reader is unlikely to feel, to the extent that he does with critics
after Dryden, that he is engaged in a dialogue with a reader who
can be imagined to share precisely his own kind of interest in
literature.

The special character of Sidney's *Apology* can help us determine
the nature of Spenser's own prose criticism. (The 'E.K.' who
wrote the prefatory epistle to *The Shepheardes Calender* has never
been identified. We shall probably never know whether Spenser
had a hand in writing this preface; for our purposes, it is sufficient
to say that he associated himself with it.) No one, reading the
Apology, could fail to see that it is excellent, sometimes noble,
prose, and that it addresses itself to fundamental questions of
poetic theory. Yet for all the distinction of mind Sidney displays,
it is very difficult to say how he answers the questions he poses.
He espouses a variety of critical stands (hence there has been
endless debate about whether he is an Aristotelian, a Platonist, or

something else), and unlike his Italian contemporaries, who were nurtured on Aristotle, he seems not at all concerned with analytic discourse that produces philosophical decisions. He is literally writing an 'apology' or 'defence', as the work was sometimes titled: his aim is to make the reader assent to the spiritual power and worth of imaginative literature. Hence the work is unashamedly eclectic, because it is willing to enlist a great number of the traditional arguments for the value of poetry. In the same way, E.K. enlists a variety of arguments for Spenser's use of archaic words in *The Shepheardes Calender*; the modern reader who seeks out a single, 'true' explanation among all that are offered will be simply baffled. By the same token, the Letter to Raleigh defends using poetry to teach moral doctrine in ways that imply divergent, perhaps even contradictory, estimates of the trustworthiness and use of earthly phenomena and sensory experience. Spenser first says that the times are such that 'all things [are] accounted by their shows' and then argues, as Sidney does, that moral instruction is 'much more profitable and gracious ... by ensample [of epic heroes] than by rule.'

E.K.'s and Spenser's purposes are not so directly rhetorical as Sidney's, but their aims in general are to persuade and proclaim, rather than to argue and analyse. Their message is clear – that with Spenser's pastorals and his heroic poem, English literature has established itself as a branch of European literature. The political, artistic, and linguistic nationalism that characterize Renaissance civilization all come together in the effort of European poets to rival the ancient epics of Homer and Virgil. European and patriotic motives balance each other in such works. They are written in the vernacular, but the style is modelled on Virgil's Latin. (The potential conflict here is evident in E.K.'s defence of Spenser's archaic and rustic terms and in Sidney's condemnation of them.) They are often intensely nationalistic – thus Spenser chooses Prince Arthur as his hero and celebrates the triumph of the

English over the Roman Church – and at the same time concern fundamental aspects of human nature: in the Letter to Raleigh, Spenser describes the heroic poems on which his is modelled in terms of the moral virtues their heroes exemplify. Given the dreary situation of English poetry in 1579, one can well understand the enthusiasm with which E.K. proclaims that England has a young Virgil and that English is now a fit language for poetry. But even in subsequent decades Spenser's work (especially *The Faerie Queene*) is praised not simply for what it is in itself, but as the rival and superior of works by poets of other countries and times.

The Letter to Raleigh, of course, purports to do more than proclaim that England now has its own epic. It seems to give an analytic account of *The Faerie Queene* itself, and readers who take it at face value quickly see that it raises more problems than it solves. There is a lengthy bibliography on these problems, and this is not the place to develop a full argument about them. But it seems to me that they are less pressing than has been thought and that two broad considerations support this view. (a) The main difficulty the Letter presents is that it describes the action of Books II and III as beginning at the court of the Fairy Queen, whereas in the poem they begin as accidental encounters in the woods. But this variance is truly significant only if we assume that for Spenser the plot (in Aristotle's sense) is the fundamental structuring reality in a poem. Modern Spenserians are more and more coming to agree that this is not the case (see the studies by Lewis, Nelson, Roche, Tuve, Alpers, and Sale in the bibliography). The discrepancy between Letter and poem, then, is not evidence that Spenser changed his mind about his poem or had insufficient control over it. Rather his describing all the adventures as beginning from the Fairy Queen's court is a device to help the reader of the Letter, in his own words, 'as in a handful, grip all the discourse'.

(b) There is strong bibliographical evidence *against* assuming, as an eminent American scholar put it, that 'every re-examination of the *Faerie Queene* must commence with the Letter to Raleigh. For whatever its relation to the composition of the poem, the Letter is clearly Spenser's introduction to a reading of it.' Accepting this view, modern editors usually print the Letter as a preface to *The Faerie Queene*. Spenser himself, on the other hand, placed it at the end of the first edition of *The Faerie Queene* (1590, Books I–III) and withdrew it entirely when all six books were published in 1596. The Letter did not appear in the first folio edition of 1609, in which the *Mutability Cantos* first appeared. The Letter reappears in the 1611–1617 folio editions of Spenser's complete works, but again as an appendix to *The Faerie Queene*, not as a preface. The Letter first appears as a preface exactly when one would expect it to, in the first eighteenth-century edition (edited by John Hughes, 1715) – that is, at a time when an editor might well believe that prefatory explanations were needed to make the poem accessible to readers of a later age. (Hughes himself wrote a fine preface, which is reprinted in this volume, page 78.)

The Letter to Raleigh, then, is valuable not as critical analysis and description, but as a historical document that indicates assumptions and issues that other Renaissance writings deal with more fully and interestingly – for example, the idea of an epic poem as moral in conception and didactic in purpose, and the problems of the relation of poetic fictions and historical truth to moral and poetic truth. When, on the other hand, we turn to the statements about poetry that occur in Spenser's poems themselves, we are apt to underestimate their acuteness and interest as critical statements. The best literary criticism written in the English Renaissance occurs in literary works themselves, not in what officially passes as criticism. No English prose criticism of the period displays the extraordinary critical intelligence of Donne's treatment of poetic conventions, Shakespeare's examination of

the reality of roles and theatrical shows, or Ben Jonson's
domestication of the genres in which he wrote. So although the
Letter to Raleigh disappoints us, it is not surprising that
Spenser's poems consider critical problems in a precise and
subtle way, and by poetic means. Thus the October eclogue of
The Shepheardes Calender uses the traditional dialogue form to set
two critical viewpoints, two testimonies to the power of poetry,
into a mutually illuminating relationship. Or consider the proem
to Book II of *The Faerie Queene*, where Spenser defends the
truthfulness of his poem. The proem consists of a series of
questions, but these are not merely 'rhetorical' – questions in
form but assertions in fact. The questions do suggest affirmations,
but at the same time they express a sense of wonder, which
becomes explicit at the end:

What if within the Moones faire shining spheare?
What if in euery other starre vnseene
Of other worldes he happily should heare?
He wonder would much more: yet such to some appeare.

There is a beautiful poise here between a very firm sense that
something can be so, and a capacity for limitless marvelling at
what might turn out to be so. The final 'yet such to some
appeare' is so firm and decisive precisely because Spenser does not
claim to be one of those 'some'. He has made the affirmation
hold true even when the fact exceeds what we can conceive.
He thus does in a positive and powerful way what Sidney's
Apology does only by negation. Spenser's stanzas enact the
affirmation that is only implicit in Sidney's famous dictum, 'The
poet nothing affirms and therefore never lieth'.

If Elizabethan writers characteristically exercised their critical
intelligence in verse not prose, it is not surprising to find that
there is little sustained commentary on Spenser's work during
his lifetime and in the fifty years after his death. Quite the

contrary, the most famous statements about him are brief
remarks – Ben Jonson's assertion that he 'writ no language' and
Milton's reference to 'our sage and serious poet Spenser'. This,
however, does not mean that Spenser's contemporaries and near
contemporaries did not read him perceptively. Unfortunately
we cannot include a passage like these lines from the description
of Eden in *Paradise Lost*:

Another side, umbrageous Grots and Caves
Of cool recess, o'er which the mantling Vine
Lays forth her purple Grape, and gently creeps
Luxuriant.

(IV 257–60)

Milton is not simply 'influenced' by Spenser here. The sudden
producing and isolating of the word 'luxuriant' directly uses a
rhetorical technique that Spenser made his own in describing the
Bower of Bliss (*The Faerie Queene*, II xii) – pleasing or alluring
the reader and then suddenly revealing moral danger, often by
making us feel the menacing moral meanings in words that, in
other contexts, could be innocent or merely descriptive.
Milton, of course, stands the technique on its head: he uses it
precisely to remind us, here with a genuine shock of recognition,
that this garden, unlike Spenser's, is the true Eden. The point
for us to observe is that such a use of Spenser involves active,
critical awareness of his poetic achievement. Like any good critic,
Milton appreciates Spenser's rhetorical device both for its verbal
craftsmanship and for the way it renders and evaluates man's
visions of and longing for a paradise on earth. We cannot include
such passages in this anthology, because they assume rather
than state critical understanding. But we should remember that
in an age that accepted the reality of poetic genres and
conventions, writing a poem was often an act of literary
criticism. Much implicit commentary on Spenser is therefore

to be found in the poems of his contemporaries and successors, and it must be rediscovered by every reader of these poems.

We also cannot include in this collection some materials, like marginal comments, quotations and allusions, that give us some evidence about the way Spenser's contemporaries read him. There is a sufficiency, though not more, of this material, but recent attempts to evaluate it have been rather hag-ridden by the modern image of 'the sixteenth-century reader'. The usual view of that hypothetical creature can be seen in an article by Graham Hough, 'First Commentary on *The Faerie Queene*' (*T.L.S.*, 9 April 1964, p. 294). Hough summarizes the annotations made in 1597 by a man named John Dixon in a copy of the 1590 quarto of the first three books of *The Faerie Queene*. Three types of note predominate – biblical allusions, historical information and allegory, and moral commentary. An example of the latter is the comment on II xii 32–3 – stanzas whose attractiveness a reader like Milton would surely have acknowledged: 'womanish alluringe baites, and perswasions, wherby fonde intemperat men, are ofte over-come, to the hurte both of soull and bodye.' Hough summarizes these notes in the following way:

Their great interest is that we can see in them for the first time how *The Faerie Queene* impressed itself on a literate but not particularly literary reader in its own day. Dixon reads the poem largely as a celebration of religious and national history, while the romantic element is given very perfunctory attention or none at all. It is also noteworthy that he is as a rule extremely sure-footed in interpreting the allegory while he makes muddles about the surface narrative. Again and again he dives right through the story to the moral purpose underneath. It may be that in this he was not untypical of the readers of Spenser's day.

Hough's closing speculation is sufficiently tentative, but it is nevertheless characteristic of the modern reader's tendency to exaggerate the solemnity of the Elizabethan reader. Hough would not have made such a remark about the two annotators, mentioned in Alastair Fowler's survey of early copies of *The Faerie Queene*, who assiduously mark similes and nothing else. Fowler remarks that 'this fondness for Spenser's similes is a feature common to many of the annotators' ('Oxford and London Marginalia to *The Faerie Queene*', N. & Q., n.s. vol. 8, 1961, p. 417). Surely they are as typical of Spenser's audience as John Dixon? We need only be reminded of Peele's imitation of a particularly glamorous description of the sun rising,[1] or of Marlowe's imitation of the description of Arthur's helmet,[2] to recognize that 'the sixteenth-century reader' would have assented to the praise of Spenser in *The Return from Parnassus:*

A sweeter Swan then euer song in Poe,
A shriller Nightingale then euer blest
The prouder groues of selfe admiring Rome.
Blith was each vally, and each sheapeard proud,
While he did chaunt his rurall minstralsye.
Attentiue was full many a dainty eare,
Nay, hearers hong vpon his melting tong,
While sweetly of his Faiery Queene he song,
While to the waters fall he tun'd her fame,
And in each barke engrau'd Elizaes name.[3]

The last six lines are a pastiche of Spenserian phrases, and one of the passages the author is remembering is one that John Dixon would have reviled: 'Eftsoones they heard a most melodious sound, | Of all that mote delight a daintie eare' (II xii 70). In the sixteenth century, as in the twentieth, some readers of

1 *David and Bethsabe*, vii 58–66; cf. *The Faerie Queene*, I v 2.
2 *2 Tamburlane*, iv iii 116–24; cf. *The Faerie Queene*, I vii 32.
3 Part 2, lines 210–19, in *The Three Parnassus Plays*, ed. J. B. Leishman, London, 1949.

The Faerie Queene especially prize the verse when it is sensuous and decorative, while others, in Hough's phrase, dive through the surface of the poem to the presumed moral purpose underneath.

As a collection the passages that follow introduce us to some of the most important debates in the history of Spenser criticism. The most obvious of these is the debate concerning the propriety and nature of Spenser's poetic diction, particularly his archaisms. This particular problem is closely connected with a larger point at issue that appears in several of the passages that follow: is Spenser a contemporary poet, or is he outmoded and to be praised as an 'ancient'? (In later times this problem takes the form: is Spenser a living presence and influence to poets and readers, or is he, if not merely a curiosity, of decidedly historical interest and importance?) Finally, several of the passages included here state or imply views on two problems broached by Spenser in the Letter to Raleigh: what is the nature of moral meanings in *The Faerie Queene*, and how (and how well) are they conveyed by the surface devices, both narrative and rhetorical, of the poem? These are problems that concern every new reader of *The Faerie Queene*. And though one would hardly send a novice to these Renaissance critics for his first instruction in the ways of the poem, the reader who has begun to sense the security and multifariousness with which the poem unfolds can learn a good deal from, and will certainly feel some kinship with, these contemporaries of Spenser's.

E.K.

Dedicatory Epistle to *The Shepheardes Calender* 1579

To the most excellent and learned both orator and poet, Master Gabriel Harvey, his very special and singular good friend E.K. commendeth the good liking of this his labour and the patronage of the new poet.

'Uncouthe unkiste,' said the old famous poet Chaucer, whom for his excellency and wonderful skill in making, his scholar Lydgate, a worthy scholar of so excellent a master, calleth the lodestar of our language and whom our Colin Clout in his aeglogue called Tityrus, the god of shepherds, comparing him to the worthiness of the Roman Tityrus, Virgil. Which proverb, mine own good friend Master Harvey, as in that good old poet it served well Pandare's purpose for the bolstering of his bawdy brokage, so very well taketh place in this our new poet, who for that he is uncouth (as said Chaucer), is unkist, and unknown to most men, is regarded but of few. But I doubt not, so soon as his name shall come into the knowledge of men and his worthiness be sounded in the trump of fame, but that he shall be not only kist, but also beloved of all, embraced of the most and wondered at of the best. No less I think deserveth his wittiness in devising, his pithiness in uttering, his complaints of love so lovely, his discourses of pleasure so pleasantly, his pastoral rudeness, his moral wiseness, his due observing of decorum everywhere – in personages, in seasons, in matter, in speech and generally in all seemly simplicity of handling his matter and framing his words, the which of many things which in him be strange I know will seem the strangest, the words themselves being so ancient, the knitting of them so short and intricate and the whole period and compass of speech so delightsome for the roundness and so grave for the strangeness. And first of the words to speak, I grant they be something hard and of most men unused, yet both English and also used of most excellent authors and most famous poets. In whom, whenas this our poet hath been much travelled and thoroughly read, how could it be (as that worthy orator said) but that walking in the sun, although for other cause he walked, yet needs he mought[1] be sunburnt and, having the sound of those ancient poets still ringing in his ears, he mought needs in singing hit out some of their tunes? But whether he useth them by such casualty and custom or of set purpose and choice, as thinking them fittest for such rustical rudeness of shepherds, either for that their rough sound would make his rhymes more ragged and rustical or else because such old and obsolete words are most used of country folk, sure I think (and think I think not amiss) that they bring great grace and, as one would say, authority to the verse. For albe[2] amongst many other faults it specially be objected of Valla against Livy and of other against Sallust that with overmuch study they affect antiquity, as coveting thereby credence and honour of elder years; yet I am of opinion, and eke the best-learned are of the like, that those ancient solemn words are a great ornament both in the one and in the other, the one labouring to set forth in his work an eternal image of antiquity and the other carefully discoursing matters of gravity and importance. For if my memory fail not, Tully, in that book wherein he endeavoureth to set forth the pattern of a perfect orator, saith that ofttimes an ancient word maketh the style seem grave and, as it were, reverend, no otherwise than we honour and reverence grey hairs for a certain religious regard which we have of old age. Yet neither everywhere must old words be stuffed in nor the common dialect and manner of speaking so corrupted thereby that, as in old buildings, it seem disorderly and ruinous. But all as in most exquisite pictures they use to blaze and portrait not only the dainty lineaments of beauty, but also round about it to shadow the rude thickets and craggy clifts, that by the baseness of such parts more excellency may accrue to the principal. For ofttimes we find ourselves, I know not how, singularly delighted with the show of such natural rudeness and take great pleasure in that disorderly order. Even so do those rough and harsh terms enlumine and make more clearly to appear the brightness of brave and glorious words. So oftentimes a discord in music maketh a comely concordance; so great delight took the worthy poet Alcaeus to behold a blemish in the joint of a well-shaped body. But if any will rashly blame such his purpose in choice of old and unwonted[3] words, him may I more justly blame and condemn or of witless headiness[4] in

---

1 must   2 although   3 unaccustomed   4 hastiness, rashness

judging or of heedless hardiness in condemning; for not marking the
compass of his bent, he will judge of the length of his cast. For in my
opinion it is one special praise of many which are due to this poet that
he hath laboured to restore, as to their rightful heritage, such good and
natural English words as have been long time out of use and almost
clean disherited.[1] Which is the only cause that our mother tongue,
which truly of itself is both full enough for prose and stately enough
for verse, hath long time been counted most bare and barren of both.
Which default whenas some endeavoured to salve and recure, they
patched up the holes with pieces and rags of other languages, borrow-
ing here of the French, there of the Italian, everywhere of the Latin –
not weighing how ill those tongues accord with themselves, but how
much worse with ours! So now they have made our English tongue a
gallimaufry[2] or hodgepodge of all other speeches. Other some, not so
well seen in the English tongue as perhaps in other languages, if they
happen to hear an old word, albeit very natural and significant, cry
out straightway that we speak not English but gibberish, or rather
such as in old time Evander's mother spake. Whose first shame is that
they are not ashamed in their own mother tongue strangers to be
counted and aliens. The second shame, no less than the first, that
whatso they understand not they straightway deem to be senseless and
not at all to be understood, much like to the mole in Aesop's fable
that, being blind herself, would in nowise be persuaded that any beast
could see. The last, more shameful than both, that of their own country
and natural speech, which together with their nurse's milk they
sucked, they have so base regard and bastard judgement that they will
not only themselves not labour to garnish and beautify it, but also
repine that of other it should be embellished, like to the dog in the
manger, that himself can eat no hay and yet barketh at the hungry
bullock that so fain would feed – whose currish kind, though it cannot
be kept from barking, yet I con[3] them thank that they refrain from
biting.

Now for the knitting of sentences, which they call the joints and
members thereof, and for all the compass of the speech, it is round
without roughness and learned without hardness, such indeed as may

1 dispossessed, banished from its rightful domain
2 jumble, medley
3 can

be perceived of the least, understood of the most, but judged only of the learned. For what in most English writers useth to be loose and as it were ungirt, in this author is well-grounded, finely framed and strongly trussed up together. In regard whereof, I scorn and spew out the rakehelly[1] rout of our ragged rhymers (for so themselves use to hunt the letter), which without learning boast, without judgement jangle, without reason rage and foam, as if some instinct of poetical spirit had newly ravished them above the meanness of common capacity. And being in the midst of all their bravery, suddenly, either for want of matter or of rhyme, or having forgotten their former conceit, they seem to be so pained and travailed in their remembrance as it were a woman in childbirth or as that same Pythia when the trance came upon her:

Os rabidum fera corda domans, etc.[2]

Netheless, let them, a God's name, feed on their own folly, so they seek not to darken the beams of others' glory. As for Colin, under whose person the author self is shadowed, how far he is from such vaunted titles and glorious shows both himself showeth, where he saith,

Of Muses Hobbinol, I conne[3] no skill:

and

Enough is me to paint out my unrest, etc.

and also appeareth by the baseness of the name, wherein it seemeth he chose rather to unfold great matter of argument covertly than, professing it, not suffice thereto accordingly. Which moved him rather in aeglogues than otherwise to write, doubting perhaps his ability, which he little needed, or minding to furnish our tongue with this kind, wherein it faulteth, or following the example of the best and most ancient poets, which devised this kind of writing, being both so base for the matter and homely for the manner, at the first to try their abilities and, as young birds that be newly crept out of the nest, by little first to prove their tender wings before they make a greater

1 worthless, rascally
2 Taming her foaming mouth and wild heart.
3 know

flight. So flew Theocritus, as you may perceive he was already full fledged. So flew Virgil, as not yet well feeling his wings. So flew Mantuan, as being not full summed.[1] So Petrarch. So Boccace; so Marot, Sannazzarus, and also divers other excellent both Italian and French poets, whose footing this author everywhere followeth, yet so as few but they be well-scented[2] can trace him out. So finally flieth this our new poet, as a bird whose principals[3] be scarce grown out, but yet as that in time shall be able to keep wing with the best.

Now as touching the general drift and purpose of his aeglogues I mind not to say much, himself labouring to conceal it. Only this appeareth: that his unstaid[4] youth had long wandered in the common labyrinth of love, in which time, to mitigate and allay the heat of his passion or else to warn (as he saith) the young shepherds, scilicet his equals and companions, of his unfortunate folly, he compiled these twelve aeglogues, which, for that they be proportioned to the state of the twelve months, he termeth the *Shepheardes Calender*, applying an old name to a new work.

Edmund Spenser

'October', *The Shepheardes Calender* 1579

Argument

In Cuddie is set out the perfecte paterne of a Poete, whiche finding no maintenaunce of his state and studies, complayneth of the contempte of Poetrie, and the causes thereof: Specially hauing bene in all ages, and euen amongst the most barbarous alwayes of singular accounpt and honor, and being indede so worthy and commendable an arte: or rather no arte, but a diuine gift and heauenly instinct not to bee gotten by laboure and learning, but adorned with both: and poured into the witte by a certaine *enthousiasmos* and celestiall inspiration, as the Author hereof els where at large discourseth, in his booke called the English

1 property of a hawk, having the full complement of feathers
2 gifted with keen perception
3 the two principal feathers in each wing
4 unsteady

Poete, which booke being lately come to my hands, I mynde also by Gods grace vpon further aduisement[1] to publish.

        PIERCE   CVDDIE
Cvddie, for shame hold vp thy heauye head,
And let vs cast[2] with what delight to chace,
And weary thys long lingring *Phœbus* race.
Whilome[3] thou wont[4] the shepheards laddes to leade,
In rymes, in ridles, and in bydding base: [5]
Now they in thee, and thou in sleepe art dead.

CVDDYE
Piers, I haue pyped erst[6] so long with payne,
That all mine Oten reedes bene rent and wore:
And my poore Muse hath spent her spared[7] store,
Yet little good hath got, and much lesse gayne.
Such pleasaunce makes the Grashopper so poore,
And ligge so layd,[8] when Winter doth her straine:[9]

The dapper ditties, that I wont deuise,
To feede youthes fancie, and the flocking fry,[10]
Delighten much: what I the bett[11] for thy?[12]
They han the pleasure, I a sclender prise.
I beate the bush, the byrds to them doe flye:
What good thereof to Cuddie can arise?

PIERS
Cuddie, the prayse is better, then the price,
The glory eke much greater then the gayne:
O what an honor is it, to restraine
The lust of lawlesse youth with good aduice:
Or pricke them forth[13] with pleasaunce of thy vaine,[14]
Whereto thou list their trayned willes entice.

1 advice, counsel, consideration   2 consider
3 formerly, once   4 were accustomed
5 prisoner's base (a children's game)   6 lately
7 saved   8 be so subdued
9 constrain, force   10 young creatures
11 better   12 therefore, because
13 spur them on   14 poetic vein

Soone as thou gynst to sette thy notes in frame,
O how the rurall routes[1] to thee doe cleaue:
Seemeth thou dost their soule of sence bereaue,
All as the shepheard, that did fetch his dame
From *Plutoes* balefull bowre withouten leaue:
His musicks might the hellish hound did tame.

CVDDIE

So praysen babes the Peacoks spotted traine,
And wondren at bright *Argus* blazing eye:
But who rewards him ere the more for thy?
Or feedes him once the fuller by a graine?
Sike[2] prayse is smoke, that sheddeth in the skye,
Sike words bene wynd, and wasten soone in vayne.

PIERS

Abandon then the base and viler clowne,
Lyft vp thy selfe out of the lowly dust:
And sing of bloody Mars, of wars, of giusts,[3]
Turne thee to those, that weld[4] the awful crowne.
To doubted[5] Knights, whose woundlesse armour rusts,
And helmes vnbruzed wexen[6] dayly browne.

There may thy Muse display her fluttryng wing,
And stretch her selfe at large from East to West:
Whither thou list[7] in fayre *Elisa* rest,
Or if thee please in bigger notes to sing,
Aduaunce the worthy whome shee loueth best,
That first the white beare to the stake did bring.[8]

1 crowd, troop   2 such
3 joust, tournament   4 bear
5 redoubted   6 grow, become
7 wish, desire, choose
8 'He meaneth (as I guesse) the most honorable and renowned the Erle of
Leycester, whom by his cognisance (although the same be also proper to other)
rather then by his name he bewrayeth, being not likely, that the names of
noble princes be known to country clowne.' [E.K.'s note.]

And when the stubborne stroke of stronger stounds,[1]
Has somewhat slackt the tenor of thy string:
Of loue and lustihead[2] tho[3] mayst thou sing,
And carrol[4] lowde, and leade the Myllers rownde,
All[5] were *Elisa* one of thilke[6] same ring.
So mought our *Cuddies* name to Heauen sownde.

CVDDYE
Indeede the Romish *Tityrus*, I heare,
Through his *Mecænas* left his Oaten reede,
Whereon he earst had taught his flocks to feede,
And laboured lands to yield the timely eare,
And eft[7] did sing of warres and deadly drede,
So as the Heauens did quake his verse to here.

But ah *Mecænas* is yclad in claye,
And great *Augustus* long ygoe is dead:
And all the worthies liggen wrapt in leade,
That matter made for Poets on to play:
For euer, who in derring doe[8] were dreade,
The loftie verse of hem was loued aye.

But after vertue gan for age to stoupe,
And mighty manhode brought a bedde of ease:
The vaunting Poets found nought worth a pease,[9]
To put in preace[10] emong the learned troupe.
Tho gan the streames of flowing wittes to cease,
And sonnebright honour pend in shamefull coupe.

And if that any buddes of Poesie,
Yet of the old stocke gan to shoote agayne:
Or[11] it mens follies mote be forst to fayne,
And rolle with rest in rymes of rybaudrye:
Or as it sprong, it wither must agayne:
Tom Piper makes vs better melodie.

1 strokes, blows 2 lustiness, pleasure 3 then
4 sing a lively or joyous strain 5 although 6 this 7 afterwards
8 daring deeds 9 of no value 10 to put in practice 11 Either

PIERS

O pierlesse Poesye, where is then thy place?
If nor in Princes pallace thou doe sitt:
(And yet is Princes pallace the most fitt)
Ne brest of baser birth doth thee embrace.
Then make thee winges of thine aspyring wit,
And, whence thou camst, flye backe to heauen apace.

CVDDIE

Ah *Percy* it is all to weake and wanne,
So high to sore, and make so large a flight:
Her peeced[1] pyneons bene not so in plight,[2]
For *Colin* fittes[3] such famous flight to scanne:[4]
He, were he not with loue so ill bedight,[5]
Would mount as high, and sing as soote[6] as Swanne.

PIERS

Ah fon,[7] for loue does teach him climbe so hie,
And lyftes him vp out of the loathsome myre:
Such immortall mirrhor, as he doth admire,
Would rayse ones mynd aboue the starry skie.
And cause a caytiue corage[8] to aspire,
For lofty loue doth loath a lowly eye.

CVDDIE

All otherwise the state of Poet stands,
For lordly loue is such a Tyranne fell:[9]
That where he rules, all power he doth expell.
The vaunted verse a vacant head demaundes,
Ne wont with crabbed care the Muses dwell.
Vnwisely weaues, that takes two webbes in hand.

1 pierced, imperfect   2 condition   3 to be fitting
4 to attempt   5 stricken   6 sweetly   7 fool   8 base mind   9 fierce

Who euer casts to compasse weightye prise,
And thinks to throwe out thondring words of threate:
Let powre in lauish cups and thriftie bitts of meate,
For *Bacchus* fruite is frend to *Phœbus* wise.
And when with Wine the braine begins to sweate,
The nombers flowe as fast as spring doth ryse.

Thou kenst not *Percie* howe the ryme should rage.
O if my temples were distaind[1] with wine,
And girt in girlonds of wild Yuie twine,
How I could reare the Muse on stately stage,
And teache her tread aloft in bus-kin[2] fine,
With queint[3] *Bellona* in her equipage.[4]

But ah my corage cooles ere it be warme,
For thy, content vs in thys humble shade:
Where no such troublous tydes[5] han vs assayde,[6]
Here we our slender pipes may safely charme.

PIERS
And when my Gates shall han their bellies layd[7]:
Cuddie shall haue a Kidde to store his farme.

Edmund Spenser

from a letter to Gabriel Harvey, *Three Proper and Witty Familiar Letters* 1580

I like your late English hexameters so exceedingly well that I also enure my pen sometime in that kind, which I find indeed, as I have heard you often defend in word, neither so hard nor so harsh that it will easily and fairly yield itself to our mother tongue. For the only or chiefest hardness which seemeth is in the accent, which sometime

1 stained   2 buskin = tragedy   3 strange   4 equipment, retinue
5 times   6 afflicted   7 reduced

gapeth and, as it were, yawneth ill-favouredly, coming short of that it should, and sometime exceeding the measure of the number – as in 'carpenter', the middle syllable being used short in speech, when it shall be read long in verse seemeth like a lame gosling that draweth one leg after her; and 'heaven', being used short as one syllable, when it is in verse stretched out with a diastole is like a lame dog that holds up one leg. But it is to be won with custom, and rough words must be subdued with use. For why, a God's name, may not we, as else the Greeks, have the kingdom of our own language and measure our accents by the sound, reserving the quantity to the verse?

Gabriel Harvey

from a letter to Edmund Spenser, *Three Proper and Witty Familiar Letters* 1580

... I like your *Dreams* passingly well, and the rather because they savour of that singular extraordinary vein and invention which I ever fancied most and in a manner admired only in Lucian, Petrarch, Aretine, Pasquill, and all the most delicate and fine-conceited Grecians and Italians (for the Romans, to speak of, are but very ciphers in this kind), whose chiefest endeavour and drift was to have nothing vulgar, but in some respect or other – and especially in lively hyperbolical amplifications – rare, quaint and odd in every point and, as a man would say, a degree or two at least above the reach and compass of a common scholar's capacity. In which respect notwithstanding, as well for the singularity of the manner as the divinity of the matter, I heard once a divine prefer Saint John's Revelation before all the veriest metaphysical visions and jolliest conceited dreams or ecstacies that ever were devised by one or other, how admirable or super-excellent soever they seemed otherwise to the world. And truly I am so confirmed in this opinion that when I bethink me of the very notablest and most wonderful prophetical or poetical vision that ever I read or heard, me seemeth the proportion is so unequal that there hardly appeareth any semblance of comparison, no more in a manner (specially for poets) than doth between the incomprehensible wisdom of God and the sensible wit of man. But what needeth this digression

between you and me? I dare say you will hold yourself reasonably
well satisfied if your *Dreams* be but as well esteemed of in England as
Petrarch's *Visions* be in Italy – which I assure you, is the very worst I
wish you. But see how I have the art memorative at commandment!
In good faith, I had once again nigh forgotten your *Faerie Queene*,
howbeit by good chance I have now sent her home at the last, neither
in better nor worse case than I found her. And must you of necessity
have my judgement of her indeed? To be plain, I am void of all judgement if your *Nine Comedies* – whereunto, in imitation of Herodotus,
you give the names of the nine muses (and in one man's fancy, not un-
worthily) – come not nearer Ariosto's *Comedies*, either for the fineness
of plausible elocution or the rareness of poetical invention, than that
Elvish Queen doth to his *Orlando Furioso*, which, notwithstanding,
you will needs seem to emulate and hope to overgo, as you flatly professed yourself in one of your last letters. Besides that you know it hath
been the usual practice of the most exquisite and odd wits in all
nations, and specially in Italy, rather to show and advance themselves
that way than any other, as namely those three notorious discoursing
heads, Bibiena, Machiavel and Aretine, did (to let Bembo and Ariosto
pass), with the great admiration and wonderment of the whole
country, being indeed reputed matchable in all points, both for conceit of wit and eloquent deciphering of matters, either with Aristo-
phanes and Menander in Greek or with Plautus and Terence in Latin
or with any other in any other tongue. But I will not stand greatly
with you in your own matters. If so be the Fairy Queen be fairer in
your eye than the nine muses, and Hobgoblin run away with the
garland from Apollo, mark what I say – and yet I will not say that I
thought, but there an end for this once, and fare you well till God or
some good angel put you in a better mind.

Sir Philip Sidney

from *An Apology for Poetry* 1595 (but written about 1582)

The Shepheardes Calender hath much poetry in his eclogues, indeed
worthy the reading, if I be not deceived. That same framing of his
style to an old rustic language I dare not allow, since neither

Theocritus in Greek, Virgil in Latin, nor Sannazaro in Italian did affect it. Besides these [*The Shepheardes Calender*, Chaucer's *Troilus and Criseyde*, *A Mirror for Magistrates*, the Earl of Surrey's lyrics], do I not remember to have seen but few (to speak boldly) printed that have poetical sinews in them. For proof whereof, let but most of the verses be put in prose and then ask the meaning, and it will be found that one verse did but get another, without ordering at the first what should be at the last; which becomes a confused mass of words, with a tingling sound of rhyme, barely accompanied with reason.

William Webbe

from *Of English Poetry*   1586

I will now speak a little of another kind of poetical writing, which might notwithstanding, for the variableness of the argument therein usually handled, be comprehended in those kinds before declared. That is, the compiling aeglogues, as much to say as goatherds' tales, because they be commonly dialogues or speeches framed or supposed between shepherds, neatherds, goatherds or suchlike simple men – in which kind of writing many have obtained as immortal praise and commendation as in any other.

The chiefest of these is Theocritus in Greek; next him, and almost the very same, is Virgil in Latin. After Virgil in like sort writ Titus Calpurnius and Baptista Mantuan, with many other, both in Latin and other languages very learnedly. Although the matter they take in hand seemeth commonly in appearance rude and homely, as the usual talk of simple clowns, yet do they indeed utter in the same much pleasant and profitable delight. For under these persons, as it were in a cloak of simplicity, they would either set forth the praises of their friends, without the note of flattery, or inveigh grievously against abuses, without any token of bitterness.

Somewhat like unto these works are many pieces of Chaucer, but yet not altogether so poetical. But now yet at the last hath England hatched up one poet of this sort, in my conscience comparable with the best in any respect: even Master Sp., author of the *Shepheardes Calender*, whose travail in that piece of English poetry I think verily is so commendable as none of equal judgement can yield him less praise for his excellent skill and skilful excellency showed forth in the same than they would to either Theocritus or Virgil, whom in mine opinion, if the coarseness of our speech (I mean the course of custom, which he would not infringe) had been no more let unto him than their pure native tongues were unto them, he would have (if it might be) surpassed them. What one thing is there in them so worthy admiration whereunto we may not adjoin something of his of equal desert? Take Virgil and make some little comparison between them, and judge as ye shall see cause.

Virgil hath a gallant report of Augustus covertly comprised in the first Aeglogue; the like is in him of Her Majesty, under the name of Eliza. Virgil maketh a brave-coloured complaint of unsteadfast friendship in the person of Corydon; the like is him in his fifth Aeglogue. Again, behold the pretty pastoral contentions of Virgil in the third Aeglogue; of him in the eighth Aeglogue. Finally, either in comparison with them or respect of his own great learning, he may well wear the garland and step before the best of all English poets that I have seen or heard; for I think no less 'deserveth' (thus saith E.K. in his commendations) 'his wittiness in devising, his pithiness in uttering, his complaints of love so lovely, his discourses of pleasure so pleasantly, his pastoral rudeness, his moral wiseness, his due observing of decorum everywhere – in personages, in season[s], in matter, in speech and generally in all seemly simplicity of handling his matter and framing his words.' The occasion of his work is a warning to other young men, who, being entangled in love and youthful vanities, may learn to look to themselves in time and to avoid inconveniences which may breed if they be not in time prevented. Many good moral lessons are therein contained, as the reverence which young men owe to the aged (in the second Aeglogue), the caveat or warning to beware a subtle professor of friendship (in the fifth Aeglogue), the commendation of good pastors and shame and dispraise of idle and ambitious goatherds (in the seventh), the loose and reckless living of popish prelates (in the ninth), the learned and sweet complaint of the contempt of learning under the name of poetry (in the tenth). There is also much matter uttered somewhat covertly – especially the abuses of some whom he would not be too plain withall – in which, though it be not apparent to everyone what his special meaning was, yet so skilfully is it handled as any man may take much delight at his learned conveyance and pick out much good sense in the most obscurest of it. His notable praise deserved in every parcel of that work, because I cannot express as I would and as it should, I will cease to speak any more of, the rather because I never heard as yet any that hath read it which hath not with much admiration commended it. One only thing therein have I heard some curious heads call in question, viz., the motion of some unsavoury love, such as in the sixth Aeglogue he seemeth to deal withall, which (say they) is scant allowable to English ears and might well have been left for the Italian defenders of loathsome beastliness, of whom perhaps he learned it. To this objection I have often answered (and I think truly) that their nice opinion overshooteth the poet's meaning, who, though he in that as in other things imitateth the ancient poets, yet doth not mean – no more did they before him – any disordered love or the filthy lust of the devilish *pederastice* taken in the worse sense, but rather to show how the dissolute life of young men, entangled in love of women, do neglect the friendship and league with their old friends and familiars. Why, say they, yet he should give no occasion of suspicion nor offer to the view of Christians any token of such filthiness, how good soever his meaning were. Whereunto I oppose the simple conceit they have of matters which concern learning or wit, willing them to give poets leave to use their vein as they see good. It is their foolish construction, not his writing that is blameable. We must prescribe to no writers (much less to poets) in what sort they should utter their conceits. . . .

Edmund Spenser

Letter to Sir Walter Raleigh   1590

A letter of the author's, expounding his whole intention in the course of this work, which, for that it giveth great light to the reader, for the better understanding is hereunto annexed.

To the right noble and valorous Sir Walter Raleigh, Knight, Lord

Warden of the Stanneries and Her Majesty's Lieutenant of the County of Cornwall:

Sir, knowing how doubtfully all allegories may be construed and this book of mine, which I have entitled the *Faerie Queene*, being a continued allegory, or dark conceit, I have thought good, as well for avoiding of jealous opinions and misconstructions as also for your better light in reading thereof, being so by you commanded, to discover unto you the general intention and meaning which in the whole course thereof I have fashioned, without expressing of any particular purposes or by-accidents therein occasioned. The general end, therefore, of all the book is to fashion a gentleman or noble person in virtuous and gentle discipline, which for that I conceived should be most plausible and pleasing being coloured with an historical fiction – the which the most part of men delight to read rather for variety of matter than for profit of the ensample – I chose the history of King Arthur, as most fit for the excellency of his person, being made famous by many men's former works, and also furthest from the danger of envy and suspicion of present time. In which I have followed all the antique poets historical: first Homer, who in the persons of Agamemnon and Ulysses hath ensampled a good governor and a virtuous man, the one in his *Ilias*, the other in his *Odysseis*; then Virgil, whose like intention was to do in the person of Aeneas; after him Ariosto comprised them both in his Orlando; and lately Tasso dissevered them again and formed both parts in two persons, namely that part which they in philosophy call *ethice*, or virtues of a private man, coloured in his Rinaldo, the other, named *politice*, in his Godfredo. By ensample of which excellent poets I labour to portrait in Arthur, before he was king, the image of a brave knight perfected in the twelve private moral virtues, as Aristotle hath devised – the which is the purpose of these first twelve books, which if I find to be well accepted, I may be perhaps encouraged to frame the other part of politic virtues in his person after that he came to be king. To some I know this method will seem displeasant, which had rather have good discipline delivered plainly in way of precepts or sermoned at large, as they use, than thus cloudily enwrapped in allegorical devises. But such, me seem, should be satisfied with the use of these days, seeing all things accounted by their shows and nothing esteemed of that is not delightful and pleasing to common sense. For this cause is Xenophon preferred before Plato: for that the one, in the exquisite depth of his judgement, formed a commonwealth such as it should be, but the other, in the person of Cyrus and the Persians, fashioned a government such as might best be. So much more profitable and gracious is doctrine by ensample than by rule. So have I laboured to do in the person of Arthur, whom I conceive, after his long education by Timon (to whom he was by Merlin delivered to be brought up so soon as he was born of the Lady Igraine), to have seen in a dream or vision the Fairy Queen, with whose excellent beauty ravished, he awaking resolved to seek her out; and so, being by Merlin armed and by Timon thoroughly instructed, he went to seek her forth in Fairyland. In that Fairy Queen I mean glory in my general intention, but in my particular I conceive the most excellent and glorious person of our sovereign the Queen, and her kingdom in Fairyland. And yet, in some places else I do otherwise shadow her. For considering she beareth two persons – the one of a most royal queen or empress, the other of a most virtuous and beautiful lady – this latter part in some places I do express in Belphoebe, fashioning her name according to your own excellent conceit of Cynthia, Phoebe and Cynthia being both names of Diana. So in the person of Prince Arthur I set forth magnificence in particular, which virtue, for that (according to Aristotle and the rest) it is the perfection of all the rest and containeth in it them all, therefore, in the whole course I mention the deeds of Arthur appliable to that virtue which I write of in that book. But of the twelve other virtues I make twelve other knights the patrons, for the more variety of the history, of which these three books contain three: the first of the knight of the Red Cross, in whom I express holiness, the second of Sir Guyon, in whom I set forth temperance, the third of Britomartis, a lady knight, in whom I picture chastity. But because the beginning of the whole work seemeth abrupt and as depending upon other antecedents, it needs that ye know the occasion of these three knights' several adventures. For the method of a poet historical is not such as of an historiographer. For an historiographer discourseth of affairs orderly as they were done, accounting as well the times as the actions, but a poet thrusteth into the midst, even where it most concerneth him, and there recoursing to the things forepassed and divining of things to come, maketh a pleasing analysis of all. The beginning therefore of my history, if it were to be told by an historiographer, should be the twelfth book, which is the last, where I devise that the Fairy Queen kept her annual feast twelve days, upon which twelve several days the occasions of the twelve several adventures happened, which, being undertaken by twelve several knights, are in these twelve books severally handled and discoursed. The first was this: in the beginning of the feast there presented himself a tall, clownish young man, who, falling before the Queen of Fairies, desired a boon (as the manner then was), which during that feast she might not refuse, which was that he might have the achievement of any adventure which during that feast should happen. That being granted, he rested him on the floor, unfit through his rusticity for a better place. Soon after entered a fair lady in mourning weeds, riding on a white ass with a dwarf behind her leading a warlike steed, that bore the arms of a knight, and his spear in the dwarf's hand. She, falling before the Queen of Fairies, complained that her father and mother, an ancient king and queen, had been by an huge dragon many years shut up in a brazen castle, who thence suffered them not to issue, and therefore besought the Fairy Queen to assign her some one of her knights to take on him that exploit. Presently that clownish person, upstarting, desired that adventure, whereat the Queen much wondering and the lady much gainsaying, yet he earnestly importuned his desire. In the end the lady told him that unless that armour which she brought would serve him (that is, the armour of a Christian man specified by Saint Paul v. Ephes.), that he could not succeed in that enterprise, which being forthwith put upon him with due furnitures thereunto, he seemed the goodliest man in all that company and was well liked of the lady. And eftsoons taking on him knighthood and mounting on that strange courser, he went forth with her on that adventure, where beginneth the first book, viz.,

A gentle knight was pricking on the plaine, etc.

The second day there came in a palmer bearing an infant with bloody hands, whose parents he complained to have been slain by an enchantress called Acrasia and therefore craved of the Fairy Queen to appoint him some knight to perform that adventure, which being assigned to Sir Guyon, he presently went forth with that same palmer – which is the beginning of the second book and the whole subject thereof. The third day there came in a groom who complained before the Fairy Queen that a vile enchanter, called Busirane, had in hand a most fair lady, called Amoretta, whom he kept in most grievous torment because she would not yield him the pleasure of her body. Whereupon Sir Scudamour, the lover of that lady, presently took on him that adventure. But being unable to perform it by reason of the hard enchantments, after long sorrow, in the end met with Britomartis, who succoured him and rescued his love.

But by occasion hereof, many other adventures are inter-meddled, but rather as accidents than intendments – as the love of Britomart, the overthrow of Marinell, the misery of Florimell, the virtuousness of Belphoebe, the lasciviousness of Hellenora, and many the like.

Thus much, Sir, I have briefly overrun to direct your understanding to the wellhead of the history, that from thence gathering the whole intention of the conceit, ye may, as in a handful, grip all the discourse, which otherwise may happily seem tedious and confused. So humbly craving the continuance of your honourable favour towards me and the eternal establishment of your happiness, I humbly take leave.

23 January 1589 [old style, i.e. 1590]
Yours most humbly affectionate,
Ed. Spenser

Edmund Spenser

Dedicatory Sonnets to *The Faerie Queene* 1590

To the right honourable Sir Christopher Hatton,
Lord high Chauncelor of England, etc.

Those prudent heads, that with theire counsels wise
   Whylom the Pillours of th'earth did sustaine,
   And taught ambitious *Rome* to tyrannise,
   And in the neck of all the world to rayne,
Oft from those graue affaires were wont abstaine,
   With the sweet Lady Muses for to play:
   So *Ennius* the elder Africane,
   So *Maro* oft did *Cæsars* cares allay.

So you great Lord, that with your counsell sway
   The burdeine of this kingdom mightily,
   With like delightes sometimes may eke delay,
   The rugged brow of carefull Policy:
And to these ydle rymes lend litle space,
   Which for their titles sake may find more grace.

To the right honourable the Lo. Burleigh Lo. high Threasurer of England

To you right noble Lord, whose carefull brest
   To menage of most graue affaires is bent,
   And on whose mightie shoulders most doth rest
   The burdein of this kingdomes gouernement,
As the wide compasse of the firmament,
   On *Atlas* mighty shoulders is vpstayd;
   Vnfitly I these ydle rimes present,
   The labor of lost time, and wit vnstayd:
Yet if their deeper sence be inly wayd,
   And the dim vele, with which from comune vew
   Their fairer parts are hid, aside be layd.
Perhaps not vaine they may appeare to you.
Such as they be, vouchsafe them to receaue,
   And wipe their faults out of your censure graue.

To the right honourable the Earle of Cumberland

Redoubted Lord, in whose corageous mind
   The flowre of cheualry now bloosming faire,
   Doth promise fruite worthy the noble kind,
   Which of their praises haue left you the haire;
To you this humble present I prepare,
   For loue of vertue and of Martiall praise,
   To which though nobly ye inclined are,
   As goodlie well ye shew'd in late assaies,
Yet braue ensample of long passed daies,
   In which trew honor yee may fashiond see,
   To like desire of honor may ye raise,

And fill your mind with magnanimitee.
Receiue it Lord therefore as it was ment,
   For honor of your name and high descent.

Edmund Spenser

from *The Faerie Queene*   1590–96

Proem to Book II

Right well I wote most mighty Soueraine,
That all this famous antique history,
Of some th'aboundance of an idle braine
Will iudged be, and painted forgery,
Rather then matter of iust memory,
Sith none, that breatheth liuing aire, does know,
Where is that happy land of Faery,
Which I so much do vaunt, yet no where show,
But vouch antiquities, which no body can know.

But let that man with better sence aduize,
That of the world least part to vs is red:
And dayly how through hardy enterprize,
Many great Regions are discouered,
Which to late age were neuer mentioned.
Who euer heard of th'Indian *Peru*?
Or who in venturous vessell measured
The *Amazons* huge riuer now found trew?
Or fruitfullest *Virginia* who did euer vew?

Yet all these were, when no man did them know;
Yet haue from wisest ages hidden beene:
And later times things more vnknowne shall show.
Why then should witlesse man so much misweene[1]
That nothing is, but that which he hath seene?
What if within the Moones faire shining spheare?

[1] have a wrong opinion, think wrongly

What if in euery other starre vnseene
Of other worldes he happily should heare?
He wonder would much more: yet such to some appeare.

Of Faerie lond yet if he more inquire,
By certaine signes here set in sundry place
He may it find; ne let him then admire,
But yield[1] his sence to be too blunt and bace,
That no'te[2] without an hound fine footing trace.
And thou, O fairest Princesse vnder sky,
In this faire mirrhour maist behold thy face,
And thine owne realmes in lond of Faery,
And in this antique Image thy great auncestry.

The which O pardon me thus to enfold
In couert vele, and wrap in shadowes light,
That feeble eyes your glory may behold,
Which else could not endure those beames bright,
But would be dazled with exceeding light.
O pardon, and vouchsafe with patient eare
The braue aduentures of this Faery knight
The good Sir *Guyon* gratiously to heare,
In whom great rule of Temp'raunce goodly doth appeare.

Proem to Book IV

The rugged forhead that with graue foresight
Welds[3] kingdomes causes, and affaires of state,
My looser rimes (I wote) doth sharply wite,[4]
For praising loue, as I haue done of late,
And magnifying louers deare debate;
By which fraile youth is oft to follie led,
Through false allurement of that pleasing baite,
That better were in vertues discipled,
Then with vaine poemes weeds to haue their fancies fed.

1 admit, grant   2 cannot
3 governs, manages, controls   4 blame, censure

Such ones ill iudge of loue, that cannot loue,
Ne in their frosen hearts feele kindly flame:
For thy they ought not thing vnknowne reproue,
Ne naturall affection faultlesse blame,
For fault of few that haue abusd the same.
For it of honor and all vertue is
The roote, and brings forth glorious flowres of fame,
That crowne true louers with immortall blis,
The meed[1] of them that loue, and do not liue amisse.

Which who so list looke backe to former ages,
And call to count the things that then were donne,
Shall find, that all the workes of those wise sages,
And braue exploits which great Heroes wonne,
In loue were either ended or begunne:
Witnesse the father of Philosophie,
Which to his *Critias*, shaded oft from sunne,
Of loue full manie lessons did apply,
The which these Stoicke censours cannot well deny.

To such therefore I do not sing at all,
But to that sacred Saint my soueraigne Queene,
In whose chast breast all bountie naturall,
And treasures of true loue enlocked beene,
Boue all her sexe that euer yet was seene;
To her I sing of loue, that loueth best,
And best is lou'd of all aliue I weene:
To her this song most fitly is addrest,
The Queene of loue, and Prince of peace from heauen blest.

Which that she may the better deigne to heare,
Do thou dred infant, *Venus* dearling doue,
From her high spirit chase imperious feare,
And vse of awfull Maiestie remoue:
In sted thereof with drops of melting loue,
Deawd with ambrosiall kisses, by thee gotten
From thy sweete smyling mother from aboue,
Sprinckle her heart, and haughtie courage[2] soften,
That she may hearke to loue, and reade this lesson often.

1 reward, gain   2 nature

Proem to Book VI, stanzas 1-3

The waies, through which my weary steps I guyde,
In this delightfull land of Faery,
Are so exceeding spacious and wyde,
And sprinckled with such sweet variety,
Of all that pleasant is to eare or eye,
That I nigh rauisht with rare thoughts delight,
My tedious trauell doe forget thereby;
And when I gin to feele decay of might,
It strength to me supplies, and chears my dulled spright.

Such secret comfort, and such heauenly pleasures,
Ye sacred imps, that on *Parnasso* dwell,
And there the keeping haue of learnings threasures,
Which doe all worldly riches farre excell,
Into the mindes of mortall men doe well,
And goodly fury into them infuse;
Guyde ye my footing, and conduct me well
In these strange waies, where neuer foote did vse,
Ne none can find, but who was taught them by the Muse.

Reuele to me the sacred noursery
Of vertue, which with you doth there remaine,
Where it in siluer bowre does hidden ly
From view of men, and wicked worlds disdaine.
Since it at first was by the Gods with paine
Planted in earth, being deriu'd at furst
From heauenly seedes of bounty soueraine,
And by them long with carefull labour nurst,
Till it to ripenesse grew, and forth to honour burst.

Sir Walter Raleigh

A Vision upon this Conceit of 'The Faerie Queene', published in
the first edition of *The Faerie Queene* 1590

Me thought I saw the grave, where Laura lay,

Within that temple, where the vestal flame
Was wont to burn, and passing by that way,
To see that buried dust of living fame,
Whose tomb fair love and fairer virtue kept,
All suddenly I saw the Fairy Queen:
At whose approach the soul of Petrarch wept,
And from thenceforth those graces were not seen.
For they this queen attended, in whose stead
Oblivion laid him down on Laura's hearse;
Hereat the hardest stones were seen to bleed,
And groans for buried ghosts the heavens did perse:[1]
   Where Homer's spright did tremble all for grief,
   And cursed th'access of that celestial thief.

Joseph Hall

from *His Defiance to Envy*, prefaced to *Virgidemiarum* 1597

Would she [his Muse] but shade her tender brows with bay,
That now lie bare in careless, wilful rage,
And trance herself in that sweet ecstasy,
That rouseth drooping thoughts of bashful age,
   Though now these bays and that aspired thought
   In careless rage she sets at worse than nought.

Or would we loose her plumy pinion,
Manacled long with bands of modest fear,
Soon might she have those kestrels[2] proud outgone,
Whose flighty wings are dewed with wetter air,
   And hopen now to shoulder from above
   The eagle from the stairs of friendly Jove.

Or list she rather in late triumph rear
Eternal trophies to some conqueror,
Whose dead deserts slept in his sepulchre,
And never saw nor life nor light before,
   To lead sad Pluto captive with my song,
   To grace the triumphs he obscured so long.

1 pierce   2 small falcon

Or scour the rusted swords of elvish knights,
Bathèd in pagan blood, or sheath them new
In misty moral types, or tell their fights
Who mighty giants or who monsters slew,
   And by some strange enchanted spear and shield
   Vanquished their foe and won the doubtful field.

Maybe she might in stately stanzas frame
Stories of ladies and adventurous knights,
To raise her silent and inglorious name
Unto a reachless pitch of praises height,
   And somewhat say, as more unworthy done,
   Worthy of brass and hoary marble stone.

Then might vain Envy waft her duller wing,
To trace the airy steps she spiting sees,
And vainly faint in hopeless following
The clouded paths her native dross denies;
   But now such lowly satires here I sing,
   Not worth our Muse, not worth their envying.

                 (31–66)

Joseph Hall

from *Virgidemiarum*   1597

Too popular is tragic poesy,
Straining his tip-toes for a farthing fee,
And doth besides on rhymeless numbers tread –
Unbid iambics flow from careless head.
Some braver brain in high heroic rhymes
Compileth worm-eat stories of old times,
And he like some imperious Maronist,
Conjures the Muses that they him assist.
Then strives he to bombast his feeble lines
With far-fetched phrase –
And maketh up his hard-betaken tale
With strange enchantments, fetched from darksome vale,

Of some Melissa, that by magic doom
To Tuscan soil transporteth Merlin's tomb.
Painters and poets hold your ancient right:
Write what you will, and write not what you might.
Their limits be their list, their reason will.
But if some painter in presuming skill
Should paint the stars in center of the earth,
Could ye forbear some smiles and taunting mirth?
But let no rebel satire dare traduce
Th'eternal legends of thy Fairy Muse,
Renownèd Spenser, whom no earthly wight
Dares once to emulate, much less dares despite.
Sallust of France and Tuscan Ariost,
Yield up the laurel garland ye have lost,
And let all others willow wear with me,
Or let their undeserving temples barèd be.

(Book 1, Satire 4)

Everard Guilpin

from *Skialetheia*   1598

Some blame deep Spenser for his grandam words,
Others protest that in them he records
His masterpiece of cunning, giving praise
And gravity to his profound-pricked lays.

(Satire 6)

Anonymous

from *The Second Part of the Return from Parnassus*   1602

INGENIOSO: Good men and true, stand together; hear your censure.
What's thy judgement of Spenser?
IUDICIO: A sweeter swan than ever sung in Po,
A shriller nightingale than ever blessed

The prouder groves of self-admiring Rome.
Blithe was each valley and each shepherd proud,
While he did chant his rural minstralsy.
Attentive was full many a dainty ear,
Nay, hearers hung upon his melting tongue,
While sweetly of his Fairy Queen he sung,
While to the waters' fall he tuned her fame,
And in each bark engraved Eliza's name.
And yet for all, this unregarding soil
Unlaced the line of his desired life,
Denying maintenance for his dear relief:
Careless e'er to prevent his exequy,
Scarce deigning to shut up his dying eye.
INGENIOSO: Pity it is that gentler wits should breed
Where thick-skin chuffs laugh at a scholar's need.
But softly may our Homer's ashes rest,
That lie by merry Chaucer's noble chest.

(208–28)

Edmund Bolton

from *Hypercritica, or A Rule of Judgement for Writing or
Reading our Histories* ?1618

[The following passages are from a discussion of stylistic models for a
historian.]

In verse there are Edmund Spenser's Hymns. I cannot advise the
allowance of other his poems as for practic English, no more than I
can do Geoffrey Chaucer, Lydgate, Piers Plowman, or Laureate
Skelton. It was laid as a fault to the charge of Sallust that he used some
old outworn words, stolen out of Cato his books *De Originibus*. And
for an historian in our tongue to affect the like out of those our poets
would be accounted a foul oversight. . . . My judgement is nothing at
all in poems or poesy, and therefore I dare not go far, but will simply
deliver my mind concerning those authors among us whose English
hath in my conceit most propriety, and is nearest to the phrase of

court and to the speech used among the noble and among the better sort in London – the two sovereign seats and, as it were, Parliament tribunals to try the question in. . . .

[Bolton praises works by, among other poets, George Chapman (translation of the *Iliad*), Samuel Daniel, Michael Drayton (*England's Heroical Epistles*), Robert Southwell, Henry Constable, Thomas Sackville (Induction to the *Mirror for Magistrates* and *Gorboduc*), Sir Thomas Wyatt, Henry Howard Earl of Surrey (sonnets and translation of the *Aeneid*), Sir Walter Raleigh, John Donne, and Fulke Greville. He concludes:]

. . . But if I should declare mine own rudeness rudely, I should then confess that I never tasted English more to my liking, nor more smart and put to the height of use in poetry, than in that vital, judicious and most practicable language of Benjamin Jonson's poems.

Robert Salter

from *Wonderful Prophecies from the Beginning of the Monarchy of this Land*   1626 (second edition 1627)

Here is in this quadripartite parable described unto us a fourfold state of the man in Christ.

The first is the state of nature, originally derived unto him from his parents. . . .

The second is the state of his adoption and childhood in Christ through Grace. . . .

The third is his full growth and strength of manhood in Christ. . . .

The fourth is the glory of the man's consummation. By the which although he do yet walk in the flesh, assailed on every side with the spears thereof as with so many lions, notwithstanding he doth not war after the flesh that he should stand in fear of them, or be annoyed by them, because he liveth in Christ. As, for as much as he is able in the brightness of a good conscience to bear witness to himself with the apostle ('I have kept faith'), therefore he doth conclude that neither tribulation, nor distress, nor persecution, nor famine, nor nakedness, nor peril, nor sword shall separate betwixt Christ and him. For in all these we are more than conquerors, as we find Daniel amidst the lions in the fourth period.

And even this very mystery is it that a right learned and virtuous gentleman[1] hath so lively deciphered in his legend of the Patron of True Holiness, the Knight of the Red Cross; whereby, and by the rest of his lovely raptures, he hath justly purchased the laurel of honourable memory, while the pilgrimage of those his worthies are to endure.

He there hath brought forth our noble Saint George, at the first only in the state of a swain, before his glorious Queen cast down on the ground, uncouth, unkest, unacknown, uncared of as a dead trunk, and only fit for the fire, as in our first period.

But when he had arrayed himself in the armour of his dying Lord, his presence is then become gracious, and his person promising great things, as one for sad encounters fit. Which he first passively (as in our second period) and after actively (as in our third period) doth so victoriously pass through and finish that at the length (as in our fourth period) he is become altogether impassible, whether of assaults of the frailty of nature within, or affronts of adversaries without, as being fully possessed of that Kingdom, against which there is none to stand up.

(41–3)

Henry Reynolds

from *Mythomystes* 1632

From the multitude, I say, of the common rhymers in these our modern times and modern tongues, I will exempt some few, as of a better rank and condition than the rest. . . . Chaucer, for some of his poems, chiefly his *Troilus and Criseyde*. Then the generous and ingenious Sidney, for his smooth and artful *Arcadia*, and who I could wish had chose rather to have left us of his pen an encomiastic poem in honour, than prose apology in defence, of his favourite, the excellent art of poesy. Next I must approve the learned Spenser, in the rest of his poems no less than his *Faerie Queene*, an exact body of the ethic doctrine; though some good judgements have wished, and

1 Mr Edmund Spenser. The great contentment I sometimes enjoyed by his sweet society suffereth not this to pass me without respective mention of so true a friend.

perhaps not without cause, that he had therein been a little freer of his fiction, and not so close riveted to his moral.

[Reynolds is a champion of esoteric Neoplatonism, of the sort that flourished in Renaissance Italy. The rationale of his judgement of Spenser appears in the following passage.]

Our rhymes, say they [modern poets], are full of moral doctrine. Be it so; but why not delivered then in plain prose, and as openly to everyman's understanding as it deserves to be taught and commonly known by every one? The ancients, say they, were authors of fables, which they sung in measured numbers, as we in imitation of them do. True; but sure enough their meanings were of more high nature and more difficult to be found out than any book of manners we shall readily meet withal affords; else they had not writ them so obscurely, or we should find them out more easily and make some use of them; whereas not understanding nor seeking to understand, we make none at all. We live in a mist, blind and benighted, and since our first father's disobedience poisoned himself and our posterity, man is become the imperfectest and most deficient animal of all the field; for then he lost that instinct that the beast retains, though with him the beast, and with it the whole vegetable and general terrene nature also suffered, and still groans under the loss of their first purity, occasioned by his fall. What concerns him now so nearly as to attend to the cultivating or refining, and thereby advancing, of his rational part, to the purchase and regaining of his first lost felicity? And what means to conduce to this purchase can there be, but the knowledge first and love next (for none can love but what he first knows) of his Maker, for whose love and service he was only made? And how can this blind, lame and utterly imperfect man, with so great a load to boot of original and actual offence upon his back, hope to approach this supreme altitude and immensity ... but by two means only: the one, by laying his burden on him that on his cross bore the burthen of all our defects, and interpositions between us and the hope of the vision of his blessed essence face to face hereafter; and the other, by careful search of him here in this life (according to St Paul's instruction) in his works, who tells us (Romans i, 20), 'Those invisible things of God are clearly seen, being understood by the things that are made,' or by the works of his blessed hands? So as between these two main and only means of acquiring here the knowledge and hereafter the vision of him wherein all our present and future happiness consists, what middle place (to descend to my former discourse) can these men's moral philosophy (trow we) challenge? Which in its first masters' and teachers' time, before there was any better divinity known, might well enough pass for a coarse kind of divinity, but, however, such a one as (with the leave of our poets) needs no fiction to clothe or conceal it. And therefore utterly unfit to be the subject of poems, since it contains in it but the obvious restraints or impulsions of the human sense and will, to or from what it inly beforehand, without extrinsic force or law, feels and knows it ought to shun or embrace.

Ben Jonson

from *Timber, or Discoveries*   before 1637 (published posthumously 1640)

As it is fit to read the best authors to youth first, so let them be of the openest and clearest, as Livy before Sallust, Sidney before Donne; and beware of letting them taste Gower or Chaucer at first, lest falling too much in love with antiquity, and not apprehending the weight, they grow rough and barren in language only. When their judgements are firm and out of danger, let them read both the old and the new; but no less take heed that their new flowers and sweetness do not as much corrupt as the others' dryness and squalor, if they choose not carefully. Spenser, in affecting the ancients, writ no language; yet I would have him read for his matter, but as Virgil read Ennius.

Sir Kenelm Digby

'Concerning Spenser that I wrote at Mr May's Desire'   1638

Whosoever will deliver a well-grounded opinion and censure of any learned man must at the least stand upon the same level with him in matter of judgement and ability. For otherwise, whiles remaining on the lower ground he looketh up at him, he shall have but a superficial view of the most prominent parts, without being able to make any discovery into the large continent that lieth behind those, wherein usually is the richest soil. This consideration maketh me very unwilling to say anything in this kind of our late admirable poet Edmund Spenser, who is seated so high above the reach of my weak eyes as, the more I look to discern and descry his perfections, the more faint and dazzled they grow through the distance and splendour of the object. Yet to comply with your desire, I will here briefly deliver you (though with a hoarse voice and trembling hand) some of those rude and undigested conceptions that I have of him – not daring to look too far into the sacrary of the Muses and of learning, where to handle anything with boldness were impiety.

His learned works confirm me in the belief that our northern climate may give life to as well-tempered a brain and to as rich a mind as where the sun shineth fairest. When I read him methinks our country needeth not to envy either Greece, Rome or Tuscany, for if affection deceive me not very much, their poets excel in nothing but he is admirable in the same. And in this he is the more admirable: that what perfections they have severally you may find all in him alone, as though Nature had strived to show in him that when she pleaseth to make a masterpiece, she can give in one subject all those excellencies that to be in height would seem to require, every one of them, a different temper and complexion. And if at any time he plucketh a flower out of their gardens, he transplanteth it so happily into his own that it groweth there fairer and sweeter than it did where first it sprang up. His works are such as, were their true worth known abroad, I am persuaded the best wits and most learned men of other parts would study our long-neglected language to be capable of his rich conceptions and smooth delivery of them; for certainly weight of matter was never better joined with propriety of language and with majesty and sweetness of verse than by him. And if any should except against his reviving some obsolete words and using some ancient forms of speech, in my opinion he blameth that which deserveth much praise. For Spenser doth not that out of any affectation (although his assiduity in Chaucer might make his language familiar to him), but only then when they serve to express more lively and more concisely what he would say; and whensoever he useth them, he doth so polish their native rudeness as, retaining the majesty of antiquity, they want nothing of the elegance of our freshest speech. I hope that what he hath written will be a means that the English tongue will now receive no more alterations and changes but will remain and continue settled in that form it now hath. For excellent authors do draw unto them the study of posterity, and whosoever is delighted with what he readeth in another feeleth in himself a desire to express like things in a like manner; and the more resemblance his elocutions have to his author's, the nearer he persuadeth himself he arriveth to perfection; and thus, much conversation and study in what he would imitate begetteth a habit of doing the like. This is the cause that after the great lights of learning among the Grecians, their language received no further alterations, and that the Latin hath ever since remained in the same state whereunto it was reduced by Cicero, Virgil and the other great men of that time; and the Tuscan tongue is at this day the same as it was left about three hundred years ago by Dante, Petrarch and Boccace. It is true that the vicissitudes of things (change being a necessary and inseparable condition of all sublunary creatures) and the inundations of barbarous nations may overgrow and overrun the vulgar practice of the perfectest languages, as we see of the fore-mentioned Greek and Latin. Yet the use of those tongues will flourish among learned men as long as those excellent authors remain in the world. Which maketh me confident that no fate nor length of time will bury Spenser's works and memory nor indeed alter that language that out of his school we now use, until some general innovation happen that may shake as well the foundations of our nation as of our speech – from which hard law of stepmother Nature what empire or kingdom hath ever yet been free? And herein Spenser hath been very happy: that he hath had one immediately succeeding him of parts and power to make what he planted take deep roots and to build up that work whose foundations he so fairly laid. For it is beyond the com-pass and reach of our short life and narrow power to have the same man begin and perfect any great thing. No empire was ever settled to long continuance but in the first beginnings of it there was an un-interrupted succession of heroic and brave men to extend and confirm it. A like necessity is in languages, and in ours we may promise our-selves a long and flourishing age, when divine Spenser's sun was no sooner set but in Jonson a new one rose with as much glory and brightness as ever any shone withall – who being himself most ex-cellent and admirable in the judicious compositions that in several kinds he hath made, thinketh no man more excellent and more admirable than this his late predecessor in the laurel crown. To his wise and knowing judgement faith may be given, whereas my weak one may be called in question upon any other occasion than this, where the conspicuity of truth beareth it out.

Spenser in what he saith hath a way of expression peculiar to himself; he bringeth down the highest and deepest mysteries that are contained in human learning to an easy and gentle form of delivery – which showeth he is master of what he treateth of, he can wield it as he pleaseth. And he hath done this so cunningly that if one heed him not with great attention, rare and wonderful conceptions will unperceived slide by him that readeth his works, and he will think he hath met with nothing but familiar and easy discourses; but let one dwell awhile upon them and he shall feel a strange fullness and roundness in all he saith. The most generous wines tickle the palate least, but they are no sooner in the stomach but by their warmth and strength there, they discover what they are; and those streams that steal away with least noise are usually deepest and most dangerous to pass over.

His knowledge in profound learning, both divine and human, appeareth to me without controversy the greatest that any poet before him ever had excepting Virgil, whom I dare not meddle withall otherwise than as witty Scaliger did, erecting an altar to him. And this his knowledge was not such as many poets are contented withall, which is but a mere sprinkling of several sciences of which they have some general and superficial notions to beautify their poems with. But he had a solid and deep insight in theology, philosophy (especially the Platonic) and the mathematical sciences, and in what others depend of these three – as indeed all others do. He was a master in every one of them, and where he maketh use of any of them, it is not by gathering a posy out of other men's works, but by spending of his own stock.

And lastly, where he treateth moral or political learning, he giveth evidence of himself that he had a most excellently composed head to observe and govern men's actions and might have been eminent in the active part that way, if his own choice or fortune had given him employment in the commonwealth.

Sir Kenelm Digby

from *Observations on the Twenty-Second Stanza in the Ninth Canto of the Second Book of Spenser's 'Faerie Queene'*   1644

In this staff [*Faerie Queene*, II ix 22, a numerological allegory of the human body] the author seems to me to proceed in a different manner from what he doth elsewhere generally through his whole book. For in other places, although the beginning of his allegory or mystical sense may be obscure, yet in the process of it he doth himself declare his own conceptions, in such sort as they are obvious to any ordinary capacity. But in this he seems only to glance at the profoundest notions that any science can deliver us, and then on a sudden, as it were, recalling himself out of an enthusiasm, he returns to the gentle relation of the allegorical history he had begun, leaving his readers to wander up and down in much obscurity, and to come within much danger of erring at his intention in these lines. Which I conceive to be dictated by such a learned spirit and so generally a knowing soul, that were there nothing else extant of Spenser's writing, yet these few words would make me esteem him no whit inferior to the most famous men that ever have been in any age – as giving evident testimony herein that he was thoroughly versed in the mathematical sciences, in philosophy, and in divinity, to which this might serve for an ample theme to make large commentaries upon.

John Milton

from *Areopagitica*   1644

As therefore the state of man now is, what wisdom can there be to choose, what continence to forbear without the knowledge of evil? He that can apprehend and consider vice with all her baits and seeming pleasures, and yet abstain, and yet distinguish, and yet prefer that which is truly better, he is the true warfaring Christian. I cannot praise a fugitive and cloistered virtue, unexercised and unbreathed, that never sallies out and sees her adversary, but slinks out of the race where that immortal garland is to be run for, not without dust and heat. Assuredly we bring not innocence into the world, we bring impurity much rather: that which purifies us is trial, and trial is by what is contrary. That virtue therefore which is but a youngling in the contemplation of evil, and knows not the utmost that vice promises to her followers, and rejects it, is but a blank virtue, not a pure; her whiteness is but an excremental whiteness; which was the reason why our sage and serious poet Spenser, whom I dare be known to think a better teacher than Scotus or Aquinas, describing true temperance under the person of Guyon, brings him in with his palmer through the cave of Mammon and the bower of earthly bliss, that he might see and know, and yet abstain.

Sir William Davenant

from the Preface to *Gondibert* 1650

Spenser may stand here as the last of this short file of heroic poets – men whose intellectuals were of so great a making (though some have thought them liable to those few censures we have mentioned) as perhaps they will in worthy memory outlast even makers of laws and founders of empires and all but such as must therefore live equally with them, because they have recorded their names and, consequently, with their own hands led them to the Temple of Fame. And since we have dared to remember those exceptions which the curious have against them, it will not be expected I should forget what is objected against Spenser, whose obsolete language we are constrained to mention, though it be grown the most vulgar accusation that is laid to his charge.

Language, which is the only creature of man's creation, hath like a plant seasons of flourishing and decay, like plants is removed from one soil to another and, by being so transplanted, doth often gather vigour and increase. But as it is false husbandry to graft old branches upon young stocks, so we may wonder that our language (not long before his time created out of a confusion of others and then beginning to flourish like a new plant) should, as helps to its increase, receive from his hand new grafts of old, withered words. But this vulgar exception shall only have the vulgar excuse, which is, that the unlucky choice of his stanza hath by repetition of rhyme brought him to the necessity of many exploded words.

If we proceed from his language to his argument, we must observe with others that his noble and most artful hands deserved to be employed upon matter of a more natural and therefore of a more useful kind – his allegorical story, by many held defective in the connexion, resembling, methinks, a continuance of extraordinary dreams, such as excellent poets and painters, by being over-studious, may have in the beginning of fevers. And those moral visions are just of so much use to human application as painted history, when with the cozenage of lights it is represented in scenes, by which we are much less informed than by actions on the stage.

Part Two Neoclassical and Romantic Criticism

Introduction

> But now the mystic tale, that pleased of yore,
> Can charm an understanding age no more.

So Addison spoke of *The Faerie Queene*, and the impression he gives is one that many readers have – that Augustan writers, often enough prone to cultural smugness, found Spenser's poetry inaccessible and merely curious. Against this view a number of facts can be marshalled. There are first of all the tributes of Dryden, Prior and Pope, and widespread testimony among critics to Spenser's genius and powers. Second, the eighteenth century laid the foundations of Spenserian scholarship, and did so, as Thomas Warton's remarks indicate, in a spirit of aesthetic admiration and critical discrimination. Warton's *Observations on 'The Faerie Queene'* (1754) is a major compilation of sources and background materials. Of the various editions, John Hughes' of the *Works* is prefaced by an important critical essay, while John Upton's of *The Faerie Queene* provided annotations of such learning and intelligence that they are still the most helpful and interesting to be found in the modern Variorum edition. Finally we may note Pope's telling Joseph Spence that Addison had not even read *The Faerie Queene* at the time he wrote the passage quoted.

Nevertheless, Addison's damning Spenser with faint praise does have representative significance. It is not simply that critics like Thomas Rymer and William Temple spoke of Spenser in similar terms. Even Spenser's warmest admirers feel the constraints of neoclassical canons and criteria. 'At no other period of English history,' F. R. Leavis remarks in discussing Johnson, 'have literary interests been governed by a literary tradition so positive.' The observation explains some puzzling facts about Spenser criticism in the eighteenth century. There is very little positive criticism in the form of concrete elucidation and analysis, even though most of what there is is excellent. Conversely, a writer like

Joseph Spence can bestow warm general praise on Spenser and
then proceed to damn almost every detail he notices. Thomas
Warton noted this situation in a 'postscript' to his *Observations*.
He admits that he has remarked faults rather than beauties, and
all but says that a critic's judgement (as opposed to his appreciative
enthusiasm) can only serve this function. What can have made
Warton take such a position? Why should he not have given us
many more positive analyses than the few – almost all memorable
and helpful – that the reader will find on the following pages?
In an age when, more than in any other, the vocabulary of
criticism represented a sense of literature shared by all cultivated
readers, what can it mean to say, 'In reading Spenser, if the
critic is not satisfied, yet the reader is transported'? The answer
to these questions lies in the eighteenth-century commonplace
that Spenser is a poet of the fancy or (almost synonymous) the
imagination. It is obvious that *The Faerie Queene* – with its
endlessly detailed, vividly pictorial but unrealistic poetry – would
seem a monument to the faculty of the mind that renders
ordinary sense impressions in new sequences and combinations,
and thus is responsible for the power of poetry to surprise,
enrapture, and excite. But however poetical in this sense,
The Faerie Queene seemed notoriously lacking in other properties
equally essential to a poem – form and structure, which have their
source in the mental faculty of judgement. The Augustan debate
about the structure of *The Faerie Queene* is thus much more vital
a matter than an attempt to bring the poem into line with
irrelevant rules. Eighteenth-century critics obviously found the
poem powerfully appealing, yet at the same time it must have
seemed to them radically incomplete – in the words of the modern
critic, G. Wilson Knight, 'more a storehouse for poets of the
future than itself a poem'. So deep are the contradictions of the
situation that Richard Hurd – the very critic who resolved the
problem of structure by analysing *The Faerie Queene* on 'Gothic'

principles – exemplifies the Gothic virtues of sublimity and force of imagination by quoting Shakespeare, Milton and Tasso – but not Spenser, whom he nevertheless says 'still ranks highest among the poets'.

There is one other important reflection of Augustan uneasiness with *The Faerie Queene* – the appeal to history to explain its characteristics and defects. For example, the triumphant praise of Spenser and of the fancy which ends Hurd's book is preceded by an apologetic account of the Elizabethan tastes for allegory and chivalry. An apologetic use of history is not necessarily meaningless or shallow. Behind much historical discussion of Spenser in the eighteenth century is an attitude that has its noblest statement in Johnson's *Preface to Shakespeare*:

Those whom my arguments cannot persuade to give their approbation to the judgement of Shakespeare, will easily, if they consider the condition of his life, make some allowance for his ignorance. Every man's performances, to be rightly estimated, must be compared with the state of the age in which he lived, and with his own particular opportunities; and though to the reader a book be not worse or better for the circumstances of the author, yet as there is always a silent reference of human works to human abilities, and as the inquiry, how far man may extend his designs, or how high he may rate his native force, is of far greater dignity than in what rank we shall place any particular performance, curiosity is always busy to discover the instruments, as well as to survey the workmanship, to know how much is to be ascribed to original powers, and how much to casual and adventitious help.

This is a splendid critique of a narrow concern for literary judgement. Yet it is very far from the modern assumption that the first use of historical knowledge is to enable us to read a work 'on its own terms'. Johnson's terms – as is clear when

he goes on to discuss the vulgarity and childish credulity of
Shakespeare's audience – are decidedly those of his time. By
the same token, the eighteenth-century critics who invoke
Elizabethan tastes and manners to explain *The Faerie Queene*
are essentially giving a generous and favourable version of
Rymer's harsh strictures.

   Why then, apart from historical interests of our own, should
we read eighteenth-century criticism of *The Faerie Queene*?
Because when it is good, it displays the security, independence
and clarity of formulation that Leavis rightly identifies, in
Johnson's case, as the strengths that accompany and correspond
to the inevitable limitations of a criticism based on a strong, often
complacent, sense of a common culture. When their criticism is
positive and concrete, these critics display to a remarkable
degree the 'sense of fact' – the grasp of what is relevant and
demonstrable – that Eliot has praised as the essential qualification
of a critic.[1] On larger issues, like allegory and structure, their
limitations of course become very apparent. And yet even on
these matters they are concerned with aspects of *The Faerie
Queene* that every reader must come to terms with. And they
have so well and literally 'come to terms' themselves – a critic
like John Hughes so well understands the grounds of his arguments
and discriminations – that no reader of the poem can fail to
benefit from taking them seriously, by way of either emulation
or disagreement.

   For all the strengths of eighteenth-century criticism, it is clear
that its limitations produced corresponding blindnesses to
qualities of *The Faerie Queene*. Sensitivity to some of these
qualities is perhaps the first thing we notice when we come to
the criticism of the romantic period, or think of the ways in
which romantic poets are indebted to Spenser. But the

1 Readers of Christopher Ricks' *Milton's Grand Style* will recall the presence of
this quality in eighteenth-century commentaries on *Paradise Lost*.

importance of romantic criticism for the reader of Spenser goes
far beyond the specific new emphases that come from specific
tastes and awarenesses. The romantics, with Coleridge foremost
among them, brought about fundamental advances in our
notions of poems, of poets and – what most concerns us here –
of the reader's relation to poems. Romantic critics give us, in a
way neoclassic critics do not, a sense of dealing directly with the
felt qualities of a poem. For example, it was not a novelty to call
Spenser a dreamer, as the romantics commonly did: it was a
perfectly obvious notion, in the eighteenth century, that the play
of fancy uncontrolled by judgement was like the mind's activity
in dreaming. But no eighteenth-century critic would have been
capable of Lamb's discriminating the images in a real dream from
those of the Cave of Mammon episode. By comparison with
Lamb's immediate sense of psychic and literary experience,
eighteenth-century criticism seems mere deduction from a
psychology. It is important to emphasize the achievement of
romantic criticism in this respect, precisely because we assume it
to be inherent in any criticism. But eighteenth-century treatments
of rhetoric, thought and structure seem externalized and, in a
limiting sense, objective, when we consider the apprehension of
sensibility that underlies Coleridge's characterization of Spenser's
style and his defence of Spenser's prolixity, Hazlitt's comparison
of Spenser and Milton or his characterization of *The Faerie Queene*.

It is also important that the reader should not underestimate the
specific achievements of the romantics in interpreting *The
Faerie Queene*. Hazlitt's essay, for example, states what is by now
the most tired and hackneyed view of the poem, one that is justly
outmoded because unfruitful, and one that we are likely to think
of as the typical romantic view of Spenser. Hazlitt's
characterization of Spenser's passivity, sensuousness and love of
beauty – with its clear affinities with aspects of Keats' and Shelley's
poetry – makes *The Faerie Queene* seem a monument to

'poeticalness' in a bad sense. But in fact this view, in its specialized and stultifying form, is not to be laid to Hazlitt's charge. It is, however, found in James Russell Lowell's Victorian statement of it, one of the most influential essays in the history of Spenser criticism. It is Lowell who denies that Spenser's allegory can be in any way poetic and who values only what is 'innocently sensuous'. Hazlitt was laying the ground for this attitude, but he was not espousing it when he said:

Some people will say that all this may be very fine, but that they cannot understand it on account of the allegory. They are afraid of the allegory, as if they thought it would bite them: they look at it as a child looks at a painted dragon, and think it will strangle them in its shining folds. This is very idle. If they do not meddle with the allegory, the allegory will not meddle with them. Without minding it at all, the whole is as plain as a pike-staff.

Where Lowell treats moral aspects of *The Faerie Queene* as a foreign element (coming upon them, he says, is like finding a bit of gravel in a dish of strawberries and cream), Hazlitt's counsel is to accept, as frankly and directly as possible, whatever the poem offers. Hence Hazlitt is able to praise a much wider range of passages and effects than Lowell can; for all his bias towards the picturesque in Spenser, he praises allegorical characters and moralistic statements in a generous and unfussy way. Rightly understood, his statement about Spenser's allegory is still the most essential piece of advice to the reader: put away vain fears that inaccessible knowledge and attitudes are the key to *The Faerie Queene*; trust the verse, and take the poem as it comes. The best witness to the essential soundness of Hazlitt's position is C. S. Lewis' puzzlement about it:

Though such studies [of Spenser's philosophical and icono-graphical background] are enrichments they are not necessary for all readers. For those who can surrender themselves simply to the story Spenser himself will provide guidance enough. The allegory that really matters is usually unmistakable. Hazlitt can hardly have meant what he said on that subject. Few poets are so radically allegorical as Spenser.

On the contrary Hazlitt meant what he said and Lewis agreed with him; but Lewis rightly felt that he could not accept Hazlitt's terms.

Lowell's essay presents one side of a debate that for half a century set the terms for understanding *The Faerie Queene*. The other side is represented by Edward Dowden's 'Spenser, the Poet and Teacher,' for at least a generation the most admired essay on *The Faerie Queene*. Dowden argues that our watchword in reading Spenser should be Milton's praise of him as 'sage and serious', 'a better teacher than Scotus or Aquinas'. Like Lowell's essay, Dowden's has its roots in the romantics, and by this fact bears witness to the breadth and fullness of their creative engagement with Spenser. Dowden's Spenser, as he makes perfectly explicit, is Wordsworth's. Where Lowell saw in Spenser a purified sensuousness (thus making him a prototype of Keats and Tennyson), Dowden saw a purified and exalted sense of human character.

Dowden's essay unquestionably takes the right side in the Victorian debate on *The Faerie Queene*, and for that very reason it is puzzling to find that it continually strikes a false note. It would be easy enough to invoke the Victorianism of the essay – to draw a contrast between Wordsworth the poet and Dowden the professor, between Wordsworth's writing on Spenser, luminous and incisive in both verse and prose, and Dowden's falsely poetic prose. We need not bother to excuse Dowden by observing that the 'Victorian' Wordsworth was very much the poet's own creation. It is much more important to remark that what now

seems weak in Dowden is due to a positive understanding of
Wordsworth's achievement and of Spenser's – after all, we only
feel the presence of false notes when the true tune seems within
range. But Dowden, for all the rightness of his emphases, could
not give a just account of the seriousness of *The Faerie Queene*,
because by the time he wrote, readers had almost entirely lost
a sense of Spenser's allegory. And this is precisely because the
Victorian critics, in this respect, were true to their romantic
heritage. Lowell's view of allegory comes directly from
Coleridge's – that allegory is essentially unpoetic, because it
refers and is tied to realities external to the poem itself.
Wordsworth and the tradition that derives from him would
seem to respect more justly the spiritual realities with which
The Faerie Queene is concerned. But whereas an allegorical poet
treats spiritual realities precisely as such – permanent constituents
of man's psychological and moral nature – Wordsworth and the
Victorians treat them as idealizations in an ethical sense. Hence
the women in *The Faerie Queene* – 'pure types' in one sense, since
they present fundamental aspects of spiritual and erotic
experience – become 'pure' in another sense in Dowden's essay,
and Spenser's clear-sighted, free intelligence is represented as a
rapturous prudery. The villain here is the notion that Spenser
is an 'idealist', a notion that depends on the view (characteristic
of the great age of the English novel) that man is 'of the earth,
earthy' and that reality is physical and secular, limited in all ways.
It is understandable that Wordsworth would have fathered such a
misconception of Spenser, for his work was devoted to
redeeming the earth for the human spirit, and to joining separate
individuals and their separate lives and histories into a common
human nature. But for Spenser, Wordsworth's goals were
assumptions and starting points: he would have called himself a
realist and scarcely understood the term 'idealist'. Except for
Ruskin, however, no Victorian critic saw this fact; fully grasping

and conveying its significance was perhaps the greatest contribution of Lewis, the greatest of modern Spenserians.

This brings us to the threshold of the last section of this anthology. It remains only to remark that this section ends with an essay by a figure ideally suited to make the transition from historical to contemporary criticism of Spenser. Yeats' roots were in the romantic tradition, and for him Spenser was a master. On the other hand, he was born late enough to have a critical attitude towards the tradition: where Dowden simply equates Spenser and Wordsworth, Yeats (however questionable the specific terms of his historical analysis) sees that Spenser and Shelley come from quite different phases of English civilization. Finally, given the nature of this anthology, it is agreeable to reflect that the vigour and directness of Yeats' prose owe something to the essentially eighteenth-century culture that he knew in Ireland.

Thomas Rymer

from the Preface to his translation of Rapin's *Reflections on Aristotle's Treatise of Poesie*   1674

Spenser, I think, may be reckoned the first of our heroic poets: he had a large spirit, a sharp judgement, and a genius for heroic poesy, perhaps above any that ever writ since Virgil. But our misfortune is, he wanted a true idea, and lost himself by following an unfaithful guide. Though besides Homer and Virgil he had read Tasso, yet he rather suffered himself to be misled by Ariosto, with whom blindly rambling on marvellous adventures, he makes no conscience of probability. All is fanciful and chimerical, without any uniformity, without any foundation in truth; his poem is perfect Fairyland.

They who can love Ariosto will be ravished with Spenser, whilst men of juster thoughts lament that such great wits have miscarried in their travels for want of direction to set them in the right way. But the truth is, in Spenser's time Italy itself was not well satisfied with Tasso, and few amongst them would then allow that he had excelled their divine Ariosto. And it was the vice of those times to affect superstitiously the allegory, and nothing would then be current without a mystical meaning. We must blame the Italians for debauching great Spenser's judgement; and they cast him on the unlucky choice of the stanza, which in no wise is proper for our language.

John Dryden

from 'Discourse Concerning Satire'   1692

There is no uniformity in the design of Spenser: he aims at the accomplishment of no one action; he raises up a hero for every one of his adventures; and endows each of them with some particular moral virtue, which renders them all equal, without subordination or preference. Every one is most valiant in his own legend: only we must do him that justice to observe that magnanimity, which is the character of Prince Arthur, shines throughout the whole poem, and succours the rest when they are in distress. The original of every knight was then living in the court of Queen Elizabeth, and he attributed to each of them that virtue which he thought was most conspicuous in them – an ingenious piece of flattery, though it turned not much to his account. Had he lived to finish his poem, in the six remaining legends, it had certainly been more of a piece, but could not have been perfect, because the model was not true. But Prince Arthur, or his chief patron Sir Philip Sidney, whom he intended to make happy by the marriage of his Gloriana, dying before him, deprived the poet both of means and spirit to accomplish his design. For the rest, his obsolete language and the ill choice of his stanza are faults but of the second magnitude; for, notwithstanding the first, he is still intelligible, at least after a little practice; and for the last, he is the more to be admired, that, labouring under such a difficulty, his verses are so numerous, so various, and so harmonious, that only Virgil, whom he profestly imitated, has surpassed him among the Romans; and only Mr Waller among the English.

Joseph Addison

from *Account of the Greatest English Poets* 1694

Old Spenser next, warmed with poetic rage,
In ancient tales amused a barb'rous age;
An age that yet uncultivate and rude,
Where'er the poet's fancy led, pursued
Through pathless fields and unfrequented floods,
To dens of dragons and enchanted woods.
But now the mystic tale, that pleased of yore,
Can charm an understanding age no more;
The long-spun allegories fulsome grow,
While the dull moral lies too plain below.
We view well pleased at distance all the sights
Of arms and palfries, battles, fields and fights,
And damsels in distress, and courteous knights.
But when we look too near, the shades decay,
And all the pleasing landscape fades away.
(17–31)

John Dryden

from the Dedication to his translation of Virgil's *Pastorals* 1697

Our own nation has produced a third poet in this kind [the pastoral], not inferior to the two former [Theocritus and Virgil]. For the *Shepheardes Calender* of Spenser is not to be matched in any modern language, not even by Tasso's *Aminta*, which infinitely transcends Guarini's *Pastor Fido*, as having more of nature in it and being almost wholly clear from the wretched affectation of learning. I will say nothing of the *Piscatory Eclogues*, because no modern Latin can bear criticism. ... But Spenser, being master of our northern dialect and skilled in Chaucer's English, has so exactly imitated the Doric of Theocritus that his love is a perfect image of that passion which God infused into both sexes, before it was corrupted with the knowledge of arts and the ceremonies of what we call good manners.

John Dryden

from the Dedication to his translation of Virgil's *Aeneid* 1697

Spenser wanted only to have read the rules of Bossu; for no man was ever born with a greater genius, or had more knowledge to support it. ...

I must acknowledge that Virgil in Latin and Spenser in English have been my masters. Spenser has also given me the boldness to make use sometimes of his Alexandrine line, which we call, though improperly, the Pindaric, because Mr Cowley has often employed it in his *Odes*. ...

When I mentioned the Pindaric line, I should have added, that I take another licence in my verses: for I frequently make use of triplet rhymes, and for the same reason, because they bound the sense. And therefore I generally join these two licences together, and make the last verse of the triplet a Pindaric: for, besides the majesty which it gives, it confines the sense within the barriers of three lines, which would languish if it were lengthened into four. Spenser is my example for both these privileges of English verses, and Chapman has followed him in his translation of Homer. Mr Cowley has given into them after both, and all succeeding writers after him. I regard them now as the *Magna Charta* of heroic poetry, and am too much an Englishman to lose what my ancestors have gained for me. Let the French and Italians value themselves on their regularity; strength and elevation are our standard.

Alexander Pope

from 'A Discourse on Pastoral Poetry' 1704

Spenser's *Calender*, in Mr Dryden's opinion, is the most complete work of this kind which any nation has produced ever since the time of Virgil. Not but that he may be thought imperfect in some few points. His eclogues are somewhat too long if we compare them with the ancients. He is sometimes too allegorical, and treats of matters of religion in a pastoral style as Mantuan had done before him. He has employed the lyric measure, which is contrary to the practice of the old poets. His stanza is not still the same, nor always well chosen. This last may be the reason his expression is sometimes not concise enough: for the tetrastic has obliged him to extend his sense to the length of four lines, which would have been more closely confined in the couplet.

In the manners, thoughts and characters, he comes near to Theocritus himself, though notwithstanding all the care he has taken, he is certainly inferior in his dialect. For the Doric had its beauty and propriety in the time of Theocritus; it was used in part of Greece and frequent in the mouths of many of the greatest persons; whereas the old English and country phrases of Spenser were either entirely obsolete or spoken only by people of the lowest condition. As there is a difference between simplicity and rusticity, so the expression of simple thoughts should be plain but not clownish. The addition he has made of a calendar to his eclogues is very beautiful, since by this, besides the general moral of innocence and simplicity, which is common to other authors of pastoral, he has one peculiar to himself: he compares human life to the several seasons, and at once exposes to his readers a view of the great and little worlds in their various changes and aspects. Yet the scrupulous division of his pastorals into months has obliged him either to repeat the same description in other words for three months together, or when it was exhausted before, entirely to omit it: whence it comes to pass that some of his eclogues (as the sixth, eighth and tenth, for example) have nothing but their titles to distinguish them. The reason is evident: because the year has not that variety in it to furnish every month with a particular description, as it may every season.

Matthew Prior

from the Preface to *An Ode, Humbly Inscribed to the Queen.
On the Glorious Success of Her Majesty's Arms. Written in Imitation
of Spenser's Style* 1706

When I first thought of writing upon this occasion, I found the ideas so great and numerous that I judged them more proper for the warmth of an ode than for any other sort of poetry. I therefore set Horace before me for a pattern, and particularly his famous ode, the fourth of the fourth book, ... which he wrote in praise of Drusus after his expedition into Germany, and of Augustus upon his happy choice of that general. And in the following poem, though I have endeavoured to imitate all the great strokes of that ode, I have taken the liberty to go off from it and to add variously, as the subject and my own imagination carried me. As to the style, the choice I made of following the ode in Latin determined me in English to the stanza; and herein it was impossible not to have a mind to follow our great countryman Spenser. Which I have done (as well at least as I could) in the manner of my expression and the turn of my number, having only added one verse to his stanza – which I thought made the number more harmonious – and avoided such of his words as I found too obsolete. I have however retained some few of them, to make the colouring look more like Spenser's. 'Behest', command; 'band', army; 'prowess', strength; 'I weet', I know; 'I ween', I think; 'whilom', heretofore; and two or three more of that kind, which I hope the ladies will pardon me and not judge my muse less hand-some, though for once she appears in a farthingale. I have also, in

Spenser's manner, used 'Caesar' for the Emperor, 'Boya' for Bavaria, 'Bavar' for that prince, 'Ister' for Danube, 'Iberia' for Spain, etc. . . .

My two great examples, Horace and Spenser, in many things resemble each other. Both have a height of imagination and a majesty of expression in describing the sublime; and both know to temper those talents and sweeten the description, so as to make it lovely as well as pompous. Both have equally that agreeable manner of mixing morality with their story, and that *curiosa felicitas* in the choice of their diction which every writer aims at and so very few have reached. Both are particularly fine in their images and knowing in their numbers.

John Hughes

from 'An Essay on Allegorical Poetry' and 'Remarks on *The Faerie Queene*' in his edition of Spenser's *Works* 1715

It is a misfortune, as Mr Waller observes, which attends the writers of English poetry that they can hardly expect their works should last long in a tongue which is daily changing; that whilst they are new, envy is apt to prevail against them, and as that wears off, our language itself fails. Our poets, therefore, he says, should imitate judicious statuaries, that choose the most durable materials, and should carve in Latin or Greek if they would have their labours preserved forever.

Notwithstanding the disadvantage he has mentioned, we have two ancient English poets, Chaucer and Spenser, who may perhaps be reckoned as exceptions to this remark. These seem to have taken deep root, like old British oaks, and to flourish in defiance of all the injuries of time and weather. The former is indeed much more obsolete in his style than the latter; but it is owing to an extraordinary native strength in both that they have been able thus far to survive amidst the changes of our tongue and seem rather likely, among the curious at least, to preserve the knowledge of our ancient language than to be in danger of being destroyed with it and buried under its ruins.

Though Spenser's affection to his master Chaucer led him in many things to copy after him, yet those who have read both will easily observe that these two geniuses were of a very different kind. Chaucer excelled in his characters; Spenser in his descriptions. The first studied humour, was an excellent satirist and a lively but rough painter of the manners of that rude age in which he lived; the latter was of the serious turn, had an exalted and elegant mind, a warm and boundless fancy and was an admirable imager of virtues and vices, which was his particular talent. The embellishments of description are rich and lavish in him beyond comparison; and as this is the most striking part of poetry, especially to young readers, I take it to be the reason that he has been the father of more poets among us than any other of our writers – poetry being first kindled in the imagination, which Spenser writes to more than anyone, and the season of youth being the most susceptible of the impression. It will not seem strange, therefore, that Cowley, as he himself tells us, first caught his flame by reading Spenser; that our great Milton owned him for his original, as Mr Dryden assures us; and that Dryden studied him and has bestowed more frequent commendations on him than on any other English poet.

The most known and celebrated of his works, though I will not say the most perfect, is *The Faerie Queene*. It is conceived, wrought up and coloured with a stranger fancy and discovers more the particular genius of Spenser than any of his other writings. The author, in a letter to Sir Walter Raleigh, having called this poem 'a continued Allegory, or dark Conceit', it may not be improper to offer some remarks on allegorical poetry in general, by which the beauties of this work may more easily be discovered by ordinary readers. I must at the same time beg the indulgence of those who are conversant with critical discourses to what I shall here propose, this being a subject something out of the way and not expressly treated upon by those who have laid down rules for the art of poetry.

An allegory is a fable or story in which under imaginary persons or things is shadowed some real action or instructive moral; or, as I think it is somewhere very shortly defined by Plutarch, it is that 'in which one thing is related and another thing is understood'. It is a kind of poetical picture, or hieroglyphic, which by its apt resemblance conveys instruction to the mind by an analogy to the senses and so amuses the fancy whilst it informs the understanding. Every allegory has therefore two senses, the literal and the mystical; the literal sense is like a dream or vision, of which the mystical sense is the true meaning or interpretation.

This will be more clearly apprehended by considering that as a simile is but a more extended metaphor, so an allegory is a kind of continued simile or an assemblage of similitudes drawn out at full length. Thus when it is said that 'Death is the offspring of Sin', this is a metaphor to signify that the former is produced by the latter as a child is brought into the world by its parent. Again, to compare death to a meager and ghastly apparition starting out of the ground, moving towards the spectator with a menacing air and shaking in his hand a bloody dart is a representation of the terrors which attend that great enemy to human nature. But let the reader observe in Milton's *Paradise Lost* with what exquisite fancy and skill this common metaphor and simile, and the moral contained in them, are extended and wrought up into one of the most beautiful allegories in our language.

The resemblance which has been so often observed in general between poetry and painting is yet more particular in allegory, which, as I said before, is a kind of picture in poetry. Horace has in one of his odes pathetically described the ruinous condition of his country after the civil wars and the hazard of its being involved in new dissensions, by the emblem of a ship shattered with storms and driven into port with broken masts, torn sails and disabled rigging and in danger of being forced by new storms out to sea again. There is nothing said in the whole ode but what is literally applicable to a ship, but it is generally agreed that the thing signified is the Roman State. Thus Rubens, who had a good allegorical genius in painting, has in his famous work of the Luxembourg Gallery figured the government of France, on Louis the Thirteenth's arriving at age, by a galley. The king stands at the helm; Mary of Medicis, the queen mother and regent, puts the rudder in his hand; Justice, Fortitude, Religion and Public Faith are seated at the oars; and other Virtues have their proper employments in managing the sails and tackle.

By this general description of allegory it may easily be conceived that in works of this kind there is a large field open to invention, which among the ancients was universally looked upon to be the principal part of poetry. The power of raising images or resemblances of things, giving them life and action and presenting them as it were before the eyes was thought to have something in it like creation. And it was probably for this fabling part that the first authors of such works were called 'poets', or 'makers' as the word signifies and as it is literally translated and used by Spenser; though the learned Gerard Vossius is of opinion that it was rather for the framing their verses. However, by this art of fiction or allegory more than by the structure of their numbers, or what we now call 'versification', the poets were distinguished from historians and philosophers, though the latter sometimes invaded the province of the poet and delivered their doctrines likewise in allegories or parables. And this, when they did not purposely make them obscure in order to conceal them from the common people, was a plain indication that they thought there was an advantage in such methods of conveying instruction to the mind and that they served for the more effectual engaging the attention of the hearers and for leaving deeper impressions on their memories.

Plutarch, in one of his discourses, gives a very good reason for the use of fiction in poetry: because Truth of itself is rigid and austere and cannot be moulded into such agreeable forms as fiction can. 'For neither the numbers,' says he, 'nor the ranging of the words, nor the elevation and elegance of the style have so many graces as the artful contrivance and disposition of the fable.' For this reason, as he relates it after Plato, when the wise Socrates himself was prompted by a particular impulse to the writing of verses, being by his constant employment in the study of truth a stranger to the art of inventing, he chose for his subject the fables of Aesop, 'not thinking', says Plutarch, 'that anything could be poetry which was void of fiction'. The same author makes use of a comparison in another place which I think may be most properly applied to allegorical poetry in particular: that as grapes on a vine are covered by the leaves which grow about them, so under the pleasant narrations and fictions of the poets there are couched many useful morals and doctrines.

It is for this reason – that is to say, in regard to the moral sense – that allegory has a liberty indulged to it beyond any other sort of writing whatsoever; that it often assembles things of the most contrary kinds in nature and supposes even impossibilities – as that a golden bough should grow among the common branches of a tree, as Virgil has described it in the Sixth Book of his *Aeneis*. Allegory is indeed the fairyland of poetry, peopled by imagination; its inhabitants are so many apparitions; its woods, caves, wild beasts, rivers, mountains

and palaces are produced by a kind of magical power and are all
visionary and typical; and it abounds in such licenses as would be
shocking and monstrous if the mind did not attend to the mystic
sense contained under them. Thus in the fables of Aesop, which are
some of the most ancient allegories extant, the author gives reason and
speech to beasts, insects and plants, and by that means covertly instructs mankind in the most important incidents and concerns of their
lives.

I am not insensible that the word 'allegory' has been sometimes
used in a larger sense than that to which I may seem here to have
restrained it and has been applied indifferently to any poem which
contains a covered moral, though the story or fable carries nothing in
it that appears visionary or romantic. It may be necessary, therefore,
to distinguish allegory into the two following kinds.

The first is that in which the story is framed of real or historical
persons and probable or possible actions, by which however some
other persons and actions are typified or represented. In this sense the
whole *Aeneis* of Virgil may be said to be an allegory, if we consider
Aeneas as representing Augustus Caesar and his conducting the
remains of his countrymen from the ruins of Troy to a new settlement
in Italy as emblematical of Augustus' modelling a new government
out of the ruins of the aristocracy and establishing the Romans, after
the confusion of the civil war, in a peaceable and flourishing condition.
It does not, I think, appear that Homer had any such design in his
poems or that he meant to delineate his contemporaries or their
actions under the chief characters and adventures of the Trojan War.
And though the allusion I have mentioned in Virgil is a circumstance
which the author has finely contrived to be coincident to the general
frame of his story, yet he has avoided the making it plain and particular
and has thrown it off in so many instances from a direct application
that his poem is perfect without it. This then, for distinction, should,
I think, rather be called a parallel than an allegory; at least, in allegories framed after this manner, the literal sense is sufficient to satisfy
the reader, though he should look no further, and without being considered as emblematical of some other persons or action, may of itself
exhibit very useful morals and instructions. Thus the morals which
may be drawn from the *Aeneis* are equally noble and instructive
whether we suppose the real hero to be Aeneas or Augustus Caesar.

The second kind of allegory, and which I think may more properly challenge the name, is that in which the fable or story consists for the most part of fictitious persons or beings, creatures of the poet's brain, and actions surprising and without the bounds of probability or nature. In works of this kind it is impossible for the reader to rest in the literal sense, but he is of necessity driven to seek for another meaning under these wild types and shadows. This grotesque invention claims, as I have observed, a licence peculiar to itself and is what I would be understood in this discourse more particularly to mean by the word 'allegory'. Thus Milton has described it in his poem called *Il Penseroso*, where he alludes to the *Squire's Tale* in Chaucer:

Or call up him that left half told
The story of Cambuscan bold,
Of Cambal and of Algarsife,
And who had Canace to wife:
That own'd the virtuous ring and glass,
And of the wondrous horse of brass,
On which the Tartar King did ride;
And if ought else great bards beside
In sage and solemn tunes have sung
Of tourneys and of trophies hung,
Of forests and enchantments drear,
Where more is meant than meets the ear.

(109–20)

It may be proper to give an instance or two, by which the distinction of this last kind of allegory may more plainly appear.

The story of Circe in the *Odysses* is an allegorical fable of which there are perhaps more copies and imitations than of any other whatever. Her offering a cup filled with intoxicating liquor to her guests, her mingling poison with their food and then by magical arts turning them into the shapes of swine, and Ulysses resisting her charms by the virtue of an herb called moly, which he had received from the God Mercury, and restoring his companions to their true persons are all fictions of the last kind I have mentioned. The person of the goddess is likewise fictitious and out of the circle of the Grecian divinities, and the adventures are not to be understood but in a mystical sense. The episode of Calypso, though somewhat of the same kind, approaches nearer to nature and probability. But the story of Dido in the *Aeneis*, though copied from the Circe and Calypso and formed on the same moral – namely, to represent a hero obstructed by the allurements of pleasure and at last breaking from them – and though Mercury likewise assists in it to dissolve the charm, yet is not necessarily to be looked upon as an allegory. The fable does not appear merely imaginary or emblematical; the persons are natural; and excepting the distance of time which the critics have noted between the real Aeneas and Dido (a circumstance which Virgil, not being bound to historical truth, wilfully neglected), there is nothing which might not really have happened. Ariosto's Alcina and the Armida of Tasso are copies from the same original. These again are plainly allegorical: the whole literal sense of the latter is a kind of vision, or scene of imagination, and is everywhere transparent, to show the moral sense which is under it. The Bower of Bliss, in the Second Book of *The Faerie Queene*, is in like manner a copy from Tasso; but the ornaments of description, which Spenser has transplanted out of the Italian poem, are more proper in his work, which was designed to be wholly allegorical, than in an epic poem, which is superior in its nature to such lavish embellishments. There is another copy of the Circe in the dramatic way in a masque by our famous Milton, the whole plan of which is allegorical and is written with a very poetical spirit on the same moral, though with different characters.

I have here instanced in one of the most ancient and best-imagined allegories extant. Scylla, Charybdis and the Sirens in the same poem are of the same nature and are creatures purely allegorical. But the Harpies in Virgil, which disturbed Aeneas and his followers at their banquet, as they do not seem to exhibit any certain moral, may probably have been thrown in by the poet only as an omen and to raise what is commonly called 'the wonderful', which is a property as essential to epic poetry as probability. Homer's giving speech to the River Xanthus in the *Iliad* and to the horses of Achilles seem to be inventions of the same kind, and might be designed to fill the reader with astonishment and concern and with an apprehension of the greatness of an occasion which, by a bold fiction of the poet, is supposed to have produced such extraordinary effects.

As allegory sometimes, for the sake of the moral sense couched under its fictions, gives speech to brutes and sometimes introduces creatures which are out of nature – as goblins, chimeras, fairies and the like – so it frequently gives life to virtues and vices, passions and diseases, to natural and moral qualities and represents them acting as divine, human or infernal persons. A very ingenious writer calls these characters 'shadowy Beings'[1] and has with good reason censured the employing them in just epic poems. Of this kind are Sin and Death, which I mentioned before, in Milton and Fame in Virgil. We find likewise a large group of these shadowy figures placed, in the Sixth Book of the *Aeneis*, at the entrance into the infernal regions; but as they are only shown there and have no share in the action of the poem, the description of them is a fine allegory and extremely proper to the place where they appear: [quotes *Aeneid*, v 273–84].

As persons of this imaginary life are to be excluded from any share of action in epic poems, they are yet less to be endured in the drama; yet we find they have sometimes made their appearance on the ancient stage. Thus in a tragedy of Aeschylus, Strength is introduced assisting Vulcan to bind Prometheus to a rock, and in one of Euripides, Death comes to the house of Admetus to demand Alcestis, who had offered herself to die to save her husband's life. But what I have here said of epic and dramatic poems does not extend to such writings, the very frame and model of which is designed to be allegorical – in which therefore, as I said before, such unsubstantial and symbolical actors may be very properly admitted.

Every book of *The Faerie Queene* is fruitful of these visionary beings, which are invented and drawn with a surprising strength of imagination. I shall produce but one instance here, which the reader may compare with that just mentioned in Virgil, to which it is no way inferior. It is in the Second Book where Mammon conducts Guyon through a cave underground to show him his treasure:

> At length they came into a larger space,
> That stretcht it selfe into an ample plaine,
> Through which a beaten broad high way did trace,
> That streight did lead to *Plutoes* griesly raine:
> By that wayes side, there sat infernall Payne,
> And fast beside him sat tumultuous Strife:

---

1 *Spectator*, vol. 4, no. 273.

The one in hand an yron whip did straine,
  The other brandished a bloudy knife,
And both did gnash their teeth, and both did threaten life.

  On thother side in one consort there sate
  Cruell Reuenge, and rancorous Despight,
  Disloyall Treason, and hart-burning Hate,
  But gnawing Gealosie out of their sight
  Sitting alone, his bitter lips did bight,
  And trembling Feare still to and fro did fly,
  And found no place, where safe he shroud him might,
  Lamenting Sorrow did in darknesse lye,
And Shame his vgly face did hide from liuing eye.

  And ouer them sad Horrour with grim hew,
  Did alwayes sore, beating his yron wings;
  And after him Owles and Night-rauens flew,
  The hatefull messengers of heauy things,
  Of death and dolour telling sad tidings;
  Whiles sad *Celeno*, sitting on a clift,
  A song of bale and bitter sorrow sings,
  That hart of flint a sunder could haue rift:
Which hauing ended, after him she flyeth swift.

(II vii 21–3)

The posture of Jealousy and the motion of Fear in this description are particularly fine. These are instances of allegorical persons which are shown only in one transient view. The reader will everywhere meet with others in this author which are employed in the action of the poem and which need not be mentioned here.

Having thus endeavoured to give a general idea of what is meant by allegory in poetry and shown what kinds of persons are frequently employed in it, I shall proceed to mention some properties which seem requisite in all well-invented fables of this kind.

There is no doubt but men of critical learning, if they had thought fit, might have given us rules about allegorical writing, as they have done about epic and other kinds of poetry; but they have rather chosen to let this forest remain wild, as if they thought there was something in the nature of the soil which could not so well be restrained and cultivated in enclosures. What Sir William Temple observes about rules in general may perhaps be more particularly applicable to this: that they may possibly hinder some from being very bad Poets, but are not capable of making any very good one. Notwithstanding this, they are useful to help our observation in distinguishing the beauties and the blemishes in such works as have been already produced. I shall, therefore, beg leave to mention four qualities which I think are essential to every good allegory, the three first of which relate to the fable and the last to the moral.

The first is that it be lively and surprising. The fable, or literal sense, being that which most immediately offers itself to the reader's observation, must have this property in order to raise and entertain his curiosity. As there is, therefore, more invention employed in a work of this kind than in mere narration or description or in general amplifications on any subject, it consequently requires a more than ordinary heat of fancy in its first production. If the fable, on the contrary, is flat, spiritless or barren of invention, the reader's imagination is not affected nor his attention engaged, though the instruction conveyed under it be ever so useful or important.

The second qualification I shall mention is elegance, or a beautiful propriety and aptness in the fable to the subject on which it is employed. By this quality the invention of the poet is restrained from taking too great a compass or losing itself in a confusion of ill-sorted ideas, such representations as that mentioned by Horace of 'dolphins in a wood' or 'boars in the sea' being fit only to surprise the imagination without pleasing the judgement. The same moral may likewise be expressed in different fables, all of which may be lively and full of spirit yet not equally elegant – as various dresses may be made for the same body, yet not equally becoming. As it therefore requires a heat of fancy to raise images and resemblances, it requires a good taste to distinguish and range them and to choose the most proper and beautiful where there appears an almost distracting variety. I may compare this to Aeneas searching in the wood for the golden bough: he was at a loss where to lay his hand till his mother's doves, descending in his sight, flew before him and perched on the tree where it was to be found.

Another essential property is that the fable be everywhere consistent with itself. As licentious as allegorical fiction may seem in some respects, it is nevertheless subject to this restraint. The poet is indeed at liberty in choosing his story and inventing his persons, but after he has introduced them, he is obliged to sustain them in their proper characters as well as in more regular kinds of writing. It is difficult to give particular rules under this head; it may suffice to say that this wild nature is, however, subject to an economy proper to itself, and though it may sometimes seem extravagant, ought never to be absurd. Most of the allegories in *The Faerie Queene* are agreeable to this rule, but in one of his other poems the author has manifestly transgressed it. The poem I mean is that which is called *Prothalamion*. In this the two brides are figured by two beautiful swans sailing down the River Thames. The allegory breaks before the reader is prepared for it, and we see them at their landing in their true shapes without knowing how this sudden change is effected. If this had been only a simile, the poet might have dropped it at pleasure, but as it is an allegory, he ought to have made it of a piece or to have invented some probable means of coming out of it.

The last property I shall mention is that the allegory be clear and intelligible. The fable, being designed only to clothe and adorn the moral but not to hide it, should methinks resemble the draperies we admire in some of the ancient statues, in which the folds are not too many nor too thick, but so judiciously ordered that the shape and beauty of the limbs may be seen through them.

It must be confessed that many of the ancient fables appear to us at this distance of time very perplexed and dark, and if they had any moral at all, it is so closely couched that it is very difficult to discover it. Whoever reads the Lord Bacon's *Wisdom of the Ancients* will be convinced of this. He has employed a more than ordinary penetration to decipher the most known traditions in the heathen mythology, but his interpretations are often farfetched and so much at random that the reader can have no assurance of their truth. It is not to be doubted that a great part of these fables were allegorical, but others might have been stories designed only to amuse or to practice upon the credulity of the vulgar; or the doctrines they contained might be purposely clouded to conceal them from common knowledge. But though, as I hinted in the former part of this discourse, this may have been a reason among philosophers, it ought not to be admitted among poets. An allegory which is not clear is a riddle, and the sense of it lies at the mercy of every fanciful interpreter.

Though the epic poets, as I have shown, have sprinkled some allegories through their poems, yet it would be absurd to endeavour to understand them everywhere in a mystical sense. We are told of one Metrodorus Lampsacenus, whose works are lost, that turned the whole writings of Homer into an allegory. It was doubtless by some such means that the principles of all arts and sciences whatever were discovered in that single author, for nothing can escape an expositor who proceeds in his operations like a Rosicrucian and brings with him the gold he pretends to find.

It is surprising that Tasso, whose *Jerusalem* was, at the time when he wrote it, the best plan of an epic poem after Virgil, should be possessed with this affectation and should not believe his work perfect till he had turned it into a mystery. I cannot help thinking that the 'Allegory', as it is called, which he has printed with it, looks as if it were invented after the poem was finished. He tells us that the Christian army represents Man; the City of Jerusalem, Civil Happiness; Godfrey, the Understanding; Rinaldo and Tancred, the other Powers of the Soul; and that the Body is typified by the common soldiers – with a great deal more that carries in it a strong cast of enthusiasm. He is indeed much more intelligible when he explains the flowers, the fountains, the nymphs and the musical instruments to figure to us Sensual Pleasures under the false appearance of Good. But for the rest, I appeal to anyone who is acquainted with that poem whether he would ever have discovered these mysteries if the poet had not let him into them or whether, even after this, he can keep them long in his mind while he is reading it.

Spenser's conduct is much more reasonable: as he designed his poem upon the plan of the virtues by which he has entitled his several books, he scarce ever loses sight of this design, but has almost everywhere taken care to let it appear. Sir William Temple, indeed, censures this as a fault and says that though his flights of fancy were very noble and high, yet his moral lay so bare that it lost the effect. But I confess I do not understand this. A moral which is not clear is in my apprehension next to no moral at all.

It would be easy to enumerate other properties which are various according to the different kinds of allegory or its different degrees of perfection. Sometimes we are surprised with an uncommon moral which ennobles the fable that conveys it, and at other times we meet with a known and obvious truth placed in some new and beautiful point of light and made surprising by the fiction under which it is exhibited. I have thought it sufficient to touch upon such properties only as seem to be the most essential, and perhaps many more might be reduced under one or other of these general heads. . . .

After what has been said it must be confessed that, excepting Spenser, there are few extraordinary instances of this kind of writing among the moderns. The great mines of invention have been opened long ago, and little new ore seems to have been discovered or brought to light by latter ages. With us the art of framing fables, apologues and allegories, which was so frequent among the writers of antiquity, seems to be, like the art of painting upon glass, but little practised and in a great measure lost. Our colours are not so rich and transparent and are either so ill prepared or so unskillfully laid on that they often sully the light which is to pass through them rather than agreeably tincture and beautify it. Boccalini must be reckoned one of the chief masters of allegory; yet his fables are often flat and ill-chosen, and his invention seems to have been rather fruitful than elegant. I cannot, however, conclude this essay on allegory without observing that we have had the satisfaction to see this kind of writing very lately revived by an excellent genius among ourselves, in the true spirit of the ancients. I need only mention the visions in the *Tatler* and *Spectator* by Mr Addison to convince everyone of this. The Table of Fame, the Vision of Justice, that of the different Pursuits of Love, Ambition and Avarice, the Vision of Mirza and several others, and especially that admirable fable of the two families of Pain and Pleasure – which are all imagined and writ with the greatest strength and delicacy – may give the reader an idea more than anything I can say of the perfection to which this kind of writing is capable of being raised.

(I, xxv–lvi)

By what has been offered in the foregoing discourse on allegorical poetry we may be able, not only to discover many beauties in *The Faerie Queene*, but likewise to excuse some of its irregularities. The chief merit of this poem consists in that surprising vein of fabulous invention which runs through it and enriches it everywhere with imagery and descriptions more than we meet with in any other modern poem. The author seems to be possessed of a kind of poetical magic; and the figures he calls up to our view rise so thick upon us that we are at once pleased and distracted by the exhaustless variety of them, so that his faults may in a manner be imputed to his excellencies. His abundance betrays him into excess, and his judgement is over-borne by the torrent of his imagination.

That which seems the most liable to exception in this work is the model of it and the choice the author has made of so romantic a story. The several books appear rather like so many several poems than one entire fable; each of them has its peculiar knight and is independent of the rest, and though some of the persons make their appearance in different books, yet this has very little effect in connecting them. Prince Arthur is, indeed, the principal person and has, therefore, a share given him in every legend, but his part is not considerable enough in any one of them. He appears and vanishes again like a spirit, and we lose sight of him too soon to consider him as the hero of the poem.

These are the most obvious defects in the fable of *The Faerie Queene*. The want of unity in the story makes it difficult for the reader to carry it in his mind and distracts too much his attention to the several parts of it; and indeed the whole frame of it would appear monstrous if it were to be examined by the rules of epic poetry as they have been drawn from the practice of Homer and Virgil. But as it is plain the author never designed it by those rules, I think it ought rather to be considered as a poem of a particular kind, describing in a series of allegorical adventures or episodes the most noted virtues and vices. To compare it, therefore, with the models of antiquity would be like drawing a parallel between the Roman and the Gothic archi-tecture. In the first there is doubtless a more natural grandeur and simplicity; in the latter we find great mixtures of beauty and bar-barism, yet assisted by the invention of a variety of inferior ornaments. And though the former is more majestic in the whole, the latter may be very surprising and agreeable in its parts.

It may seem strange indeed, since Spenser appears to have been well acquainted with the best writers of antiquity, that he has not imitated them in the structure of his story. Two reasons may be given for this: the first is that at the time when he wrote the Italian poets, whom he has chiefly imitated and who were the first revivers of this art among the moderns, were in the highest vogue and were universally read and admired. But the chief reason was probably that he chose to frame his fable after a model which might give the greatest scope to that range of fancy which was so remarkably his talent. There is a bent in nature which is apt to determine men that particular way in which they are most capable of excelling, and though it is certain he might have formed a better plan, it is to be questioned whether he could have executed any other so well.

It is probably for the same reason that among the Italian poets he rather followed Ariosto, whom he found more agreeable to his genius, than Tasso, who had formed a better plan and from whom he has only borrowed some particular ornaments. Yet it is but justice to say that his plan is much more regular than that of Ariosto. In the *Orlando Furioso* we everywhere meet with an exuberant invention joined with great liveliness and facility of description, yet debased by frequent mixtures of the comic genius as well as many shocking indecorums. Besides, in the huddle and distraction of the adventures, we are for the most part only amused with extravagant stories without being instructed in any moral. On the other hand, Spenser's fable, though often wild, is, as I have observed, always emblematical; and this may very much excuse likewise that air of romance in which he has followed the Italian author. The perpetual stories of knights, giants, castles, and enchantments and all that train of legendary adventures would indeed appear very trifling if Spenser had not found a way to turn them all into allegory or if a less masterly hand had filled up his draught. But it is surprising to observe how much the strength of the painting is superior to the design. It ought to be considered too that at the time when our author wrote the remains of the old gothic chivalry were not quite abolished. It was not many years before that the famous Earl of Surrey, remarkable for his wit and poetry in the reign of King Henry the Eighth, took a romantic journey to Florence, the place of his mistress's birth, and published there a challenge against all nations in defence of her beauty. Jousts and tournaments were held in England in the time of Queen Elizabeth. Sir Philip Sidney tilted at one of these entertainments, which was made for the French ambassador when the treaty of marriage was on foot with the Duke of Anjou. And some of our historians have given us a very particular and formal account of preparations, by marking out lists and appointing judges, for a trial by combat in the same reign which was to have decided the title to a considerable estate, and in which the whole ceremony was perfectly agreeable to the fabulous descriptions in books of knight-errantry. This might render his story more familiar to his first readers, though knights in armour and ladies errant are as antiquated figures to us as the court of that time would appear if we could see them now in their ruffs and farthingales.

There are two other objections to the plan of *The Faerie Queene*, which, I confess, I am more at a loss to answer. I need not, I think, be scrupulous in mentioning freely the defects of a poem which, though it was never supposed to be perfect, has always been allowed to be admirable.

The first is that the scene is laid in Fairyland and the chief actors are fairies. The reader may see their imaginary race and history in the Second Book, at the end of the Tenth Canto, but if he is not prepared beforehand, he may expect to find them acting agreeably to the common stories and traditions about such fancied beings. Thus Shakespeare, who has introduced them in his *Midsummer Night's Dream*, has made them speak and act in a manner perfectly adapted to their supposed characters; but the fairies in this poem are not distinguished from other persons. There is this misfortune likewise attends the choice of such actors: that having been accustomed to conceive of them in a diminutive way, we find it difficult to raise our ideas and to imagine a fairy encountering with a monster or a giant. Homer has pursued a contrary method and represented his heroes above the size and strength of ordinary men, and it is certain that the actions of the *Iliad* would have appeared but ill proportioned to the characters if we were to have imagined them all performed by pygmies.

But as the actors our author has chosen are only fancied beings, he might possibly think himself at liberty to give them what stature, customs and manners he pleased. I will not say he was in the right in this; but it is plain that by the literal sense of Fairyland he only designed an utopia, an imaginary place, and by his fairies, persons of whom he might invent any action proper to human kind without being restrained as he must have been if he had chosen a real scene and historical characters. As for the mystical sense, it appears both by the work itself and by the author's explanation of it that his Fairyland is

England and his Fairy Queen, Queen Elizabeth, at whose command
the adventure of every legend is supposed to be undertaken.

The other objection is that, having chosen an historical person,
Prince Arthur, for his principal hero – who is no fairy, yet is mingled
with them – he has not, however, represented any part of his history. He
appears here, indeed, only in his minority and performs his exercises
in Fairyland as a private gentleman, but we might at least have expected that the fabulous accounts of him and of his victories over the
Saxons should have been worked into some beautiful vision or
prophecy. And I cannot think Spenser would wholly omit this, but
am apt to believe he had done it in some of the following books
which were lost.

In the moral introductions to every book, many of which have a
great propriety and elegance, the author has followed the example of
Ariosto. I will only beg leave to point out some of the principal
beauties in each book, which may yet more particularly discover the
genius of the author.

(I, lviii–lxvii)

There is one episode in this book [Book One] which I cannot but
particularly admire: I mean that in the Fifth Canto, where Duessa the
witch seeks the assistance of Night to convey the body of the wounded
pagan to be cured by Aesculapius in the regions below. The author
here rises above himself and is got into a track of imitating the
ancients, different from the greatest part of his poem. The speech in
which Duessa addresses Night is wonderfully great and stained with
that impious flattery which is the character of Falsehood, who is the
speaker:

O thou most auncient Grandmother of all,
More old than *Ioue*, whom thou at first didst breede,
Or that great house of Gods cælestiall,
Which wast begot in *Dæmogorgons* hall,
And sawst the secrets of the world vnmade.

(I v 22)

As Duessa came away hastily on this expedition and forgot to put
off the shape of Truth, which she had assumed a little before, Night
does not know her; this circumstance and the discovery afterwards,

when she owns her for her daughter, are finely emblematical. The images of horror are raised in a very masterly manner. Night takes the witch into her chariot, and being arrived where the body lay, they alight:

> And all the while she stood vpon the ground,
> The wakefull dogs did neuer cease to bay,
> As giuing warning of th'vnwonted sound,
> With which her yron wheeles did them affray,[1]
> And her darke griesly looke them much dismay;
> The messenger of death, the ghastly Owle
> With drearie shriekes did also her bewray;[2]
> And hungry Wolues continually did howle,
> At her abhorred face, so filthy and so fowle.
>
> (I v 30)

They steal away the body and carry it down through the cave Avernus to the realms of Pluto. What strength of painting is there in the following lines!

> ... on euery side them stood
> The trembling ghosts with sad amazed mood,
> Chattring their yron teeth, and staring wide
> With stonie eyes; and all the hellish brood
> Of feends infernall flockt on euery side,
> To gaze on earthly wight, that with the Night durst ride.
>
> (I v 32)

Longinus, commending a description in Euripides of Phaeton's journey through the heavens, in which the turnings and windings are marked out in a very likely manner, says that the soul of the poet seems to mount the chariot with him and to share all his dangers. The reader will find himself in a like manner transported throughout this whole episode, which shows that it has in it the force and spirit of the most sublime poetry.

(I, lxx-lxii)

These are such passages as we may imagine our excellent Milton

---

1 frighten, terrify
2 reveal, betray

to have studied in this author. And here, by the way, it is remarkable that as Spenser abounds with such thoughts as are truly sublime, so he is almost everywhere free from the mixture of little conceits and that low affectation of wit which so much infected both our verse and prose afterwards and from which scarce any writer of his own time, besides himself, was free.

(I, lxxvii)

Alexander Pope

in conversation   February 1744   (from Joseph Spence, *Observations, Anecdotes and Characters*, ed James M. Osborn, 1966)

'After my reading a canto in Spenser two or three days ago to an old lady between seventy and eighty, she said that I had been showing her a collection of pictures,' [said Spence.]

She said very right, and I don't know how it is but there's something in Spenser that pleases me as strongly in one's old age as it did in one's youth. I read *The Faerie Queene* when I was about twelve with a vast deal of delight, and I think it gave me as much when I read it over about a year or two ago.

Joseph Spence

from *Polymetis*   1747

The Defects of our Modern Poets in their Allegories, Instanced from Spenser's *Faerie Queene*

... Where Spenser does introduce the allegories of the ancient poets, he does not always follow them so exactly as he might. And in the allegories which are purely of his own invention, though his invention is one of the richest and most beautiful that perhaps ever was, I am sorry to say that he does not only fall very short of that simplicity and propriety which is so remarkable in the works of the ancients, but runs now and then into thoughts that are quite unworthy so great a genius. I shall mark out some of these faults to you, that appear, even through all his beauties, and which may perhaps look quite gross to you when they are thus taken from them and laid together by themselves; but if they should prejudice you at all against so fine a writer, read almost any one of his entire cantos and it will reconcile you to him again. The reason of my producing these instances to you is only to show what faults the greatest allegorist may commit whilst the manner of allegorizing is left upon so unfixed and irregular a footing as it was in his time and is still among us.

The first sort of fault I shall mention to you from such allegories of Spenser as are purely of his own invention is their being sometimes too complicated or overdone. Such, for example, are his representations of Scandal, Discord and Pride. Scandal is what Spenser calls 'the Blatant Beast', and indeed, he has made a very strange beast of him. He says that his mouth was as wide as a peck (VI xii 26) and that he had a thousand tongues in it of dogs, cats, bears, tigers, men and serpents (VI xii 27). There is a duplicity in his figure of Discord which is carried on so far as to be quite preposterous. He makes her hear double and look two different ways; he splits her tongue and even her heart in two and makes her act contrarily with her two hands and walk forward with one foot and backward with the other at the same time (IV i 27–9).

There is a great deal of apparatus in Spenser's manner of introducing Pride in a personal character, and she has so many different things and attributes about her that, was this show to be represented (in the manner of our old pageants), they would rather set one aguessing what they meant themselves than serve to point out who the principal figure should be. She makes her appearance exalted in a high chariot drawn by six different creatures, every one of them carrying a Vice, as a postilion, on his back, and all drove on by Satan as charioteer (I iv 18–36). The six Vices are Idleness, on an ass; Gluttony, on a hog; Lechery, on a goat; Avarice, on a camel laden with gold; Envy, eating a toad and riding on a wolf; and Wrath, with a firebrand in his hand, on a lion. The account of each of these particular vices in Spenser is admirable; the chief fault I find with it is that it is too complex a way of characterizing Pride in general and may possibly be as improper in some few respects as it is redundant in others.

There is another particular in some of Spenser's allegories which I cannot but look upon as faulty, though it is not near so great a fault as the former. What I mean is his affixing such filthy ideas to some of his personages or characters, that it half turns one's stomach to read his account of them. Such, for example, is the description of Error in the very first canto of the poem (I i 20), of which we may very well say in the poet's own words on a like occasion,

Such loathly matter were small lust to speake, or thinke.

(v xi 31)

The third fault in the allegories of Spenser's own invention is that they are sometimes stretched to such a degree that they appear rather extravagant than great, and that he is sometimes so minute in pointing out every particular of its vastness to you that the object is in danger of becoming ridiculous instead of being admirable. This is not common in Spenser; the strongest instance of the few I can remember is in his description of the dragon killed by the Knight of the Red Cross in the last canto [sic] of his first book. The tail of this dragon, he tells you, wanted by very little of being three furlongs in length, (I xi 11); the blood that gushes from his wound is enough to drive a water mill (I xi 22); and his roar is like that of a hundred hungry lions (I xi 37).

The fourth class of faults in Spenser's allegories consists of such as arise from their not being well invented. You will easily, I believe, allow me here the three following *postulata:* that in introducing allegories, one should consider whether the thing is fit to be represented as a person or not; secondly, that if you choose to represent it as a human personage, it should not be represented with anything inconsistent with the human form or nature; and thirdly, that when it is represented as a man, you should not make it perform any action which no man in his senses would do.

Spenser seems to have erred against the first of these maxims in those lines in his description of the cave of Care:

... they for nought would from their worke refraine,
Ne let his speeches come vnto their eare.
And eke the breathfull bellowes blew amaine,
Like to the Northren winde, that none could heare:
Those *Pensifenesse* did moue; and *Sighes* the bellows weare.

(IV v 38)

Was a poet to say that sighs are 'the bellows that blow up the fire of love', that would be only a metaphor – a poor one indeed, but not at all improper; but here they are realized, or rather metamorphized into bellows, which I could never persuade myself to think any way proper. Spenser is perhaps guilty of the same sort of fault in making Gifts, or Munera, a woman in the second canto of the fifth book (stanzas 9 ff.), though that may be only a misnomer; for if he had called her Bribery, one should not have the same objection. But the grossest instance in him of this kind is in the ninth canto of the second book, where he turns the human body into a castle, the tongue into the porter that keeps the gate, and the teeth into two and thirty warders dressed in white (stanzas 21, 25 and 26).

Spenser seems to have erred against the second of these maxims in representing the rigid execution of the laws under the character of a man all made up of iron (v i 12) and Bribery – or the lady Munera, before mentioned – as a woman with golden hands and silver feet (v ii 10); and against the third where he describes Desire as holding coals of fire in his hands and blowing them up into a flame (III xii 9) – which last particular is some degrees worse than Ariosto's bringing in Discord, in his *Orlando Furioso* (XVIII 34), with a flint and steel to strike fire in the face of Pride.

The fifth sort of faults is when the allegorical personages, though well invented, are not well marked out. There are many instances of this in Spenser which are but too apt to put one in mind of the fancifulness and whims of Ripa and Vaenius. Thus, in one canto, Doubt is represented as walking with a staff that shrinks under him (III xii 10), Hope with an aspergoire, or the instrument the Roman Catholics use for sprinkling sinners with holy water (stanza 13), Dissimulation as twisting two clews of silk together (stanza 14), Grief with a pair of pincers (stanza 16) and Pleasure with an humblebee in a phial (stanza 18). And in another – in the procession of the months and seasons – February is introduced in a wagon drawn by two fishes (VII vii 43), May as riding on Castor and Pollux (stanza 34); June is mounted on a crab (stanza 35), October on a scorpion (stanza 39); and November comes in on a centaur, all in a sweat because (as the poet observes) he had just been fatting his hogs (stanza 40).

This might full as well have been ranged under my sixth and last class of faults in Spenser's allegories, consisting of such instances as I fear can scarce be called by any softer name than that of 'ridiculous imaginations'. Such, I think, is that idea of Ignorance in the first book, where he is made to move with the back part of his head foremost (I viii 31), and that of Danger in the fourth, with Hatred, Murder, Treason, etc., in his back (IV x 16, 17, 20). Such is the sorrowful lady with a bottle for her tears and a bag to put her repentance into and both running out almost as fast as she puts them in (VI viii 24); such the thought of a vast giant's shrinking into an empty form, like a bladder (I viii 24); the horses of Night foaming tar (I v 28); Sir Guyon putting a padlock on the tongue of Occasion (II iv 12); and Remorse nipping St George's heart (I x 27).

(303–7)

Samuel Johnson

from *The Rambler*, no. 37   24 July 1750

Other writers, having the mean and despicable condition of a shepherd always before them, conceive it necessary to degrade the language of pastoral by obsolete terms and rustic words, which they very learnedly call Doric, without reflecting that they thus become authors of a mangled dialect which no human being ever could have spoken, that they may as well refine the speech as the sentiments of their personages, and that none of the inconsistencies which they endeavour to avoid is greater than that of joining elegance of thought with coarseness of diction. Spenser begins one of his pastorals with studied barbarity.

Diggon Dauie, I bidde her god day:
Or Diggon her is, or I missaye.
DIGGON: Her was her, while it was daye light,
But now her is a most wretched wight.

(*Shepheardes Calender*, 'September')

What will the reader imagine to be the subject on which speakers like these exercise their eloquence? Will he not be somewhat disappointed when he finds them met together to condemn the corruptions of the church of Rome? Surely, at the same time that a shepherd learns theology, he may gain some acquaintance with his native language.

Thomas Warton

from *Observations on 'The Faerie Queene' of Spenser* 1754 (second edition 1762)

It may be asked with great propriety, how does Arthur execute the grand, simple and ultimate design intended by the poet? It may be answered, with some degree of plausibility, that by lending his respective assistance to each of the twelve knights who patronize the twelve virtues, in his allotted defence of each, Arthur approaches still nearer and nearer to Glory, till at last he gains a complete possession. But surely to assist is not a sufficient service. This secondary merit is inadequate to the reward. The poet ought to have made this 'brave knight' the leading adventurer. Arthur should have been the principal agent in vindicating the cause of holiness, temperance, and the rest. If our hero had thus, in his own person, exerted himself in the protection of the twelve virtues, he might have been deservedly styled the perfect pattern of all, and consequently would have succeeded in the task assigned, the attainment of glory. At present he is only a subordinate or accessory character. The difficulties and obstacles which we expect him to surmount, in order to accomplish his final achievement, are removed by others. It is not he who subdues the dragon, in the first book, or quells the magician Busirane, in the third. These are the victories of St George and of Britomart. On the whole, the twelve Knights do too much for Arthur to do anything; or at least, so much as may be reasonably required from the promised plan of the poet. While we are attending to the design of the hero of the book, we forget that of the hero of the poem. Dryden remarks, 'We must do Spenser that justice to observe that magnanimity [magnificence], which is the true character of Prince Arthur, shines throughout the whole poem, and succours the rest when they are in distress.' If the magnanimity of Arthur did, in reality, thus shine in every part of the poem with a superior and steady lustre, our author would fairly stand acquitted. At present it bursts forth but seldom, in obscure and interrupted flashes. 'To succour the rest when they are in distress' is, as I have hinted, a circumstance of too little importance in the character of this universal champion. It is a service to be performed in the cause of the hero of the epic poem by some dependent or inferior chief, the business of a Gyas or a Cloanthus.

(I, 6–8)

But it is absurd to think of judging either Ariosto or Spenser by precepts which they did not attend to. We who live in the days of writing by rule, are apt to try every composition by those laws which we have been taught to think the sole criterion of excellence. Critical taste is universally diffused, and we require the same order and design which every modern performance is expected to have, in poems where they never were regarded or intended. Spenser, and the same may be said of Ariosto, did not live in an age of planning. His poetry is the careless exuberance of a warm imagination and a strong sensibility. It was his business to engage the fancy and to interest the attention by bold and striking images, in the formation and the disposition of which, little labour or art was applied. The various and the marvellous were the chief sources of delight. Hence we find our author ransacking alike the regions of reality and romance, of truth and fiction, to find the proper decorations and furniture for his fairy structure. Born in such an age, Spenser wrote rapidly from his own feelings, which at the same time were naturally noble. Exactness in his poem would have been like the cornice which a painter introduced in the grotto of Calypso. Spenser's beauties are like the flowers in Paradise.

Which not nice art
In beds and curious knots, but Nature boon
Pour'd forth profuse, on hill, and dale, and plain;
Both where the morning sun first warmly smote
The open field, or where the unpierced shade
Imbrown'd the noon-tide bowers.

(Paradise Lost, IV 241–6)

If The Faerie Queene be destitute of that arrangement and economy which epic severity requires, yet we scarcely regret the loss of these, while their place is so amply supplied by something which more powerfully attracts us: something which engages the affections, the feelings of the heart, rather than the cold approbation of the head. If there be any poem whose graces please, because they are situated beyond the reach of art, and where the force and faculties of creative imagination delight, because they are unassisted and unrestrained by those of deliberate judgement, it is this. In reading Spenser, if the critic is not satisfied, yet the reader is transported.

(1, 15–16)

[On the value of studying Spenser's sources]

We feel a sort of malicious triumph in detecting the latent and obscure source from whence an original author has drawn some celebrated description: yet this, it must be granted, soon gives way to the rapture that naturally results from contemplating the chemical energy of true genius, which can produce so noble a transmutation; and whose virtues are not less efficacious and vivifying in their nature than those of the miraculous water here displayed by Spenser [*Faerie Queene*, 1 xi 49].

(1, 54)

Our author's imagination was entirely possessed with that species of reading which was the fashion and the delight of his age. The lovers of Spenser, I hope, will not think I have been too tedious in a disquisition, which has contributed not only to illustrate many particular passages in their favourite poet, but to display the general cast and colour of his poem. Some there are who will censure what I have collected on this subject as both trifling and uninteresting; but such readers can have no taste for Spenser.

(1, 65)

Of Spenser's Use and Abuse of Ancient History and Mythology

As Spenser sought to produce surprise by extravagant incidents and fantastic descriptions, great part of classical history and mythology afforded ample materials for such a design, and properly coincided with the general aim of his romantic plan. He has accordingly adopted some of their most extraordinary fictions, in many of which he has departed from the received tradition, as his purpose and subject occasionally required or permitted. But with regard to our author's misrepresentation of ancient fable, it may be justly urged that from those arguments which are produced against his fidelity, new proofs arise in favour of his fancy. Spenser's native force of invention would not suffer him to pursue the letter of prescribed fiction with scrupulous observation and servile regularity. In many particulars he varies from antiquity only to substitute new beauties, and from a slight mention of one or two leading circumstances in ancient fable, takes an opportunity to display some new fiction of his own coinage. He sometimes, in the fervour of composition, misrepresents these matters through haste and inattention. His allusions to ancient history are likewise very frequent, which he has not scrupled to violate, with equal freedom, and for the same reasons.

(I, 66–7)

He is describing Envy:

> ... still did chaw[1]
> Betweene his cankred teeth a venemous tode,
> That all the poison ran about his chaw.[2]
>
> (I iv 30)

Ovid feigns (*Met*. ii, 76) that Envy was found eating the flesh of vipers, a fiction not much unlike Spenser's picture. But our author has heightened this circumstance to a most disgusting degree; for he adds, that the poison ran about his jaw. This is perhaps one of the most loathsome images which Spenser has given us; though he paints very strongly,

> ... she spewd out of her filthy maw
> A floud of poyson horrible and blacke,
> Full of great lumpes of flesh and gobbets raw,
> Which stunck so vildly,[3] that it forst him slacke
> His grasping hold ...
>
> (I i 20)

As also in the discovery of Duessa, I viii 47, 48. He is likewise very indelicate where he speaks of Serena's wounds.

For now her wounds corruption gan to breed.

(VI v 31)

1 chew   2 jaw   3 vilely

And to forbear disagreeable citations, see VII vii 31 and VII vii 40. The truth is, the strength of our author's imagination could not be suppressed on any subject; and, in some measure, it is owing to the fulness of his stanza and the reiteration of his rhymes, that he describes these offensive objects so minutely.

But to return to his Envy. This personage is again introduced, v xii 29, chewing a snake, of which a most beautiful use is made, stanza 39.

> Then from her mouth the gobbet she does take,
> The which whyleare she was so greedily
> Deuouring, euen that halfe-gnawen snake,
> And at him throwes it most despightfully.
> The cursed Serpent, though she hungrily
> Earst chawd thereon, yet was not all so dead,
> But that some life remayned secretly,
> And as he past afore withouten dread,
> Bit him behind, that long the marke was to be read.

It may be objected that Spenser drew the thought of Envy throwing her snake at Arthegall, from Alecto's attack upon Amata.

> Huic Dea caeruleis unum de crinibus anguem
> Conjicit, inque sinus praecordia ad intima condit.[1]

(*Aeneid*, VII 346)

But Spenser's application of this thought is surely a stronger effort of invention than the thought itself. The rancour, both of Envy and of her snake, could not have been expressed by more significant strokes. Although the snake was her constant food, yet she was tempted to part with her only sustenance, while she could render it an instrument of injuring another; and although the snake, by being thus constantly fed upon, was nearly dead, 'some life', as he finely says, 'remaining secretly', yet its natural malignity enabled it to bite with violence.

(I, 69–71)

1 The goddess threw at her one of the snakes from her dark blue hair, and plunged it into her bosom and deep into her heart.

Of Spenser's Stanza, Versification and Language

Spenser's favourite Chaucer had made use of the *ottava rima*, or stanza of eight lines, yet it seems probable that Spenser was principally induced to adopt it, with the addition of one line, from the practice of Ariosto and Tasso, the most fashionable poets of his age. But Spenser, in choosing this stanza, did not sufficiently consider the genius of the English language, which does not easily fall into a frequent repetition of the same termination – a circumstance natural to the Italian, which deals largely in identical cadences.

Besides, it is to be remembered that Tasso and Ariosto did not embarrass themselves with the necessity of finding out so many similar terminations as Spenser. Their *ottava rima* has only three similar endings, alternately rhyming. The last lines formed a distinct rhyme. But in Spenser, the second rhyme is repeated four times, and the third three.

This constraint led our author into many absurdities, the most striking and obvious of which seem to be the following.

I. It obliged him to dilate the thing to be expressed, however unimportant, with trifling and tedious circumlocutions, viz.

> Now hath faire *Phœbe* with her siluer face
> Thrise seene the shadowes of the neather world,
> Sith last I left that honorable place,
> In which her royall presence is enroll'd.
>
> (II ii 44)

That is, 'it is three months since I left her palace.'

II. It necessitated him, when matter failed towards the close of a stanza, to run into a ridiculous redundancy and repetition of words, viz.

> In which was nothing pourtrahed nor wrought,
> Nor wrought, nor pourtrahed, but easie to be thought.
>
> (II ix 33)

III. It forced him, that he might make out his complement of rhymes, to introduce a puerile or impertinent idea, viz.

> Nor that proud towre of *Troy*, though richly *guilt*.
>
> (II ix 45)

Being here laid under the compulsion of producing a consonant word to *spilt* and *built*, which are preceding rhymes, he has mechanically given us an image at once little and improper.

To the difficulty of a stanza so injudiciously chosen, I think we may properly impute the great number of his ellipses, some of which will be pointed out at large in another place; and it may be easily conceived how that constraint which occasioned superfluity should at the same time be the cause of omission.

Notwithstanding these inconveniencies flow from Spenser's measure, it must yet be owned, that some advantages arise from it; and we may venture to affirm that the fullness and significancy of Spenser's descriptions is often owing to the prolixity of his stanza and the multitude of his rhymes. The discerning reader is desired to consider the following stanza, as an instance of what is here advanced. Guyon is binding Furor.

> With hundred yron chaines he did him bind,
> And hundred knots that did him sore constraine:
> Yet his great yron teeth he still did grind,
> And grimly gnash, threatning reuenge in vaine;
> His burning eyen, whom bloudie strakes[1] did staine,
> Stared full wide, and threw forth sparkes of fire,
> And more for ranck despight,[2] then for great paine,
> Shakt his long lockes, colourd like copper-wire,
> And bit his tawny beard to shew his raging ire.
>   (II iv 15)

In the subsequent stanza there are some images, which perhaps were produced by a multiplicity of rhymes.

> He all that night, that too long night did passe.
> And now the day out of the Ocean mayne
> Began to peepe aboue this earthly masse,
> With pearly dew sprinkling the morning grasse:
> Then vp he rose like heauie lumpe of lead,
> That in his face, as in a looking glasse,
> The signes of anguish one mote plainely read.
>   (IV v 45)

1 streaks   2 anger, defiance

Dryden, I think, somewhere remarks that rhyme often helped him into a thought – an observation which, probably, Spenser's experience had likewise supplied him with. Spenser, however, must have found more assistance in this respect, from writing in rhyme, than Dryden, in proportion as his stanza obliged him to a more repeated use of it.

(I, 113–17)

Notwithstanding our author's frequent and affected usage of obsolete words and phrases, yet it may be affirmed that his style, in general, has great perspicuity and facility. It is also remarkable that his lines are seldom broken by transpositions, antitheses, or parentheses. His sense and sound are equally flowing and uninterrupted.

(I, 122–3)

Spenser, perhaps, in this minute and particular enumeration of various trees [Faerie Queene, 1 i 8–9], has incurred less censure than some of the Roman authors mentioned above. In some of those, indeed, such a description will be found superfluous and impertinent; but upon this occasion it is highly consistent, and even expedient, that the poet should dwell, for some time, on the beauty of this grove, in describing its variety of trees, as that circumstance tends to draw the Red Cross Knight and his companions farther and farther into the shade, 'till at length they are imperceptibly invited to the Cave of Error, which stood in the thickest part of it. This description is so far from being puerile or ill-placed, that it serves to improve and illustrate the allegory. But notwithstanding this may be affirmed in vindication of Spenser, I am apt to think that the impropriety of introducing such a description would not have appeared a sufficient reason to our poet for not admitting it.

(I, 137–8)

I do not deny that Spenser was, in great measure, tempted by the Orlando Furioso to write an allegorical poem. Yet it must still be acknowledged that Spenser's peculiar mode of allegorizing seems to have been dictated by those spectacles [pageants, masques, etc.], rather than by the fictions of Ariosto. In fact, Ariosto's species of allegory does not so properly consist in impersonating the virtues, vices, and affections of the mind, as in the adumbration of moral doctrine under the actions of men and women. On this plan Spenser's allegories are sometimes formed: as in the first book where the Red Cross Knight, or a *True Christian*, defeats the wiles of Archimago, or the *Devil*, etc. These indeed are fictitious personages; but he proves himself a much more ingenious allegorist where his imagination *bodies* forth unsubstantial things, *turns them to shape*, and marks out the nature, powers and effects of that which is ideal and abstracted, by visible and external symbols; as in his delineations of Fear, Despair, Fancy, Envy, and the like. Ariosto gives us but few symbolical beings of this sort, for a picturesque invention was by no means his talent; while those few which we find in his poem are seldom drawn with that characteristical fullness and significant expression so striking in the fantastic portraits of Spenser. And that Spenser painted these figures in so distinct and animated a style, may we not partly account for it from this cause: that he had been long habituated to the sight of these emblematical personages, visibly decorated with their proper attributes, and actually endued with speech, motion and life?

(II, 90–92)

Instead of entering into a critical examination of Spenser's manner of allegorizing and of the poetical conduct of his allegories, which has been done with an equally judicious and ingenious discernment by Mr Spence, I shall observe that our author frequently introduces an allegory under which no meaning is couched, viz. II ix 21. Alma is the mind, and her Castle the body. The tongue is the porter of this castle, the nose the portcullis, and the mouth the porch, about the inside of which are placed twice sixteen warders clad in white, which are the teeth; these Alma passes by, who rise up and do obeisance to her (st. 26). But how can the teeth be said to rise up and bow to the mind? Spenser here forgot that he was allegorizing, and speaks as if he was describing, without any latent meaning, a real Queen with twice sixteen real warders, who, as such, might, with no impropriety, be said to rise and bow to their queen. Many instances of his confounding allegory with reality occur through this whole canto and the two next; particularly where he is describing the kitchen of this castle, which is the belly, he gives us a formal description of such a kitchen as was to be seen in his time in castles and great houses, by no means expressive of the thing intended. Again, the occult meaning of his bringing Scudamore to the house of Care, IV v 32, clashes with what he had before told us. By this allegory of Scudamore coming to Care's house, it should be *understood*, that 'Scudamore, from a happy, passed into a miserable state'. For we may reasonably suppose that before he came to Care's house he was unacquainted with Care; whereas the poet had before represented him as involved in extreme misery. It would be tedious, by an allegation of particular examples, to demonstrate how frequently his allegories are mere descriptions; and that, taken in their literal sense, they contain an improper, or no signification. I shall, however, mention one. The Blatant Beast is said to break into the monasteries, to rob their chancels, cast down the desks of the monks, deface the altars, and destroy the images found in their churches. By the Blatant Beast is understood Scandal, and by the havoc just mentioned as effected by it, is implied the suppression of religious houses and popish superstition. But how can this be properly said to have been brought about by Scandal? And how could Spenser, in particular, with any consistency say this, who was, as appears by his pastorals, a friend to the reformation, as was his heroine Elizabeth?

(II, 95–7)

[III viii 40–41] The use which the poet here makes of Proteus's power of changing his shape is artful enough, having a novelty founded on propriety.

(II, 167)

[v iii 25] When the false Florimel is placed by the side of the true, the former vanishes into nothing; and as suddenly, says the poet, as all the glorious colours of the rainbow fade and perish. With regard to the sudden evanescence in each, the comparison is just and elegant; but if we consider that a rainbow exists by the presence of the sun, the similitude by no means is made out. However, it is the former of these circumstances alone which the poet insists upon, so that a partial correspondence only is expected.

(II, 206)

And for more horror and more crueltie,
Vnder that cursed Idols altar stone
An hideous monster doth in darknesse lie,

Whose dreadfull shape was neuer seene of none
That liues on earth. . . .

(v x 29)

We are apt to conceive something very wonderful of those mysterious things which are thus said to be unknown to us, and to be out
of the reach and compass of man's knowledge and apprehension. Thus
a cave is said to be,

A dreadfull depth, how deepe no man can tell.

(v ix 6)

If the poet had limited the depth of this cave to a very great, but to a
certain number of fathoms, the fancy could still have supposed and
added more; but as no determinate measure is assigned, our imagination is left at liberty to exert its utmost arbitrary stretch, to add fathom
to fathom, and depth to depth, till it is lost in its own attempt to grasp
the idea of that which is unbounded or infinite. *Omne ignotum pro
magnifico est*, says Tacitus, somewhere – a writer of the strongest
imagination.

From a concealment of this kind arises the Sublime, in the following
passage.

. . . There *Merlin* stayd,
As ouercomen of the spirites powre,
Or other ghastly spectacle dismayd,

That *secretly* he *saw, yet note*[1] *discoure*.

This is finely heightened by the consternation of the beholders.

Which suddein fit, and halfe extatick stoure[2]
When the two fearefull women saw, they grew
Greatly confused in behauioure.

(III iii 50)

Here is a striking instance of the force of additional figures. The
whole is a fine subject for a picture.

(II, 220–21)

***

1 could, might not   2 fit, paroxysm

Joseph Warton

from *An Essay on the Genius and Writings of Pope* 1756 (fourth edition 1782)

[Pope's] imitation of Spenser . . . is a description of an alley of fish-women. He that was unacquainted with Spenser and was to form his ideas of the turn and manner of his genius from this piece would undoubtedly suppose that he abounded in filthy images and excelled in describing the lower scenes of life. But the characteristics of this sweet and amiable allegorical poet are not only strong and circumstantial imagery, but tender and pathetic feeling, a most melodious flow of versification, and a certain pleasing melancholy in his sentiments – the constant companion of an elegant taste – that casts a delicacy and grace over all his compositions. To imitate Spenser on a subject that does not partake of the pathos is not giving a true representation of him, for he seems to be more awake and alive to all the softnesses of nature than almost any writer I can recollect. . . .

Pope represents some allegorical figures, of which his original was so fond:

Hard by a sty, beneath a roof of thatch
Dwelt Obloquy, who in her early days,
Baskets of fish at Billingsgate did watch,
Cod, whiting, oyster, mackerel, sprat or plaice:
There learn'd she speech from tongues that never cease.
Slander beside her, like a magpie chatters,
With Envy (spitting cat) dread foe to peace;
Like a curs'd cur, Malice before her clatters,
And vexing every wight, tears cloaths and all to tatters.

But these personages of Obloquy, Slander, Envy and Malice are not marked with any distinct attributes; they are not those living figures whose attitudes and behaviour Spenser has minutely drawn with so much clearness and truth that we behold them with our eyes as plainly as we do on the ceiling of the banqueting house. For in truth, the pencil of Spenser is as powerful as that of Rubens, his brother allegorist – which two artists resembled each other in many respects, but Spenser had more grace and was as warm a colourist. Among a multitude of objects delineated with the utmost force which we might select on this occasion, let us stop a moment and take one attentive look at the allegorical figures that rise to our view in the following lines:

> By that wayes side, there sate infernall Payne,
> And fast beside him sat tumultuous Strife:
> The one in hand an yron whip did straine,[1]
> The other brandished a bloudy knife,
> And both did gnash their teeth, and both did threaten life.
>
> But gnawing Gealosie out of their sight
> Sitting alone, his bitter lips did bight,
> And trembling Feare still to and fro did fly,
> And found no place, where safe he shroud him might,
> Lamenting Sorrow did in darknesse lye,
> And Shame his vgly face did hide from liuing eye.
>
> (II vii 21–2)

To show the richness of his fancy, he has given us another picture of Jealousy, conceived with equal strength, in a succeeding book:

> Into the same he creepes, and thenceforth there
> Resolu'd to build his balefull mansion,
> In drery darkenesse, and continuall feare
> Of that rockes fall, which euer and anon
> Threates with huge ruine him to fall vpon,
> That he dare neuer sleepe, but that one eye
> Still ope he keepes for that occasion;
> Ne euer rests he in tranquillity,
> The roring billowes beat his bowre so boystrously.
>
> (III x 58)

Here all is in life and motion; here we behold the true Poet or Maker; this is creation; it is here, might we cry out to Spenser, it is here that you display to us, that you make us feel, the sure effects of genuine poetry, 'when carried away by enthusiasm and passion, you think you see what you describe, and you place it before the eyes of your hearers' (Longinus, *On the Sublime*, sec. 15).

It has been fashionable of late to imitate Spenser, but the likeness of

1 wield

most of these copies hath consisted rather in using a few of his ancient expressions than in catching his real manner. Some, however, have been executed with happiness and with attention to that simplicity, that tenderness of sentiment and those little touches of nature that constitute Spenser's character. I have a peculiar pleasure in mentioning two of them, *The School-Mistress*, by Mr Shenstone, and the *Education of Achilles*, by Mr Bedingfield. To these must be added that exquisite piece of wild and romantic imagery, Thomson's *Castle of Indolence*, the first canto of which in particular is marvellously pleasing, and the stanzas have a greater flow and freedom than his blank verse.

(II, 30–37)

Richard Hurd

from *Letters on Chivalry and Romance*, Letter 8   1762

When an architect examines a Gothic structure by Grecian rules, he finds nothing but deformity. But the Gothic architecture has its own rules, by which when it comes to be examined, it is seen to have its merit as well as the Grecian. The question is not which of the two is conducted in the simplest or truest taste, but whether there be not sense and design in both, when scrutinized by the laws on which each is projected.

The same observation holds of the two sorts of poetry. Judge of *The Faerie Queene* by the classic models and you are shocked with its disorder; consider it with an eye to its Gothic original and you find it regular. The unity and simplicity of the former are more complete, but the latter has that sort of unity and simplicity which results from its nature.

The Faerie Queene then, as a Gothic poem, derives its method, as well as the other characters of its composition, from the established modes and ideas of chivalry.

It was usual in the days of knight errantry, at the holding of any great feast, for knights to appear before the prince who presided at it, and claim the privilege of being sent on any adventure to which the solemnity might give occasion. For it was supposed that when such a 'throng of knights and barons bold' as Milton speaks of were got together, the distressed would flock in from all quarters, as to a place where they knew they might find and claim redress for all their grievances. . . .

Now laying down this practice as a foundation for the poet's design, you will see how properly *The Faerie Queene* is conducted.

'I devise,' says the poet himself in his letter to Sir W. Raleigh, 'that the Fairy Queen kept her annual feast twelve days: upon which twelve several days, the occasions of the twelve several adventures happened; which being undertaken by twelve several knights, are in these twelve books severally handled.' Here you have the poet delivering his own method and the reason of it. It arose out of the order of his subject. And would you desire a better reason for his choice?

Yes, you will say; a poet's method is not that of his subject. I grant you, as to the order of *time* in which the recital is made; for here, as Spenser observes – and his own practice agrees to the rule – lies the main difference between the 'poet historical' and the 'historiographer', the reason of which is drawn from the nature of epic composition itself and holds equally, let the subject be what it will, and whatever the system of manners be on which it is conducted. Gothic or classic makes no difference in this respect.

But the case is not the same with regard to the general plan of a work, or what may be called the order of *distribution*, which is and must be governed by the subject matter itself. It was as requisite for *The Faerie Queene* to consist of the adventures of twelve knights as for the *Odyssey* to be confined to the adventures of one hero. Justice had otherwise not been done to his subject.

So that if you will say anything against the poet's method, you must say that he should not have chosen this subject. But this objection arises from your classic ideas of unity, which have no place here and are in every view foreign to the purpose, if the poet has found means to give his work, though consisting of many parts, the advantage of unity. For in some reasonable sense or other, it is agreed, every work of art must be *one*, the very idea of a work requiring it.

If you ask then, what is this unity of Spenser's poem? I say, it consists in the relation of its several adventures to one common *original*, the appointment of the Fairy Queen, and to one common *end*, the completion of the Fairy Queen's injunctions. The knights issued forth on their adventures on the breaking up of this annual feast; and the next annual feast, we are to suppose, is to bring them together again from the achievement of their several charges.

This, it is true, is not the classic unity, which consists in the representation of one entire action; but it is an unity of another sort, an unity resulting from the respect which a number of related actions have to one common purpose. In other words, it is an unity of *design*, and not of action.

This Gothic method of design in poetry may be, in some sort, illustrated by what is called the Gothic method of design in gardening. A wood or grove cut out into many separate avenues or glades was amongst the most favourite of the works of art which our fathers attempted in this species of cultivation. These walks were distinct from each other, had, each, their several destination, and terminated on their own proper objects. Yet the whole was brought together and considered under one view by the relation which these various openings had, not to each other, but to their common and concurrent centre. You and I are, perhaps, agreed that this sort of gardening is not of so true a taste as that which Kent and Nature have brought us acquainted with, where the supreme art of the designer consists in disposing his ground and objects into an *entire landscape* and grouping them, if I may use the term, in so easy a manner that the careless observer, though he be taken with the symmetry of the whole, discovers no art in the combination. . . . This, I say, may be the truest taste in gardening, because the simplest. Yet there is a manifest regard to unity in the other method, which has had its admirers – as it may have again – and is certainly not without its *design* and beauty.

But to return to our poet. Thus far he drew from Gothic ideas, and these ideas, I think, would lead him no farther. But, as Spenser knew what belonged to classic composition, he was tempted to tie his subjects still closer together by one expedient of his own and by another taken from his classic models.

His own was to interrupt the proper story of each book by dispersing it into several, involving by this means, and as it were intertwisting, the several actions together in order to give something like the appearance of one action to his twelve adventures. And for this conduct, as absurd as it seems, he had some great examples in the Italian poets, though I believe they were led into it by different motives.

The other expedient which he borrowed from the classics was by adopting one superior character which should be seen throughout. Prince Arthur, who had a separate adventure of his own, was to have his part in each of the other; and thus several actions were to be embodied by the interest which one principal hero had in them all. It is even observable that Spenser gives this adventure of Prince Arthur, in quest of Gloriana, as the proper subject of his poem. And upon this idea the late learned editor[1] of *The Faerie Queene* has attempted, but I think without success, to defend the unity and simplicity of its fable. The truth was, the violence of classic prejudices forced the poet to affect this appearance of unity, though in contradiction to his Gothic system. And as far as we can judge of the tenor of the whole work from the finished half of it, the adventure of Prince Arthur, whatever the author pretended and his critic too easily believed, was but an afterthought and, at least with regard to the *historical fable* – which we are now considering – was only one of the expedients by which he would conceal the disorder of his Gothic plan.

And if this was his design, I will venture to say that both his expedients were injudicious. Their purpose was to ally two things in nature incompatible, the Gothic and the classic unity, the effect of which misalliance was to discover and expose the nakedness of the Gothic.

I am of opinion then, considering *The Faerie Queene* as an epic or narrative poem constructed on Gothic ideas, that the poet had done well to affect no other unity than that of *design*, by which his subject was connected. But his poem is not simply narrative: it is throughout *allegorical* (he calls it 'a perpetual allegory or dark conceit'), and this character, for reasons I may have occasion to observe hereafter, was even predominant in *The Faerie Queene*. His narration is subservient to his moral and but serves to colour it. This he tells us himself at setting out:

Fierce warres and faithfull loues shall *moralize* my song,

that is, shall serve for a vehicle or instrument to convey the moral.

Now, under this idea the unity of *The Faerie Queene* is more apparent. His twelve knights are to exemplify as many virtues, out of which one illustrious character is to be composed. And in this view the part of Prince Arthur in each book becomes *essential* and yet not

1 John Upton

principal, exactly as the poet has contrived it. They who rest in the literal story – that is, who criticize it on the footing of a narrative poem – have constantly objected to this management. They say it necessarily breaks the unity of design. Prince Arthur, they affirm, should either have had no part in the other adventures, or he should have had the chief part. He should either have done nothing or more. And the objection is unanswerable; at least, I know of nothing that can be said to remove it but what I have supposed above might be the purpose of the poet and which I myself have rejected as insufficient.

But how faulty soever this conduct be in the literal story, it is perfectly right in the *moral*, and that for an obvious reason, though his critics seem not to have been aware of it. His chief hero was not to have the twelve virtues in the *degree* in which the knights had, each of them, their own – such a character would be a monster. But he was to have so much of each as was requisite to form his superior character. Each virtue, in its perfection, is exemplified in its own knight; they are all, in a due degree, concentred in Prince Arthur.

This was the poet's moral. And what way of expressing this moral in the history but by making Prince Arthur appear in each adventure and in a manner subordinate to its proper hero? Thus, though inferior to each in his own specific virtue, he is superior to all by uniting the whole circle of their virtues in himself. And thus he arrives, at length, at the possession of that bright form of Glory, whose ravishing beauty, as seen in a dream or vision, had led him out into these miraculous adventures in the land of Fairy.

The conclusion is that, as an allegorical poem, the method of *The Faerie Queene* is governed by the justness of the moral; as a narrative poem, it is conducted on the ideas and usages of chivalry. In either view, if taken by itself, the plan is defensible. But from the union of the two designs there arises a perplexity and confusion which is the proper, and only considerable, defect of this extraordinary poem.

Samuel Johnson

from *Preface to Shakespeare* 1765

To him [Shakespeare] we must ascribe the praise, unless Spenser may divide it with him, of having first discovered to how much smoothness and harmony the English language could be softened.

S. T. Coleridge

from a notebook entry on prolixity   May 1804

... Whether we gain or lose by that dread of prolixity which is the passion of highly polished states of society – from the diffusion of critical knowledge and of the habit of criticism, from the multitude of competitors, etc. Still, are those who never did consider the *Paradise Lost* as a task; those who, taking Spenser and reading him by small portions at a time with his own 'believing mind', only wish and regret that lost half, in a more or less enviable state? Does not this dread of prolixity in ourselves, and criticism of it in others, tend to make all knowledge superficial as well as desultory – incompatible with the pleasure derived from seeing things as they are, as far as the nature of language permits it to be exhibited? Apply this to Wordsworth's *Pedlar* [i.e. *The Ruined Cottage*].

William Wordsworth

from *The Prelude*   1850 (but first drafted 1805–6)

Sometimes the ambitious Power of choice, mistaking
Proud spring-tide swellings for a regular sea,
Will settle on some British theme, some old
Romantic tale by Milton left unsung;
More often turning to some gentle place
Within the groves of Chivalry, I pipe
To shepherd swains, or seated harp in hand,
Amid reposing knights by a river side
Or fountain, listen to the grave reports
Of dire enchantments faced and overcome
By the strong mind, and tales of warlike feats,
Where spear encountered spear, and sword with sword

Fought, as if conscious of the blazonry
That the shield bore, so glorious was the strife;
Whence inspiration for a song that winds
Through ever changing scenes of votive quest
Wrongs to redress, harmonious tribute paid
To patient courage and unblemished truth,
To firm devotion, zeal unquenchable,
And Christian meekness hallowing faithful loves.

(I 166–85)

[Residence at Cambridge]

Beside the pleasant Mill of Trompington
I laughed with Chaucer in the hawthorn shade;
Heard him, while birds were warbling, tell his tales
Of amorous passion. And that gentle Bard,
Chosen by the Muses for their Page of State –
Sweet Spenser, moving through his clouded heaven
With the moon's beauty and the moon's soft pace,
I called him Brother, Englishman, and Friend!

(III 278–85)

William Wordsworth

from the Preface to the 1815 edition of *Lyrical Ballads*

Imagination, in the sense of the word as giving title to a class of the following Poems, has no reference to images that are merely a faithful copy, existing in the mind, of absent external objects; but is a word of higher import, denoting operations of the mind upon those objects, and processes of creation or of composition, governed by certain fixed laws. I proceed to illustrate my meaning by instances. A parrot *hangs* from the wires of his cage by his beak or by his claws; or a monkey from the bough of a tree by his paws or his tail. Each creature does so literally and actually. In the first Eclogue of Virgil, the shepherd, thinking of the time when he is to take leave of his farm, thus addresses his goats:

Non ego vos posthac viridi projectus in antro
Dumosa *pendere* procul de rupe videbo.[1]

. . . half way down
Hangs one who gathers samphire,

(*King Lear*, IV VI 16)

is the well-known expression of Shakespeare, delineating an ordinary
image upon the cliffs of Dover. In these two instances is a slight
exertion of the faculty which I denominate imagination, in the use
of one word: neither the goats nor the samphire-gatherer do literally
hang, as does the parrot or the monkey; but, presenting to the senses
something of such an appearance, the mind in its activity, for its
own gratification, contemplates them as hanging.

As when far off at sea a fleet descried
Hangs in the clouds, by equinoctial winds
Close sailing from Bengala, or the isles
Of Ternate or Tidore, whence merchants bring
Their spicy drugs; they on the trading flood
Through the wide Ethiopian to the Cape
Ply, stemming nightly toward the Pole: so seemed
Far off the flying Fiend.

(*Paradise Lost*, II 636–43)

Here is the full strength of the imagination involved in the word
hangs, and exerted upon the whole image: first, the fleet, an aggre-
gate of many ships, is represented as one mighty person, whose
track, we know and feel, is upon the waters; but, taking advantage
of its appearance to the senses, the Poet dares to represent it as *hanging
in the clouds*, both for the gratification of the mind in contemplating
the image itself, and in reference to the motion and appearance of the
sublime objects to which it is compared. . . .

Thus far of images independent of each other, and immediately
endowed by the mind with properties that do not inhere in them,
upon an incitement from properties and qualities the existence of
which is inherent and obvious. These processes of imagination are
carried on either by conferring additional properties upon an object,

[1] I, lying in a green cave, will not see you after this hanging in the distance
from a bushy rock.

or abstracting from it some of those which it actually possesses, and thus enabling it to re-act upon the mind which hath performed the process, like a new existence.

I pass from the Imagination acting upon an individual image to a consideration of the same faculty employed upon images in a conjunction by which they modify each other. The Reader has already had a fine instance before him in the passage quoted from Virgil, where the apparently perilous situation of the goat, hanging upon the shaggy precipice, is contrasted with that of the shepherd contemplating it from the seclusion of the cavern in which he lies stretched at ease and in security. Take these images separately, and how unaffecting the picture compared with that produced by their being thus connected with, and opposed to, each other!

As a huge stone is sometimes seen to lie
Couched on the bald top of an eminence,
Wonder to all who do the same espy
By what means it could thither come, and whence,
So that it seems a thing endued with sense,
Like a sea-beast crawled forth, which on a shelf
Of rock or sand reposeth, there to sun himself.

Such seemed this Man; not all alive or dead
Nor all asleep, in his extreme old age.

. . . . . .

Motionless as a cloud the old Man stood,
That heareth not the loud winds when they call,
And moveth altogether if it move at all.

(*Resolution and Independence,*
57–65, 75–7)

In these images, the conferring, the abstracting, and the modifying powers of the Imagination, immediately and mediately acting, are all brought into conjunction. The stone is endowed with something of the power of life to approximate it to the sea-beast; and the sea-beast stripped of some of its vital qualities to assimilate it to the stone; which intermediate image is thus treated for the purpose of bringing the original image, that of the stone, to a nearer resemblance to the figure and condition of the aged Man; who is divested of so much of the indications of life and motion as to bring him to the point where the two objects unite and coalesce in just comparison. After what has been said, the image of the cloud need not be commented upon.

Thus far of an endowing or modifying power: but the Imagination also shapes and *creates*; and how? By innumerable processes; and in none does it more delight than in that of consolidating numbers into unity, and dissolving and separating unity into number, – alternations proceeding from, and governed by, a sublime consciousness of the soul in her own mighty and almost divine powers. Recur to the passage already cited from Milton. When the compact Fleet, as one Person, has been introduced 'sailing from Bengala', 'They', *i.e.* the 'merchants', representing the fleet resolved into a multitude of ships, 'ply' their voyage towards the extremities of the earth: 'So', (referring to the word 'As' in the commencement) 'seemed the flying Fiend'; the image of his Person acting to recombine the multitude of ships into one body, – the point from which the comparison set out. 'So seemed', and to whom seemed? To the heavenly Muse who dictates the poem, to the eye of the Poet's mind, and to that of the Reader, present at one moment in the wide Ethiopian, and the next in the solitudes, then first broken in upon, of the infernal regions!

Modo me Thebis, modo ponit Athenis.[1]
(Horace, Epistles, II 213)

Hear again this mighty Poet, – speaking of the Messiah going forth to expel from heaven the rebellious angels,

Attended by ten thousand thousand Saints
He onward came: far off his coming shone,
(Paradise Lost, VI 767–8)

the retinue of Saints, and the Person of the Messiah himself, lost almost and merged in the splendour of that indefinite abstraction 'His coming!' . . .

---

[1] Now he places me in Thebes, now in Athens.

The grand store-houses of enthusiastic and meditative Imagination, of poetical, as contra-distinguished from human and dramatic Imagination, are the prophetic and lyrical parts of the Holy Scriptures, and the works of Milton; to which I cannot forbear to add those of Spenser. I select these writers in preference to those of ancient Greece and Rome, because the anthropomorphitism of the Pagan religion subjected the minds of the greatest poets in those countries too much to the bondage of definite form; from which the Hebrews were preserved by their abhorrence of idolatry. This abhorrence was almost as strong in our great epic Poet, both from circumstances of his life, and from the constitution of his mind. However imbued the surface might be with classical literature, he was a Hebrew in soul; and all things tended in him towards the sublime. Spenser, of a gentler nature, maintained his freedom by aid of his allegorical spirit, at one time inciting him to create persons out of abstractions; and, at another, by a superior effort of genius, to give the universality and permanence of abstractions to his human beings, by means of attributes and emblems that belong to the highest moral truths and the purest sensations, – of which his character of Una is a glorious example. Of the human and dramatic Imagination the works of Shakspeare are an inexhaustible source.

I tax not you, ye Elements, with unkindness,
I never gave you kingdoms, call'd you Daughters!
(*King Lear*, III ii 16–17)

William Wordsworth

Dedication to *The White Doe of Rylstone* 1815

In trellised shed with clustering roses gay,
And, Mary! oft beside our blazing fire,
When years of wedded life were as a day
Whose current answers to the heart's desire,
Did we together read in Spenser's Lay
How Una, sad of soul – in sad attire,
The gentle Una, of celestial birth,
To seek her Knight went wandering o'er the earth.

Ah, then, Belovèd! pleasing was the smart,
And the tear precious in compassion shed
For Her, who, pierced by sorrow's thrilling dart,
Did meekly bear the pang unmerited;
Meek as that emblem of her lowly heart
The milk-white Lamb which in a line she led, –
And faithful, loyal in her innocence,
Like the brave Lion slain in her defence.

Notes could we hear as of a faery shell
Attuned to words with sacred wisdom fraught;
Free Fancy prized each specious miracle,
And all its finer inspiration caught;
Till in the bosom of our rustic Cell,
We by a lamentable change were taught
That 'bliss with mortal Man may not abide':
How nearly joy and sorrow are allied!

For us the stream of fiction ceased to flow,
For us the voice of melody was mute.
– But, as soft gales dissolve the dreary snow,
And give the timid herbage leave to shoot,
Heaven's breathing influence failed not to bestow
A timely promise of unlooked-for fruit,
Fair fruit of pleasure and serene content
From blossoms wild of fancies innocent.

It soothed us – it beguiled us – then, to hear
Once more of troubles wrought by magic spell;
And griefs whose aery motion comes not near
The pangs that tempt the Spirit to rebel:
Then, with mild Una in her sober cheer,
High over hill and low adown the dell
Again we wandered, willing to partake
All that she suffered for her dear Lord's sake.

Then, too, this Song of mine once more could please,
Where anguish, strange as dreams of restless sleep,
Is tempered and allayed by sympathies
Aloft ascending, and descending deep,

Even to the inferior Kinds; whom forest-trees
Protect from beating sunbeams, and the sweep
Of the sharp winds; – fair Creatures! – to whom Heaven
A calm and sinless life, with love, hath given.

This tragic Story cheered us; for it speaks
Of female patience winning firm repose;
And, of the recompense that conscience seeks,
A bright, encouraging, example shows;
Needful when o'er wide realms the tempest breaks,
Needful amid life's ordinary woes; –
Hence, not for them unfitted who would bless
A happy hour with holier happiness.

He serves the Muses erringly and ill,
Whose aim is pleasure light and fugitive:
O, that my mind were equal to fulfil
The comprehensive mandate which they give –
Vain aspiration of an earnest will!
Yet in this moral Strain a power may live,
Belovèd Wife! such solace to impart
As it hath yielded to thy tender heart.

William Hazlitt

from 'On the Character of Milton's Eve', *The Examiner*   1816
(collected in *The Round Table*)

The character which a living poet has given of Spenser, would be
much more true of Milton:

. . . Yet not more sweet
Than pure was he, and not more pure than wise;
High Priest of all the Muses' mysteries.
                              (Southey, *Carmen Nuptiale*,
                              Proem)

Spenser, on the contrary, is very apt to pry into mysteries which do not belong to the Muses. Milton's voluptuousness is not lascivious or sensual. He describes beautiful objects for their own sakes. Spenser has an eye to the consequences, and steeps everything in pleasure, often not of the purest kind.

S. T. Coleridge
from *Biographia Literaria*, chapter 19   1817

It might appear from some passages in the former part of Mr Wordsworth's preface that he meant to confine his theory of style, and the necessity of a close accordance with the actual language of men, to those particular subjects from low and rustic life which by way of experiment he had purposed to naturalize as a new species in our English poetry. But from the train of argument that follows, from the reference to Milton and from the spirit of his critique on Gray's sonnet, those sentences appear to have been rather courtesies of modesty than actual limitations of his system. Yet so groundless does this system appear on a close examination, and so strange and over-whelming in its consequences, that I cannot, and I do not, believe that the poet did ever himself adopt it in the unqualified sense in which his expressions have been understood by others and which indeed according to all the common laws of interpretation they seem to bear. What then did he mean? I apprehend that in the clear perception, not unaccompanied with disgust or contempt, of the gaudy affectations of a style which passed too current with too many for poetic diction (though in truth it had as little pretensions to poetry as to logic or common sense), he narrowed his view for the time; and feeling a justifiable preference for the language of nature and of good sense, even in its humblest and least ornamented forms, he suffered himself to express, in terms at once too large and too exclusive, his predilec-tion for a style the most remote possible from the false and showy splendor which he wished to explode. It is possible that this predilec-tion, at first merely comparative, deviated for a time into direct partiality. But the real object which he had in view was, I doubt not, a species of excellence which had been long before most happily characterized by the judicious and amiable Garve, whose works are so justly beloved and esteemed by the Germans, in his remarks on Gellert, from which the following is literally translated:

The talent that is required in order to make excellent
verses is perhaps greater than the philosopher is ready to admit,
or would find it in his power to acquire; the talent to seek only
the apt expression of the thought, and yet to find at the same
time with it the rhyme and the metre. Gellert possessed this
happy gift, if ever any one of our poets possessed it; and nothing
perhaps contributed more to the great and universal impression
which his fables made on their first publication or conduces more
to their continued popularity. It was a strange and curious
phenomenon, and such as in Germany had been previously unheard
of, to read verses in which every thing was expressed
just as one would wish to talk, and yet all dignified, attractive and
interesting; and all at the same time perfectly correct as to the
measure of the syllables and the rhyme. It is certain that
poetry when it has attained this excellence makes a far greater
impression than prose. So much so indeed, that even the
gratification which the very rhymes afford becomes then no longer
a contemptible or trifling gratification.

However novel this phenomenon may have been in Germany at the
time of Gellert, it is by no means new nor yet of recent existence in
our language. Spite of the licentiousness with which Spenser occasionally compels the orthography of his words into a subservience to his
rhymes, the whole *Faerie Queene* is an almost continued instance of this
beauty. Waller's song *Go, lovely Rose* is doubtless familiar to most of
my readers; but if I had happened to have had by me the poems of
Cotton, more but far less deservedly celebrated as the author of the
Virgil travestied, I should have indulged myself, and I think have
gratified many who are not acquainted with his serious works, by
selecting some admirable specimens of this style. There are not a few
poems in that volume, replete with every excellence of thought,
image and passion which we expect or desire in the poetry of the
milder muse; and yet so worded that the reader sees no one reason
either in the selection or the order of the words why he might not have
said the very same in an appropriate conversation and cannot conceive
how indeed he could have expressed such thoughts otherwise, without
loss or injury to his meaning.

But in truth our language is, and from the first dawn of poetry ever has been, particularly rich in compositions distinguished by this excellence. The final *e*, which is now mute, in Chaucer's age was either sounded or dropped indifferently. We ourselves still use either *beloved* or *belov'd* according as the rhyme, or measure, or the purpose of more or less solemnity may require. Let the reader then only adopt the pronunciation of the poet and of the court at which he lived, both with respect to the final *e* and to the accentuation of the last syllable: I would then venture to ask what even in the colloquial language of elegant and unaffected women (who are the peculiar mistresses of 'pure English and undefiled'), what could we hear more natural, or seemingly more unstudied, than the following stanzas from Chaucer's *Troilus and Creseyde:* [quotes v 603-37, 645-51].

Another exquisite master of this species of style where the scholar and the poet supplies the material, but the perfect well-bred gentleman the expressions and the arrangement, is George Herbert. As from the nature of the subject and the too frequent quaintness of the thoughts, his *Temple, or Sacred Poems and Private Ejaculations* are comparatively but little known, I shall extract two poems. The first is a Sonnet [*The Bosom Sin*], equally admirable for the weight, number and expression of the thoughts, and for the simple dignity of the language (unless indeed a fastidious taste should object to the latter half of the sixth line). The second is a poem of greater length [*Love Unknown*], which I have chosen not only for the present purpose, but likewise as a striking example and illustration of an assertion hazarded in a former page of these sketches: namely that the characteristic fault of our elder poets is the reverse of that which distinguishes too many of our more recent versifiers; the one conveying the most fantastic thoughts in the most correct and natural language; the other in the most fantastic language conveying the most trivial thoughts. The latter is a riddle of words; the former an enigma of thoughts.

William Hazlitt

from a review of Coleridge's *Biographia Literaria, Edinburgh Review*, vol. 28   1817

There is, no doubt, a simple and familiar language, common to almost all ranks, and intelligible through many ages, which is the best fitted for the direct expression of strong sense and deep passion, and which, consequently, is the language of the best poetry as well as of the best prose. But it is not the exclusive language of poetry. There is another language peculiar to this manner of writing, which has been called *poetic diction*, – those flowers of speech, which, whether natural or artificial, fresh or faded, are strewed over the plainer ground which poetry has in common with prose: a paste of rich and honeyed words, like the candied coat of the auricula; a glittering tissue of quaint conceits and sparkling metaphors, crusting over the rough stalk of homely thoughts. Such is the style of almost all our modern poets; such is the style of Pope and Gray; such, too, very often, is that of Shakespear and Milton; and, notwithstanding Mr Coleridge's decision to the contrary, of Spenser's *Faerie Queene*. Now this style is the reverse of one made up of *slang* phrases; for, as they are words associated only with mean and vulgar ideas, poetic diction is such as is connected only with the most pleasing and elegant association; and *both* differ essentially from the middle or natural style, which is a mere transparent medium of the thoughts, neither degrading nor setting them off by any adventitious qualities of its own, but leaving them to make their own impression, by the force of truth and nature. Upon the whole, therefore, we should think this ornamented and coloured style, most proper to descriptive or fanciful poetry, where the writer has to lend a borrowed, and, in some sort, meretricious lustre to outward objects, which he can best do by enshrining them in a language that, by custom and long prescription, reflects the image of a poetical mind, – as we think the common or natural style is the truly dramatic style, that in which he can best give the impassioned, unborrowed, unaffected thoughts of others. The pleasure derived from poetic diction is the same as that derived from classical diction. It is in like manner made up of words dipped in 'the dew of Castalie', – tinged with colours borrowed from the rainbow, – 'sky-tinctured', warmed with the glow of genius, purified by the breath of time, – that soften into distance, and expand into magnitude, whatever is seen through their medium, – that varnish over the trite and commonplace, and lend a gorgeous robe to the forms of fancy, but are only an incumbrance and a disguise in conveying the true touches of nature, the intense strokes of passion. The beauty of poetic diction is, in short, borrowed and artificial. It is a glittering veil spread over the forms of things and the feelings of the heart; and is best laid aside, when we wish to show either the one or the other in their naked beauty or deformity. As the dialogues in *Othello* and *Lear* furnish the most striking instances of plain, point-blank speaking, or of the real language of nature and passion, so the Choruses in *Samson Agonistes* abound in the fullest and finest adaptations of classic and poetic phrases to express distant and elevated notions, born of fancy, religion and learning.

William Hazlitt

from *Lectures on the English Poets*   1818

Spenser, as well as Chaucer, was engaged in active life; but the genius of his poetry was not active: it is inspired by the love of ease, and relaxation from all the cares and business of life. Of all the poets, he is the most poetical. Though much later than Chaucer, his obligations to preceding writers were less. He has in some measure borrowed the plan of his poem (as a number of distinct narratives) from Ariosto; but he has engrafted upon it an exuberance of fancy, and an endless voluptuousness of sentiment, which are not to be found in the Italian writer. Further, Spenser is even more of an inventor in the subject-matter. There is an originality, richness, and variety in his allegorical personages and fictions, which almost vies with the splendour of the ancient mythology. If Ariosto transports us into the regions of romance, Spenser's poetry is all fairy-land. In Ariosto, we walk upon the ground, in a company, gay, fantastic, and adventurous enough. In Spenser, we wander in another world, among ideal beings. The poet takes and lays us in the lap of a lovelier nature, by the sound of softer streams, among greener hills and fairer valleys. He paints nature, not as we find it, but as we expected to find it; and fulfils the delightful promise of our youth. He waves his wand of enchantment – and at once embodies airy beings, and throws a delicious veil over all actual objects. The two worlds of reality and of fiction are poised on the wings of his imagination. His ideas, indeed, seem more distinct than his perceptions. He is the painter of abstractions, and describes them with dazzling minuteness. In the Mask of Cupid he makes the God of Love 'clap on high his coloured winges *twain*'; and it is said of Gluttony, in the Procession of the Passions,

In greene vine leaues he was right fitly clad.

At times he becomes picturesque from his intense love of beauty; as where he compares Prince Arthur's crest to the appearance of the almond tree: [quotes 1 vii 32, quoted below, p. 144]. The love of beauty, however, and not of truth, is the moving principle of his mind; and he is guided in his fantastic delineations by no rule but the impulse of an inexhaustible imagination. He luxuriates equally in scenes of Eastern magnificence; or the still solitude of a hermit's cell – in the extremes of sensuality or refinement.

In reading *The Faerie Queene*, you see a little withered old man by a wood-side opening a wicket, a giant, and a dwarf lagging far behind, a damsel in a boat upon an enchanted lake, wood-nymphs, and satyrs; and all of a sudden you are transported into a lofty palace, with tapers burning, amidst knights and ladies, with dance and revelry, and song, 'and mask, and antique pageantry'. What can be more solitary, more shut up in itself, than his description of the house of Sleep, to which Archimago sends for a dream:

And more, to lulle him in his slumber soft,
A trickling streame from high rocke tumbling downe
And euer-drizling raine vpon the loft,
Mixt with a murmuring winde, much like the sowne[1]
Of swarming Bees, did cast him in a swowne:
No other noyse, nor peoples troublous cryes,
As still are wont t'annoy the walled towne,
Might there be heard: but carelesse Quiet lyes,
Wrapt in eternall silence farre from enemyes.

(1 i 41)

It is as if 'the honey-heavy dew of slumber' had settled on his pen in writing these lines. How different in the subject (and yet how like in beauty) is the following description of the Bower of Bliss:

Eftsoones they heard a most melodious sound,
Of all that mote delight a daintie eare,
Such as att once might not on liuing ground,

1 sound

Saue in this Paradise, be heard elswhere:
Right hard it was, for wight, which did it heare,
To read, what manner musicke that mote bee:
For all that pleasing is to liuing eare,
Was there consorted[1] in one harmonee,
Birdes, voyces, instruments, windes, waters, all agree.

The ioyous birdes shrouded in chearefull shade,
Their notes vnto the voyce attempred[2] sweet;
Th' Angelicall soft trembling voyces made
To th' instruments diuine respondence meet:[3]
The siluer sounding instruments did meet
With the base murmure of the waters fall:
The waters fall with difference discreet,
Now soft, now loud, vnto the wind did call:
The gentle warbling wind low answered to all.

(II xii 70–71)

The remainder of the passage has all that voluptuous pathos, and
languid brilliancy of fancy, in which this writer excelled: [quotes
II xii 74–8].

The finest things in Spenser are, the character of Una, in the first
book; the House of Pride; the Cave of Mammon, and the Cave of
Despair; the account of Memory, of whom it is said, among other
things,

The warres he well remembred of king *Nine*,
Of old *Assaracus*, and *Inachus* diuine;

(II ix 56)

the description of Belphoebe; the story of Florimel and the Witch's
son; the Gardens of Adonis, and the Bower of Bliss; the Mask of
Cupid; and Colin Clout's vision, in the last book. But some people
will say that all this may be very fine, but that they cannot understand
it on account of the allegory. They are afraid of the allegory, as if
they thought it would bite them: they look at it as a child looks at a
painted dragon, and think it will strangle them in its shining folds.

1 combined, united   2 attuned, harmonized   3 fitting, proper

This is very idle. If they do not meddle with the allegory, the allegory will not meddle with them. Without minding it at all, the whole is as plain as a pike-staff. It might as well be pretended that, we cannot see Poussin's pictures for the allegory, as that the allegory prevents us from understanding Spenser. For instance, when Britomart, seated amidst the young warriors, lets fall her hair and discovers her sex, is it necessary to know the part she plays in the allegory, to understand the beauty of the following stanza?

> And eke that straunger knight emongst the rest
> Was for like need enforst to disaray:
> Tho whenas vailed[1] was her loftie crest,
> Her golden locks, that were in tramels[2] gay
> Vpbounden, did them selues adowne display,
> And raught[3] vnto her heeles; like sunny beames,
> That in a cloud their light did long time stay,
> Their vapour vaded,[4] shew their golden gleames,
> And through the persant aire shoote forth their azure streames.
>
> (III ix 20)

Or is there any mystery in what is said of Belphoebe, that her hair was sprinkled with flowers and blossoms which had been entangled in it as she fled through the woods? Or is it necessary to have a more distinct idea of Proteus, than that which is given of him in his boat, with the frighted Florimel at his feet, while

> . . . the cold ysickles from his rough beard,
> Dropped adowne vpon her yuorie brest.
>
> (III viii 35)

Or is it not a sufficient account of one of the sea-gods that pass by them, to say –

> That was *Arion* crowned; . . .
> So went he playing on the watery plaine.
>
> (IV xi 23–4)

Or to take the Procession of the Passions that draw the coach of

1 let down   2 nets (for the hair)
3 reached   4 vanished

Pride, in which the figures of Idleness, of Gluttony, of Lechery, of Avarice, of Envy, and of Wrath speak, one should think, plain enough for themselves; such as this of Gluttony: [quotes I iv 21–2]. Or this of Lechery: [quotes I iv 24–5].

> Inconstant man, that loued all he saw,
> And lusted after all, that he did loue,
> Ne would his looser life be tide to law,
> But ioyd weake wemens hearts to tempt and proue
> If from their loyall loues he might them moue.
>
>   (I iv 26)

This is pretty plain-spoken. Mr Southey says of Spenser:

> . . . Yet not more sweet
> Than pure was he, and not more pure than wise;
> High priest of all the Muses' mysteries!

On the contrary, no one was more apt to pry into mysteries which do not strictly belong to the Muses.

Of the same kind with the Procession of the Passions, as little obscure, and still more beautiful, is the Mask of Cupid, with his train of votaries: [quotes III xii 7–13, 22–3]. The description of Hope, in this series of historical portraits, is one of the most beautiful in Spenser: and the triumph of Cupid at the mischief he has made, is worthy of the malicious urchin deity. In reading these descriptions, one can hardly avoid being reminded of Ruben's allegorical pictures; but the account of Satyrane taming the lion's whelps and lugging the bear's cubs along in his arms while yet an infant, whom his mother so naturally advises to 'go seek some other play-fellows', has even more of this high picturesque character. Nobody but Rubens could have painted the fancy of Spenser; and he could not have given the sentiment, the airy dream that hovers over it!

With all this, Spenser neither makes us laugh nor weep. The only jest in his poem is an allegorical play upon words, where he describes Malbecco as escaping in the herd of goats, 'by the help of his fayre hornes on hight.' But he has been unjustly charged with a want of passion and of strength. He has both in an immense degree. He has not indeed the pathos of immediate action or suffering, which is more properly the dramatic; but he has all the pathos of sentiment

and romance – all that belongs to distant objects of terror, and uncertain, imaginary distress. His strength, in like manner, is not strength
of will or action, of bone and muscle, nor is it coarse and palpable –
but it assumes a character of vastness and sublimity seen through the
same visionary medium, and blended with the appalling associations of
preternatural agency. We need only turn, in proof of this, to the
Cave of Despair, or the Cave of Mammon, or to the account of the
change of Malbecco into Jealousy. The following stanzas, in the description of the Cave of Mammon, the grisly house of Plutus, are
unrivalled for the portentous massiness of the forms, the splendid
chiaroscuro, and shadowy horror.

> That houses forme within was rude and strong,
> Like an huge caue, hewne out of rocky clift,
> From whose rough vaut[1] the ragged breaches[2] hong,
> Embost with massy gold of glorious gift,
> And with rich metall loaded euery rift,
> That heauy ruine they did seeme to threat;
> And ouer them *Arachne* high did lift
> Her cunning web, and spred her subtile net,
> Enwrapped in fowle smoke and clouds more blacke then Iet.

> Both roofe, and floore, and wals were all of gold,
> But ouergrowne with dust and old decay,
> And hid in darkenesse, that none could behold
> The hew thereof: for vew of chearefull day
> Did neuer in that house it selfe display,
> But a faint shadow of vncertain light;
> Such as a lamp, whose life does fade away:
> Or as the Moone cloathed with clowdy night,
> Does shew to him, that walkes in feare and sad affright.

> • • • • •

> And ouer them sad Horrour with grim hew,
> Did alwayes sore, beating his yron wings;
> And after him Owles and Night-rauens flew,
> The hatefull messengers of heauy things,
> Of death and dolour telling sad tidings;

1 vault   2 fissures

Whiles sad *Celeno*, sitting on a clift,
A song of bale and bitter sorrow sings,
That hart of flint a sunder could haue rift:
Which hauing ended, after him she flyeth swift.

(II vii 28-9, 23)

The Cave of Despair is described with equal gloominess and power of
fancy; and the fine moral declamation of the owner of it, on the evils
of life, almost makes one in love with death. In the story of Malbecco,
who is haunted by jealousy, and in vain strives to run away from his
own thoughts –

High ouer hilles and ouer dales he fled –

(III x 55)

the truth of human passion and the preternatural ending are equally
striking. – It is not fair to compare Spenser with Shakspeare, in point
of interest. A fairer comparison would be with *Comus*; and the result
would not be unfavourable to Spenser. There is only one work of the
same allegorical kind, which has more interest than Spenser (with
scarcely less imagination): and that is *The Pilgrim's Progress*. The
three first books of *The Faerie Queene* are very superior to the three
last. One would think that Pope, who used to ask if any one had ever
read *The Faerie Queene* through, had only dipped into these last. The
only things in them equal to the former, are the account of Talus, the
Iron Man, and the delightful episode of Pastorella.

The language of Spenser is full, and copious, to overflowing: it is
less pure and idiomatic than Chaucer's, and is enriched and adorned
with phrases borrowed from the different languages of Europe, both
ancient and modern. He was, probably, seduced into a certain licence
of expression by the difficulty of filling up the moulds of his complicated rhymed stanza from the limited resources of his native language.
This stanza, with alternate and repeatedly recurring rhymes, is borrowed from the Italians. It was peculiarly fitted to their language,
which abounds in similar vowel terminations, and is as little adapted
to ours, from the stubborn, unaccommodating resistance which the
consonant endings of the northern languages make to this sort of
endless sing-song. – Not that I would, on that account, part with the
stanza of Spenser. We are, perhaps, indebted to this very necessity of
finding out new forms of expression, and to the occasional faults to

which it led, for a poetical language rich and varied and magnificent beyond all former, and almost all later example. His versification is, at once, the most smooth and the most sounding in the language. It is a labyrinth of sweet sounds, 'in many a winding bout of linked sweetness long drawn out' – that would cloy by their very sweetness, but that the ear is constantly relieved and enchanted by their continued variety of modulation – dwelling on the pauses of the action, or flowing on in a fuller tide of harmony with the movement of the sentiment. It has not the bold dramatic transitions of Shakspeare's blank verse, nor the high-raised tone of Milton's; but it is the perfection of melting harmony, dissolving the soul in pleasure, or holding it captive in the chains of suspense. Spenser was the poet of our waking dreams; and he has invented not only a language, but a music of his own for them. The undulations are infinite, like those of the waves of the sea: but the effect is still the same, lulling the senses into a deep oblivion of the jarring noises of the world, from which we have no wish to be ever recalled.

S. T. Coleridge

from notes for lectures and marginal notes in a copy of *The Faerie Queene* 1818

Allegory

Substitute a simile for the thing it resembles, instead of annexing it, and it becomes a metaphor: thus if in speaking of the Duke of Wellington's campaign in Portugal against Massena we should say, 'At length he left his mountain strongholds and fell on the rear of the retreating army, as a cloud from the hill tops,' it is a simile; if more briefly we say, 'At length the cloud descended from its hill and discharged itself in thunder and lightning on the plain,' it becomes a metaphor, and a metaphor is a fragment of an allegory. But if it be asked, how do you define an allegory so as to distinguish it from a fable, I can reply only by a confession of my ignorance and inability. The fact is, that allegory must be used in two senses – the one including, while the other is defined by excluding, fable. Fable is a shorter and simpler sort of allegory – this is the past sense – and again whatever of this kind is not a fable, not only is, but is called, an allegory. So a pony is a smaller sort of horse: and horses that are not ponies are called horses. A shrub is a smaller sort of tree: and we are in no risk of being misunderstood when we say, the laurel is but a shrub in this country, but in the south of Europe it is a tree. It may indeed be justly said, that in a fable no allegoric agent or image should be used which has not had some one paramount quality universally attributed to it beforehand, while in an allegory the resemblance may have been presented for the first time by the writer. This is the true cause why animals, the heathen gods, and trees, the properties of which are recalled by their very names, are almost the only proper *dramatis personae* of a fable. A bear, a fox, a tiger, a lion, Diana, an oak, a willow, are *every man's* metaphor for clumsiness, cunning, ferocious or magnanimous courage, chastity, unbendingness, and flexibility, and it would be a safe rule that what would not be at once and generally intelligible in a metaphor may be introduced in an allegory, but ought not to be in a fable. This, how-ever, is one of the conditions of a good fable rather than a definition of a fable generally, and fortunately the difficulty of defining a thing or term is almost always in an inverse proportion to the necessity. Linnaeus found no difficulty in establishing discriminating characters of the different tribes of apes, but very great in scientific contra-distinctions between the genera man and ape; but it is to be hoped that he had not met with many individuals of either kind that had pro-duced any practical hesitation in determining his judgement.

We may then safely define allegoric writing as the employment of one set of agents and images with actions and accompaniments correspondent, so as to convey, while in disguise, either moral qualities or conceptions of the mind that are not in themselves objects of the senses, or other images, agents, actions, fortunes, and circumstances, so that the difference is everywhere presented to the eye or imagina-tion while the likeness is suggested to the mind; and this connectedly so that the parts combine to form a consistent whole. Whatever composition answering to this definition is not a fable, is entitled an allegory – of which [what] may be called picture allegories, or real or supposed pictures interpreted and moralized, and satirical allegories, we have several instances among the classics – as the Tablet of Cebes, the Choice of Hercules, and Simonides' origin of women – but of narrative or epic allegories scarce any, the multiplicity of their gods and goddesses precluding it – unless we choose rather to say that all the machinery of their poets is allegorical. Of a people who raised altars to fever, to sport, to fright, etc., it is impossible to determine how far they meant a personal power or a personification of a power. This only is certain, that the introduction of these agents could not have the same unmixed effect as the same agents used allegorically produce on our minds, but something more nearly resembling the effect produced by the introduction of characteristic saints in the Roman Catholic poets, or of Moloch, Belial, and Mammon in the second Book of *Paradise Lost* compared with his Sin and Death.

The most beautiful allegory ever composed, the Tale of Cupid and Psyche, tho' composed by an heathen, was subsequent to the general spread of Christianity, and written by one of those philosophers who attempted to Christianize a sort of Oriental and Egyptian Platonism enough to set it up against Christianity; but the first allegory completely modern in its form is the *Psychomachia* or *Battle of the Soul* by Prudentius, a Christian poet of the fifth century – facts that fully explain both the origin and nature of narrative allegory, as a substitute for the mythological imagery of polytheism, and differing from it only in the more obvious and intentional distinction of the sense from the symbol, and the known unreality of the latter – so as to be a kind of intermediate step between actual persons and mere personifications. But for this very cause it is incapable of exciting any lively interest for any length of time, for if the allegoric personage be strongly individualized so as to interest us, we cease to think of it as allegory; and if it does not interest us, it had better be away. The dullest and most defective parts of Spenser are those in which we are compelled to think of his agents as allegories – and how far the Sin and Death of Milton are exceptions to this censure, is a delicate problem which I shall attempt to solve in another lecture; but in that admirable allegory, the first Part of *Pilgrim's Progress*, which delights every one, the interest is so great that [in] spite of all the writer's attempts to force the allegoric purpose on the reader's mind by his strange names – Old Stupidity of the Tower of Honesty, etc., etc. – his piety was baffled by his genius, and the Bunyan of Parnassus had the better of Bunyan of the conventicle; and with the same illusion as we read any tale known to be fictitious, as a novel, we go on with his characters as real persons, who had been nicknamed by their neighbours. But the most decisive verdict against narrative allegory is to be found in Tasso's own account of what he would have the reader understand by the persons and events of his Jerusalem. Apollo be praised! not a thought like it would ever enter of its own accord into any mortal mind; and what is an additional good feature, when put there, it will not stay, having the very opposite quality that snakes have – they come out of their holes into open view at the sound of sweet music, while the allegoric meaning slinks off at the very first notes, and lurks in murkiest oblivion – and utter invisibility.

Spenser

There is this difference, among many others, between Shakespeare and Spenser: Shakespeare is never coloured by the customs of his age; what appears of contemporary character in him is merely negative; it is just not something else. He has none of the fictitious realities of the classics, none of the grotesqueness of chivalry, none of the allegory of the middle ages; there is no sectarianism either of politics or religion, no miser, no witch, – no common witch, – no astrology – nothing impermanent of however long duration; but he stands like the yew tree in Lorton vale, which has known so many ages that it belongs to none in particular; a living image of endless self-reproduction, like the immortal tree of Malabar. In Spenser the spirit of chivalry is entirely predominant, although with a much greater infusion of the poet's own individual self into it than is found in any other writer. He has the wit of the southern with the deeper inwardness of the northern genius. . . .

As characteristic of Spenser, I would call your particular attention in the first place to the indescribable sweetness and fluent projection of his verse, very clearly distinguishable from the deeper and more in-woven harmonies of Shakespeare and Milton. This stanza is a good instance of what I mean:

Yet she, most faithfull Ladie all this while
Forsaken, wofull, solitarie mayd
Farre from all peoples prease,[1] as in exile,
In wildernesse and wastfull deserts strayd,

1 multitude, press

> To seeke her knight; who subtilly betrayd
> Through that late vision, which th' Enchaunter wrought,
> Had her abandond. She of nought affrayd,
> Through woods and wastnesse wide him daily sought;
> Yet wished tydings none of him vnto her brought.
>
> (I iii 3)

Combined with this sweetness and fluency, the scientific construction of the metre of *The Faerie Queene* is very noticeable. One of Spenser's arts is that of alliteration, and he uses it with great effect in doubling the impression of an image:

> In *w*ildernesse and *w*astfull deserts . . .

> Through *w*oods and *w*astnesse *w*ide . . .

> They pas the bitter waues of *Acheron*,
> Where many soules sit *w*ailing *w*oefully,
> And come to *f*iery *f*lood of *Ph*legeton,
> Whereas the damned ghosts in torments fry,
> And with *s*harpe *s*hrilling *s*hriekes doe bootlesse cry . . .
>
> (I v 33)

He is particularly given to an alternate alliteration, which is, perhaps, when well used, a great secret in melody:

> A *r*amping Lyon *r*ushed suddainly,
>
> (I iii 5)

> And *s*ad to *s*ee her *s*orrowfull constraint,
>
> (I iii 8)

> And on the grasse her *d*aintie *l*imbes *d*id *l*ay.
>
> (I iii 4)

You cannot read a page of *The Faerie Queene*, if you read for that purpose, without perceiving the intentional alliterativeness of the words; and yet so skilfully is this managed, that it never strikes any unwarned ear as artificial, or other than the result of the necessary movement of the verse.

Spenser displays great skill in harmonizing his descriptions of external nature and actual incidents with the allegorical character and epic activity of the poem. Take these two beautiful passages as illustrations of what I mean:

By this the Northerne wagoner had set
His seuenfold teme behind the stedfast starre,
That was in Ocean waues yet neuer wet,
But firme is fixt, and sendeth light from farre
To all, that in the wide deepe wandring arre;
And chearefull Chaunticlere with his note shrill
Had warned once, that *Phœbus* fiery carre
In hast was climbing vp the Easterne hill,
Full enuious that night so long his roome did fill.

When those accursed messengers of hell,
That feigning dreame, and that faire-forged Spright
Came, etc. . . . .

(1 ii 1–2)

At last the golden Orientall gate
Of greatest heauen gan to open faire,
And *Phœbus* fresh, as bridegrome to his mate,
Came dauncing forth, shaking his deawie haire:
And hurld his glistring beames through gloomy aire.
Which when the wakeful Elfe perceiu'd streight way
He started vp, and did him selfe prepaire,
In sun-bright armes, and battailous[1] array:
For with that Pagan proud he combat will that day.

(1 v 2)

Observe also the exceeding vividness of Spenser's descriptions. They are not, in the true sense of the word, picturesque; but are composed of a wondrous series of images, as in our dreams. Compare the following passage with anything you may remember in *pari materia* in Milton or Shakespeare:

His haughtie helmet, horrid[2] all with gold,
Both glorious brightnesse, and great terrour bred;
For all the crest a Dragon did enfold

1 ready for battle, warlike   2 bristling, rough

With greedie pawes, and ouer all did spred
His golden wings: his dreadfull hideous hed
Close couched on the beuer, seem'd to throw
From flaming mouth bright sparkles fierie red,
That suddeine horror to faint harts did show;
And scaly tayle was stretcht adowne his backe full low.

Vpon the top of all his loftie crest,
A bunch of haires discolourd diuersly,
With sprincled pearle, and gold full richly drest,
Did shake, and seem'd to daunce for iollity,
Like to an Almond tree ymounted hye
On top of greene *Selinis* all alone,
With blossomes braue bedecked daintily;
Whose tender locks do tremble euery one
At euery little breath, that vnder heauen is blowne.

(I vii 31–2)

You will take especial note of the marvellous independence and
true imaginative absence of all particular space or time in *The Faerie
Queene*. It is in the domains neither of history or geography; it is
ignorant of all artificial boundary, all material obstacles; it is truly in
land of Fairy, that is, of mental space. The poet has placed you in a
dream, a charmed sleep, and you neither wish, nor have the power, to
inquire where you are, or how you got there. It reminds me of some
lines of my own:

Oh! would to Alla!
The raven or the sea-mew were appointed
To bring me food! – or rather that my soul
Might draw in life from the universal air!
It were a lot divine in some small skiff
Along some ocean's boundless solitude
To float for ever with a careless course,
And think myself the only being alive!

(*Remorse*, IV 3)

Indeed Spenser himself, in the conduct of his great poem, may be
represented under the same image, his symbolizing purpose being his
mariner's compass:

As Pilot well expert in perilous waue,
That to a stedfast starre his course hath bent,
When foggy mistes, or cloudy tempests haue
The faithfull light of that faire lampe yblent,[1]
And couer'd heauen with hideous dreriment,[2]
Vpon his card and compas firmes[3] his eye,
The maisters of his long experiment,
And to them does the steddy helme apply,
Bidding his winged vessell fairely forward fly.

(II vii 1)

So the poet through the realms of allegory.

You should note the quintessential character of Christian chivalry in all his characters, but more especially in his women. The Greeks, except, perhaps, in Homer, seem to have had no way of making their women interesting, but by unsexing them, as in the instances of the tragic Medea, Electra, etc. Contrast such characters with Spenser's Una, who exhibits no prominent feature, has no particularization, but produces the same feeling that a statue does, when contemplated at a distance:

From her faire head her fillet[4] she vndight,[5]
And laid her stole[6] aside. Her angels face
As the great eye of heauen shyned bright,
And made a sunshine in the shadie place;
Did neuer mortall eye behold such heauenly grace.

(I iii 4)

In Spenser we see the brightest and purest form of that nationality which was so common a characteristic of our elder poets. There is nothing unamiable, nothing contemptuous of others, in it. To glorify their country – to elevate England into a queen, an empress of the heart – this was their passion and object; and how dear and important an object it was or may be, let Spain, in the recollection of her Cid, declare! There is a great magic in national names. What a damper to all

1 blinded   2 dreariness
3 fastens   4 ribbon for the head
5 took off   6 mantle

interest is a list of native East Indian merchants! Unknown names are non-conductors; they stop all sympathy. No one of our poets has touched this string more exquisitely than Spenser; especially in his chronicle of the British Kings (ii 10), and the marriage of the Thames with the Medway (iv 11), in both which passages the mere names constitute half the pleasure we receive. To the same feeling we must in particular attribute Spenser's sweet reference to Ireland:

> Ne thence the Irishe Riuers absent were,
> Sith no lesse famous then the rest they bee,
>
> (IV xi 40)

And Mulla mine, whose waues I whilom taught to weep.

> (IV xi 41)

And there is a beautiful passage of the same sort in the *Colin Clovts Come Home Againe*:

> One day (quoth he) I sat, (as was my trade)
> Vnder the foote of *Mole* etc.
>
> (56–7)

Lastly, the great and prevailing character of Spenser's mind is fancy under the conditions of imagination, as an ever present but not always active power. He has an imaginative fancy, but he has not imagination, in kind or degree, as Shakespeare and Milton have; the boldest effort of his powers in this way is the character of Talus. Add to this a feminine tenderness and almost maidenly purity of feeling, and above all, a deep moral earnestness which produces a believing sympathy and acquiescence in the reader, and you have a tolerably adequate view of Spenser's intellectual being.

Notes on *The Faerie Queene*

[I v 6: And burning blades about their heads do blesse.]
Licentiously careless as Spenser is in the orthography of words, varying the final vowels as the rhyme requires, I scarcely can reconcile myself to the belief that he would misuse a word in so arbitrary a manner as to employ 'bless' for 'brandish'. May it not have been 'class' for 'clash'?

[Later.] May not 'blesse' mean 'to wound'? French, *blesser*? To wound the air: so *Macbeth*. Not unusual.

[III xii 14 Dissemblaunce: And her bright browes were deckt with borrowed haire.]

Here, as too often in this great poem, that which is and may be known, but cannot *appear* from the given point of view, is confounded with the visible. It is no longer a mask-figure, but the character, of a Dissembler. Another common fault in stanza 16: Grief represents two incompatibles, the grieved and the aggriever.

[*Griefe* all in sable sorrowfully clad,
  Downe hanging his dull head with heauy chere,

        .   .   .   .   .

  A paire of Pincers in his hand he had,
  With which he pinched people to the hart.]

Indeed, this confusion of agent and patient occurs so frequently in his allegorical personages that Spenser seems to have deemed it within the laws and among the legitimate principles of allegory.

John Keats

Verses written in a copy of *The Faerie Queene*, at the close of Book V Canto ii   1821

In after-time, a sage of mickle lore
Yclep'd Typographus, the Giant took,
And did refit his limbs as heretofore,
And made him read in many a learned book,
And into many a lively legend look;
Thereby in goodly themes so training him,
That all his brutishness he quite forsook,
When, meeting Artegall and Talus grim,
The one he struck stone-blind, the other's eyes wox
    dim.

Charles Lamb

'Sanity of True Genius', *New Monthly Magazine*   1826
(collected in *Last Essays of Elia*)

So far from the position holding true, that great wit (or genius, in
our modern way of speaking), has a necessary alliance with insanity,
the greatest wits, on the contrary, will ever be found to be the sanest
writers. It is impossible for the mind to conceive of a mad Shakespeare.
The greatness of wit, by which the poetic talent is here chiefly to be
understood, manifests itself in the admirable balance of all the faculties.
Madness is the disproportionate straining or excess of any one of them.
'So strong a wit,' says Cowley, speaking of a poetical friend,

> . . . did Nature to him frame,
> As all things but his judgement overcame,
> His judgement like the heavenly moon did show,
> Tempering that mighty sea below.

The ground of the mistake is, that men, finding in the raptures of the
higher poetry a condition of exaltation, to which they have no parallel
in their own experience, besides the spurious resemblance of it in
dreams and fevers, impute a state of dreaminess and fever to the poet.
But the true poet dreams being awake. He is not possessed by his
subject, but has dominion over it. In the groves of Eden he walks
familiar as in his native paths. He ascends the empyrean heaven, and is
not intoxicated. He treads the burning marl without dismay; he wins
his flight without self-loss through realms of chaos 'and old night'.
Or if, abandoning himself to that severer chaos of a 'human mind
untuned', he is content awhile to be mad with Lear, or to hate mankind (a sort of madness) with Timon, neither is that madness, nor this
misanthropy, so unchecked, but that, – never letting the reins of
reason wholly go, while most he seems to do so, – he has his better
genius still whispering at his ear, with the good servant Kent suggesting
saner counsels, or with the honest steward Flavius recommending kindlier resolutions. Where he seems most to recede from humanity, he will be found the truest to it. From beyond the scope of Nature
if he summon possible existences, he subjugates them to the law of her
consistency. He is beautifully loyal to that sovereign directress, even

when he appears most to betray and desert her. His ideal tribes submit to policy; his very monsters are tamed to his hand, even as that wild sea-brood, shepherded by Proteus. He tames, and he clothes them with attributes of flesh and blood, till they wonder at themselves, like Indian Islanders forced to submit to European vesture. Caliban, the Witches, are as true to the laws of their own nature (ours with a difference), as Othello, Hamlet and Macbeth. Herein the great and the little wits are differenced; that if the latter wander ever so little from nature or actual existence, they lose themselves, and their readers. Their phantoms are lawless; their visions nightmares. They do not create, which implies shaping and consistency. Their imaginations are not active – for to be active is to call something into act and form – but passive, as men in sick dreams. For the super-natural, or something super-added to what we know of nature, they give you the plainly non-natural. And if this were all, and that these mental hallucinations were discoverable only in the treatment of subjects out of nature, or transcending it, the judgement might with some plea be pardoned if it ran riot, and a little wantonized: but even in the describing of real and every day life, that which is before their eyes, one of these lesser wits shall more deviate from nature – show more of that inconsequence, which has a natural alliance with frenzy, – than a great genius in his 'maddest fits', as Withers somewhere calls them. We appeal to any one that is acquainted with the common run of Lane's novels, – as they existed some twenty or thirty years back, – those scanty intellectual viands of the whole female reading public, till a happier genius arose, and expelled for ever the innutritious phantoms, – whether he has not found his brain more 'betossed', his memory more puzzled, his sense of when and where more confounded, among the improbable events, the incoherent incidents, the inconsistent characters, or no-characters, of some third-rate love intrigue – where the persons shall be a Lord Glendamour and a Miss Rivers, and the scene only alternate between Bath and Bond-street – a more bewildering dreaminess induced upon him, than he has felt wandering over all the fairy grounds of Spenser. In the productions we refer to, nothing but names and places is familiar; the persons are neither of this world nor of any other conceivable one; an endless string of activities without purpose, of purposes destitute of motive: – we meet phantoms in our known walks; *fantasques* only christened. In the poet we have names which announce fiction; and we have absolutely no place at all, for the things and persons of *The Faerie Queene* prate not of their 'whereabout'. But in their inner nature, and the law of their speech and actions, we are at home and upon acquainted ground. The one turns life into a dream; the other to the wildest dreams gives the sobrieties of every day occurrences. By what subtile art of tracing the mental processes it is effected, we are not philosophers enough to explain, but in that wonderful episode of the cave of Mammon, in which the Money God appears first in the lowest form of a miser, is then a worker of metals, and becomes the god of all the treasures of the world; and has a daughter, Ambition, before whom all the world kneels for favours – with the Hesperian fruit, the waters of Tantalus, with Pilate washing his hands vainly, but not impertinently, in the same stream – that we should be at one moment in the cave of an old hoarder of treasures, at the next at the forge of the Cyclops, in a palace and yet in hell, all at once, with the shifting mutations of the most rambling dream, and our judgement yet all the time awake, and neither able nor willing to detect the fallacy, – is a proof of that hidden sanity which still guides the poet in his widest seeming-aberrations.

It is not enough to say that the whole episode is a copy of the mind's conceptions in sleep; it is, in some sort – but what a copy! Let the most romantic of us, that has been entertained all night with the spectacle of some wild and magnificent vision, recombine it in the morning, and try it by his waking judgement. That which appeared so shifting, and yet so coherent, while that faculty was passive, when it comes under cool examination, shall appear so reasonless and so unlinked, that we are ashamed to have been so deluded; and to have taken, though but in sleep, a monster for a god. But the transitions in this episode are every whit as violent as in the most extravagant dream, and yet the waking judgement ratifies them.

Sir Walter Scott

from a review of Robert Southey's edition of *The Pilgrim's Progress*, *Quarterly Review*, vol. 43   September 1830

In a style of composition, rendered thus venerable by its antiquity, and still more so by the purposes to which it has been applied, John Bunyan, however uneducated, was a distinguished master. For our part, we are inclined to allow him, in the simplicity of his story, and his very shrewdness, and, if the reader pleases, homely bluntness of style, a superiority over the great poet to whom he has been compared by D'Israeli, – which, considering both writers as allegorists, may, in some respect, counter-balance the advantages of a mind fraught with education, a head full of poetic flight and grace – in a word, the various, the unutterable distinction between the friend of Sidney and of Raleigh, the fascinating poet of fairy land, and our obscure tinker of Elstow, the self-erected holder-forth to the anabaptists of Bedford. Either has told a tale expressive of the progress of religion and morality – Spenser's under the guise of a romance of chivalry, while that of Bunyan recalls the outline of a popular fairy tale, with its machinery of giants, dwarfs, and enchanters. So far they resemble each other; and if the later writer must allow the earlier the advantage of a richer imagination, and a taste incalculably more cultivated, the uneducated man of the people may, in return, claim over Spenser the superiority due to a more simple and better concocted plan, from which he has suffered no temptation to lead him astray.

This will appear more evident, if we observe that Spenser (the first book, perhaps, excepted, where he has traced, in the adventures of the Red Cross Knight, with considerable accuracy, the history and changes of the Christian world) has, in other cantos, suffered his story to lead him astray from his moral, and engages his knights, by whom we are to understand the abstract virtues, in tilts and tournaments, not to be easily reconciled with the explanation of the allegory. What are we to understand by Britomart overthrowing Arthegal, if we regard the lady as the representative of chastity, and the knight as that of justice? many discrepances of the same kind could be pointed out; and probably some readers may agree with us in thinking that those passages of the poem are sometimes not the least amusing in which Spenser forgets his allegory, and becomes a mere romancer like Ariosto. But, besides the allegory by which Spenser designs to present the pageant of the moral virtues, assigning a knight as the representative of each virtue, by whom the opposing appetites should be curbed and overthrown; he has embodied in his story a second and political allegory. Not only is Gloriana the imaginary concentration of the glory sought by every true knight – she is Queen Elizabeth too; not only does King Arthur present the spirit and essence of pure chivalry – he is likewise Spenser's (unworthy) patron, the Earl of Leicester; and many of the adventures which describe the struggles of virtue and vice also shadow forth anecdotes and intrigues of the English court, invisible to those, as Spenser himself insinuates,

That n'ote[1] without an hound fine footing trace.
(II Proem 4)

This complication of meanings may render *The Faerie Queene* doubly valuable to the antiquary who can explore its secret sense; but it must always be an objection to Spenser's plan, with the common reader, that the attempt at too much ingenuity has marred the simplicity of his allegory, and deprived it, in a great degree, of consistency and coherence.

In this essential point the poet is greatly inferior to the prose allegorist: indeed they write with very different notions of the importance of their subject. Spenser desired, no doubt, to aid the cause of virtue, but it was in the character of a cold and unimpassioned moralist, easily seduced from that part of his task by the desire to pay a compliment to some courtier, or some lady, or the mere wish to give a wider scope to his own fancy. Bunyan, on the contrary, in recommending his own religious opinions to the readers of his romance was impressed throughout with the sense of the sacred importance of the task for which he had lived through poverty and captivity, and was, we doubt not, prepared to die. To gain the favour of Charles and all his court he would not, we are confident, have guided Christian one foot off the narrow and strait path; and his excellence above Spenser's is, that his powerful thoughts were all directed to one solemn end, and his fertile imagination taxed for everything which could give life and vivacity to his narrative, vigour and consistency to the spirit of his allegory. His every thought is turned to strengthen and confirm the reasoning on which his argument depends; and nothing is more admirable than the acuteness of that fancy with which, still keeping an eye on his principal purpose, Bunyan contrives to extract, from the slightest particulars, the means of extending and fortifying its impression.

I cannot

John Ruskin

from *The Stones of Venice*, vol. 2, chapter 8 1853

The system of Spenser is unfinished, and exceedingly complicated, the same vices and virtues occurring under different forms in different places, in order to show their different relations to each other. The peculiar superiority of his system is in its exquisite setting forth of Chastity under the figure of Britomart; not monkish chastity, but that of the purest Love. In completeness of personification no one can approach him; not even in Dante do I remember anything quite so great as the description of the Captain of the Lusts of the Flesh:

> As pale and wan as ashes was his looke,
> His bodie leane and meagre as a rake,
> And skin all withered like a dryed rooke,
> Thereto as cold and drery as a Snake,
> That seem'd to tremble euermore, and quake:
> *All in a canuas thin he was bedight,*[1]
> *And girded with a belt of twisted brake,*[2]
> Vpon his head he wore an Helmet light,
> Made of a dead mans skull. . .
> (II xi 22)

He rides upon a tiger, and in his hand is a bow, bent;

> And many arrowes vnder his right side,
>
> .   .   .   .   .   .
>
> Headed with flint, and feathers bloudie dide.
> (II xi 21)

The horror and the truth of this are beyond everything that I know, out of the pages of Inspiration. Note the heading of the arrows with flint, because sharper and more subtle in the edge than steel, and because steel might consume away with rust, but flint not; and consider in the whole description how the wasting away of body and soul together, and the *coldness* of the heart, which unholy fire has consumed into ashes, and the loss of all power, and the kindling of all terrible impatience, and the implanting of thorny and inextricable griefs, are

1 equipped   2 fern, bracken

set forth by the various images, the belt of brake, the tiger steed, and the *light* helmet, girding the head with death.

John Ruskin

from *Modern Painters*, vol. 3, chapter 8   1856

A fine grotesque is the expression, in a moment, by a series of symbols thrown together in bold and fearless connexion, of truths which it would have taken a long time to express in any verbal way, and of which the connexion is left for the beholder to work out for himself; the gaps, left or overleaped by the haste of the imagination, forming the grotesque character.

For instance, Spenser desires to tell us, (1) that envy is the most untamable and unappeasable of the passions, not to be soothed by any kindness; (2) that with continual labour it invents evil thoughts out of its own heart; (3) that even in this, its power of doing harm is partly hindered by the decaying and corrupting nature of the evil it lives in; (4) that it looks every way, and that whatever it sees is altered and discoloured by its own nature; (5) which discolouring, however, is to it a veil, or disgraceful dress, in the sight of others; (6) and that it never is free from the most bitter suffering, (7) which cramps all its acts and movements, enfolding and crushing it while it torments. All this it has required a somewhat long and languid sentence for me to say in unsymbolical terms, – not, by the way, that they *are* unsymbolical altogether, for I have been forced, whether I would or not, to use *some* figurative words; but even with this help the sentence is long and tiresome, and does not with any vigour represent the truth. It would take some prolonged enforcement of each sentence to make it felt, in ordinary ways of talking. But Spenser puts it all into a grotesque, and it is done shortly and at once, so that we feel it fully, and see it, and never forget it. I have numbered above the statements which had to be made. I now number them with the same numbers, as they occur in the several pieces of the grotesque:

    And next to him malicious *Enuie* rode,
  (1) Vpon a rauenous wolfe, and (2, 3) still did chaw

Betweene his cankred teeth a venemous tode,
That all the poison ran about his chaw;[1]

. . . . . .

(4, 5) All in a kirtle[2] of discolourd say[3]
He clothed was, ypainted full of eyes;

(6) And in his bosome secretly there lay
An hatefull Snake, the which his taile vptyes

(7) In many folds, and mortall sting implyes.[4]

(1 iv 30–31)

There is the whole thing in nine lines; or, rather in one image, which will hardly occupy any room at all on the mind's shelves, but can be lifted out, whole, whenever we want it. All noble grotesques are concentrations of this kind, and the noblest convey truths which nothing else could convey; and not only so, but convey them, in minor cases with a delightfulness, – in the higher instances with an awfulness, – which no mere utterance of the symbolized truth would have possessed, but which belongs to the effort of the mind to unweave the riddle, or to the sense it has of there being an infinite power and meaning in the thing seen, beyond all that is apparent therein, giving the highest sublimity even to the most trivial object so presented and so contemplated.

'Jeremiah, what seest thou?'
'I see a seething pot; and the face thereof is toward the north.
Out of the north an evil shall break forth upon all the inhabitants of
    the land.'

(Jeremiah i, 13)

And thus in all ages and among all nations, grotesque idealism has been the element through which the most appalling and eventful truth has been wisely conveyed, from the most sublime words of true Revelation, to the 'ἀλλ' ὅτ ἂν ἡμίονος βασιλεύς',[5] etc., of the oracles, and the more or less doubtful teaching of dreams; and so down to ordinary poetry. No element of imagination has a wider range, a more magnificent use, or so colossal a grasp of sacred truth.

1 jaw   2 tunic   3 light woollen cloth   4 enfolds
5 whenever the ass is king (Herodotus, The Histories, 1 55)

James Russell Lowell

from 'Spenser' 1875 (published in *The Writings of James Russell Lowell*, 1892, vol. 4)

Yet, with a purity like that of thrice-bolted snow, he had none of its coldness. He is, of all our poets, the most truly sensuous, using the word as Milton probably meant it when he said that poetry should be 'simple, sensuous, and passionate'. A poet is innocently sensuous when his mind permeates and illumines his senses; when they, on the other hand, muddy the mind, he becomes sensual. Every one of Spenser's senses was as exquisitely alive to the impressions of material, as every organ of his soul was to those of spiritual beauty. Accordingly, if he painted the weeds of sensuality at all, he could not help making them 'of glorious feature'. It was this, it may be suspected, rather than his 'praising love', that made Lord Burleigh shake his 'rugged forehead'. Spenser's gamut, indeed, is a wide one, ranging from a purely corporeal delight in 'precious odors fetched from far away' upward to such refinement as

> Vpon her eyelids many Graces sate,
> Vnder the shadow of her euen browes,
>
> (II iii 25)

where the eye shares its pleasure with the mind. He is court-painter in ordinary to each of the senses in turn, and idealizes these frail favorites of his majesty King Lusty Juventus, till they half believe themselves the innocent shepherdesses into which he travesties them. . . .

The true type of the allegory is the *Odyssey*, which we read without suspicion as pure poem, and then find a new pleasure in divining its double meaning, as if we somehow got a better bargain of our author than he meant to give us. But this complex feeling must not be so exacting as to prevent our lapsing into the old Arabian Nights simplicity of interest again. The moral of a poem should be suggested, as when in some mediaeval church we cast down our eyes to muse over a fresco of Giotto, and are reminded of the transitoriness of life by the mortuary tablets under our feet. The vast superiority of Bunyan over Spenser lies in the fact that we help make his allegory out of our own experience. Instead of striving to embody abstract passions and temptations, he has given us his own in all their pathetic simplicity. He is the Ulysses of his own prose-epic. This is the secret of his power and his charm, that, while the representation of what *may* happen to all men comes home to none of us in particular, the story of any one man's real experience finds its startling parallel in that of every one of us. The very homeliness of Bunyan's names and the everydayness of his scenery, too, put us off our guard, and we soon find ourselves on as easy a footing with his allegorical beings as we might be with Adam or Socrates in a dream. Indeed, he has prepared us for such incongruities by telling us at setting out that the story was of a dream. The long nights of Bedford jail had so intensified his imagination, and made the figures with which it peopled his solitude so real to him, that the creatures of his mind become *things*, as clear to the memory as if we had seen them. But Spenser's are too often mere names, with no bodies to back them, entered on the Muses' muster-roll by the specious trick of personification. There is, likewise, in Bunyan, a childlike simplicity and taking-for-granted which win our confidence. His Giant Despair, for example, is by no means the Ossianic figure into which artists who mistake the vague for the sublime have misconceived it. He is the ogre of the fairy-tales, with his malicious wife; and he comes forth to us from those regions of early faith and wonder as something beforehand accepted by the imagination. These figures of Bunyan's are already familiar inmates of the mind, and, if there be any sublimity in him, it is the daring frankness of his verisimilitude. Spenser's giants are those of the later romances, except that grand figure with the balances in the second Canto of Book V, the most original of all his conceptions, yet no real giant, but a pure eidolon of the mind. . . .

Charles Lamb made the most pithy criticism of Spenser when he called him the poets' poet. We may fairly leave the allegory on one side, for perhaps, after all, he adopted it only for the reason that it was in fashion, and put it on as he did his ruff, not because it was becoming, but because it was the only wear. The true use of him is as a gallery of pictures which we visit as the mood takes us, and where we spend an hour or two at a time, long enough to sweeten our perceptions, not so long as to cloy them. He makes one think always of Venice; for not only is his style Venetian, but as the gallery there is housed in the shell of an abandoned convent, so his in that of a deserted allegory. And again, as at Venice you swim in a gondola from Gian Bellini to Titian, and from Titian to Tintoret, so in him, where other cheer is wanting, the gentle sway of his measure, like the rhythmical impulse of the oar, floats you lullingly along from picture to picture.

If all the pens that ever poet held
Had fed the feeling of their master's thoughts,
And every sweetness that inspired their hearts
Their minds and muses on admirèd themes,
If all the heavenly quintessence they still
From their immortal flowers of poesy,
If these had made one poem's period,
And all combined in beauty's worthiness;
Yet should there hover in their restless heads
One thought, one grace, one wonder at the best,
Which into words no virtue can digest.

(Marlowe, *1 Tamburlaine*, v ii)

Spenser at his best, has come as near to expressing this unattainable something as any other poet. He is so purely poet that with him the meaning does not so often modulate the music of the verse as the music makes great part of the meaning and leads the thought along its pleasant paths. No poet is so splendidly superfluous as he; none knows so well that in poetry enough is not only not so good as a feast, but is a beggarly parsimony. He spends himself in a careless abundance only to be justified by incomes of immortal youth. . . .

This delicious abundance and overrunning luxury of Spenser appear in the very structure of his verse. He found the *ottava rima* too monotonously iterative; so, by changing the order of his rhymes, he shifted the couplet from the end of the stave, where it always seems to put on the brakes with a jar, to the middle, where it may serve at will as a brace or a bridge; he found it not roomy enough, so first ran it over into another line, and then ran that added line over into an alexandrine, in which the melody of one stanza seems forever longing and feeling forward after that which is to follow. There is no ebb and flow in his metre more than on the shores of the Adriatic, but wave follows wave with equable gainings and recessions, the one sliding back in fluent music to be mingled with and carried forward by the next. In all this there is soothingness indeed, but no slumberous monotony; for Spenser was no mere metrist, but a great composer. By the variety of his pauses – now at the close of the first or second foot, now of the third, and again of the fourth – he gives spirit and energy to a measure whose tendency it certainly is to become languorous. He knew how to make it rapid and passionate at need, as in such verses as,

> But he my Lyon, and my noble Lord,
> How does he find in cruell hart to hate
> Her that him lou'd, and euer most adord,
As the God of my life? why hath he me abhord?
>> (I iii 7)

or this,

> Come hither, come hither, O come hastily!
>> (II viii 3)

. . . His natural tendency is to shun whatever is sharp and abrupt. He loves to prolong emotion, and lingers in his honeyed sensations like a bee in the translucent cup of a lily. So entirely are beauty and delight in it the native element of Spenser, that, whenever in *The Faerie Queene* you come suddenly on the moral, it gives you a shock of unpleasant surprise, a kind of grit, as when one's teeth close on a bit of gravel in a dish of strawberries and cream. He is the most fluent of our poets. Sensation passing through emotion into revery is a prime quality of his manner. And to read him puts one in the condition of revery, a state of mind in which our thoughts and feelings float motionless, as one sees fish do in a gentle stream, with just enough vibration of their fins to keep themselves from going down with the current, while their bodies yield indolently to all its soothing curves. He chooses his language for its rich canorousness rather than for intensity of meaning. To characterize his style in a single word, I should call it *costly*. None but the daintiest and nicest phrases will serve him, and he allures us from one to the other with such cunning baits of alliteration, and such sweet lapses of verse, that never any word seems more eminent than the rest, nor detains the feeling to eddy around it, but you must go on to the end before you have time to stop and muse over the wealth that has been lavished on you. But he has characterized and exemplified his own style better than any description could do:

For round about, the wals yclothed were
With goodly arras of great maiesty,
Wouen with gold and silke so close and nere,
That the rich metall lurked priuily,
As faining to be hid from enuious eye;
Yet here, and there, and euery where vnwares
It shewd it selfe, and shone vnwillingly;
Like a discolourd Snake, whose hidden snares
Through the greene gras his long bright burnisht backe
        declares.
                                            (III xi 28)

And of the lulling quality of his verse take this as a sample: [quotes
1 i 41, quoted above, p. 132].

In the world into which Spenser carries us there is neither time nor
space, or rather it is outside of and independent of them both, and so is
purely ideal, or, more truly, imaginary; yet it is full of form, color,
and all earthly luxury, and so far, if not real, yet apprehensible by the
senses. There are no men and women in it, yet it throngs with airy
and immortal shapes that have the likeness of men and women, and
hint at some kind of foregone reality. Now this place, somewhere
between mind and matter, between soul and sense, between the actual
and the possible, is precisely the region which Spenser assigns (if I have
rightly divined him) to the poetic susceptibility of impression, –

To raine in th' aire from earth to highest skie.
                                            (*Muiopotmos*, 212)

Underneath every one of the senses lies the soul and spirit of it, dor-
mant till they are magnetized by some powerful emotion. Then whatever is imperishable in us recognizes for an instant and claims kindred
with something outside and distinct from it, yet in some inconceivable
way a part of it, that flashes back on it an ideal beauty which impover-
ishes all other companionship. This exaltation with which love
sometimes subtilizes the nerves of coarsest men so that they feel and
see, not the thing as it seems to others, but the beauty of it, the joy of it,
the soul of eternal youth that is in it, would appear to have been the
normal condition of Spenser. While the senses of most men live in
the cellar, his 'were laid in a large upper chamber which opened
toward the sunrising'.

His berth was of the wombe of Morning dew,
And his conception of the ioyous Prime.
                    (III vi 3)

... In the *Epithalamion* there is an epithet which has been much
admired for its felicitous tenderness:

Behold whiles she before the altar stands
Hearing the holy priest that to her speakes
And blesseth her with his two *happy* hands.
                    (223–5)

But the purely impersonal passion of the artist had already guided
him to this lucky phrase. It is addressed by Holiness – a dame surely as
far abstracted from the enthusiasms of love as we can readily conceive
of – to Una, who, like the visionary Helen of Dr Faustus, has every
charm of womanhood except that of being alive, as Juliet and Beatrice
are.

        O happie earth,
    Whereon thy innocent feet doe euer tread!
                    (I x 9)

Can we conceive of Una, the fall of whose foot would be as soft as
that of a rose-leaf upon its mates already fallen, – can we conceive of
her treading anything so sordid? No; it is only on some unsubstantial
floor of dream that she walks securely, herself a dream. And it is only
when Spenser has escaped thither, only when this glamour of fancy
has rarefied his wife till she is grown almost as purely a creature of the
imagination as the other ideal images with which he converses, that
his feeling becomes as nearly passionate – as nearly human, I was on
the point of saying – as with him is possible. I am so far from blaming
this idealizing property of his mind, that I find it admirable in him. It
is his quality, not his defect. Without some touch of it life would be
unendurable prose. If I have called the world to which he transports
us a world of unreality, I have wronged him. It is only a world of
unrealism. It is from pots and pans and stocks and futile gossip and
inch-long politics that he emancipates us, and makes us free of that
tomorrow, always coming and never come, where ideas shall reign
supreme.
                    (317–33)

Edward Dowden

from 'Spenser, the Poet and Teacher', *Transcripts and Studies*   1888
(first published 1882)

In *The Shepheardes Calender* we discern much of the future writer of
The Faerie Queene. It contains the poetical record of his personal griefs
as a lover; it expresses his enthusiasm for his art as a poet; his loyalty
to the crown as a servant of the Queen; his loyalty to the Reformation
as an English churchman; his delight in natural beauty, and in the fair-
ness of woman. It is now gay and sportive, now staid and serious;
sensuous ardour and moral wisdom are united in it; the allegorical
form in miniature is already employed; it exhibits a mode of idealized
treatment of contemporary public affairs not dissimilar in essentials
from that afterwards put to use in his romantic epic. The pastoral,
with its ideals of peace and simplicity, possessed a singular charm for
Europe in the high-wrought and artificial age of the Renaissance. It
had a charm for Spenser; but his is not the Arcadian pastoral of
Sannazaro and Sidney. Colin and Cuddie keep their flocks upon the
hills of Kent; the disdainful Rosalinde, 'the widow's daughter of the
glen', is a North-country lass. Spenser's power of taking up real objects, persons and incidents, of plunging these in some solvent of the
imagination, and then of recreating them – the same and not the same
– is manifest throughout. Everything has been submitted to the shaping
power of the imagination; everything has been idealized; yet
Spenser does not remove from real life, does not forsake his own
country and his own time; he does not shrink from taking a side in
controversies then troubling the English Church; he is primarily a
poet, but while a poet, he also aspires to be what Milton named him –
a teacher. In these poems the little archer, Love, shoots his roguish
shafts; Pan is the patron of shepherds; Cynthia sits crowned upon the
grassy green. The poet freely appropriates what pleases his fancy in
classical or neo-classical mythology; yet at heart he is almost Puritan.
Not indeed Puritan in any turning away from innocent delights; not
Puritan in casting dishonour on our earthly life, its beauty, its splendour, its joy, its passion; but Puritan as Milton was when he wrote
Lycidas, in his weight of moral purpose, in his love of a grave plain-
ness in religion and of humble laboriousness in those who are shepherds
under Christ.

The tenth eclogue of the *Calender*, that for the month of October, is especially characteristic of its author. In it, as stated in the argument, is set out 'the perfect pattern of a poet'. In what way does Spenser conceive of poetry? We know how in periods which are not creative, periods which are not breathed upon by divine ideas, which are not driven by the urge of strong emotions, poetry comes to be looked on as primarily an art, or even as an accomplishment, and it is treated as if its function were to decorate life much as the artistic upholsterer decorates our houses. At such a time great regard is had to the workmanship of verse exclusive of the burden and inspiration of the song, and elegant little specimens of mosaic or of enamelling are turned out of the workshops of skilled artists; until the thing descends into a trade. In the creative periods there is not less devotion to form and workmanship; but the devotion is of a less self-conscious kind, because generative powers work in the poet with a rapturous blindness of love, and he thinks of himself less as a master of technique (though he is also this) than as a man possessed by some influence out of and beyond himself, some dominant energy of Nature or of God, to which it is his part to submit, which he cannot lay claim to as if it were an attainment of skill, and which he dare not call his own. At such times poetry aims at something more than to decorate life; it is spoken of as if it possessed some imperial authority, a power to bind and to loose, to sway man's total nature, to calm, to regulate and restrain, and also to free, to arouse, to dilate the spirit – power not to titillate a particular sense, but to discipline the will and mould a character. In such a tone of high assumption Spenser speaks of poetry.

(278–80)

'A poet at that time,' says the Dean of St Paul's, commenting on this passage, 'still had to justify his employment by presenting himself in the character of a professed teacher of morality.' But this is hardly in accordance with the facts. It was not as a professed teacher of morality that Chaucer had told his *Canterbury Tales*; it was not as a professed teacher of morality that Marlowe wrote his *Hero and Leander*, or Shakespeare his *Venus and Adonis*. 'Every great poet,' said Wordsworth, 'is a teacher: I wish either to be considered as a teacher, or as nothing.' May it not be that Spenser had higher thoughts than of justifying his employment? may not he, like Wordsworth, but unlike Chaucer and Marlowe, have really aimed at edification – such edification as is proper to a poet? 'You have given me praise,' Wordsworth wrote to John Wilson, 'for having reflected faithfully in my poems the feelings of human nature. I would fain hope that I have done so. But a great poet ought to do more than this: he ought, to a certain degree, to rectify men's feelings, to give them new compositions of feeling, to render their feelings more sane, pure, and permanent; in short, more consonant to nature and the great moving spirit of things.' To render men's feelings more sane, pure and permanent – this surely was included in the great design of *The Faerie Queene*; it was deliberately kept before him as an object by Spenser – 'our sage and serious Spenser, whom I dare to name a better teacher than Scotus or Aquinas'.

How, then, should we read *The Faerie Queene*? Is it poetry? or is it philosophy? Are we merely to gaze on with wide-eyed expectancy as at a marvellous pageant or procession, in which knights and ladies, Saracens and wizards, anticks and wild men, pass before our eyes? or are these visible shows only a rind or shell, which we must break or strip away in order to get at that hidden wisdom which feeds the spirit? Neither of these things are we to do. The mere visible shows of Spenser's poem are indeed goodly enough to beguile a summer's day in some old wood, and to hold us from morning to evening in a waking dream. The ethical teaching of Spenser extracted from his poetry is worthy a careful study. Raphael drew his fainting Virgin Mother as a skeleton in his preparatory study, and the student of Raphael may well consider the anatomy of the figure, because whatever an artist has put into his work, that a critic may try to take out of it. So the moral philosophy of Spenser even apart from his poetry may rightly form a subject of study. But the special virtue of *The Faerie Queene* will be found only by one who receives it neither as pageantry nor as philosophy, but in the way in which Spenser meant that it should be received – as a living creature of the imagination, a spirit incarnate, 'one altogether', 'of a reasonable soul and human flesh subsisting'.

(285–6)

These lapses and declensions we may pardon and forget. Upon the whole *The Faerie Queene*, if nothing else, is at least a labyrinth of beauty, a forest of old romance in which it is possible to lose oneself more irrecoverably amid the tangled luxury of loveliness than elsewhere in

English poetry. Spenser's delight in the beauty of external nature is often of a high-wrought and elaborated kind, and yet no poet has written a line of more faultless simplicity than that which tells how Calepine when recovered from his wound goes forth 'to take the air and hear the thrush's song'. But Spenser's rare sensibility to beauty would have found itself ill content if he had merely solitudes of nature, however fair, to contemplate. In his perfect joy in the presence of human beauty he is thoroughly a man of the Renaissance. The visions which he creates of man and woman cast a spell over their creator; they subdue and they exalt him; he cannot withdraw his gaze from the creatures of his imagination; he must satiate his senses with their loveliness; all his being is thrilled with a pure ecstasy as he continues to gaze. . . .

But more than any other form of beauty that of womanhood charms Spenser, renders his imagination (to use a favourite word of his own) 'empassioned', or calms and completely satisfies it. There is Una, with face sad under her wimpled veil, yet, however sad, luminous like an angel's, and making, when stole and fillet have been laid aside, 'a sunshine in the shady place'. There is Belphoebe, no lily but a rose of chastity, the ideal of virginal freedom, vigour, health, and hardihood, her face clear as the sky, with the glow in it of the quickened blood, her eyes two living lamps, her broad ivory forehead a table for love to engrave his triumphs on, her voice resonant like silver, her moving fleet and firm, a boar-spear in her hand, her brown hair the lovelier for flowers and leaves of the forest which she has borne away in her speed. There is Britomart, of sterner virginal force, yet made for the love of Artegall, tall and large of limb, a martial maid. Let us remember Britomart as she appears when, roused from quiet sleep by the treachery of Malecasta – now standing for a moment in snow-white smock, with locks unbound, her advanced sword in her hand, and now flying with the flame of wronged and insulted maidenhood in her heart at the dastard knights who would do her shame. And there is Amoret, the type of perfect womanhood, as Belphoebe is of maidenhood; Amoret, brought up by Psyche in the garden of Adonis,

> To be th' ensample of true loue alone,
> And Lodestarre of all chaste affectione;
>
> (III vi 52)

Amoret, the most tried and true of wives, whom I like best to remember as pictured in the first form of the legend, rescued from the snares and tortures of the enchanter Busirane, and now lost in the happy secrecy of one long embrace:

> Lightly he clipt her twixt his armes twaine,
> And streightly did embrace her body bright,
> Her body, late the prison of sad paine,
> Now the sweet lodge of loue and deare deli**ght**:
> But she faire Lady ouercommen quight
> Of huge affection, did in pleasure melt,
> And in sweete rauishment pourd out her spright:
> No word they spake, nor earthly thing they felt,
> But like two senceles stocks in long embracement dwelt.
>
> (III xii 45)

And there is Florimell, who seems like the spirit of some inland stream, but irresistibly drawn seaward by her bold lover, Marinell. And there is Serena, scarcely seen in her loveliness by the light of stars, unclothed upon the woodland altar and prepared for death. And there is Calidore's shepherdess maiden gathering strawberries in the greenwood – a sister of Shakespeare's Perdita. And there is Charissa, the fruitful mother, hung upon by her multitude of babes. And there is Dame Celia, the reverend lady of the 'House of Holiness', who bows over Una, and embraces her with the protectiveness of age and experience towards youth. And there is Spenser's own Elizabeth, whom Sir Calidore espies encircled by the Graces, and danced around by the hundred naked maidens, lily white.

Now, this sensibility to beauty – the beauty of earth and sky, the beauty of man and woman – does it bring with it any peculiar dangers, any temptations and seductions? Every noble sensibility, every high faculty of man, it may be answered, brings with it some peculiar danger. Spenser certainly was conscious of risks attending this sensibility to beauty. Puritanism was also aware of these risks; and Puritanism, when it had attained to full strength, said, 'Lest thy right eye offend thee straightway pluck it out.' Spenser said, 'See that it offend thee not.' Ascetic in the best sense of that word Spenser assuredly was: he desired to strengthen every part of our nature by heroic discipline, and to subordinate the lower parts to the higher, so that, if strong, they might be strong for service, not for mastery. But Spenser was almost as free as Wordsworth from asceticism in its evil sense, and for the same reason as Wordsworth. To Spenser and to Wordsworth it could not seem desirable to put out the right eye, because to both the eye was an inlet of divine things for the uses of the spirit. With respect to beauty, Spenser's teaching is that true beauty is always sacred, always ennobling to the spirit which is itself sane and pure, but the sensual mind will put even beauty to sensual uses. And he declares further that there is a forged or feigned beauty, which is no more than a fair illusion covering inward foulness and shame. The true beauty, according to Spenser, may be recognized by a certain illuminating quality; it is not mere pasture for the eye; rather it smites the gazer, long accustomed to the dimness of common things, as if with sudden and exquisite light; it is indeed a ray derived from God, the central Luminary of the universe.

But neither the Aristotelian doctrine of the mean, nor Platonic conceptions of love and beauty, serve best to protect and deliver us from the temptations of sense as set forth in Spenser's poetry. By his enthusiasm on behalf of the noblest moral qualities, by his strenuous joy in presence of the noblest human creatures – man and woman – Spenser breathes into us a breath of life, which has an antiseptic power, which kills the germs of disease, and is antagonistic to the relaxed fibre, the lethargy, the dissolution, or disintegrating life-in-death of sensuality. Any heroism of man or woman is like wine to gladden Spenser's heart; we see through the verse how it quickens the motion of his blood. A swift clear flame of sympathy, like an answering beacon lit upon the high places of his soul, leaps up in response to the beacon-fire of chivalric virtue in another soul, even though it be an imagined one, summoning his own. The enchantress Acrasia in her rosy bower is so bewitchingly fair and soft that it goes hard with us to see her garden defaced and herself rudely taken captive. Or it would go hard with us did we not know the faithfulness and soft invincibility of Amoret, the virgin joy and vigour of Belphoebe, the steadfastness and animating trust in Una's eyes, – or had we not beheld the face of Britomart shining beneath her umbriere[1] like daydawn to a belated wanderer, and then all that is vain and false and sensual becomes to us

1 a defence for the face, attached to the helmet

what those ignoble knights of Malecasta were to the warrior virgin, –
no more than shadows:

> All were faire knights, and goodly well beseene,
> But to faire *Britomart* they all but shadowes beene.
>
> (III i 45)

We have no need to inspect the rout of monsters degraded from manhood by Acrasia's witchcraft. Britomart has clean delivered us from
Acrasia.

(288–93)

Spenser's conception of life was Puritan in its seriousness; yet we
think with wonder of the wide space that lies between *The Faerie
Queene* and our other great allegory, *The Pilgrim's Progress*. To escape
from the City of Destruction and to reach the Celestial City is
Christian's one concern; all his recompense for the countless trials of
the way lies upon the other side of the river of death. His consuming
thought is this: 'What must I do to be saved?' Spenser is spiritual, but
he is also mundane; he thinks of the uses of noble human creatures to
this world in which we move. His general end in the poem is 'to fashion
a gentleman or noble person in virtuous and gentle discipline'. 'A
grand self-culture,' I have elsewhere said, 'is that about which Spenser
is concerned; not, as with Bunyan, the escape of the soul to heaven;
not the attainment of supernatural grace through a point of mystical
contact, like the vision which was granted to the virgin knight,
Galahad, in the medieval allegory. Self-culture, the formation of a
complete character for the uses of earth, and afterwards, if need be, for
the uses of heaven, – this was subject sufficient for the twenty-four
books designed to form the epic of the age of Elizabeth. And the
means of that self-culture are of an active kind – namely, warfare, –
warfare, not for its own sake, but for the generous accomplishment of
unselfish ends.' Bunyan, with whom the visionary power was often
involuntary, who would live for a day and a night in some metaphor
that had attacked his imagination, transcribed into allegory his own
wonderful experience of terrors and of comfort. Spenser is more
impersonal: he can refashion Aristotle in a dream. But behind him
lies all the sentiment of Christian chivalry, and around him all the
life of Elizabethan England; and from these diverse elements arises a

rich and manifold creation, which, if it lacks the personal, spiritual passion of Bunyan's allegory, compensates by its moral breadth, its noble sanity, its conciliation of what is earthly and what is divine . . .

'A better teacher than Scotus or Aquinas.' Yet we are told by the Dean of St Paul's, that in giving himself credit for a direct purpose to instruct, Spenser 'only conformed to the curiously utilitarian spirit which pervaded the literature of the time'. It is the heresy of modern art that only useless things should be made beautiful. We want beauty only in playthings. In elder days the armour of a knight was as beautiful as sunlight, or as flowers. 'In unaffected, unconscious, artistic excellence of invention,' says one of our chief living painters [G. F. Watts], 'approaching more nearly to the strange beauty of nature, especially in vegetation, medieval armour perhaps surpasses any other effort of human ingenuity.' What if Spenser wrought armour for the soul, and, because it was precious and of finest temper, made it fair to look upon? That which gleams as bright as the waters of a sunlit lake is perhaps a breastplate to protect the heart; that which appears pliant as the blades of summer grass may prove at our need to be a sword of steel.

(301–4)

Walter Raleigh

From *Milton* 1901

[Milton's] poetry is like the eloquence of the Lord Chancellor Bacon, as described by Ben Jonson: 'No man ever spake more neatly, more pressly, more weightily, or suffered less emptiness, less idleness in what he uttered. No member of his speech but consisted of his own graces. His hearers could not cough, or look aside from him, without loss.' It is this quality of Milton's verse that makes the exercise of reading it aloud a delight and a trial. Every word is of value. There is no mortar between the stones, each is held in place by the weight of the others, and helps to uphold the building. In reading, every word must be rendered clearly and articulately; to drop one out, or to slur it over, is to take a stone from an arch. Indeed, if Lamb and Hazlitt are right in thinking that Shakespeare's greatest plays cannot be acted, by the

same token Milton's greatest poems cannot be read aloud. For his most
sonorous passages the human voice is felt to be too thin an instrument;
the lightest word in the line demands some faint emphasis, so that the
strongest could not be raised to its true value unless it were roared
through some melodious megaphone.

The carefully jewelled mosaic style was practised very early by
Milton. It occurs already in the hymn on the Nativity:

See how from far upon the eastern road
The star-led wizards haste with odours sweet:
O run, prevent them with thy humble ode
And lay it lowly at his blessed feet.

(22–5)

The same deliberateness and gentle pause of words one after another
rounding and falling like clear drops is found in the song of the Spirit
in *Comus*:

Sabrina fair,
    Listen where thou art sitting
Under the glassy, cool, translucent wave,
    In twisted braids of lilies knitting
The loose train of thy amber-dropping hair.

(859–63)

This is the effect which Sir Henry Wotton, Milton's earliest critic,
speaks of, in a letter to Milton, as 'a certain Doric delicacy in your
songs and odes, whereunto I must plainly confess to have seen yet
nothing parallel in our language.'

There are poems, and good poems among the number, written on a
more diffuse principle. If you miss one line you find the idea repeated
or persisting in the next. It is quite possible to derive pleasure from
The Faerie Queene by attending to the leading words, and, for the rest,
floating onward on the melody. You can catch the drift with ease.
The stream circles in so many eddies that to follow it laboriously
throughout its course is felt to be hardly necessary: miss it once and
you can often join it again at very near the same point. 'But a reader
of Milton,' as an early critic of Milton remarks, 'must be always upon
duty; he is surrounded with sense; it rises in every line, every word is

to the purpose. There are no lazy intervals: all has been considered, and demands and merits observation. Even in the best writers you sometimes find words and sentences which hang on so loosely, you may blow them off. Milton's are all substance and weight: fewer would not have served his turn, and more would have been superfluous. His silence has the same effect, not only that he leaves work for the imagination, when he has entertained it and furnished it with noble materials; but he expresses himself so concisely, employs words so sparingly, that whoever will possess his ideas must dig for them, and oftentimes pretty far below the surface.'

An illustration and contrast may serve to point the moral. Here is an example of Spenser's diffuser style, taken from the second book of *The Faerie Queene*. Guyon, escaped from the cave of Mammon, is guarded, during his swoon, by an angel:

Beside his head there sate a faire young man,

(This announces the theme, as in music.)

Of wondrous beautie, and of freshest yeares,

(The fair young man was fair and young.)

Whose tender bud to blossome new began,

(The fair young man was young.)

And flourish faire aboue his equall peares.

(The fair young man was fair, fairer even than his equals, who were also his peers.)

In the remaining lines of the stanza the comparison of his hair to the rays of the sun is played with in the same way:

His snowy front curled with golden heares,
Like *Phœbus* face adornd with sunny rayes,
Diuinely shone, and two sharpe winged sheares,
Decked with diuerse plumes, like painted Iayes,
Were fixed at his backe, to cut his ayerie wayes.

(II viii 5)

The whole stanza is beautiful, and musical with the music of redundance. Nothing could be less like Milton's mature style. His verse, 'with frock of mail, Adamantean proof', advances proudly and irresistibly, gaining ground at every step. He brings a situation before us in two lines, every word contributing its share:

Betwixt these rocky pillars Gabriel sat,
Chief of the angelic guards, awaiting night.

(Paradise Lost, IV 549–50)

With as decisive a touch he sketches the story of Jacob –

... in the field of Luz,
Dreaming by night under the open sky,
And waking cried, *This is the gate of Heaven.*

(Paradise Lost, III 513–15)

Or the descent of Raphael:

Like Maia's son he stood,
And shook his plumes, that heavenly fragrance filled
The circuit wide.

(Paradise Lost, V 285–7)

(198–202)

W. B. Yeats

from 'Edmund Spenser', Introduction to his edition of *Poems of Spenser* 1902 (collected in *The Cutting of an Agate*)

When Spenser was buried in Westminster Abbey many poets read verses in his praise, and then threw their verses and the pens that had written them into his tomb. Like him they belonged, for all the moral zeal that was gathering like a London fog, to that indolent, demonstrative Merry England that was about to pass away. Men still wept when they were moved, still dressed themselves in joyous colours, and spoke with many gestures. Thoughts and qualities sometimes come to their perfect expression when they are about to pass away, and Merry England was dying in plays, and in poems, and in strange adventurous men. ... He had lived in the last days of what we may call the Anglo-French nation, the old feudal nation that had been established when the Norman and the Angevin made French the language of court and market. In the time of Chaucer English poets still wrote much in French, and even English labourers lilted French songs over their work; and I cannot read any Elizabethan poem or romance without feeling the pressure of habits of emotion, and of an order of life, which were conscious, for all their Latin gaiety, of a quarrel to the death with that new Anglo-Saxon nation that was arising amid Puritan sermons and Marprelate pamphlets. This nation had driven out the language of its conquerors, and now it was to over-throw their beautiful haughty imagination and their manners, full of abandon and wilfulness, and to set in their stead earnestness and logic and the timidity and reserve of a counting-house. . . .

He was, I think, by nature altogether a man of that old Catholic feudal nation, but, like Sidney, he wanted to justify himself to his new masters. He wrote of knights and ladies, wild creatures imagined by the aristocratic poets of the twelfth century, and perhaps chiefly by English poets who had still the French tongue; but he fastened them with allegorical nails to a big barn-door of common sense, of merely practical virtue. Allegory itself had risen into general importance with the rise of the merchant class in the thirteenth and fourteenth cen-turies; and it was natural when that class was about for the first time to shape an age in its image, that the last epic poet of the old order should mix its art with his own long-descended, irresponsible, happy art. . . .

One cannot think that he should have occupied himself with moral and religious questions at all. He should have been content to be, as Emerson thought Shakespeare was, a Master of the Revels to mankind. I am certain that he never gets that visionary air which can alone make allegory real, except when he writes out of a feeling for glory and passion. He had no deep moral or religious life. He has never a line like Dante's 'His Will is our Peace', or like Thomas à Kempis's 'The Holy Spirit has liberated me from a multitude of opinions', or even like Hamlet's objection to the bare bodkin. He had been made a poet by what he had almost learnt to call his sins. If he had not felt it necessary to justify his art to some serious friend, or perhaps even to 'that rugged forehead', he would have written all his life long, one thinks, of the loves of shepherdesses and shepherds, among whom there would have been perhaps the morals of the dovecot. One is persuaded that his morality is official and impersonal – a system of life which it was his duty to support – and it is perhaps a half understanding of this that has made so many generations believe that he was the first Poet Laureate, the first salaried moralist among the poets. His processions of deadly sins, and his houses, where the very cornices are arbitrary images of virtue, are an unconscious hypocrisy, an undelighted obedience to the 'rugged forehead', for all the while he is thinking of nothing but lovers whose bodies are quivering with the memory or the hope of long embraces. When they are not together, he will indeed embroider emblems and images much as those great ladies of the courts of love embroidered them in their castles; and when these are imagined out of a thirst for magnificence and not thought out in a mood of edification, they are beautiful enough; but they are always tapestries for corridors that lead to lovers' meetings or for the walls of marriage chambers. He was not passionate, for the passionate feed their flame in wanderings and absences, when the whole being of the beloved, every little charm of body and of soul, is always present to the mind, filling it with heroical subtleties of desire. He is a poet of the delighted senses, and his song becomes most beautiful when he writes of those islands of Phaedria and Acrasia, which angered 'that rugged forehead', as it seems, but gave to Keats his *Belle Dame sans merci* and his 'perilous seas in faery lands forlorn', and to William Morris his 'Water of the Wondrous Isles'.

The dramatists lived in a disorderly world, reproached by many, persecuted even, but following their imagination wherever it led them. Their imagination, driven hither and thither by beauty and sympathy, put on something of the nature of eternity. Their subject was always the soul, the whimsical, self-awakening, self-exciting, self-appeasing soul. They celebrated its heroical, passionate will going by its own path to immortal and invisible things. Spenser, on the other hand, except among those smooth pastoral scenes and lovely effeminate islands that have made him a great poet, tried to be of his time, or rather of the time that was all but at hand. Like Sidney, whose charm, it may be, led many into slavery, he persuaded himself that we enjoy Virgil because of the virtues of Aeneas, and so planned out his immense poem that it would set before the imagination of citizens, in whom there would soon be no great energy, innumerable blameless

Aeneases. He had learned to put the State, which desires all the abundance for itself, in the place of the Church, and he found it possible to be moved by expedient emotions, merely because they were expedient, and to think serviceable thoughts with no self-contempt. . . . Spenser had learned to look to the State not only as the rewarder of virtue but as the maker of right and wrong, and had begun to love and hate as it bid him. The thoughts that we find for ourselves are timid and a little secret, but those modern thoughts that we share with large numbers are confident and very insolent. We have little else today, and when we read our newspaper and take up its cry, above all, its cry of hatred, we will not think very carefully, for we hear the marching feet. When Spenser wrote of Ireland he wrote as an official, and out of thoughts and emotions that had been organized by the State. He was the first of many Englishmen to see nothing but what he was desired to see. Could he have gone there as a poet merely, he might have found among its poets more wonderful imaginations than even those islands of Phaedria and Acrasia. He would have found among wandering story-tellers, not indeed his own power of rich, sustained description, for that belongs to lettered ease, but certainly all the kingdom of Faery, still unfaded, of which his own poetry was often but a troubled image. He would have found men doing by swift strokes of the imagination much that he was doing with painful intellect, with that imaginative reason that soon was to drive out imagination altogether and for a long time. He would have met with, at his own door, storytellers among whom the perfection of Greek art was indeed as unknown as his own power of sustained description, but who, none the less, imagined or remembered beautiful incidents and strange, pathetic outcrying that made them of Homer's lineage. . . .

There are moments when one can read neither Milton nor Spenser, moments when one recollects nothing but that their flesh had partly been changed to stone, but there are other moments when one recollects nothing but those habits of emotion that made the lesser poet especially a man of an older, more imaginative time. One remembers that he delighted in smooth pastoral places, because men could be busy there or gather together there, after their work, that he could love handiwork and the hum of voices. One remembers that he could still rejoice in the trees, not because they were images of loneliness and meditation, but because of their serviceableness. He could praise 'the builder oake', 'the aspine, good for staves', 'the cypresse funerall', 'the eugh, obedient to the bender's will', 'the birch for shaftes', 'the sallow for the mill', 'the mirrhe sweete bleeding in the bitter wound', 'the fruitful olive', and 'the carver holme'. He was of a time before undelighted labour had made the business of men a desecration. He carries one's memory back to Virgil's and Chaucer's praise of trees, and to the sweet-sounding song made by the old Irish poet in their praise.

I got up from reading *The Faerie Queene* the other day and wandered into another room. It was in a friend's house, and I came of a sudden to the ancient poetry and to our poetry side by side – an engraving of Claude's *Mill* hung under an engraving of Turner's *Temple of Jupiter*. Those dancing countrypeople, those cowherds, resting after the day's work, and that quiet mill-race made one think of Merry England with its glad Latin heart, of a time when men in every land found poetry and imagination in one another's company and in the day's labour. Those stately goddesses, moving in slow procession towards that marble architrave among mysterious trees, belong to Shelley's thought, and to the religion of the wilderness – the only religion possible to poetry today. Certainly Colin Clout, the companionable shepherd, and Calidore, the courtly man-at-arms, are gone, and Alastor is wandering from lonely river to river finding happiness in nothing but in that Star where Spenser too had imagined the fountain of perfect things. This new beauty, in losing so much, has indeed found a new loftiness, a something of religious exaltation that the old had not. It may be that those goddesses, moving with a majesty like a procession of the stars, mean something to the soul of man that those kindly women of the old poets did not mean, for all the fullness of their breasts and the joyous gravity of their eyes. Has not the wilderness been at all times a place of prophecy?

Our poetry, though it has been a deliberate bringing back of the Latin joy and the Latin love of beauty, has had to put off the old marching rhythms, that once could give delight to more than expedient hearts, in separating itself from a life where servile hands have become powerful. It has ceased to have any burden for marching shoulders, since it learned ecstasy from Smart in his mad cell, and from Blake, who made joyous little songs out of almost unintelligible visions, and from Keats, who sang of a beauty so wholly preoccupied with itself that its contemplation is a kind of lingering trance. The poet, if he would not carry burdens that are not his and obey the orders of servile lips, must sit apart in contemplative indolence playing with fragile things.

If one chooses at hazard a Spenserian stanza out of Shelley and compares it with any stanza by Spenser, one sees the change, though it would be still more clear if one had chosen a lyrical passage. I will take a stanza out of *Laon and Cythna*, for that is story-telling and runs nearer to Spenser than the meditative *Adonais*:

The meteor to its far morass returned:
The beating of our veins one interval
Made still; and then I felt the blood that burned
Within her frame, mingle with mine, and fall
Around my heart like fire; and over all
A mist was spread, the sickness of a deep
And speechless swoon of joy, as might befall
Two disunited spirits when they leap
In union from this earth's obscure and fading sleep.

The rhythm is varied and troubled, and the lines, which are in Spenser like bars of gold thrown ringing one upon another, are broken capriciously. Nor is the meaning the less an inspiration of indolent Muses, for it wanders hither and thither at the beckoning of fancy. It is now busy with a meteor and now with throbbing blood that is fire, and with a mist that is a swoon and a sleep that is life. It is bound together by the vaguest suggestion, while Spenser's verse is always rushing on to some preordained thought. A 'popular poet' can still indeed write poetry of the will, just as factory girls wear the fashion of hat or dress the moneyed classes wore a year ago, but 'popular poetry' does not belong to the living imagination of the world. Old writers gave men four temperaments, and they gave the sanguineous temperament to men of active life, and it is precisely the sanguineous temperament that is fading out of poetry and most obviously out of what is most subtle and living in poetry – its pulse and breath, its rhythm. Because poetry belongs to that element in every race which is most strong, and therefore most individual, the poet is not stirred to imaginative activity by a life which is surrendering its freedom to ever new elaboration, organization, mechanism. He has no longer a poetical will, and must be content to write out of those parts of himself which are too delicate and fiery for any deadening exercise. Every generation has more and more loosened the rhythm, more and more broken up and disorganized, for the sake of subtlety of detail, those great rhythms which move, as it were, in masses of sound. Poetry has become more spiritual, for the soul is of all things the most delicately organized, but it has lost in weight and measure and in its power of telling long stories and of dealing with great and complicated events. *Laon and Cythna*, though I think it rises sometimes into loftier air than *The Faerie Queene* and *Endymion*, though its shepherds and wandering divinities have a stranger and more intense beauty than Spenser's, has need of too watchful and minute attention for such lengthy poems. In William Morris, indeed, one finds a music smooth and unexacting like that of the old story-tellers, but not their energetic pleasure, their rhythmical wills. One too often misses in his *Earthly Paradise* the minute ecstasy of modern song without finding that old happy-go-lucky tune that had kept the story marching.

Spenser's contemporaries, writing lyrics or plays full of lyrical moments, write a verse more delicately organized than his and crowd more meaning into a phrase than he, but they could not have kept one's attention through so long a poem. A friend who has a fine ear told me the other day that she had read all Spenser with delight and yet could remember only four lines. When she repeated them they were from the poem by Matthew Roydon, which is bound up with Spenser because it is a commendation of Sir Philip Sidney:

A sweet, attractive kind of grace,
A full assurance given by looks,
Continual comfort in a face,
The lineaments of Gospel books.

Yet if one were to put even these lines beside a fine modern song one would notice that they had a stronger and rougher energy, a featherweight more, if eye and ear were fine enough to notice it, of the active will, of the happiness that comes out of life itself.

(xxii–xliv)

Part Three **Modern Views**

Introduction

In a mocking list of the opinions of 'the commonplace critic',
Hazlitt includes: 'He cannot get through Spenser's *Faerie Queene*,
and pronounces all allegorical poetry tedious.' One hundred
years later this was the opinion of our most distinguished critic:
'Who, except scholars, and except the eccentric few who are
born with a sympathy for such work, or others who have
deliberately studied themselves into the right appreciation, can now
read through the whole of *The Faerie Queene* with delight?'
This remark is striking not simply because Eliot thought he could
dismiss *The Faerie Queene* so easily, but also because it accurately
indicates the state of Spenser's reputation in 1930. At about
that time, F. R. Leavis was beginning to present, in the pages of
Scrutiny, the series of 'revaluations' of English poets that appeared
in 1936 in the book of that name. It is a sign of the moribund
condition of Spenser's reputation that Leavis did not subject
The Faerie Queene to the kind of searching examination he gave
Milton's verse. 'Spenser,' he says in his introduction, 'in his own
way a fact of the first importance in the tradition of English
poetry, is too simple a fact to need examining afresh.' Leavis's
essay on Milton initiated the modern 'Milton controversy'. But
neither he nor (it seemed) anyone else was interested in a Spenser
controversy.

The reader will think of C. S. Lewis, whose rehabilitation of
Spenser began in the great final chapter of *The Allegory of Love*,
published in the same year as *Revaluation*. But although (or
perhaps because?) he was a great proselytizer, Lewis was not much
interested in controversy. The man who thought of Spenser as
having 'the brave appeal of a cause nearly lost' would say more
openly, in a more polemical work:

It is not that [Dr Leavis] and I see different things when we look
at *Paradise Lost*. He sees and hates the very same that I see and
love. Hence the disagreement between us tends to escape from
the realm of literary criticism. We differ not about the nature

of Milton's poetry, but about the nature of man, or even the nature of joy itself.

Such an attitude does not lessen the fundamental truth and importance of what Lewis says about Spenser, but it did make him less persuasive an apologist for *The Faerie Queene*. Because he seemed complacent about his own beliefs and unwilling to take other views seriously, he could not seriously challenge the reader who did not agree with him. So that despite the considerable impact of *The Allegory of Love*, it did not initiate much public discussion of Spenser. And those who felt the power of Lewis' case for Spenser and the passion of his writing were perhaps too much persuaded that admiration for *The Faerie Queene* entailed a whole set of social, educational, and moral values.

The selections on the following pages well indicate the history of the understanding and enjoyment of Spenser in this century. (They were not chosen for this purpose, but solely for their interest and helpfulness; but when they are arranged chronologically, there is a revealing pattern.) The selections written before the Second World War are all, except Lewis's, tangential to the critics' main interests. William Empson's brilliant paragraphs are explicitly an aside in the first chapter of *Seven Types of Ambiguity*; G. Wilson Knight, a great critic of Shakespeare and the romantics, confesses that he does not feel at home in *The Faerie Queene*; Derek Traversi is hostile to the poem and writes challengingly about it only because, in the best *Scrutiny* tradition, he is committed to responsible argument. Now consider the essays by Northrop Frye, Frank Kermode and Rosemond Tuve. All were written in the 1960s, and Spenser is a central figure in each author's work. Frye is known primarily as a theorist, but *The Faerie Queene* is for him a compendium of poetry, not simply another poem: his most important work, *Anatomy of Criticism*, began (he tells us in his

preface) as a book on *The Faerie Queene*. Kermode has quite
consciously accepted the challenge of Leavis' revaluations and is
the leading English champion of Spenser and Milton. Miss Tuve,
whose profound and sympathetic love of *The Faerie Queene* was
matched only by Lewis', fought the same battle in America
against the New Critics. Finally the essays by Harry Berger Jr,
Martha Craig, Roger Sale, and the editor of this volume
are the work of younger academics for whom Spenser is a normal
subject of critical and scholarly investigation. We have at last
reached the point where writing about *The Faerie Queene* is not
taking up a special cause, but writing as one would about any
work one loves and finds interesting, and about which one feels
there is still something to be discovered or explained.

Settled and purposeful study of Spenser did not begin until
after the Second World War, when literary criticism became
almost entirely academic. There is an obvious significance to this
fact – that criticism of *The Faerie Queene* had to await historical
understanding. This is true in a rough sense, but the issues are not
nearly so simple as they might appear to new readers of the
poem. In the first place, academic critics are the beneficiaries of
lessons learned from criticism of the twenties and thirties – work
that was often anti-academic in spirit and that was
characteristically written by men who did not teach in
universities or, if they did, were conspicuous outsiders. Second,
the historic conflict between criticism and scholarship resulted,
happily, not in victory for one side over the other, but in the
recognition that each informs and assists the other. The career
of Rosemond Tuve, the greatest academic student of
Renaissance literature of her generation, is very instructive in
this respect. Miss Tuve's first and most famous work,
Elizabethan and Metaphysical Imagery, was acclaimed as a major
triumph of scholarship over the ignorance and arrogance of
modern critics. Miss Tuve herself did not conceive it in so

ungenerous a way, but the book gave an impression of that sort;
it also gave the impression (despite some specific disavowals)
that all sixteenth- and seventeenth-century poets were 'the same'
and that one could understand them only after reading stacks of
unpalatable and unilluminating treatises of rhetoric and logic. But
in her last two books, *Images and Themes in Five Poems by
Milton* and *Allegorical Imagery*, Miss Tuve's critical intelligence, her
knowledge, and her powers of historical imagination are
inseparable. She is continually asking, 'How should we read
these poems?' and one cannot find a dividing line between critical
analysis and historical awareness as she sets about restoring
imaginative modes that have become alien to us by the passage of
time. Miss Tuve's writings show how – and, of course, are a
means by which – the study of English has advanced to the point
where a young critic like Martha Craig feels no anxieties about
whether she is doing 'criticism' or 'scholarship' when she
addresses the classic problem of Spenser's archaisms.

The central problem for modern students of Spenser has been,
'How does one read *The Faerie Queene*?' One answer to this
question is 'easily', and it is not a silly or trivial answer. The
student who apologetically says that he likes reading the poem
for the story has (as Lewis would have told him) been doing just
the right thing. Perhaps he has not found, or is not able to
produce from the poem, very much by way of a true dramatic
narration; but what he means is that he has, in Addison's phrase,
'Where'er the poet's fancy led, pursued'. The real problem of
'how to read' the poem lies in understanding and assessing the
experience of reading it. We get a very good view of our
difficulties in G. Wilson Knight's essay. Knight obviously
enjoys and admires the poem, and his description of what it is
like to read substantially agrees with the testimony of readers in
all ages. Yet when he reflects on his experience with the poem,
he finds it difficult to possess and come to terms with. It is at this

stage that a sense of history can come to our aid. One occasionally finds an essay like Frank Kermode's, in which historical evidence and argument are persuasively brought to bear upon a critical problem, without much appeal to critical analysis and argumentation. But the kind of interaction between knowledge and criticism that we find in Lewis and Miss Tuve is probably a truer model of the way in which a reader learns to deal with *The Faerie Queene*.

We should also recognize that the issue is *essentially* one of imaginative sympathy with *The Faerie Queene* – however achieved – and not of combining critical perception with a sense of history. Consider the very first episode in the poem, in which the Red Cross Knight and Una are driven by a storm into a wood (1 i 6–10). Spenser does not pretend to describe a real wood, but instead devotes two stanzas to an obviously literary and conventional catalogue of trees, at the end of which the knight and lady find themselves lost in the wood – later revealed to be the Wandering Wood, home of the dragon Error. Now no reader should have difficulty seeing, or being taught to see, the two main aesthetic facts about this passage: that the wood is an allegorical image of human life (the trees are described according to the variety of human uses they serve), and that the passage makes us, by the very act of reading, enter the wood with the knight and lady and thus share their plight (compare Warton's praise of the passage, above p. 108). Our essential difficulties with *The Faerie Queene* lie in relating such separate facts to a secure sense of and confidence in the ways of the poem. We may see 'what is there', but we may still have difficulty believing that a poet can be so easily and unselfconsciously concerned with general truths; that he should feel liberated not constrained by a literary convention that (to him) sums up much human wisdom; that he so directly thinks of men as Man and so little respects separate individuals that knight, lady, and reader

participate in a single entrance into a wood that, indeed, we have
all entered simply by being human. Seeking confidence in writing
like this, we feel how inadequate it is to speak in the negative
terms of a 'willing suspension of disbelief'. What is needed is
belief itself in the poem – which means not that we must allow
it to tell us what to think, but that we must be able to enter,
participate in it, trust its ways as we are reading. Clearly there is
no one way of achieving such imaginative sympathy with
The Faerie Queene. Miss Tuve's way was that of traditional
scholarship; at the other extreme, Roger Sale has come to terms
with the poem by purely critical means. In this matter, as in
many other things Spenserian, the all-embracing figure is Lewis.
Who can say what was the source of *his* imaginative sympathy
with Spenser – temperament, knowledge, critical intelligence,
self-reflection, hostility to modernism?

In making the selections for this volume, there was no
question about giving Lewis pride of place. He is the first critic
to whom any reader of *The Faerie Queene* should turn – especially
readers of this anthology, since his imagination is so rooted in
the nineteenth century, against whose version of Spenser he was
reacting. The other selections involved more complicated decisions,
not simply because of my own biases and limitations, but also
because more than one need was to be served. For example, in
Rosemond Tuve's, Roger Sale's, and my own books there are
sections with a greater amount of summary and generalization
than is to be found in the selections included here. But I hope the
passages I have chosen will directly help the reader as reader –
that is, help him to follow and trust the verse of *The Faerie
Queene* and to keep his bearings in the poem. There are additional
reasons for choosing the passages from Miss Tuve's book: they
deal with a traditional problem of Spenser criticism, and in
explaining the structure of books of *The Faerie Queene* by
reference to both intellectual history and the aesthetics of

medieval romance, Miss Tuve well shows how scholarly
knowledge can serve the broadest literary purposes. I have already
mentioned the interrelation of criticism and scholarship in
Kermode's and Craig's essays; Miss Craig's subject has the additional
advantage of combining the modern reader's most immediate
difficulty with *The Faerie Queene* and what is historically the
oldest critical problem about it.

Rather different considerations underlie some other selections.
It is the intent, in this series of Penguin anthologies, to represent
a variety of viewpoints. Even without such a policy, the essays by
Traversi and Knight have a strong claim on our attention.
Traversi's, by invoking notions of concrete reality to criticize
The Faerie Queene, states a difficulty that any modern reader
must feel – and that I hope the other essays will help overcome.
Knight's essay seems to me the best dissenting opinion on *The
Faerie Queene*: it has a keen sense of the imaginative qualities
of the poem and is frank and sympathetic in its dealings with it,
but it does not take the poem at its own (or modern
Spenserians') valuation. Harry Berger Jr's essay is a cogent
presentation of a view that has been attractive to recent critics –
that the true subject of *The Faerie Queene* is the poetic process
itself – but that seems to me inherently to involve minimizing or
ignoring Spenser's concern with and poetic revelation of his
ostensible subject, man's moral and psychological nature.
Finally the essay by Northrop Frye is an especially engaging and
stimulating statement of a way of dealing with *The Faerie Queene*
with which I myself feel little sympathy. Too much of what
Kermode calls the presence of the poem – both its historical reality
and its existence as a reading experience for each of us – seems to
me to be lost in the attempt to 'figure out' and structure the
poem on the basis of an absolute, theoretical poetics. Whatever
the justice of this objection, the fact is that Frye's views have
been very influential and that his assumptions about what a critic

of *The Faerie Queene* should do are widely held.

Two other aspects of modern Spenser studies should be mentioned here, both having to do with the relation of historical knowledge to interpretation of *The Faerie Queene*. Within the academic world, the dominant tradition has been that of American scholarship: one of its monuments, as they say, is the Johns Hopkins Variorum edition of Spenser's works. Miss Tuve's book and Hallett Smith's essay on *The Shepheardes Calender* represent this tradition, but my selection as a whole probably does not suggest how much the reader will feel its presence in other books and essays he may consult. The hallmark of this mode of scholarship is the marshalling of large quantities of historical material by way of creating a context into which individual poems fit. Probably the finest product of the method, as applied to Spenser, is A. S. P. Woodhouse's article, 'Nature and Grace in *The Faerie Queene*'. As for the sense of Spenser conveyed by the American scholarly tradition, the reader can encounter it in a sympathetic and civilized form in William Nelson's *The Poetry of Edmund Spenser*.

Finally this collection represents with only one essay, Alastair Fowler's, a subject that is becoming of some importance in the study of *The Faerie Queene*: the role of iconography, the historical study of symbols, which has had so great an impact in the field of art history. The issue is not whether but how understanding the details and assumptions of Renaissance iconography can illuminate Spenser's work. At present there is rather a sharp split between those who treat *The Faerie Queene* as an esoteric poem, employing a symbolism accessible only to initiates, and those who think it enacts the idea of common wisdom and makes its meanings open to all who have the sympathy and patience to read. There is some useful controversy here and I had hoped to include some of it. But a disproportionate amount of space would have been required to include all the evidence and arguments marshalled on both sides. The reader interested in this subject should consult Lewis' posthumous *Spenser's Images of Life*, Miss Tuve's *Allegorical Imagery*, Kermode's influential essay on the Cave of Mammon, chapters 7 and 8 of my book, Thomas P. Roche's *The Kindly Flame*, and all the work of Alastair Fowler, the most formidably learned Spenserian in this field.

Having rattled off a list of books on a subject that carries suggestions of vast and intimidating learning, let me assure the reader that there is *not* a large body of Spenserian scholarship that he must master before he can trust his own dealings with the poem. Given the nature of *The Faerie Queene*, the amount of scholarship on it is amazingly little when compared with the amount devoted to *Paradise Lost*. The explanation for this, it seems to me, is the nature of the poem itself. As Lewis has said, Spenser

assumed from the outset that the truth about the universe was knowable and in fact known. If that were so, then of course you would expect agreements between the great teachers of all ages just as you expect agreements between the reports of different explorers. ... What some call his philosophy he would have called common knowledge.

It is this that makes the thought of *The Faerie Queene*, as Professor Osgood says, 'somehow unmeasurable'. Spenser expected his readers to find in it not his philosophy but their own experience – everyone's experience – loosened from its particular contexts by the universalizing power of allegory.

Hence of the few really impressive scholarly works on Spenser, Robert Ellrodt's concludes that Spenser's neoplatonism was traditional, syncretistic, and widely accessible, while Rosemond Tuve's is directly concerned with the aesthetic realities of the poetry. No one, least of all Lewis, would say that the reader of Spenser does not need historical understanding. But such understanding is not a matter of working up special knowledge; one acquires it by a sympathetic reading of Renaissance writings. There is therefore every reason to acquire our understanding of *The Faerie Queene* by reading the poem itself – by encountering it, as Thoreau said we should encounter nature, with a corresponding trust and magnanimity.

William Empson

from *Seven Types of Ambiguity*   1930 (revised 1947)

I have mentioned Spenser, whom no discussion of rhythm can ignore.
To show the scale of his rhythm, it may be enough to list some of the
ways in which he gave movement to the stanza of *The Faerie Queene*;
it is by the delicacy of this movement that he shows his attitude
towards his sentences, rather than by devices of implication in the
sentences themselves. At the same time, once such an attitude has been
fixed, it is more easily described in terms of the meaning of the words
than in terms of the meaning of the rhythm; in the next example,
from Sidney, I shall use this other mode of approach.

Spenser concentrates the reader's attention on to the movement of
his stanza: by the use of archaic words and constructions, so that one
is at a safe distance from the exercise of an immediate judgement, by
the steady untroubled flow of similar lines, by making no rapid
change of sense or feeling, by sustained alliteration, parallel adjectives,
and full statement of the accessories of a thought, and by the dreamy
repetition of the great stanza perpetually pausing at its close. *Ababbcbcc*
is a unit which may be broken up into a variety of metrical forms, and
the ways in which it is successively broken up are fitted into enormous patterns. The first quatrain usually gratifies the ear directly and
without surprise, and the stanzas may then be classified by the grammatical connexions of the crucial fifth line, which must give a soft
bump to the dying fall of the first quatrain, keep it in the air, and
prevent it from falling apart from the rest of the stanza.

It may complete the sense of the quatrain, for instance, with a
couplet, and the stanza will then begin with a larger, more narrative
unit, *ababb*, and wander garrulously down a perspective to the alexandrine. Or it may add to the quatrain as by an afterthought, as if with a
childish earnestness it made sure of its point without regard to the
metre, and one is relieved to find that the metre recovers itself after all.
For more energetic or serious statements it will start a new quatrain at
the fifth line, with a new sentence; there are then two smaller and
tighter, repeatedly didactic, or logically opposed, historically or
advancing, units, whose common rhyme serves to insist upon their
contrast, which are summed up and reconciled in the final solemnity

of the alexandrine. In times of excitement the fifth line will be connected both ways, so as to ignore the two quatrains, and, by flowing straight on down the stanza with an insistence on its unity, show the accumulated energy of some enormous climax; and again, by being connected with neither, it will make the stanza into an unstressed conversational device without overtones of rhythm, picking up stray threads of the story with almost the relief of prose. It would be interesting to take one of the vast famous passages of the work and show how these devices are fitted together into larger units of rhythm, but having said that every use of the stanza includes all these uses in the reader's apprehension of it I may have said enough to show the sort of methods Spenser had under his control; why it was not necessary for him to concentrate on the lightning flashes of ambiguity.

The size, the possible variety, and the fixity of this unit give something of the blankness that comes from fixing your eyes on a bright spot; you have to yield yourself to it very completely to take in the variety of its movement, and, at the same time, there is no need to concentrate the elements of the situation into a judgement as if for action. As a result of this, when there are ambiguities of idea, it is whole civilizations rather than details of the moment which are their elements; he can pour into the even dreamwork of his fairyland Christian, classical, and chivalrous materials with an air, not of ignoring their differences, but of holding all their systems of values floating as if at a distance, so as not to interfere with one another, in the prolonged and diffused energies of his mind.

(33-4)

C. S. Lewis

from *The Allegory of Love*   1936

There is no *situation* in *The Faerie Queene*, no when nor where. Ariosto begins with a situation – Roland's return from the East and Agramant's invasion of France. *The Faerie Queene* begins quite differently. A knight and a lady ride across our field of vision. We do not know where they are, nor in what period; the poet's whole energy is devoted to telling us what they look like. Ariosto begins like a man telling us, very well and clearly, a series of events which he has heard: Spenser begins like a man in a trance, or a man looking through a window, telling us what he sees. And however deep we dig in Spenser we shall never get to a situation, and never find a context in the objective world for the shapes he is going to show us.

But this does not mean that he is all surface. He, too, has his lower levels, though they are much harder to describe than those of the Italians. In one sense, of course, we know already what they are going to be: Spenser has allegorized the romantic epic (that is the only formal novelty of his work) and what lies below the surface of his poem will therefore be something subjective and immaterial. But, for the moment, it will be better to proceed inductively – to notice what lies beneath his poetry from moment to moment without yet inquiring into his 'continued' allegory.

Let us return to the Knight and the Lady in the opening stanzas. The knight has a red cross on a silver shield; the lady is leading a lamb. The lamb has puzzled many readers; but we now know that it had a real function in earlier versions of the legend of St George, and (what is much more important) we know that the lady was commonly represented leading her lamb in the pageants of St George and the dragon. In other words, the two figures which meet us at the beginning of *The Faerie Queene* were instantly recognized by Spenser's first readers, and were clothed for them not in literary or courtly associations, but in popular, homely, patriotic associations. They spoke immediately to what was most universal and child-like in gentle and simple alike. This at once suggests an aspect of Spenser's poetry which it will be fatal for us to neglect, and which is abundantly illustrated in the First Book. The angels who sing at Una's wedding probably come from the same pageant source as the lamb. The well in which St George is refreshed during his fight with the dragon comes from *Bevis of Southampton*. The whole similarity between his allegory and that of Bunyan, which has exercised many scholars, is best explained by the fact that they have a common source – the old-fashioned sermon in the village church still continuing the allegorical tradition of the medieval pulpit. Innumerable details come from the Bible, and specially from those books of the Bible which have meant much to Protestantism – the Pauline epistles and the Revelation. His anti-papal allegories strike the very note of popular, even of rustic, Protestant aversion; they can be understood and enjoyed by the modern reader (whatever his religion) only if he remembers that Roman Catholicism was in Spenser's day simply the most potent contemporary symbol for something much more primitive – the sheer Bogey, who often changes his name but never wholly retires from the popular mind. Foxe's *Book of Martyrs* was in every one's hands; horrible stories of the Inquisition and the galleys came from overseas; and every nervous child must have heard tales of a panel slid back at twilight in a seeming innocent manor house to reveal the pale face and thin, black body of a Jesuit. The ghosts crying from beneath the altar in Orgoglio's chapel and the mystery of iniquity beneath that other altar of Gerioneo are accurate embodiments of popular contemporary horror at these things. Gerioneo himself, who

> laught so loud, that all his teeth wide bare
> One might haue seene enraung'd disorderly,
> Like to a rancke of piles, that pitched are awry
> (v xi 9)

is the genuine raw-head and bloody-bones of our remembered night nurseries. A dragon's mouth is the 'griesly mouth of hell' as in medieval drama (1 xi 12). Mammon is the gold-hoarding earthman of immemorial tradition, the gnome. The witcheries of Duessa, when she rides in Night's chariot and 'hungry Wolues continually did howle' (1 v 30), or of the hag with whom Florimel guested, are almost incomparably closer to the world of real superstition than any of the Italian enchantments. We have long looked for the origins of *The Faerie Queene* in Renaissance palaces and Platonic academies, and forgotten that it has humbler origins of at least equal importance in the Lord Mayor's show, the chap-book, the bedtime story, the family Bible, and the village church. What lies next beneath the surface in Spenser's poem is the world of popular imagination: almost, a popular mythology.

And this world is not called up, as Ariosto may call up a fragment of folk lore, in order to amuse us. On the contrary, it is used for the sake of something yet deeper which it brings up with it and which is Spenser's real concern; the primitive or instinctive mind, with all its terrors and ecstasies – that part in the mind of each of us which we should never dream of showing to a man of the world like Ariosto. Archimago and Una, in their opposite ways, are true creations of that mind. When we first meet them we seem to have known them long before; and so in a sense we have, but only the poet could have clothed them for us in form and colour. The same may be said of Despair and Malengin, of Busirane's appalling house, and of the garden of Adonis. For all of these are translations into the visible of feelings else blind and inarticulate; and they are translations made with singular accuracy, with singularly little loss. The secret of this accuracy in which, to my mind, Spenser excels nearly all poets, is partly to be sought in his humble fidelity to the popular symbols which he found ready made to his hand; but much more in his profound sympathy with that which makes the symbols, with the fundamental tendencies of human imagination as such. Like the writers of the New Testament (to whom, in the character of his symbolism, he is the closest of all English poets) he is endlessly preoccupied with such ultimate antitheses as Light and Darkness or Life and Death. It has not often been noticed – and, indeed, save for a special purpose it ought not to be noticed – that Night is hardly even mentioned by Spenser without aversion. His story leads him to describe innumerable nightfalls, and his feeling about them is always the same:

> So soone as Night had with her pallid hew
> Defast the beautie of the shining sky,
> And reft from men the worlds desired vew
> > (III ii 28)

or,

> when as chearelesse Night ycouered had
> Faire heauen with an vniversall cloud,
> That euery wight dismayd with darknesse sad
> > (III xii 1)

or, again,

> when as daies faire shinie-beame, yclowded
> With fearefull shadowes of deformed night,
> Warn'd man and beast in quiet rest be shrowded.
> > (v iv 45)

And, answering to this, in his descriptions of morning we have a never failing rapture: mere light is as sweet to Spenser as if it were a new creation. Such passages are too numerous and too widely scattered (often at unimportant places in the story) to be the result of any conscious plan: they are spontaneous and the better proof of the flawless health, the paradisal naïveté, of his imagination. They form a background, hardly noticed at a first reading, to those great passages where the conflict of light and dark becomes explicit. Such is the sleepless night of Prince Arthur in the third book, where the old description of lover's insomnia is heightened and spiritualized into a 'statement' (as the musicians say) of one of Spenser's main themes;

> Dayes dearest children be the blessed seed,
> Which darknesse shall subdew, and heauen win:
> Truth is his daughter; he her first did breed,
> Most sacred virgin, without spot of sin.
>
> (III iv 59)

It is no accident that Truth, or Una, should be mentioned here, for she is indeed the daughter of Light, and through the whole First Book runs the antithesis between her father as emperor of the East and Duessa as queen of the West – a conception possibly borrowed from *Reason and Sensuality* – and in the Fifth Canto of that book we meet Night face to face. The contrast between her 'visage deadly sad' as she comes forth from her 'darksome mew' and Duessa

> sunny bright,
> Adornd with gold and iewels shining cleare,
>
> (I v 21)

(though Duessa is but pretended, reflected light!) is, of course, a familiar example of that pictorial quality which critics have often praised in Spenser – but praised without a full understanding of those very unpictorial, unpicturable, depths from which it rises. Spenser is no dilettante, and has a low opinion of the painter's art as compared with his own (III Proem 2). He is not playing mere tricks with light and shade; and few speeches in our poetry are more serious than Night's sad sentence (the very accent of a creature *dréame bedaéled*)

> The sonnes of Day he fauoureth, I see.
>
> (I v 25)

And yet it is characteristic of him that the constant pressure of this day and night antithesis on his imagination never tempts him into dualism. He is impressed, more perhaps than any other poet, with the conflict of two mighty opposites – aware that our world is dualistic for all practical purposes, dualistic in all but the very last resort: but from the final heresy he abstains, drawing back from the verge of dualism to remind us by delicate allegories that though the conflict seems ultimate yet one of the opposites really contains, and is not contained by, the other. Truth and falsehood are opposed; but truth is the norm not of truth only but of falsehood also. That is why we find that Una's father, King of the East and enemy of the West, is yet *de jure* King of the West as well as of the East (I i 5). That is why Love and Hatred, whom the poet borrows no doubt from Empedocles, are opposites but not, as in Empedocles, mere opposites: they are both the sons of Concord (IV x 34). And that, again, in the passage we were discussing, is why Aesculapius, a creature of Night's party, asks Night the formidable question,

> Can Night defray
> The wrath of thundring *Ioue*, that rules both night and day?
> (I v 42)

(310–15)

Misconceptions about the real merit and limitation of Spenser's genius have led to his present neglect. The very phrase 'poets' poet', I believe, has done incalculable damage. The genitive of *poets'* is taken to have an intensive force and the phrase is interpreted on the analogy of *Holy of Holies*. Readers trained on such a conception open their Spenser expecting to find some quintessential 'poeticalness' in the lowest and most obvious sense of that word – something more mellifluous than Shakespeare's sonnets, more airy than Shelley, more swooningly sensuous than Keats, more dreamlike than William Morris: and then, as likely as not, what first meets their eye is something of this sort:

> But I with better reason him auiz'd,
> And shew'd him how through error and mis-thought
> Of our like persons eath[1] to be disguiz'd,
> Or his exchange, or freedome might be wrought.
> Whereto full loth was he, ne would for ought
> Consent, that I who stood all fearelesse free,

Should wilfully be into thraldome brought,
  Till fortune did perforce it so decree.
Yet ouerrul'd at last, he did to me agree.

(IV viii 58)

Such a reader, at this point, excusably throws the book away. Now you may say that I have selected a specimen of Spenser at his worst; and so I have. But this 'worst' would not matter unless Spenser had a false reputation for sheer 'poeticalness'. The reader, unless he were a fool, would be prepared for flats in a long poem: he would not be put off by one such experience from making the acquaintance of Wordsworth or Chaucer. The real trouble is that he cannot be prepared for such a flat as this in a poem such as *The Faerie Queene* is commonly supposed to be: he has been taught not to look for vigorous thought or serious issues or even coherence and sanity in his Spenser – taught that the man's only merit is voluptuousness and day dream. And if Spenser can, in any passage, do so badly the only thing he is supposed to be able to do at all, he is naturally rejected. . . .

Just as Wordsworth retains to the end many traces of the diction he revolted against, so Spenser is always liable to give us 'huge heaps of words uphoarded hideously'. His excessive alliteration is a disease of the period, and so is his tendency to abandon true poetic presentation in favour of mere eulogistic or dyslogistic adjectives. Such words as 'direfull', 'goodly', 'foul', 'fair', 'filthie', and the like (abdications of the poet's true office) are far too common in his work. And even when he is at his best the merits of his verse are not always those which critical tradition – generalizing too hastily from the Cave of Sleep and the Bower of Bliss – has led us to expect. Let us dip our hands into the lucky-bag again.

Nought vnder heauen so strongly doth allure
The sence of man, and all his minde possesse,
As beauties louely baite, that doth procure
Great warriours oft their rigour to represse,
And mighty hands forget their manlinesse;
Drawne with the powre of an heart-robbing eye,
And wrapt in fetters of a golden tresse.

(V viii 1)

1 easily

And troubled bloud through his pale face was seene
To come, and goe with tydings from the hart.

(I ix 51)

What time the natiue Belman of the night,
The bird, that warned *Peter* of his fall . . .

(v vi 27)

In all these there is undoubted poetry; but it is a poetry far more
nervous and masculine – a drier flavour and a wine with more body –
than the modern reader has been taught to anticipate. Even more
remarkable, in this context, are those passages where the pungency
of the writing depends on a deliberate approximation to the prosaic,
as this, of the amazon Radigund:

For all those Knights, the which by force or guile
She doth subdue, she fowly doth entreate.
First she doth them of warlike armes despoile,
And cloth in womens weedes: And then with threat
Doth them compell to worke, to earne their meat,
To spin, to card, to sew, to wash, to wring . . .

(v iv 31)

A few stanzas later, the same amazon, sending her ambassadors to
Arthegall, whom she hopes to conquer on the morrow and to set to
washing and wringing (how admirably the verbs were chosen!), bids
them

beare with you both wine and iuncates fit,
And bid him eate, henceforth he oft shall hungry sit.

(v iv 49)

(317–20)

But these are generalities. For the study of Spenser himself, I think
the most useful thing we can do as a preparative ('Laughing to
teach the truth, what hinders?') is to draw up two lists of epithets after
the manner of Rabelais. The first would run something like this:

Elfin Spenser: Renaissance Spenser: voluptuous Spenser: courtly
Spenser: Italianate Spenser: decorative Spenser.

For the second I propose –

English Spenser: Protestant Spenser: rustic Spenser: manly Spenser: churchwardenly Spenser: domestic Spenser: thrifty Spenser: honest Spenser.

All that I have hitherto said has been directed to persuading the reader that the second of these lists is quite as fully justified as the first – that Spenser is the master of Milton in a far deeper sense than we had supposed. It is the measure of his greatness that he deserves the epithets of both lists.

(320–21)

The charge of actual sensuality and theoretical austerity cannot be answered so briefly. The spear-head of this attack is usually directed against the Bower of Bliss, and it is sometimes strengthened by the statement that the Garden of Adonis is not sufficiently distinguished from it; and an analysis of these two places is as good a method as any other of beginning a study of Spenser's allegory. The home of Acrasia is first shown to us in the Fifth Canto of Book II, when Atin finds Cymochles there asleep. The very first words of the description are

> And ouer him, art striuing to compaire
> With nature, did an Arber greene dispred.
> (II v 29)

This explicit statement that Acrasia's garden is art not nature can be paralleled in Tasso, and would be unimportant if it stood alone. But the interesting thing is that when the Bower of Bliss reappears seven cantos later, there again the very first stanza of description tells us that it was

> goodly beautifide
> With all the ornaments of *Floraes* pride,
> Wherewith her mother Art, as halfe in scorne
> Of niggard Nature, like a pompous bride
> Did decke her, and too lauishly adorne.
> (II xii 50)

In order to be perfectly fair to Spenser's hostile critics, I am prepared to assume that this repetition of the antithesis between art and nature is accidental. But I think the hardest sceptic will hesitate when he reads, eight stanzas further,

> And that, which all faire workes doth most aggrace,
> The art, which all that wrought, appeared in no place.
>
> (II xii 58)

And if this does not satisfy him let him read on to the sixty-first stanza where we find the imitation ivy in metal which adorns Acrasia's bathing-pool. Whether those who think that Spenser is secretly on Acrasia's side, themselves approve of metal vegetation as a garden ornament, or whether they regard this passage as a proof of Spenser's abominable bad taste, I do not know; but this is how the poet describes it,

> And ouer all, of purest gold was spred,
> A trayle of yuie in his natiue hew:
> For the rich mettall was so coloured,
> That wight, who did not well auis'd[1] it vew,
> Would surely deeme it to bee yuie trew.
>
> (II xii 61)

Is it possible now to resist the conviction that Spenser's hostile critics are precisely such wights who have viewed the Bower 'not well auis'd' and therefore erroneously deemed it to be true? Let us suppose, however, that the reader is still unconvinced: let us even help him by pointing out stanza 59 where the antithesis is blurred. But we have still to deal with the garden of Adonis; and surely all suspicion that the insistence on Acrasia's artificiality is accidental must disappear if we find throughout the description of the garden of Adonis an equal insistence on its natural spontaneity. And this is just what we do find. Here, as in the description of the Bower, the very first stanza gives us the key-note: the garden of Adonis is

> So faire a place, as Nature can deuize.
>
> (III vi 29)

A few stanzas later, in lines which I have already quoted, we are told that it needs no Gardiner because all its plants grow 'of their owne accord' in virtue of the divine word that works within them. It even

[1] judiciously, with consideration

needs no water, because these plants have eternall moisture 'in them-selues' (III vi 34). Like the Bower, the Garden has an arbour, but it is an arbour

> not by art,
> But of the trees owne inclination made
>> (III vi 44)

and the ivy in this arbour is living ivy not painted metal. Finally, the Bower has the story of a false love depicted by art on its gate (II xii 44), and the Garden has faithful lovers growing as live flowers out of its soil (III vi 45). When these facts have once been pointed out, only prejudice can continue to deny the deliberate differentiation between the Bower and the Garden. The one is artifice, sterility, death: the other, nature, fecundity, life. The similarity between them is just that similarity which exists between the two gardens in Jean de Meun; the similarity of the real to the pretended and of the archetype to the imitation. *Diabolus simius Dei*.

Before continuing our analysis of the Garden and the Bower we must digress for a little to notice an important corollary which has already emerged. Spenser, as I have shown, distinguishes the good and evil paradises by a skilful contrast between nature and art; and this at once throws a flood of light upon his poetic use of the arts in general. It has often been noticed that he is fond of describing pictures or tapestries; but it has not been equally noticed that he usually puts such artefacts in places which he thinks evil. It would be rash to infer from this that the poet disliked pictures: his practice is probably a calculated symbolic device and not a mere slavish obedience to temperament. But the fact is incontestable. There is, so far as I have noticed, only one exception, and it is very easily explained. In the House of Alma, the cells of the brain are internally decorated with pictures because this is the obvious, perhaps the only, way of allegorizing the fact that the external world enters as image into the human mind (II ix 50, 53). Everywhere else Spenser uses art to suggest the artificial in its bad sense – the sham or imitation. Thus he uses pictures to suggest luxurious corruption in the house of Malecasta (III i 34 ff.); and it is deliciously characteristic of our poet (*thrifty* Spenser) that St George and Britomart at first sight of the place should wonder uneasily (like the sober English soldier and gentlewoman they are) who is paying for it all, and how (III i 33). So, again, he uses pictures to build up an unbearable silent splendour in the House of Busirane. In the Temple of Venus, on the other hand, a place 'wall'd by nature gainst inuaders wrong', we have no pictures of lovers, but the living lovers themselves: as against the pictured Cupid of Busirane we have 'a flocke of little loues', all alive and fluttering about the neck and shoulders of Venus, as birds, in another mythology, fly about the head of Aengus (IV x 42). The gardener's art which had been excluded from the home of Adonis is indeed admitted into the Temple of Venus, for a reason which will appear later; but it is allowed only to supplement Nature (IV x 21, 22), not to deceive or sophisticate as it does in the Bower of Bliss. The abiding impression is that of a place 'lauishly enricht with natures threasure', 'by nature made' (IV x 23, 24). Thus, again, Pride has a palace, Belphoebe a pavilion in the woods, and the hill where the Graces dance is adorned only 'by natures skill' (VI x 5).

Truth is an unruly subject and, once admitted, comes crowding in on us faster than we wish. I had intended only a short digression to show the deliberate contrast between nature and art (or reality and imitation) in all Spenser's good and bad places, but I find that I have stumbled on another of those great antitheses which run through his whole poem. Like Life and Death, or Light and Darkness, the opposition of natural and artificial, naïve and sophisticated, genuine and spurious, meets us at every turn. He had learned from Seneca and the Stoics about the life according to Nature; and he had learned from Plato to see good and evil as the real and the apparent. Both doctrines were congenial to the rustic and humble piety of his temper – that fine flower of Anglican sanctity which meets us again in Herbert or Walton. He is not at home in the artificialities of the court, and if, as a man, he was sometimes seduced, as a poet he never was. The rotting captives in Pride's dungeon are those who 'fell from high Princes court' after long wasting their 'thriftlesse howres' (I v 51). Guyon, like a true Stoic, rejects Mammon's offers of wealth in favour of 'vn-troubled Nature', because 'at the well head the purest streames arise' (II vii 15). Philotime's beauty is not 'her owne natiue hew, | But wrought by art', and the description of her court ('Some thought to raise themselues to high degree' etc.) is so vivid that an officer of my acquaintance thought of presenting a framed and illuminated text of that stanza to the Head Quarters Mess of the — (II vii 45, 47). The whole conception of the false Florimel, not to mention Braggadochio, expresses the same feeling; and at her making, Nature 'grudg'd to see the counterfet should shame | The thing it selfe' (III viii 5). True love is praised because it is 'naturall affection faultlesse' (IV Proem 2), whereas the false love of Paridell is an 'art' which he 'learned had of yore', and he himself 'the learned louer' equipped with 'Bransles,[1] Ballads, virelayes,[2] and verses vaine' (III ix 28, x 6, 8). The pictures in the House of Busirane have already been mentioned; but perhaps the simile with which they are introduced gives us more of the depth of Spenser's mind on these matters than the whole description that follows.

> Wouen with gold and silke so close and nere,
> That the rich metall lurked priuily
> As faining to be hid from enuious eye;
> Yet here, and there, and euery where vnwares
> It shewd it selfe, and shone vnwillingly;
> Like a discolourd Snake, whose hidden snares
> Through the greene gras his long bright burnisht backe declares.
>
> (III xi 28)

Any moralist may disapprove luxury and artifice; but Spenser alone can turn the platitude into imagery of such sinister suggestion. It is thought completely converted into immediate sensation. Even the innocent trappings of the courtly life do not attract him, and he dismisses the externals of a tournament as contemptuously as Milton himself: to describe them, he says,

> Were worke fit for an Herauld, not for me.
>
> (V iii 3)

Clothes and jewellery interest him only when they adorn his 'shining ones', and become, as a modern critic has well pointed out, the symbol of a spiritual radiance.[1] Everywhere else the pomps and vanities of the 'World' are for him illusions

> Fashion'd to please the eies of them, that pas,
> Which see not perfect things but in a glas,

[1] dances   [2] short light song or poem

and easily rejected by those who compare them with 'plaine Anti-quitie' (VI Proem 5, 4). The Noble Savage, long before Dryden gives him that name, has played his part in the Sixth Book of *The Faerie Queene*. Una's face is fairest unveiled. 'Naturals' – lions and satyrs – come to her aid. True courtesy dwells among shepherds who alone have never seen the Blatant Beast (VI ix 6).

All this is quite compatible with Spenser's horror of something else which is also commonly called 'nature'. As we had to remind our-selves in an earlier chapter, Nature may be opposed not only to the artificial or the spurious, but also to the spiritual or the civil. There is a nature of Hobbes' painting as well as of Rousseau's. Of nature in this second sense, nature as the brutal, the unimproved, the inchoate, Spenser has given us notice enough in his cannibals, brigands, and the like; and, more philosophically, in the 'hatefull darknesse' and 'deepe horrore' of the chaos whence all the fair shapes in the garden of Adonis have taken their 'substance' (III vi 36). This is what moderns tend to mean by Nature – the primitive, or original, and Spenser knows what it is like. But most commonly he understands Nature as Aristotle did – the 'nature' of anything being its unimpeded growth from within to perfection, neither checked by accident nor sophisti-cated by art. To this 'nature' his allegiance never falters, save perhaps in some regrettable compliments to the Queen which accord ill with his general feeling about the court: and when Nature personified enters his poem she turns out to be the greatest of his shining ones. In some respects, indeed, she symbolizes God Himself (VII vi 35, vii 15).

The reader may well be excused if he has, by this, forgotten that the whole subject of nature and art arose out of our analysis of the Bower of Bliss and the Garden of Adonis. But the Bower and the Garden (the very names, I trust, have now become significant) are so im-portant that we have still not exhausted them. We have dealt only with their contrast of nature and art. It still remains to consider the equally careful, and even more important, contrast between the ex-plicitly erotic imagery of the one and the other. We here approach a subject on which Spenser has been much misunderstood. He is full of pictures of virtuous and vicious love, and they are, in fact, exquisitely contrasted. Most readers seem to approach him with the vulgar ex-pectation that his distinction between them is going to be a quantita-

1 See Dr Janet Spens, *Spenser's Faerie Queene*, 1934, p. 62.

204 C. S. Lewis

tive one; that the vicious loves are going to be warmly painted and the virtuous tepidly – the sacred draped and the profane nude. It must be stated at once that in so far as Spenser's distinction is quantitative at all, the quantities are the other way round. He is at the opposite pole from the scholastic philosophers. For him, intensity of passion purifies: cold pleasure, such as the scholastics seem to approve, is corruption. But in reality the distinction has very little to do with degree or quantity.

The reader who wishes to understand Spenser in this matter may begin with one of his most elementary contrasts – that between the naked damsels in Acrasia's fountain and the equally naked (in fact rather more naked) damsels who dance round Colin Clout (II xii 53 ff.; VI x II ff.). Here, I presume, no one can be confused. Acrasia's two young women (their names are obviously Cissie and Flossie) are ducking and giggling in a bathing-pool for the benefit of a passer-by: a man does not need to go to fairie land to meet them. The Graces are engaged in doing something worth doing, – namely, dancing in a ring 'in order excellent'. They are, at first, much too busy to notice Calidore's arrival, and when they do notice him they vanish. The contrast here is almost too simple to be worth mentioning; and it is only marginal to our immediate subject, for the Graces symbolize no sexual experience at all. Let us proceed to something a little less obvious and more relevant: let us compare the pictured Venus and Adonis in the house of Malecasta with the real Venus and Adonis in the Garden. We find at once that the latter (the good and real) are a picture of actual fruition. Venus, in defiance of the forces of death, the Stygian gods,

Possesseth him, and of his sweetnesse takes her fill.

(III vi 46)

Nothing could be franker; a dainty reader might even object that the phrase 'takes her fill' brings us too close to other and more prosaic appetites. But daintiness will be rebuked (as Spenser is always ready to rebuke it) if any one tries to prefer the pictured Venus on Malecasta's wall. For she is not in the arms of Adonis: she is merely looking at him,

And whilest he bath'd, with her two crafty spyes,
She secretly would search each daintie lim.

(III i 36)

The words 'crafty', 'spies', and 'secretly' warn us sufficiently well where we have arrived. The good Venus is a picture of fruition: the bad Venus is a picture not of 'lust in action' but of lust suspended – lust turning into what would now be called *skeptophilia*. The contrast is just as clear as that in the previous example, and incalculably more important. Thus armed, we may now return to the Bower. The very first person we meet there is Cymochles. He has come there for pleasure and he is surrounded by a flock of wanton nymphs. But the wretched creature does not approach one of them: instead, he lies in the grass ('like an Adder, lurking in the weeds') and

> Sometimes he falsely faines himselfe to sleepe,
> Whiles through their lids his wanton eies do peepe.
>
> (II v 34)

The word 'peepe' is the danger signal, and once again we know where we are. If we turn to the Garden of Adonis we shall find a very different state of affairs. There 'all plentie and all pleasure flowes': the garden is full of lovers and 'Franckly each paramor his leman knowes' (III vi 41). And when we have noticed this it ought to dawn upon us that the Bower of Bliss is not a place even of healthy animalism, or indeed of activity of any kind. Acrasia herself *does* nothing: she is merely 'discovered', posed on a sofa beside a sleeping young man, in suitably semi-transparent raiment. It is hardly necessary to add that her breast is 'bare to readie spoyle| Of hungry eies' (II xii 78), for eyes, greedy eyes ('which n'ote therewith be fild') are the tyrants of that whole region. The Bower of Bliss is not a picture of lawless, that is, unwedded, love as opposed to lawful love. It is a picture, one of the most powerful ever painted, of the whole sexual nature in disease. There is not a kiss or an embrace in the island: only male prurience and female provocation. Against it we should set not only the Garden of Adonis, but the rapturous reunion of Scudamour with Amoret (III xii 43–7; 1590 ed), or the singularly fresh and frank account of Arthur's meeting with Gloriana (I ix 9–15). It is not to be supposed of course that Spenser wrote as a scientific 'sexologist' or consciously designed his Bower of Bliss as a picture of sexual perversion. Acrasia indeed does not represent sexual vice in particular, but vicious pleasure in general (II xii 1). Spenser's conscious intention, no doubt, was merely to produce a picture which should do justice both to the pleasantness and to the vice. He has done this in the only way possible – namely, by filling his Bower of Bliss with sweetness showered upon sweetness and yet contriving that there should be something subtly wrong throughout. But perhaps 'contriving' is a bad word. When he wishes to paint disease, the exquisite health of his own imagination shows him what images to exclude.

(324–33)

A few pages ago we were considering the difference between the Bower of Bliss and the Garden of Adonis. While we did so I carefully excluded a much more interesting question – that of the difference between the Bower of Bliss and the Houses of Malecasta and Busirane. It is now time to rectify this omission. The Bower, it will be remembered, turned out to be a place not of lawless loves or even lawless lusts, but of disease and paralysis in appetite itself. It will be remembered that the Bower is the home not of vicious sexuality in particular, but of vicious Pleasure in general. The poet has selected one kind of pleasure chiefly because it is the only kind that can be treated at length in serious poetry. The Bower is connected with sex at all only through the medium of Pleasure. And this is borne out by the fact – very remarkable to any one well read in previous allegory – that Cupid is never mentioned in the Bower, a clear indication that we are not yet dealing with love. The Bower is not the foe of Chastity but of Continence – of that elementary psychic integration which is presupposed even in unlawful loves. To find the real foe of Chastity, the real portrait of false love, we must turn to Malecasta and Busirane. The moment we do so, we find that Malecasta and Busirane are nothing else than the main subject of this study – Courtly Love; and that Courtly Love is in Spenser's view the chief opponent of Chastity. But Chastity for him means Britomart, married love. The story he tells is therefore part of my story: the final struggle between the romance of marriage and the romance of adultery.

Malecasta lives in Castle Joyeous amid the 'curteous | And comely glee' of gracious ladies and gentle knights (III i 31). Somebody must be paying for it all, but one cannot find out who. The Venus in her tapestries entices Adonis 'as well that art she knew' (III i 35): we are back in the world of the Vekke and the commandments of Love. In the rooms of the castle there is 'Dauncing and reueling both day and night', and 'Cupid still emongst them kindled lustfull fires' (III i 39). The six knights with whom Britomart contends at its gate (Gardante, Parlante, and the rest) might have stepped straight out of the Roman de la Rose, and in the very next stanza the simile of the rose itself occurs (III i 46). The place is dangerous to spirits who would have gone through the Bower of Bliss without noticing its existence. Britomart gets a flesh wound there (III i 65), and Holiness himself is glad to be helped in his fight against Malecasta's champions by Britomart; by which the honest poet intends, no doubt, to let us know that even a religious man need not disdain the support which a happy marriage will give him against fashionable gallantry. For Britomart is married love.

Malecasta clearly represents the dangerous attractions of courtly love – the attractions that drew a Surrey or a Sidney. Hers is the face that it shows to us at first. But the House of Busirane is the bitter ending of it. In these vast, silent rooms, dazzling with snake-like gold, and endlessly pictured with 'Cupids warres . . . and cruell battels' (III xi 29), scrawled over with 'A thousand monstrous formes' (III xi 51) of false love, where Britomart awaits her hidden enemy for a day and a night, shut in, entombed, cut off from the dawn which comes outside 'Calling men to their daily exercize' (III xii 28), Spenser has painted for us an unforgettable picture not of lust but of love – love as understood by the traditional French novel or by Guillaume de Lorris – in all its heartbreaking glitter, its sterility, its suffocating monotony. And when at last the ominous door opens and the Mask of Cupid comes out, what is this but a picture of the deep human suffering which underlies such loves?

> Vnquiet *Care*, and fond *Vnthriftihead*,[1]
> Lewd *Losse of Time*, and *Sorrow* seeming dead,
> Inconstant *Chaunge*, and false *Disloyaltie*,
> Consuming *Riotise*, and guilty *Dread*
> Of heauenly vengeance, faint *Infirmitie*,
> Vile *Pouertie*, and lastly *Death* with infamie.
>
> (III xii 25)

The Mask, in fact embodies all the sorrows of Isoud among the lepers,

1 unthriftiness

and Launcelot mad in the woods, of Guinevere at the stake or Guinevere made nun and penitent, of Troilus waiting on the wall, of Petrarch writing *vergogna è 'l frutto* and Sidney rejecting the love that reaches but to dust; or of Donne writing his fierce poems *from* the house of Busirane soon after Spenser had written *of* it. When Britomart rescues Amoret from this place of death she is ending some five centuries of human experience, predominantly painful. The only thing Spenser does not know is that Britomart is the daughter of Busirane – that his ideal of married love grew out of courtly love.

Who, then, is Amoret? She is the twin sister of Belphoebe and both were begotten by the Sun,

> Pure and vnspotted from all loathly crime,
> That is ingenerate[1] in fleshly slime.
>
> (III vi 3)

The meaning of which is best understood by comparison with Spenser's sonnet,

> More then most faire, full of the liuing fire,
> Kindled aboue vnto the maker neere.
>
> (*Amoretti*, 8)

And we know that the Sun is an image of the Good for Plato, and therefore of God for Spenser. The first important event in the life of these twins was their adoption by Venus and Diana: Diana the goddess of virginity, and Venus from whose house 'all the world deriues the glorious | Features of beautie' (III vi 12). Now the circumstances which led up to this adoption are related in one of the most medieval passages in the whole *Faerie Queene* – a *débat* between Venus and Diana (III vi 11–25); but this *débat* has two remarkable features. In the first place, the Venus who takes part in it is a Venus severed from Cupid, and Cupid, as we have already seen, is associated with courtly love. I say 'associated' because we are dealing with what was merely a feeling in Spenser's mind, not a piece of intellectual and historical knowledge, as it is to us. There is therefore no consistent and conscious identification of Cupid with courtly love, but Cupid tends to appear in one kind of context and to be absent from another kind.

1 innate

And when he does appear in contexts approved by our domestic poet, he usually appears with some kind of reservation. He is allowed into the Garden of Adonis on condition of his 'laying his sad darts | Aside' (III vi 49): in the Temple of Venus it is only his younger brothers who flutter round the neck of the goddess (IV x 42). We are therefore fully justified in stressing the fact that Venus finds Amoret only because she has lost Cupid, and finally adopts Amoret *instead of* Cupid (III vi 28). The other important novelty is that this *débat* ends with a reconciliation; Spenser is claiming to have settled the old quarrel between Venus and Diana, and that after a singularly frank statement of the claims of each. And when the two goddesses have agreed, their young wards

> twixt them two did share
> The heritage of all celestiall grace.
> That all the rest it seem'd they robbed bare,
>
> (III vi 4)

and one of them, Amoret, became

> th'ensample of true loue alone,
> And Lodestarre of all chaste affectione.
>
> (III vi 52)

She was taken by Venus to be reared in the Garden of Adonis, guarded by Genius the lord of generation, among happy lovers and flowers (the two are here indistinguishable) whose fecundity never ceases to obey the Divine Command. This was her nursery: her school or university was the Temple of Venus. This is a region neither purely natural, like the Garden, nor artificial in the bad sense, like the Bower of Bliss: a region where,

> all that nature did omit,

Art playing second natures part, supplyed it.
> (IV x 21)

Here Amoret no longer grows like a plant, but is committed to the care of Womanhood; the innocent sensuousness of the garden is replaced by '*sober Modestie*', '*comely Curtesie*',

Soft *Silence*, and submisse[1] *Obedience*,

which are gifts of God and protect His saints 'against their foes offence' (IV x 51). Indeed the whole island is strongly protected, partly by Nature (IV x 6), and partly by such immemorial champions of maidenhead in the Rose tradition, as Doubt, Delay and Daunger (IV x 12, 13, 17). But when the lover comes he defeats all these and plucks Amoret from her place among the modest virtues. The struggle in his own mind before he does so, his sense of 'Beauty too rich for use, for earth too dear', is a beautiful gift made by the humilities of medieval love poetry to Spenser at the very moment of his victory over the medieval tradition:

> my hart gan throb,
> And wade[2] in doubt, what best were to be donne:
> For sacrilege me seem'd the Church to rob,
> And folly seem'd to leaue the thing vndonne.
>
> (IV x 53)

Amoret, however, cannot withdraw her hand, and the conclusion of the adventure may be given in the words of the poet who has studied most deeply this part of *The Faerie Queene*:

> she what was Honour knew,
> And with obsequious Majestie approv'd
> My pleaded reason.
>
> (*Paradise Lost*, VIII 508–10)

The natural conclusion is marriage, but Busirane for centuries has stood in the way. That is why it is from the marriage feast that Busirane carries Amoret away (IV i 3), to pine for an indefinite period in his tomblike house. When once Britomart has rescued her thence, the two lovers become one flesh – for that is the meaning of the daring simile of the Hermaphrodite in the original conclusion of Book III. But even after this, Amoret is in danger if she strays from Britomart's side; she will then fall into a world of wild beasts where she has no comfort or guide (IV vii 2), and may even become the victim of monsters who live on the 'spoile of women' (IV vii 12).

(339–44)

1 submissive   2 go

My claim for Spenser may take the form of the old eulogy – *totam vitae imaginem expressit*; but perhaps my meaning will be clearer if we omit the word *totam*, if we say simply *vitae imaginem*. Certainly this will help to clear up a common misunderstanding. People find a 'likeness' or 'truth' to life in Shakespeare because the persons, passions and events which we meet in his plays are like those which we meet in our own lives: he excels, in fact, in what the old critics called 'nature', or the probable. When they find nothing of the sort in Spenser, they are apt to conclude that he has nothing to do with 'life' – that he writes that poetry of escape or recreation which (for some reason or other) is so intensely hated at present. But they do not notice that *The Faerie Queene* is 'like life' in a different sense, in a much more literal sense. When I say that it is like life, I do not mean that the places and people in it are like those which life produces. I mean precisely what I say – that it is like life itself, not like the products of life. It is an image of the *natura naturans*, not of the *natura naturata*. The things we read about in it are not like life, but the experience of reading it is like living. The clashing antitheses which meet and resolve themselves into higher unities, the lights streaming out from the great allegorical *foci* to turn into a hundred different colours as they reach the lower levels of complex adventure, the adventures gathering themselves together and revealing their true nature as we draw near the *foci*, the constant re-appearance of certain basic ideas, which transform themselves without end and yet ever remain the same (eterne in mutability), the unwearied variety and seamless continuity of the whole – all this is Spenser's true likeness to life. It is this which gives us, while we read him, a sensation akin to that which Hegelians are said to get from Hegel – a feeling that we have before us not so much an image as a sublime instance of the universal process – that this is not so much a poet writing about the fundamental forms of life as those forms themselves spontaneously displaying their activities to us through the imagination of a poet. The invocation of the Muse hardly seems to be a convention in Spenser. We feel that his poetry has really tapped sources not easily accessible to discursive thought. He makes imaginable inner realities so vast and simple that they ordinarily escape us as the largely printed names of continents escape us on the map – too big for our notice, too visible for sight. Milton has well selected wisdom as his peculiar excellence – wisdom of that kind which rarely penetrates into literature because it exists most often in inarticulate people. It is this that has kept children and poets true to him for three centuries, while the intellectuals (on whom the office of criticism naturally devolves) have been baffled even to irritation by a spell which they could not explain. To our own troubled and inquiring age this wisdom will perhaps show its most welcome aspect in the complete integration, the harmony, of Spenser's mind. His work is one, like a growing thing, a tree; like the world-ash-tree itself, with branches reaching to heaven and roots to hell. It reaches up to the songs of angels or the vision of the New Jerusalem and admits among its shining ones the veiled image of God Himself: it reaches down to the horror of fertile chaos beneath the Garden of Adonis and to the grotesque satyrs who protect Una or debauch Hellenore with equal truth to their nature. And between these two extremes comes all the multiplicity of human life, trans-muted but not falsified by the conventions of chivalrous romance. The 'great golden chain of Concord' has united the whole of his world. What he feels on one level, he feels on all. When the good and fair appear to him, the whole man responds; the satyrs gambol, the lances splinter, the shining ones rise up. There is a place for everything and everything is in its place. Nothing is repressed; nothing is in-subordinate. To read him is to grow in mental health.

(357–9)

D. A. Traversi

from 'Revaluation: *The Vision of Piers Plowman*', *Scrutiny*, vol. 5 1936

The poetic qualities of which this tradition [of medieval preaching] made Langland master can readily be shown in quotation; I select his picture of Covetyse in Passus C VII as typical:

Thenne cam Couetyse   ich can nat hym discryue,
So hongerliche and so holw   Heruey hym-self lokede.
He was bytelbrowed and baberlupped   with two blery eyen,
And as a letherene pors   lollid hus chekus,

Wel sydder than hys chyn   ychiueled for elde:
As bondemenne bacon   hus berd was yshaue,
With hus hod on his heued   and hus hatte bothe;
In a toren tabarde   of twelue wynter age.

The qualities of this passage are clearly visual qualities, and their ancestry is obvious. It derives from centuries of effort on the part of the preacher to bring home the great and common vices of his time to his audience. Even the alliteration is as much a device of the speaker as a traditional poetic technique; note how it falls again and again upon the descriptive epithets which are the key to the whole effect. And the words chosen are precisely those which a preacher could be certain of sharing with his audience, intense, but in no way 'poetic', if by poetic we mean a refined decoration of not too pressing emotions. These merits, once we admit them, are soon seen to be more than personal, more even than the qualities of Langland's own particular tradition; they are a general characteristic of the best English poetry. They are based upon an extraordinary ability to describe personal experience in terms of a common idiom, founded in this case on the simple but fundamental activities of a society closely connected with the land. It is unnecessary to prove Langland's close contact with rural life, for it is clear on every page of his poem. It opens with the wanderings of a shepherd on the Malvern Hills and never moves far from them in spirit. Piers Plowman, its hero, is merely a universalizing of the normal English life, the life which all readers of the poem would understand and in terms of which they could establish a common idiom with their poet. To realize how such a symbol could be given a universal significance, we have only to see how Piers appears successively as a fine and honest farmer, as the expounder of Charity and the Holy Trinity, as the Good Samaritan, and as Jesus himself. We are becoming increasingly aware of the way in which honest and active emotional responses can be fostered in people whose close contact with the soil and with traditional ways of living and working have not been undermined by the deadening forces of modern industrialism. If this can be so, even today, it is not surprising that this common social basis provided the vital idiom for the greatest English poetry.

Langland, in fact, was a great poet, and his greatness throws some light upon the nature of the English contribution to poetry. The great

English poets have always been those who have rescued English from scholarship run to seed; the genius of the language has always resisted false systems and false conventions. One should not, at this date, have to quote extensively to prove this point. Shakespeare and Donne, in their turn, were great poets because they freed English from the bondage of a dead scholarship and restored to it expressiveness and idiomatic strength. That was what Shakespeare was doing when he wrote:

> who would fardels bear,
> To *grunt* and *sweat* under a weary life . . . ?

These two verbs, so expressive in their evocation of common physical effort, should not have pleased those who followed logically the precepts of the Humanists. Nor should the sharp effect by which the 'bare bodkin' is doubly driven in by contrast with the Latin of 'quietus', so that it comes upon us with a definite effect of physical shock. Hopkins, too, was in his day the bearer to English of this new linguistic life, and his praise of Dryden for stressing 'the naked thew and sinew of the English language' is only a critical formulation of Shakespeare's practice. And their idiom was similar to that of Langland, whose language was vital English, and the alliterative metre into which it naturally fell the vital vehicle for it. . . .

Langland's metre, in fact, was the natural setting of a living language. The Victorian mechanism of scansion, with its cumbrous names and hieroglyphic signs, is only possible for a medium that has become ossified and lost contact with genuine feeling. Langland's language, as we have seen, was vital because the hideous modern plastering of the emotional life had not yet come to make men incapable of physical, mental or spiritual feeling. To adapt a phrase from *Lady Chatterley's Lover*, man's continuity with his past and with his own environment was still not mechanical, but organic. One very important indication of this was the fact that Langland, in the passage just quoted, showed that he could do what very few modern poets have been able to accomplish – that is, to handle a plain unadorned narrative, bringing out its full implications, without interrupting its natural flow. He succeeded in telling us that his poem was to be a complete survey of human life under the aspect of good and evil (for he saw – 'Al the welthe of this worlde and the woo bothe'), without in any way distracting us from the preliminary statement of the circumstances of the poem. And, since we could trust very few of even the greatest of our Romantic poets to do this, we must conclude that it was in itself a considerable achievement.

These considerations will serve, I hope, to point out how Langland is great. They will now help us to grasp the essence and value of his experience, which I propose to estimate by a comparison with the other great allegorist of English poetry – I mean Spenser. Spenser's language is clearly a different instrument from Langland's. Even at its simplest, in *Mother Hubberd's Tale* and other poems which derive from traditional sources, the divergence is obvious. In so far as his inspiration is English, and not that of the French humanists, it is clearly the decorative aspect of Chaucer that appeals to him. Even when he uses the English vocabulary which he cultivated so sedulously, the words have quite a different significance. Here he is elaborating an English subject:

Seest, howe brag[1] yond Bullocke beares,
So smirke,[2] so smoothe, his pricked eares?
His hornes bene as broade, as Rainebowe bent,
His dewelap[3] as lythe,[4] as lasse of Kent.
See howe he venteth[5] into the wynd.
Weenest of loue is not his mynd?
Seemeth thy flocke thy counsell can,[6]
So lustless[7] bene they, so weake so wan,[8]
Clothed with cold, and hoary wyth frost.

(*Shepheardes Calender*,
'February', 71–9)

This is the voice of a new sophistication. Words like 'brag', 'smirke', and 'pricked' have a traditional look about them, but their use suggests the arrival of a new poetic purpose. They are fastidiously chosen to present to the court a courtly picture of the countryside, and they are set in a rhythm which acts as a decorative border to the whole. They fit the social grace and dignity which an Elizabethan court possessed, and their effect is undoubtedly pleasing. But they suggest danger at hand. Already there is a perilous lack of root in this convention. Those

1 proudly   2 neat, trim
3 fold of loose skin hanging from the throat of cattle   4 pliant, supple
5 snuffs   6 knows   7 feeble, listless   8 feeble

whose way of life has become remote from the real soil cannot expect
to preserve for long the veneer of the soil; and that, translated into
social terms, is the meaning of *The Shepheardes Calender*. When
Spenser tries to write about the common physical experiences of
healthy mankind, his words become little more than pleasant
decorative trimmings; they are coins which have only a diminishing
reserve of real feeling behind them. When Langland desires to express
his deepest feelings, he finds it natural to rely on the simplest images.
He writes of the Incarnation in terms of the most universal physical
processes:

Loue is the plante of pees   and most preciouse of vertues;
For heuene holde hit ne mygte   so heuy hit semede,
Till hit hadde on erthe   goten hym-selue.
Was neuere lef vp-on lynde   lyghter ther-after,
As whanne hit hadde of the folde   flesch and blod ytake;
Tho was it portatyf and pershaunt   as the poynt of a nedle,
May non armure hit lette   nother hye walles;
For-thy is loue ledere   of oure lordes folke in heuene.

The issue is quite clear. Langland's language is the vehicle of a finely
integrated experience, alive and sensitive to every point of contact,
and crystallizing suavely into poetry. The effect of that adjective,
'pershaunt', followed by 'as the poynt of a nedle', for example, is not
so inferior to Shakespeare's 'bare bodkin'; it is certainly of the same
kind, and depends upon the same vitality of perception. The words
are almost transparent vehicles for the emotion that underlies them
and demands the simplest, most vital expression. Their value, so to
speak, is sacramental (the word has a peculiar relevance in view of the
nature of Langland's allegory) and the presence of universal physical
experiences is a help in indicating even the most spiritual reality. But
for Spenser these things have only a decorative value, and here too is a
philosophy at stake beneath the critical issue; body is body, and can
only meet spirit by degrading it – this was the implication of Spenser's
attraction to Neoplatonism.

Spenser, in fact, is the first great Puritan poet. The second was
Milton, who, it is well known, thought Spenser a better moral teacher
than Aquinas. No two men have done more, by their very genius, to
crush the true poetic tradition of England. It is typical of all Puritans

217 D. A. Traversi

that their attempts to escape the body and live by the 'spiritual'
faculty alone in a kind of baseless caricature of Christian sanctity leads
to the free spawning of every kind of evil. Milton's account of the
relation of Sin and Death in Book II of *Paradise Lost* is perfectly
typical. It can be amply paralleled in Spenser. The pages of *The Faerie
Queene* abound in monsters of every description, who are perfectly
unreal as moral representations of evil, but who teem with incredible
frequency and vividness. One cannot avoid feeling that Spenser got
a kind of half-horrified thrill out of this continual loathsome reproduction. Indeed, one must be struck by the vividness of Spenser's
description of evil and deformity:

> And by his side rode loathsome *Gluttony*,
> Deformed creature, on a filthie swyne,
> His belly was vp-blowne with luxury,
> And eke with fatnesse swollen were his eyne,
> And like a Crane his necke was long and fyne,
> With which he swallowd vp excessiue feast,
> For want whereof poore people oft did pyne;
> And all the way, most like a brutish beast,
> He spued vp his gorge, that all did him deteast.
>
> In greene vine leaues he was right fitly clad;
> For other clothes he could not weare for heat,
> And on his head an yuie girland had,
> From vnder which fast trickled downe the sweat:
> Still as he rode, he somewhat still did eat,
> And in his hand did beare a bouzing can,
> Of which he supt so oft, that on his seat
> His dronken corse he scarse vpholden can,
> In shape and life more like a monster, then a man.
>
> (I iv 21–2)

After that, one would not deny Spenser's greatness as a poet. But the
passage is doubly significant in view of its ancestry, which is Christian
and medieval; the 'bouzing can' is there to remind us of its connexion
with the vivid vernacular, and the contrasting reference to the poor
recalls one of the main social grievances of the English pulpit. The
whole picture, moreover, belongs to the world of the miracle plays,
where Herod died raving and rotting to pieces as Aelfric had des-

cribed him in a sermon more than five hundred years before. But there evil had always been subordinate to and less real than good, so that even Herod might easily turn into something like a joke. All was given its proper place in a theology that covered the whole of experience and centred everything upon the complete man's destined vision of God. So it was in Langland, whose allegory, like his language, grew out of his experience before transcending it. The symbol of Piers has a content that Spenser's figures lack for this very reason; he is fully natural both before and after he touches the supernatural. Langland's moral judgements are always founded on particular instances, and his portraits remind us of Ben Jonson's humours. . . .

A single example here is worth pages of generalities. The words of Lechery, a typical Langlandian personification, will serve:

To eche maide that ich mette   ich made hure a sygne
Semyinge to synne-warde   and somme gan ich teste
A-boute the mouthe, and by-nythe   by-gan ich to grope,
Til our brothers wil was on;   to werke we yeden
As wel fastyngdaies as Frydaies   and heye-feste euenes,
As lief in lent as oute of lente   all tymes liche –
Such werkus with ous   were neuere oute of season –
Til we myghte no more;   thanne hadde we murye tales
Of puterie and of paramours   and proueden thorw speches,
Handlynge and halsynge   and al-so thorw cissynge
Excitynge oure aither other   til oure old synne;
Sotilede songes   and sende out olde baudes
For to wynne to my wil   wommen with gyle;
By sorcerye some tyme   and som tyme by maistrie.
Ich lay by the louelokest   and loued hem neuere after.
Whenne ich was old and hor   and hadde lore that kynde,
Ich had lykynge to lauhe   of lecherous tales.
Now, lord, for thy leaute   of lechours haue mercy!

All the characteristics we are seeking are here. Each element in this picture could be paralleled in the pages of the didactic literature of the time; here is a related passage, one of many, taken from Owst's book:

these costumable lechours, when age suffreth hem no longer
to the dedus unclennes, yit woll thei than synge and make bost

at ther owne lewdnes in lechery; ye, and tell more therof at the taverne than ever he tolde othur thenketh to tell to his confessour all the dayes of his liff.

No two selections could do more to illustrate the origin and development of that concreteness and vitality in delineation which is the basis of the English comedy of humours and of Langland's allegorical method. The characteristics of lechery are not presented in a Spenserian abstraction, but by the mouth of a human being. The feeling is human, and not only human, but dramatic; that is the essence of the practice of humours. The human figure is simplified by that 'distortion to scale' of which we have spoken, but so simplified that its significance is not less but greater. Real human nature is given us, but given under an aspect, seen in the light of one dominating quality. Such a simplification is essential to the dramatist, and Langland foreshadows the development of the Elizabethan theatre, not only here, but time and again in his work.

But this is not all. It is essential to realize that the human figure thus revealed through a dominating aspect is firmly subordinated to a moral aim. Lechery is given, towards the end of the speech, a certain tragic quality in the bitter line:

Ich lay by the louelokest   and loued hem neuere after,

and in the vanity which is conveyed in the thought of

Whenne ich was old and hor   and hadde lore that kynde.

. . . Full value is given to the human and religious tragedy represented by the figure of Lechery. The tragedy is that of 'the expense of spirit in a waste of shame', and Langland's moral judgement fully recognizes, not only the 'waste' and the 'expense', but the fact that it is 'of spirit', and must be so in his Christian philosophy. So we emphasize once more that the allegory of *Piers Plowman* follows the principle of its writer's central doctrine – the Christian Incarnation. It starts from the real, and nothing that is real is irrelevant to it. Instead of imposing itself upon reality as a tyrannous abstraction, burdening the human and corporal with a dissociated spirituality, it works from the body to the soul, from natural life to the consummation of grace in which its author believed. And, by so doing, it teaches us the true strength of English literature.

220 D. A. Traversi

Turn once more to Spenser, and you will find yourself in a different world. The bitter Fifth Book of *The Faerie Queene* only emphasizes what is characteristic of the whole work. Consider Artegall and his servant Talus, the confessed representatives of Spenserian justice:

> Long they her sought, yet no where could they finde her,
> That sure they ween'd she was escapt away:
> But *Talus*, that could like a limehound[1] winde her,
> And all things secrete wisely could bewray,[2]
> At length found out, whereas she hidden lay
> Vnder an heape of gold. Thence he her drew
> By the faire lockes, and fowly did array,[3]
> Withouten pitty of her goodly hew,
> That *Artegall* him selfe her seemelesse plight did rew.
>
> Yet for no pitty would he change the course
> Of Iustice, which in *Talus* hand did lye;
> Who rudely hayld her forth without remorse,
> Still holding vp her suppliant hands on hye,
> And kneeling at his feete submissiuely.
> But he her suppliant hands, those hands of gold,
> And eke her feete, those feete of siluer trye,[4]
> Which sought vnrighteousnesse, and iustice sold,
> Chopt off, and nayld on high, that all might them behold.
>
> Her selfe then tooke he by the sclender wast,
> In vaine loud crying, and into the flood
> Ouer the Castle wall adowne her cast,
> And there her drowned in the durty mud:
> But the streame washt away her guilty blood.
>
> (v ii 25–7)

Once more, the technical mastery is considerable, a sure sign that Spenser was more interested than he sometimes was in his subject: I need only point to the fact that the rhymes do succeed in emphasizing the flow of the poet's indignation, and remark upon the sharp brutality of 'chopt off' as the culmination of an effective rhetorical construction. But its success only serves to show how dubious and how barbarous

1 bloodhound   2 disclose   3 give a 'dressing'   4 choice, select

221 D. A. Traversi

(in the last resort) were the interests and emotions of its author. We must remember that the whole incident is more than moral allegory. Spenser was the sort of man who is sometimes admired in the most academic circles as 'an idealist, who was also a man of the world', and the above represents the treatment that he regarded as suitable for the Irish among whom he lived. It defends a policy already put into operation by Lord Grey, the original of Artegall. That is its political meaning. Spiritually, it represents a view of Justice coloured by the bitter Puritan melancholy so typical of Spenser, and must be read in the light of his sombre reflections on decay and mutability. Puritanism is more than a mere matter of dark clothes and a nasalized psalm-singing; Spenser was a courtier and Milton's 'urbanity' was known to all his contemporaries. Its spirit can best be felt by a comparison of *The Faerie Queene* with *Piers Plowman*. The allegory of the latter is, as we have seen, a real and experienced thing, and its virtues and personifications spring out of flesh and blood. In Spenser, however, the knights and ladies are pale abstractions, so pale that their creator is unable to keep them apart in our minds as his tangled tale proceeds. Ultimately, the only reality is provided by Mutability and the Blatant Beast, for whom, one feels, the disembodied shades of Chastity, Temperance, and Courtesy are fair game. Langland's allegory is based on a hierarchy of virtues leading from the Life of Do-Well (the ordinary daily life, lived in the sight of God) to that of Do-best (the life of the saint who orders and directs the activities of the Church), and holiness is the crown of each and all of them; but Spenser's Knight of Holiness is hardly to be distinguished from his fellow who represents Temperance. Both live only in the intellect; for the emotions, they have no significance and no life. This suggests that Puritanism, as embodied in Spenser, is nothing else than the disembodied and destructive intellect preying on the body to kill the soul. That is the importance of Spenser and Milton, and their relation to the development of the English tradition. Their pallid successors are seen in the age of Tennyson and after, producing a dead poetry out of a dead 'poetic' language – sterile emotions issuing in a sterilized speech. In such a situation, Langland commends himself to the attention of all by the breadth and healthiness of his experience. To maintain the actuality of our sensible and emotional responses is at once the function and the condition of art, and it points beyond itself to a view of life which is complete and, in a true sense, orderly. Complete, because it has a catholic appreciation of good at every level, and orderly, because it teaches us to be content with no intellectual synthesis that falsifies or belittles the scope of human experience. And those two aims might pass today for a definition of the function of criticism.

(279–91)

G. Wilson Knight

'The Spenserian Fluidity', *The Burning Oracle*   1939 (revised for *Poets of Action*, 1967)

In *The Faerie Queene* (1590–96) Spenser seems to have taken all poetic impressionism as his province. It is stocked with folklore, myth, and legend of all sorts and crammed with influences Italian, medieval and classical. The poem is peculiarly rich in pagan lore. Spenser's metaphysic of fertility and creation is often nearer to the pagan and the naturalistic than to the Christian. *The Faerie Queene* is more a storehouse for poets of the future than itself a poem. In this, if in no other sense, he is 'the poets' poet', and a study of *The Faerie Queene* in detail should help any one who finds Colin Still's interpretation of *The Tempest* in terms of ancient legendary and ritualistic correspondences a fantastic conception.[1] Behind all our poetry there is a communal store of semi-consciously possessed legendary material: Spenser seems to have possessed it consciously. As so often, the Elizabethan is fully aware, his mind flooded, where later poets rely on mysterious, not-to-be-accounted-for promptings, controlled or otherwise, from unconsciousness.

But *The Faerie Queene* is not concerned mainly with ancient recollections: it is supremely Elizabethan as well. Its forked meanings are clear from Spenser's own statement in *A Letter of the Author's expounding his whole intention in the course of this work*:

In that Faery Queen I mean glory in my general intention, but in my particular I conceive the most excellent and glorious person of

1 I refer to Still's *Shakespeare's Mystery Play*, 1921; revised as *The Timeless Theme*, 1936. See my study *The Crown of Life*, [1967], p. 226.

our sovereign the Queen, and her kingdom in Faery Land. And yet in some places else, I do otherwise shadow her. . . (*Poetical Works*, ed. J. C. Smith and E. de Selincourt, 1924, p. 407).

A neat statement of the universal and particular in poetic blend, though so tight and exact a fusion as is suggested applies more generally to the work of Lyly than to that of Spenser, whose significances are often arbitrary and laxly related, as his final phrase suggests. But he is throughout more than a fancy-poet, and also more than a medieval allegorist, though both these he certainly is too. He builds a nationalist and royalist purpose into the scheme. It is 'the eulogy of a patriot addressing a united people', writes B. E. C. Davis (*Edmund Spenser*, 1933, p. 75), 'the nearest approach to a national epic in the cycle of English poetry'. He suggests that the constitution of Spenser's Fairy Land presents a happy medium between monarchy and oligarchy that reflects 'in vague outline' the commonwealth of Tudor England. The poem is dedicated to the Queen, who as Gloriana is supposed to dominate. In the introduction to Book II there is praise of the Queen; reference to recent explorations and discoveries; and a final sense of mystery and magic in the immediate and actual projected into the equation of England and Fairy Land under the 'fairest Princess under sky'. The Queen's chastity, so often found to make a neat blend in the Elizabethan mind of its two dominating positives – royalistic splendour and sexual excellence of one divine sort or another – is to be related elsewhere to Belphoebe and also to Mercilla. Prince Arthur is, in part, Leicester. Arthur's 'magnificence' is the Renaissance ideal in full show: 'The general end therefore of all the book is to fashion a gentleman or noble person in virtuous and gentle discipline' (*Poetical Works*, 1924, p. 407). Not, be it noted, to make a saint. The search for eternal truth (Una), the supplanting of deceitful semblances (Archimago and Duessa) are aspects of the humanistic ideal. Again,

So in the person of Prince Arthur I set forth magnificence in particular, which virtue for that (according to Aristotle and the rest) it is the perfection of all the rest, and containeth in it them all, therefore in the whole course I mention the deeds of Arthur applyable to that virtue, which I write of in that book (*Poetical Works*, 1924, p. 407).

224 G. Wilson Knight

That holiness would not have been one of Aristotle's 'virtues' need not trouble us. Renaissance poets try to *include* Christianity in a new, humanistic, comprehension. This is their poetic instinct, whatever their religious assertions. With them the present and actual incarnates the divine; from that sense is born their poetry. This is true equally of their royalistic and their erotic perceptions, which are not finally distinct. Both are blended with Christianity rather than subject to it.

Besides the specifically ancient or contemporary there are throughout *The Faerie Queene* essences of the universal and the timeless. I mean the vivid naturalism and imagistic grace, the luscious stanzaic woodlands and glades of impressionism and event, the featuring of beasts and people, good or evil; of lovely life and hideous fears; the use of cosmic forces, sun or earth; of the seasons; of night and day; death and life in interdependence; and of divine purposes generally.

Nevertheless the poem is, as a whole, unsatisfying. It claims more than it fulfills. The various knights and their quests are surely too shadowy, too slightly distinguished and objectified. And even if they were not, the dominating and binding presences of Gloriana and Arthur do not dominate and bind as they ought. It is difficult to feel the poem as a whole and would be even if it were finished. We get from it a vague quality rather than a structure. This is partly because the symbolic technique is faulty. Although Spenser attempts to in-weave his general thinking with the national life of his day, yet, faced by his vast self-proposed scheme, he falls back on a medievalistic allegory which he never quite controls. When one of his monsters vomits pamphlets we are shocked; too much realism in the beast's creation renders his deeper significance ludicrous; the blend of allegory and realism has not been properly performed. He misses symbol of the more profound sort: that incarnation of significance in fictional person or beast, so exactly true that every bend of the mould fits, in its degree, the desired shape of the contained fluid. Spenser's moulds are themselves undisciplined and variable. Dante had his rigid theological beliefs and the medieval allegorists normally started with some precise and ruling intellectual structure. Shakespeare has his realism, his unswerving sense of the way things happen, as well as his sources. Spenser has no such discipline: there is nothing to stop his poem going on for ever, and, worm-like, its organic perfection suffers little from its having been chopped off half-way. It is true that in Shakespeare various meanings can be drawn from one symbolic figure: Caliban, for example. But Caliban is first a unit. 'This is the law of symbolism,' writes Charles Williams in discussion of Spenser, 'that the symbol must be utterly itself before it can properly be a symbol' (*Reason and Beauty in the Poetic Mind*, 1933, p. 55). Whatever Caliban may mean, he is first Caliban, a rounded artistic whole. Spenser's significances are flat, and however many flatnesses are superimposed you do not create a multifacial globe. One sees in his work a transition between old-style allegory and a more rounded symbolism. He is struggling for it. He talks well of 'general' and 'particular' intentions, but in the completed result these are not tied up in a tight knot, it is all loose. His seeming complexity is never a complex profundity.

Though the main plan is, it seems, a magnificent failure, this does not preclude excellences in the parts. Its national, religious, and social implications are probably weaker than those personal and psychological, but these are often exquisite.

The poem is concerned heavily with man's erotic and sensuous nature, the problem of good and bad love. 'Love,' writes B. E. C. Davis (pp. 217, 220), is 'a cardinal motive' in all Spenser's poetry; it 'lies at the very foundation' of his 'cosmos'. In *The Allegory of Love* C. S. Lewis has well analysed Spenser's meticulous impressionism in conveying states of decadent and healthy sex-instincts. In the Bower of Bliss there is stress on idleness, artificiality ('metal ivy'), eye-lust, and an excessively conscious sex-appeal, as in the bathing nymphs:

> Then suddeinly both would themselues vnhele,[1]
> And th' amarous sweet spoiles to greedy eyes reuele.
>
> (II xii 64)

In contrast, the Garden of Adonis offers nature rather than art, frank sex-intercourse and a stress on creation (*The Allegory of Love*, 1936, pp. 324–6; 330–33). The naked Graces at VI x are, comments Lewis (331), 'engaged in doing something worth doing'; that is, dancing in a ring 'in order excellent' (VI x 13). Lewis analyses another related and tricky opposition: of passionate yet adulterous love, persistent in medieval poetry, to married faithfulness. The end and aim of the sex-substances in *The Faerie Queene* seems to be this marriage-ideal: a

1 disclose, uncover

thought with manifold implications for the study of Elizabethan drama. Chastity to Spenser 'means Britomart, married love'. The 'romance of marriage' replaces the 'romance of adultery' (*The Allegory of Love*, p. 340).

We must therefore not complain too readily that Spenser's attractive evils, as in the Bower of Bliss, prove him a dangerous moralist. Rather he is at work on a very subtle problem. Certain stanzas may suggest a failure, such as we find in *Comus*, to be sure about his own judgements; but then he may not be sure; which, of course, may be an artistic limitation. C. S. Lewis writes: 'The Bower of Bliss is not a place even of healthy animalism, or indeed of activity of any kind. ... It is a picture, one of the most powerful ever painted, of the whole sexual nature in disease' (p. 332). The attraction – and the accompanying descriptions are often attractive – is part of the disease, and the problem as old as the Garden of Eden. It is similarly insistent in Marlowe and Milton, though there is no trace of it in Lyly or Shakespeare. The puritan, whether Spenser or Milton, opposes, as did D. H. Lawrence, not a physical instinct but an insidious mind-perversion from which few of us can claim complete freedom. It is the enjoyment of an idea rather than a reality, and ideas can have an attractive intensity no reality quite touches. Properly to act and live an experience the mind must be subdued, dissolved, itself unpossessing; creative things are often accomplished half-aware; while excessive awareness tends to the immoral. Nevertheless some intensity of perception may perhaps be known in the very mental twist of such evil, some sense of the life-fire not known otherwise, depending partly on the breaking of conventional codes, whatever they be; an enjoyment of daring, parasitic on traditional principles. In so far as we describe or imagine an ultimate paradise, where neither creativeness nor ethical codes are properly relevant, a degree of essential freedom may again be helpful, if only to suit the perversions of our minds. Both the Bower of Bliss and the Garden of Adonis have their rights, and maybe this is why Spenser allows so much exquisite description, involving bird-song, to accompany temptation. The problem is obscure. We shall meet it again in study of Milton.

Spenser's puritanism is, in a sense, sex-flooded. In the Garden of Adonis we hear: 'Franckly each paramour his leman[1] knowes' (III vi 41); which is not true of the Bower of Bliss. The Temple of Venus is a place of 'ioy and amorous desire' (IV x 38) where, writes B. E. C. Davis (p. 219), 'every object serves to stimulate passion and the instinct to reproduce, unchecked by moral or religious scruple'. Again (p. 228), 'No moral law or religious inhibition mars the "sweete love" and "goodly merriment" of the Garden of Adonis, the "spotless pleasures" and unbridled Hedonism of Venus' Isle.' This is Spenser's central hope: untainted creative joy outside and beyond the world of good and evil, from a Shakespearean height where the Bower of Bliss will perhaps appear an insubstantial rather than evil dream. The continual search in Spenser's narrative for truth and reality, the supplanting of imposters and righting of erroneous choice, is an aspect of our problem. The conceits of lust correspond within Spenser's story to deceptive occurrences: though these may have ecclesiastical references, there are psychological references too. Spenser's humanism asserts that virtue is finally the only realism: a fulfillment of nature, not a thwarting of it. This he knows, and describes; yet does not, like Shakespeare, reveal.

His poem does not quite live the gospel it preaches. It lacks architectonic strength. It is fluid. Of the two qualities needed, that of a time-sequence and a strong, controlling, spatial design, it valuably possesses only the first. Its spatialized scheme, though vast, is unsubstantial. Exquisite descriptions of human art and various rich solids are frequent, but the poem as a whole has neither architectural stability nor solid richness. There is an addition of image to image, of verbal music to verbal music, a diffusion rather than concentration, an essentially stanzaic sequence, but no complex intertwisted multiplication of significances. There are modifying contrasts, but no dramatic intensity. Often Spenser seems more interested in his abstract doctrines than in his created world; or, if his world grips him, he seems to forget, for a stanza or two, his message, which is temporarily smothered by the luxuriant impressionism. The nature of his creation changes indecisively. Aristotle's idea that the constructing of a weighty central plot is a greater art than characterization or rhetoric comes to mind. Spenser's fluid, shifting significances make a boneless, piecemeal work. There is a lack of tough moral fibre in his constructional technique. Any amount of things happen, but you get slight sense of vital action. It is a dream-world, a 'fairy' world, perilously near decadence. It is

1 lover

sensuous, yet unreal. Janet Spens writes (pp. 69–70) that 'he never deals so much with the sensuous fact as with the mental translation of the fact – with the use which the soul's faculty makes of the impact and stir of the physical sensation; and he is more excited by the infinitely various web which man has woven to adorn and clothe the physical than by the simple physical facts themselves.' She notes elsewhere (pp. 122, 130) that the root evil in Spenser's world is the medieval *accidie*: that is, sloth, melancholia, inactivity. If this be true, there is an interesting relation between the poem's technical weakness and those sensuous and mental errors the poet so skilfully diagnoses. *The Faerie Queene* is an eye-feast, an ear-feast, a mind-feast: but it is not a shared action, it is without dramatic suspense. People do things, but at a distance, like figures on a tapestry. It is hard to feel events in relation to the whole. There is really no organic heart. Though Gloriana and Arthur are meant as such, they do not so function, do not receive from the whole action and pump back living significances. Consequently the body-structure lacks organic warmth. It tends to split, dissolve: the whole into books, books into cantos, cantos into events, events into descriptive luxuriance. The proper organic process is reversed. To compare it with a contemporary: in Thomas Sackville's Induction to *A Mirror for Magistrates* (1563) we have at least fine separate imaginative blocks (death, hell, Buckingham) in whose service images are powerfully used, thronging all their joint force into each little whole. Even in Spenser's shorter movements each whole is liable to obscurity by its parts. It is less than the sum of its parts. Instead of building up and cohering, the poem is always decomposing. Its finest units, being so independently fine, are, even if in themselves organic, rich rather with a cancerous and upstart vitality, drawing attention from that whole they should serve. Hence the baggy, bulgy, loose effect, the fluidity. 'Flowing water,' writes Miss Spens (p. 78), 'always fascinated Spenser.' Naturally. This fascination corresponds to a relaxed sensuousness, and that to an immorality of technique which just misses conviction, is over-mentalized and all but decadent. Spenser may explicitly favour his Garden of Adonis, with its upsurge of creative life; but we must go elsewhere for that. *The Faerie Queene* is itself one vast Bower of Bliss.

That is, it may be, an overstatement. I admit that I do not feel at home here. Possibly, were the poem complete and I had it in all detail and as a whole thoroughly comprehended, its design might appear satisfactory and its parts contributory. But it is very difficult to reach this, and difficult in a sense that the mental possession of Dante's poem is not. Spenser asks, and I think has undertaken, too much. It is a transition poem, aiming at an epic or medieval-heroic manner not deeply suitable to the age. Greek tragedy stands between us and Homer; the New Testament between us and Virgil; and Shakespeare between us and the *Morte d'Arthur*. The dramatic and complex continually supervene on the epic and the adventurous. A new dimension of significance interwoven with every action is, in the Renaissance world especially, urgent for expression. Spenser's poem has no *active* meaning, is not dramatically alive, because he has not found the action he believes in: action which, as in Shakespeare, is newly created, not a legendary reminiscence of a past chivalry. Greek tragedy and the New Testament are both powerfully realistic and metaphysical. Spenser's story is usually unworthy of his thought, of his metrical and stanzaic skill, of his impressionistic profusion. The action, as such, is weak.

True, Spenser with his subtle and comprehensive designing and his intention of a Gloriana and Arthur centrality attempts the typical patterning and dominant, fusing symbol that so often lend meaning and power to long works: he has the idea, though his vast scheme is too unwieldy for it. Many Shakespearian essences, moreover, are here. The heritage of the ages is combined with a contemporary royalism; human instinct, and especially Renaissance sensuousness, subtly analysed; pagan and Christian mythology entwined. Shakespeare's political thinking is forecast. I quote again from B. E. C. Davis (p. 228): 'The national pests disfiguring the land of Faerie – Error, Deceit, Tyranny, Anarchy, Lust, Detraction – all spring from the cardinal evil principle, Disorder.' The various knights are at work quelling the various forces of disorder. Spenser is, like all poets, at home among cosmic forces of all sorts; but something is wanting.

That 'something' is to be related to (i) the New Testament and great tragedy generally; (ii) individual human personality as an indissoluble and realized unit. The two are clearly related. Often in *The Faerie Queene* there is a subtle sensuous inconsistency, or if not that, an artistic indecision: he can insert a lovely bird-song stanza in his Bower of Bliss, or associate the most ghoulish horrors with an *intellectual* heresy. There is a certain want of imaginative common sense, and perhaps sincerity, as though ethical principles were not in the wider issues of this work perfectly integrated with aesthetic associations into his imaginative scheme. Though it witnesses a certain integrity, this indecision – when he is sure of evils he leaves you in no doubt, as in the masque of sins at the end of Book I – precludes the creation of strong human action and a convincing artistic structure. There is not that impact of terrific importance and native direction in the human adventure found in the New Testament drama and in Shakespeare. These generally force a dramatic, often tragic, expression. Conversely dramatic form helps to force creative profundity. Drama, with its close plot-texture and disciplinary limits, its centralized and realistic human concern, was the condition of full Elizabethan expression. The Elizabethan mind was too flooded with a diversity of ideas and images; Shakespeare knew no more than Spenser, but gained by being forced to say less. Steep banks make a stream deep, swift, and forceful – 'forceful' rather than 'fluid' – which without them is slothful, leisurely, and expansively shallow. Moreover the greatest dramatic expression depends also on a sense of human personality which I feel Spenser, to a final judgement, lacks. He is rarely inside his fictions, enduring their joys and terrors. Shakespeare writes from a hard core of trust in human personality, his own or others', which Spenser's fluid impressionism does not reach, so getting underneath his dramatic figure or action, creating from within and forcing others to share from within; and finally, the structure of his art form has, with little explicit doctrine, the tough-corded sanity of an unswerving experienced realism.

The Hymns present Spenser's visionary thought, while his sensuousness is most perfect in *Epithalamion*, wherein his fluid tendency, which becomes an explicit river-symbolism in *Prothalamion* and the union of Thames and Medway in *The Faerie Queene* (IV xi), functions beautifully in torrential celebration of his own marriage; but in referring these twin impulses, intellectual and emotional to epic action, he fails. *The Faerie Queene* has nevertheless certain passages of deep tragic meditation; its recurrent metaphysic of fertility is important; and piece, of symbolic description presenting pictures, legends in static designs sculptured figures, and so on, hold profound psychological meanings.

The poem perhaps improves after the more famous, but perhaps less powerful, first two books, moving from religious polemic towards, at times, a blazing humanism, a pagan-ritualistic apprehension wherein the closely related glories of sunfire and human love are finely advanced. The praise of Venus, sovereign of creation is especially valuable (IV x 37–47). Spenser's ranging cosmic intuition draws level with Bacon's *Advancement of Learning* and Pope's *Essay on Man*, as in the dialogue between Artegall and the Giant concerning the divine ordering of the physical universe (V ii 30–50). The poetry grows more plain, virile and athletic (as at III xi 25); with similes of sharp, realistic observation and sense of elemental vigour (see IV vi 14; V ii 50), and a remarkable projection of animal life in fierce action (see V ii 15; V xi 12). There is, once at least, a Shakespearian inwardness of dramatic sympathy in description of Britomart's varying anxiety and distress, compared finally to a child's wayward grief (V vi 1–14); and once strong action becomes itself significant in Britomart's penetration of fire to rescue Amoret from sensuous enchantment (III xi 21–xii 45). Britomart is Spenser's most satisfying person. She is a comprehensive conception, in her masculine dress and armour signifying an integration of sexual principles, as does Venus at IV x 41; a creature of romantic action, challenging purity, and – we are told, though perhaps scarcely made to feel – ardent love. Dedicated to a dream-lover, she is meant to attain successful human consummation, though her attractiveness symbolizing the feminine and finally matrimonial ideal is rather strained by her twice conquering in fight her future lord before their union. Artegall cuts a sorry figure: 'Ah my deare Lord,' says Britomart to him during a characteristic rescue, 'What May-game hath misfortune made of you?' (V vii 40). She herself, however, accurately personifies what the fiction as a whole does not attain: the marriage of strong action with emotional purity.

Spenser's expressly *gentle* humanism, which precludes any convincing presentation of heroic conflict as such and leads to excessive reliance on spiritual content as opposed to realistic form – and this is what we mean by allegory – nevertheless itself draws him finally nearer to the consistently trusting humanists, Lyly, Shakespeare and Pope, than to the somewhat aesthetically turbulent and variously forceful distrusters, Marlowe and Milton. His attempt to convey in philosophic and epic form a flooding sensuousness which penetrates so many creeks and ramifications of human desire, good or bad, heralds a new line of poetry to be concerned with (i) the erotic impulse as the central drive to an expanding apprehension of man's at once earthy–natural and fiery–cosmic setting, and (ii) the problem of action, involving conceptions royalistic and communal; while both are to be related to man's tragic destiny and the spirit, though not necessarily the dogmas, of Christianity.

(6 – 16)

Hallett Smith

from *Elizabethan Poetry* 1952

E.K., whoever he was, was a mixed blessing. His confusions and his errors have been straightened out by modern scholarship, but one of his contributions, a classification of the eclogues, seems to have been very little utilized.

This classification would read as follows:

Plaintive: 1st (January), 6th (June), 11th (November), 12th (December)
Moral: 2nd (February), 5th (May), 7th (July), 9th (September), 10th (October)
Recreative: 3rd (March), 4th (April), 8th (August)

A glance at this list will show that the three kinds, if the distinction between them is valid, are quite skillfully scattered through the pattern of the whole. There are five moral eclogues, four plaintive and three recreative. The division into kinds, even though it is of course not absolute, serves as a means to achieve variety, and it bears some relationship to the adherence of some of the eclogues to the atmosphere of the season concerned. The variety of verse forms is another means by which the *Calender* distinguishes itself. But with all this care to achieve variety, there is also a principle of continuity stronger than the mere sequence of the months. In each of the three 'forms or ranks', as E.K. calls them, two of the examples occur consecutively: the third and fourth eclogues are recreative, the ninth and tenth are moral, and the eleventh and twelfth are plaintive. The over-all structure of the *Calender*, then, is one which combines similarity and contrasts, variety and continuity. The complex relationships of theme, of style and of 'rank or form' give *The Shepheardes Calender* a vitality and interest which no other collection of pastoral eclogues in English can boast.

The *Calender* begins and ends with plaintive eclogues. This is appropriate to the winter season of January and December, and it also sets the over-all tone for the series. . . .

'January' is simple in style. The plaintive eclogues increase in complexity up through 'November' (a piece which E.K. says he prefers to all the rest), and then the style is somewhat simpler again for the final 'December'. 'January' mainly equates the lovelorn shepherd's state of mind with nature around him. The poem might be called an extended simile:

Thou barrein ground, whome winters wrath hath wasted,
Art made a myrrhour, to behold my plight.

(19–20)

Rather than a simile, it is a mirror situation; the comparison between object and image extends both ways, and each has its validity. For example, stanza 5 describes the shepherd's heart, blood and pain in terms of winter weather. The sixth stanza does the reverse: it turns the woodland into an abandoned and disconsolate lover of birds and flowers. What does this leave for the spectator as a point of view? It is impossible to keep the position of the shepherd, for he is sometimes only a reflection of nature; it is impossible to keep the point of view of nature, for it is often only a reflection of the moods and feelings of the shepherd. The result is a kind of 'distance' or objectivity, which gives us both shepherd and nature in perspective, in the round. We are not sure which is object and which is reflection because they reverse roles. Sometimes this is made explicit by means of rhetorical figures, which commentators who belong to the tribe of E.K. have noticed:

With mourning pyne I, you with pyning mourne.

(48)

This, addressed to the sheep, seems stilted and frigid under the comment of those who merely give the name for the rhetorical figure; seen as a detail which reinforces the whole mirror device of the eclogue, it acquires some artistic significance.

The device of lovers in series, or the fragmentary cross-eyed Cupid situation, is also used here. As Hobbinol is to Colin ('His clownish gifts and curtsies I disdaine', line 57), so Colin is to Rosalind ('And of my rurall musick holdeth scorne', line 64). This device also provides scale and 'distance'. Finally, it leads up to the resolution, in which Colin breaks his pipe (the symbolic significance of poetry as such is very great in the *Calender*, and this is an unobtrusive and yet powerful way of opening the theme) and concludes his outburst ...

'June', the second of the plaintive eclogues, is a dialogue in form; the complaint here derives its strength from the conflict of two situations and points of view and finally proceeds to paradox. The contrast is between Hobbinol and Colin. Hobbinol represents the standard, happy pastoral existence. He has found, according to Colin, that Paradise which Adam lost. This is one way of making the equation between mind and nature, content and Arcadia. But Colin is not so fortunate; he has grown older, sadder, and wiser. His youth was marked by love and poetry, 'But ryper age such pleasures doth reproue' (line 36); sad experience has turned him away from vain love and 'those weary wanton toyes' of poetry (line 48).

The paradox develops when Hobbinol praises his poetry: Colin was able to teach the birds themselves how to sing, and when the Muses heard him, even they had to confess themselves outdone in their art. Colin replies by denying all the ambitious implications of this praise and asserts that his aims are very modest:

But pyping lowe in shade of lowly groue,
I play to please my selfe, all be it ill.

Nought weigh I, who my song doth prayse or blame,
Ne striue to winne renowne, or passe the rest:
With shepheard sittes not, followe flying fame:
But feede his flocke in fields, where falls hem best.

(71–6)

This is, of course, the shepherd's denial of ambition, the literary form of the central pastoral philosophy of life. And Spenser uses this poetic equivalent of 'the quiet mind' as a background for Colin's proudest boast:

The God of shepheards *Tityrus* is dead,
Who taught me homely, as I can, to make.

He, whilst he liued, was the soueraigne head
Of shepheards all, that bene with loue ytake.

(81–4)

Colin, although he protests his verses are rough and rude, is still the
true heir of Chaucer. Here is the paradox: he is both uncouth and
unambitious, yet he is the pupil of great artists and proud to be in
their tradition. There is a contrast of mood, too. Chaucer, as Tityrus,
was able to dampen the flames that love bred in him and to entertain
the shepherds with merry tales to keep them awake, but Colin cannot
achieve this gaiety. Therefore, in the act of bewailing his sad state,
he says he is not able to continue, and instructs the other shepherds
(inferior to him in ability at complaints) to tell Rosalind what she has
done.

The involutions of the complaint are quite elaborately exploited
in this eclogue, and the contrasts and paradoxes might absorb all of
our attention. It is worth noticing, however, that Spenser has really
shifted the grounds for the pastoral complaint. There is a good deal
more about poetry here than about love. The unhappy love situation
is felt to be important chiefly because it is said to affect Colin's poetry.
The shift has been subtly managed, and no doubt those gullible
readers who follow E.K.'s challenge and speculate on the identity of
Rosalind miss it; but they are hardly reading the poem anyway; they
are playing with biographical puzzles. E.K. in the argument to the
eclogue says nothing about poetry, but of course poetry is the main
theme of 'June'; there is a link here with the next plaintive eclogue,
'November', and with 'October', its predecessor, also.

'November', like 'December', follows the model set by Marot in
pastoral. The November poem is a dialogue between Thenot and
Colin, leading up to the elaborate pastoral elegy which Colin composed to celebrate the death of Dido, the great shepherd's daughter.
The most interesting thing about 'November' is not the identity of
Dido, whatever the commentators say; it is the elaborateness of the
elegy, at the most formal and most elevated level of the complaint.
E.K. did not know the identity of Dido, but he declared this eclogue
his favorite, 'farre passing his [Marot's] reache, and in myne opinion
all other the Eglogues of this booke'. Plaintive poetry starts with the
complaining lover, then has to refine him out of it for the sake of the

form and objectivity of the work of art; finally, it discovers in the formal pastoral elegy a vehicle which permits elaborate verse technique together with heightened rhetorical style and a subject which is large enough to permit the expression of deeply felt personal sorrow within the limits of decorum. It is the emancipation of the lover's complaint.

Formally, 'November' contains the invocation to the Muse (line 53), the calling on others to wail (lines 63 ff.), the description of the effects of her death on Nature (line 83 ff. and 123 ff.), the parade of the nymphs (lines 143 ff.), and the change from grief to joy (lines 163 ff.), which characterize the conventional pastoral elegy. From these conventional features of the elegy the poet has his opportunity in varying and increasing the emotion. The combination of grief and joy makes a 'doleful pleasaunce', as Thenot calls it; he hesitates whether to rejoice or weep. This fine balance is what the pastoral elegy tries to achieve . . .

'November' is connected rather more definitely with the season than some of the other eclogues. The mood of the elegy is prepared for by the explanation of Colin that other types of poetry are unsuitable for this time of year. This contrast calls to mind another, that between the elaborate elegy for Dido in 'November' and the elaborate praise of Eliza in 'April'. The two are in a sense complementary, and their importance is clearly marked for us by the wealth of metrical invention Spenser lavished upon them.

'December', the final eclogue, returns to monologue and rounds out the tonal pattern 'even as the first beganne', as E.K. says. This poem, too, is dependent on Marot, but a more important influence is that of the calendars, with their symbolic representations of the four seasons as representing the stages of a man's life.[1] The career of Colin, which I take to be somewhat more fictional than the commentators do, is here summed up. In spring he experienced exuberance and freedom, felt pride in his songs. In summer he learned his craft, but was smitten with love. In harvest he reaped only a weedy crop of care. And now winter comes:

Winter is come, that blowes the balefull breath,

---

1 See Mary Parmenter, 'Spenser's *Twelve Aeglogues Proportionable to the Twelve Monethes*', *E.L.H.*, vol. 3, 1936, p. 191.

And after Winter commeth timely death.
                    (149–50)

The paradox here depends upon the idea of a calendar: it runs out
as time runs out; and yet the calendar of months is still good, it records something which is permanent. Just so the poet, saying adieu
to his delights, to his love, to his sheep and his woods, to his friend,
as Colin does in the last stanza, is by the very form in which he says
it achieving something that stops time, that contradicts and denies
the Death which is the subject. The detachment or the 'distance'
between the content or argument and the poetry itself produces a
paradoxical relationship between them. That Spenser's use of the
calendar device was useful for 'scale' was first pointed out, I think,
by Pope: 'The addition he has made of a Calendar to his Eclogues,
is very beautiful: since by this, besides that general moral of innocence and simplicity, which is common to other authors of pastoral,
he has one peculiar to himself; he compares human Life to the several
Seasons, and at once exposes to his readers a view of the great and
little worlds, in their various changes and aspects.' The missing
emblem for Colin is explained by E.K.: 'The meaning wherof is that
all thinges perish and come to theyr last end, but workes of learned
wits and monuments of Poetry abide for euer.' This is clearly the implication of the whole eclogue and, as summary, of the whole
Shepheardes Calender. Shakespeare found in Ovid the same commonplace and developed it in a non-pastoral setting in his sonnets. The
pastoral handling of the theme enjoys an added richness, for, as the
reply to Marlowe's *Passionate Shepherd* shows, time is the answer to the
pastoral ideal. But what if, in poetry, there is an answer to the answer?

The five 'moral' eclogues, 'February', 'May', 'July', 'September',
and 'October', are arranged in such a way as to develop a climax, just
as the plaintive eclogues were. In this series the climax comes in the
September eclogue, and the succeeding and final one, 'October',
turns as the plaintive series did, specifically to the subject of poetry. If
in the plaintive series the difficulty was to build out of the given state
of mind of the lovesick shepherd an expression which would do
justice to the emotion itself and yet reconcile with it the verve of the
poetry, the problem in the moral eclogues is to find a function for
poetry in the social, political, and cultural environment.

Far from being escapist, pastoral poetry was the most apt of all the kinds for serious humanistic purposes. Because of the central concern with the relative value of wealth, power, riches, and the 'contented mind', and because of its conventional machinery of shepherds, with their singing contests, debates, and complaints, the eclogue lent itself readily to indirect or slightly masked criticism of contemporary affairs. It had been so used by Virgil, and the Renaissance imitators of the greatest of Roman poets had developed the satirical, critical strain still further. Spenser's chief model in this series is Mantuan, especially his eclogues 7, 8 and 9. But he fuses with Mantuan's serious, satirical manner something from his own English Tityrus, Chaucer. It is not so apparent to us as it was to the sixteenth century that Chaucer is a very moral poet; Spenser was chiefly impressed with his use of fables. So 'February', 'May' and 'September' utilize Aesopic or pseudo-Aesopic material, told in the manner of Chaucer. The fable gives a narrative interest to these eclogues; there is something more primitive and perhaps more solid in their stories than there is in the extended emotion of the plaintive series. For this reason, perhaps, as well as to produce further variety, Spenser has devised a characteristic style for these eclogues – rough, uncouth, non-lyrical and full of dialect words. The matter is harsh, the meter is old-fashioned, suggesting the alliterative accentual verse of an earlier age in 'February', the stolid fourteeners of the 1560s and 1570s in 'July'.

'February' tells the fable of the oak and the briar, after a dramatic introduction in the form of a quarrel between the young shepherd Cuddie and the old shepherd Thenot. There is a connexion here with the time of year, for old age and winter are explicitly identified:

For Age and Winter accord full nie,
This chill, that cold, this crooked, that wrye.
(27–8)

The conflict of age and youth is very common in the pastoral mode. It is simply another form of the central problem which makes pastoral – the problem of the values inherent in the good life. Here the quarrel is resolved by a story, the briar finding out when winter comes that it has been dependent upon the old oak. So the threat of winter and rough weather or old age, when time drives the flocks from field to fold, is the basic challenge to the pastoral ideal and must be faced. The fable in the February eclogue is simple, but its theme is central.

The May eclogue first introduces what E.K. calls 'some Satyrical bitternesse'; it is an attack on Catholic pastors, who are not true shepherds but deceitful and malicious, like the fox that devoured the kid. This involves of course the equation of shepherds–pastors–priests; more significantly, it poses the question of the relative value of the gay, irresponsible pastoral life and the conscientious tending of sheep. The month of May is utilized to give the shepherd Palinode an opportunity to urge participation in the pagan revelries of May Day and to have Piers, the spokesman for the serious, Protestant, point of view, reprove these sports as follies, fit for 'Younkers' but reprehensible in men of elder wit. The connexion between this subject of true and false pastors (a theme which Milton later developed, with even more satirical bitterness, in *Lycidas*) and the personal, direct, moral effect of these eclogues lies in the subject of friendship and trust. Palinode believes that tolerance and resignation are the only ways to deal with differences between shepherds:

Let none mislike of that may not be mended:
So conteck¹ soone by concord mought be ended.
(162–3)

But Piers, who is given the advantage of being the teller of the fable, says that no peace or compromise is possible with that shepherd 'that does the right way forsake'. The story is told with more art and elaboration than the story of the oak and briar; besides, in accordance with the climactic scheme of the series, the whole eclogue is more vigorous and outspoken. A link with a later moral eclogue, 'September', is prepared in the lines (126–9) about the wolves in sheep's clothing. In the lines just preceding these, Spenser prepares for the theme of 'July'. By the time 'July' is reached, the basic theme has been so clearly introduced, through the narratives of the preceding moral eclogues, that now it can be debated directly, taken out of the fable framework, and presented dramatically. Spenser chooses the old familiar 4–3–4–3 ballad measure, that of the versified psalms and of all matter to be committed to memory, the most familiar of Elizabethan verse forms.

1 strife, discord

Thomalin, in a long speech, gives the conventional praise of shepherds derived from Mantuan, which we have already noticed. His emphasis is that the true shepherds are not ambitious, not aspiring, but humble and low. This serves as an image which works in several ways: Thomalin and Morrell represent, respectively, the valley and the hill, and the woodcut at the head of the eclogue naïvely shows them stationed at these two points while they hold their debate: Thomalin represents the Puritan ideal of a clergy unelevated, humble, and devoted to pastoral care, while Morrell represents the Catholic or Anglican clergy gloating in worldly pomp; most general and most significant of all, Thomalin represents the mean estate, the central theme of pastoralism, and Morrell embodies the aspiring mind. . . .

'September', though it has been called 'the least interesting and most difficult' (Herford) of the eclogues in *The Shepheardes Calender*, and even more harshly 'a tedious though fluent stream of commonplace complaint' (Palgrave), is really the climax of the moral series.[1] Here the bitterness about bad shepherds is stronger than in any of the other eclogues; here the verse form is a hard, punching couplet. Hobbinol and Diggon Davy do not argue, but Diggon reports to Hobbinol the sad state of things in the country he has just visited, and Hobbinol provides the choral comment. It is again the pastoral assertion:

Content who liues with tryed state,
Neede feare no chaunge of frowning fate.

(70–71)

In this eclogue, as Friedland points out,[2] the technique of the fable is brought to its climax; here the fable is an integral part of the eclogue, not just appended for illustrative interest as in 'February' and 'May'. The fable this time is a genuinely poetic idea. Spenser's source was Mantuan, as usual in the moral eclogues, but the idea, concisely expressed in Matthew vii, 15, 'Beware of false prophets, which come to you in sheep's clothing, but inwardly they are ravening wolves,' appears often in the sermons of the time,[1] and its suggestions are so wide that it provides the satisfactory image for the unification of the

1 Variorum *Minor Poems*, vol. 1, pp. 350–51.
2 L. S. Friedland, 'Spenser as a Fabulist', *S.A.B.*, vol. 12, 1937, p. 147.

pastoral, religious and social ideas in this whole group of poems. The shepherd's life is always stressed as one in which the characteristics of the mind and will are important; the conditions for human existence are most favorable, and there are few dangers from pride or ambition, but the goddesses still appear before a shepherd and demand that he choose between them. A wrong choice is always possible. The shepherd is still man seen simply, but his idyllic life is now put upon a basis of moral responsibility, and the existence of evil is recognized.

Hobbinol's statement presents an awareness of human limitations and an acceptance of them, within the pastoral framework, as sad but valuable. Here is a link, in mood, with the encompassing tone of the plaintive eclogues, and the moral poems are finding their place in the unity of the whole.

The October eclogue, which E.K. placed among the moral eclogues, has seemed to some students to belong by itself because it treats the subject of poets and their low state at the present time instead of the problem of the good pastor. But as I have shown, the plaintive series developed toward a self-conscious emphasis on poetry, and it is only according to the pattern that the moral eclogues should do so too. Herford, who separates 'October' from its group, says that 'this noble and pregnant piece is the very core of *The Shepheard's Calender*'.[2] It is interesting, by the way, to see how the critics decide what is central in the book. Greenlaw, partly because he reads the poems so heavily as historical allegory and propaganda, sees the moral eclogues together as 'the core and heart' of the *Calender*.[3] R. E. N. Dodge calls the Rosalind story 'the central theme of *S.C.*'[4] I have been trying to show that there is not a core of something wrapped up in a covering of pastoral, but that the pastoral idea, in its various ramifications, *is* the *Calender*. . . .

The shepherd as pastor is responsible for caring for his flock; he has his reward in protecting them from the wolves. What, then, are the responsibilities of the shepherd as poet? Shall he be content 'To feede youthes fancie, and the flocking fry'[1] (line 14) with his dapper

1 W. L. Renwick (ed.), *The Shepherd's Calendar*, 1930, p. 213, quotes usefully from Thomas Cartwright.

2 C. H. Herford (ed.), *Shepheards Calender*, 1907, p. xlv.

3 Variorum *Minor Poems*, vol. 1, p. 603. 4 ibid., p. 602.

ditties? Is he a mere entertainer? No, Piers replies, he can influence
them morally. Here Piers is giving voice to the justification for poetry
that runs through Elizabethan criticism from Sir Philip Sidney to
Milton:

> O what an honor is it, to restraine
> The lust of lawlesse youth with good aduice:
> Or pricke them forth[2] with pleasaunce of thy vaine,[3]
> Whereto thou list their trayned willes entice.

> (21-4)

But if the lowly are not grateful for instruction, then the poet should
turn to heroic poetry, celebrating deeds of greatness and becoming
the spokesman for the national spirit. This was the pattern followed
by Virgil, who, being favored by Maecenas, was enabled to rise above
the humble style of the pastoral and write the epic of Rome. Yet as
Cuddie recalls this, he says that in these degenerate days the poet has
no such prospect; he must make 'rymes of rybaudrye' or resign in
favor of the doggerel-monger Tom Piper.

   This concern over the place of poetry is not so much professional
as it is moral. True, some glances at the niggardly ways of patrons are
taken over from Mantuan, but the primary concern is for the use and
value of poetry, and the final conclusion is that it is holy. The Platonism which here enters the *Calender* serves this purpose. It gives a
theory of poetic inspiration which allies the poet with the priest.
Their work is in essence divine. Love is a source of such divine inspiration, and even love poetry may provide it, as is the case with
Colin. Cuddie, however, can approximate the high elevated style of
truly inspired poetry only by imagining himself aroused by wine, and
when he does we have, for a moment, heroic poetry. But the feeling
must soon subside and return within the scope of pastoral:

> But ah my corage cooles ere it be warme,
> For thy, content vs in thys humble shade:
> Where no such troublous tydes[1] han vs assayde,[2]

1 young creatures   2 spur them on
3 poetic vein

Here we our slender pipes may safely charme.
(115–18)

The contrast between the style of this eclogue and that of the other moral eclogues is very striking. It is as if Spenser deliberately made the satirical eclogues rough and uncouth for reasons of decorum and effectiveness of the moral ideas, but culminated his series in an eclogue which not only showed that the poet is as directly connected with the divine in his business as the pastor is, but that his sounds, too, are closer to heavenly music than to the sounds of Tom Piper.

(33–48)

C. S. Lewis

from *English Literature in the Sixteenth Century*   1954

Formally considered, *The Faerie Queene* is the fusion of two kinds, the medieval allegory and the more recent romantic epic of the Italians. Because it is allegory, and allegory neither strictly religious nor strictly erotic but universal, every part of the poet's experience can be brought in: because it is romantic epic, a certain unity is immediately imposed on all that enters it, for all is embodied in romantic adventures. 'Faerie land' itself provides the unity – a unity not of plot but of *milieu*. *A priori* the ways of Faerie Land might seem 'so exceeding spatious and wide' that such a unity amounted to nothing, but this is not found to be so. Few poems have a greater harmony of atmosphere. The multiplicity of the stories, far from impairing the unity, supports it; for just that multiplicity, that packed fullness of 'vehement adventures', is the quality of Faerie Land; as tragedy is the quality of Hardy's Wessex.

When I last wrote about *The Faerie Queene* some fifteen years ago, I do not think I sufficiently emphasized the originality and fruitfulness of this structural invention. Perhaps it can be best brought out by considering the problems it solves. Spenser, let us say, has experienced in himself and observed in others sensual temptation; frivolous

1 times   2 afflicted

gallantry; the imprisonment and frustration of long, serious and self-condemned passions; happy love; and religious melancholy. You could, perhaps, get all this into a lengthy, biographical novel, but that form did not exist in his time. You could get it into half a dozen plays; but only if your talent were theatrical, and only if you were ready to see these states of the heart (which were Spenser's real concern) almost smothered by the Elizabethan demands for an exciting plot and comic relief. But in Faerie Land it is all quite simple. All the states become people or places in that country. You meet the first in the Bower of Acrasia, the second in Malecasta's castle, the third in the House of Busirane, the fourth on Mount Acidale, and the fifth in Orgoglio's dungeons and Despair's cave. And this is not scissors and paste work. Such bowers, such castles, such ogres are just what we require to meet in Faerie Land: they are as necessary for filling the country as the country is for accommodating them. Whatever incidental faults the poem may have, it has, so to speak, a healthy constitution: the matter and the form fit each other like hand and glove.

This primary structural idea is reinforced by two others, the first internal to each book, and the second striding across from book to book through the whole poem. Thus in each book Spenser decided that there should be what I have called an 'allegorical core' (or shrine, or inner stage) where the theme of that book would appear disentangled from the complex adventures and reveal its unity: the House of Holiness in I, the House of Alma in II, the Garden of Adonis in III, the Temple of Venus in IV, the Church of Isis in V, Mount Acidale in VI, and the whole appeal of Mutabilitie in the unfinished book. (Since the position of the core within the book is variable, no conclusion can be based on the numbering of those two cantos.) Next in dignity to the core in each book comes the main allegorical story of the book (Guyon's or Calidore's quest). Beyond that is a loose fringe of stories which may be fully allegorical (like Scudamore's visit to the cottage of Care) or merely typical (like Paridell's seduction of Hellenore) or not allegorical at all (like the story told by the Squire of Dames to Satyrane). Thus the appearance, so necessary to the poem's quality, of pathless wandering is largely a work of deliberate and successful illusion. Spenser, for reasons I have indicated, may not always know where he is going as regards the particular stories: as regards the symphony of moods, the careful arrangement of different degrees of allegory and different degrees of seriousness, he is always in command. . . .

It is in Spenser that the myth of the visionary mistress effectively enters modern literature. His prince is the precursor of Novalis's Heinrich, of Alastor and of Keats's Endymion. Allegorically, we are told, he is Magnificence; and it is clear that, in so far as this means anything Aristotelian, it means Aristotle's Magnanimity. He is seeking Gloriana who is glory, and glory is honour, and honour is the goal of Aristotle's Magnanimous Man. The name of his foster-father, Timon, underlines this. But then glory and honour are difficult words. We found in Douglas's *Palace* that the sight of true Honour was the vision of God. We know, if we are Christians, that glory is what awaits the faithful in heaven. We know, if we are Platonists – and a reading of Boethius would make us Platonists enough for this – that every inferior good attracts us only by being an image of the single real good. The false Florimell attracts by being like the true, the true Florimell by being like Beauty itself. Earthly glory would never have moved us but by being a shadow or *idolon* of the Divine Glory, in which we are called to participate. Gloriana is 'the idole of her Makers great magnificence'. The First Fair is desired in all that is desired. It is only, I think, in the light of such conceptions that the quest of Spenser's Arthur can be understood. Arthur is an embodiment of what Professor Nygren calls 'Eros religion', the thirst of the soul for the Perfection beyond the created universe. Only this explains the terms in which Spenser describes his preliminary vision of Gloriana (i ix). The laughter of all Nature, the grassy bed shared with the 'royall Mayd', the ravishing words ('no living man like wordes did ever heare') must, it seems to me, be taken for a picture not of nascent ambition and desire for fame but either of natural or celestial love; and they are certainly not simply a picture of the former. Only this explains the scene in which Arthur pursues Florimell (iii i, iv). Those who accuse him of inconstancy forget that he had seen the glory only in a vision by night. Hence, following Florimell,

Oft did he wish, that Lady faire mote bee

His Faery Queene, for whom he did complaine:
Or that his Faery Queene were such, as shee.
                                    (iii iv 54)

The best parallel to this is the repeated (and always disappointed) belief of the Trojans in *Aeneid*, III, that they have already found the *mansuram urbem*. It is in the very nature of the Platonic quest and the Eros religion that the soul cannot know her true aim till she has achieved it. The seeker must advance, with the possibility at each step of error, beyond the false Florimells to the true, and beyond the true Florimell to the Glory. Only such an interpretation will explain the deep seriousness and the explicitly religious language of Arthur's subsequent soliloquy (55–60).

We must not, of course, forget that Gloriana is also Queen Elizabeth. This was much less chilling and shocking to the sixteenth century than it is to us. Quite apart from any prudent desire to flatter his prince (in an age when flattery had a ceremonial element in it) or from any romantic loyalty which he may have felt and probably did feel as an individual, Spenser knew that even outside poetry all reigning sovereigns were *ex officio* vicegerents and images of God. No orthodox person doubted that in this sense Elizabeth was 'an idole' of the divine magnificence. It is also easy to misunderstand the sentence 'Gloriana is Elizabeth'. She *is* Elizabeth in a sense which does not prevent Belphoebe from also being Elizabeth nor Elizabeth from being also a remote, unborn descendant of Artegall and Britomart who are contemporaries of Gloriana. Modern readers, trained on a strict *roman-à-clef* like Dryden's *Absalom*, hardly know how to sit lightly enough to what is called the 'historical allegory' in Spenser. 'Historical parallels' or 'fugitive historical allusions' would be better names. The scene we have just been discussing is a good example. Arthur may at some moments and in some senses 'be' Leicester: but the poet is certainly not meaning to proclaim to the public that Elizabeth had shared her favourite's bed. (For though Arthur met Gloriana in a vision, it was not quite a vision: there was 'pressed gras where she had lyen'.) In general it must be remembered that the identifications of Gloriana and Belphoebe are the only two in the whole poem that have Spenser's authority. That of Duessa was made so early that we may take it for certain. As for the rest, it is well to remember Spenser's own warning 'how doubtfully all allegories may be construed'. He can never have expected most of his historical meanings to be clear to more than a privileged minority of readers: it is reasonable to suppose that he seldom wrote a canto which depended on them for its main interest. No poet would embark his fame in such an unseaworthy vessel. Nor do I think that attempts in our own day to recover such meanings are at all likely to be fruitful. Great learning and skill have been spent on them. Every increase in our knowledge suggests a fresh allegory. If historical parallels were harder to come by they would convince more; but their multiplicity rather suggests to me how hard it is for a poet to feign an event which will not resemble some real event – or half a dozen real events. . . .

Hitherto I have been speaking about the structural or (in that sense) 'poetic' ideas of *The Faerie Queene*, the inventions which make it the poem it is. Critics often, however, speak of a poet's 'ideas' in quite a different sense, meaning his opinions or (in extreme cases) his philosophy. These are not often so important in a work of art as its 'idea' or 'ideas' in the first sense; the first two books of *Gulliver* depend much more on the 'idea' of big and little men than on any great novelty or profundity in Swift's 'ideas' about politics and ethics. Spenser's thought, however, has been so variously estimated that we cannot pass it over without some discussion.

Some scholars believe that in parts of *The Faerie Queene* they can find Spenser systematically expounding the doctrines of a school. But if so, the school can hardly be defined as anything narrower than Platonized Protestantism. He certainly believes in Predestination. 'Why shouldst thou then despeire, that chosen art?' says Una to the Red Cross Knight (1 ix 53). But this will hardly make Spenser Calvinist as distinct from Lutheran, nor either as distinct from Augustinian, or simply Pauline. It is also true that the virtues we meet in the House of Holiness – Humility, Zeal, Reverence, Faith, Hope, Charity, Mercy, and Contemplation – can all be paralleled in Calvin's *Institutio*; but they are not arranged in the same order, and the things themselves would be likely to occur in any Christian teaching whatever. It is argued, again, that the quests on which the faerie knights are engaged, and especially the scene (1 x 63) in which Contemplation commands St George to turn back from the vision of the New Jerusalem and finish the 'royal maides bequeathed care', reflect the activism of Protestant (and, particularly, Calvinist) ethics and its rejection of the contemplative life. They may: but it is not certain. The quests of the knights are after all allegorical. A combat with Error or with the Old Dragon does not necessarily symbolize the active life. St George's return from the mountain of Contemplation is quite as close to the return of Plato's 'guardians' (*Republic*, 519 d et seq.) as to anything in Protestant theology. And in any case, St George in the poem must return because the story must go on. It is equally true that Spenser asserts total depravity ('If any strength we haue, it is to ill', I x I) and 'loathes' this world 'this state of life so tickle' (*Mut.*, viii I), and that this fits well enough with Calvinist theology. But hardly less well with Lutheran. Indeed expressions very similar can be found in nearly all Christian writers. And something not unlike them can be found even in Platonism. When scholars claim that there is a profound difference of temper between Platonism and these world-renouncing attitudes, I do not know what they mean. There is difference of course; but few pagan systems adapt themselves so nearly to total depravity and *contemptus mundi* as the Platonic. The emotional overtones of the words 'Renaissance Platonism' perhaps help us to forget that Plato's thought is at bottom other-worldly, pessimistic and ascetic; far more ascetic than Protestantism. The natural universe is for Plato, a world of shadows, of Helens false as Spenser's false Florimell (*Rep.*, 586 A–C); the soul has come into it at all only because she lost her wings in a better place (*Phaedr.*, 246 D–248 E); and the life of wisdom, while we are here, is a practice or exercise of death (*Phaed.*, 80 D–81 A).

I am not arguing that Spenser was not a Calvinist. *A priori* it is very likely that he was. But his poetry is not so written as to enable us to pick out his own beliefs in distinct separation from kindred beliefs. When a modern writer is didactic he endeavours, like Shaw or M. Sartre, to throw his own 'ideas' into sharp relief, distinguishing them from the orthodoxy which he wants to attack. Spenser is not at all like that. Political circumstances lead him at times to stress his opposition to Roman Christianity; and if pressed, he would no doubt admit that where the pagan doctors differed from the Christian, the pagan doctors were wrong. But in general he is concerned with agreements, not differences. He is, like nearly all his contemporaries, a syncretist. He never dreamed of expounding something he could call 'his philosophy'. His business was to embody in moving images the common wisdom. It is this that may easily arouse distrust of him in a modern reader. We feel that the man who could weld together, or think that he had welded together, so many diverse elements, Protestant, chivalric, Platonic, Ovidian, Lucretian and pastoral, must have been very vague and shallow in each. But here we need to remember the difference between his basic assumption and ours. It is scepticism, despair of objective truth, which has trained us to regard diverse philosophies as historical phenomena, 'period pieces', not to be pitted against one another but each to be taken in its purest form and savoured on the historical palate. Thinking thus, we despise syncretism as we despise Victorian Gothic. Spenser could not feel thus, because he assumed from the outset that the truth about the universe was knowable and in fact known. If that were so, then of course you would expect agreements between the great teachers of all ages just as you expect agreements between the reports of different explorers. The agreements are the important thing, the useful and interesting thing. Differences, far from delighting us as precious manifestations of some unique temper or culture, are mere errors which can be neglected. Such intellectual optimism may be mistaken; but granted the mistake, a sincere and serious poet is bound to be, from our point of view, a syncretist. I believe that Sidney and Shakespeare are in this respect like Spenser, and to grasp this is one of the first duties of their critics. I do not think Shakespeare wrote a single line to express 'his' ideas. What some call his philosophy, he would have called common knowledge.

It is this that makes the thought of *The Faerie Queene*, as Professor Osgood says, 'somehow unmeasurable'. Spenser expected his readers to find in it not his philosophy but their own experience – everyone's experience – loosened from its particular contexts by the universalizing power of allegory. It is, no doubt, true that Spenser was far from being an exact thinker or a precise scholar in any department of human knowledge. Whatever he had tried to write would have had a certain vagueness about it. But most poetry is vague about something. In Milton the theology is clear, the images vague. In Racine the passions and the logic of events are clear, but the 'manners' vague and generalized. What is clear in Spenser is the image; Pyrochles beating the water while he cries 'I burne, I burne, I burne', or Disdain strutting, crane-like, on tiptoes, with legs that break but do not bleed, and as good as new, still glaring and still tiptoed, when he has been set up again. That is why it is at once so true and so misleading to call his poetry dream-like; its images have the violent clarity and precision which we often find in actual dreams, but not the dimness and evasiveness which the overtones of the word *dream-like* (based more on waking reverie than real dreaming) usually call up. These images are not founded on, but merely festooned with, philosophical conceptions. In IV x we can find, if that is our interest, the following: (1) Love as friendship; (2) Venus distinct from Love (or Cupid) as mother from son; (3) Love (Eros) as the brother of Hate (Eris) derived ultimately from Empedocles (32); (4) the hermaphroditic Venus whose obscure origins have been studied by Miss J. W. Bennett (41); (5) Love naturalistically conceived in lines adapted from Lucretius (44 et seq.). But Spenser did not set out by collecting these concepts, still less by attempting a philosophical synthesis of them. His theme is courtship and his model is medieval erotic allegory. How a gentle knight found the island fortress of true love and overcame its defenders and won meek Amoret – that is the substance. And that is all clear and vivid – the bridge with its corbes and pendants, the door where the porter Doubt peeps 'through a crevis small', the ubiquitous sound of running water, the inner paradise, the Loves fluttering round the statue, and the capture of the beloved. The philosophical matter merely adds a suggestion of depth, as if shadows of old thought played about the temple: just as fugitive memories of Donne or Dante or Patmore or Meredith might play about our own minds during a real love affair. I do not mean that Spenser thought of it quite in that way. He was too serious and too syncretistic. Everything that the wise had said about Love was worth attending to. He would not have said 'Let us shade in here a little Platonism and there a little Epicureanism'. He would have said 'Proclus *in Timaeum* doth report . . . Orpheus hath it thus . . . read the like in that place of Ficinus'. But the result is much the same. It produces that depth or thickness which is one of the excellences of *The Faerie Queene*.

This is why work on Spenser's philosophical and iconographical background seems to me so much more rewarding than work on his historical allegory. But though such studies are enrichments they are not necessary for all readers. For those who can surrender themselves simply to the story Spenser himself will provide guidance enough. The allegory that really matters is usually unmistakable. Hazlitt can hardly have meant what he said on that subject. Few poets are so radically allegorical as Spenser: it is significant that one of the few words he has given to our language, Braggadocchio, though intended by him as the name of a man, has become the name of a quality. But it is not impossible that many who thought they were obeying Hazlitt have read the poetry aright. They receive the allegory so easily that they forget they have done so, as a man in health is unaware of breathing.

(380–88)

Those who wish to attack Spenser will be wise to concentrate on his style. There alone he is seriously vulnerable. I have made no attempt to conceal or defend those places where, on any view, he must be admitted to write dully, shrilly, or clumsily. But we come to something more controversial when we consider that quality which, in his best passages no less than in his worst, will alienate many modern readers – the absence of pressure or tension. There are, indeed, metrical variations, more numerous than we always remember. But the general effect is tranquil; line by line, unremarkable. His voice never breaks, he does not pluck you by the elbow, unexpected collocations of ideas do not pour out red hot. There is no irony or ambiguity. Some now would deny the name of poetry to writing of which this must be admitted. Let us not dispute about the name. It is more important to realize that this style (when it is true to itself) is suitable for Spenser's purpose. He needs to create a certain quiet in our minds. The great images, the embodiments, as I have said, of moods or whole phases of experience, rise best if we are not flurried. A still, brooding attention, not a perpetual excitement, is what he demands. It is also probably true that the lack of tension in his verse reflects the lack of tension in his mind. His poetry does not express (though of course it often presents) discord and struggle: it expresses harmony. No poet, I think, was ever less like an Existentialist. He discovered early what things he valued, and there is no sign that his allegiance ever wavered. He was of course often, perhaps usually, disappointed. The actual court did not conform to his standard of courtesy: mutability, if philosophically accepted from the outset, might yet prove unexpectedly bitter to the taste. But disappointment is not necessarily conflict. It did not for Spenser discredit the things of which he was disappointed. It might breed melancholy or indignation, but not doubt. Why, after all, should it? Spenser inherited the Platonic and Christian dualism: heaven was set over against earth, being against becoming, eternity against time. He knew from the outset that the lower, half-unreal world must always fail to copy its archetype exactly. The worst that experience could do was to show that the degree of failure was greater than one had anticipated. If he had thought that the objects of his desire were merely 'ideals', private, subjective, constructions of his own mind, then the actual world might have thrown doubt on those ideals. But he thought no such thing. The Existentialist feels *Angst* because he thinks that man's nature (and therefore his relation to all things) has to be created or invented, without guidance, at each moment of decision. Spenser thought that man's nature was given, discoverable and discovered; he did not feel *Angst*. He was often sad: but not, at bottom, worried. To many of my readers such a state of mind must appear a total illusion. If they cannot suspend their disbelief, they should leave Spenser alone; there are plenty of other authors to read. They must not, however, suppose that he was under an illusion about the historical world. That is not where he differs from them. He differs from them in thinking that it is not the whole story. His tranquillity is a robust tranquillity that 'tolerates the indignities of time', refusing (if we may put the matter in his terms) to be deceived by them, recognizing them as truths, indeed, but only the truths, of 'a foolish world'. He would not have called himself 'the poet of our waking dreams': rather the poet of our waking.

(391–3)

Yvor Winters

from *The Function of Criticism*   1957

There is also the allegorical poem, which arose in the Middle Ages, and which was expanded to epical dimensions by Dante and Spenser.

The defects of the method are more easily seen in Spenser, since he is by far the less talented of the two poets. We may consider the dragon in the first canto of *The Faerie Queene*. The gentle knight encounters the dragon, and after many Spenserian stanzas he slays it. We eventually learn that the dragon represents Error. But the dragon in general and in all its details, and merely as a dragon, is a very dull affair; it is poorly described and poorly characterized. I do not, frankly, know what one might do to make a dragon more interesting, but it seems to me that unless one can do better than this one had better not use a dragon. In its capacity as Error, the dragon spews up a number of books and papers (along with other items), and of course the dragon is ugly, but little is done in this way to further our understanding of error: there is no functional relationship between the dragon, either in general or in detail, and that which it represents. The relationship is arbitrary, and we have to be told explicitly what the relationship is. In this example we are told in the text, though late in the incident; if we were not told in the text we would have to have it explained in a summary. The gentle knight himself suffers from exactly the same defects as the dragon, and to understand him and his actions we have to read him with a chart at our elbow, and even then the significance remains on the chart and is never functional in the poem. The poem has other defects: the clumsy and tyrannical stanza, the primitive and unvaried use of the iambic pentameter line, and an habitual redundancy; but at present I am concerned only with the incurable flaws in the method.

Dante is free of the incidental faults which I have just mentioned. In fact the corresponding virtues in Dante are striking. But much the same difficulties inhere in the form of The Divine Comedy. Too many of the allegorical spirits, demons, ascents, descents, gates, animals and monsters have only the most arbitrary relationship to that which they represent, and it would be next to impossible to determine a good many of the relationships without help. The preposterous demons in Canto XXI of The Inferno represent evil in a general way, and they are described as irrational, unpredictable and malicious, but most of the description is devoted to their physical ugliness, so that we merely get an extensive development of the obvious. The description, in fact, is little better than Spenser's description of the dragon, with these exceptions: that Dante is not hampered by Spenser's massively clumsy stanza, and he is a far more sophisticated master of the rhythm of the line, and of the relationship of syntax to rhythm, line and stanza, with the result that his description is more compact and gives us the impression of movement rather than of lethargy. The vision of Dis in the final canto of The Inferno is even more grotesque than the account of the demons in XXI, and has the same defect.

(43–5)

Alastair Fowler

'Emblems of Temperance in *The Faerie Queene*, Book II', *Review of English Studies*, n.s. vol. II 1960

It was Spenser's usual practice to build into the imagery of *The Faerie Queene*, at strategic points, the traditional emblems of the virtue whose legend he was writing. These emblems must once have helped to make at least the main drift of his allegory widely intelligible; but unfortunately it no longer works like that. In Book II, where emblems are heavily relied on for structure as well as for imagery, either their existence is now not even noticed, or else they are treated as mere surface decoration. Yet they are essential to Spenser's method, which is oblique, working indirectly through details. The golden set-square, the 'norm of temperance',[1] for instance, is only once mentioned explicitly, when Guyon says that 'with golden squire'[2] the virtue 'can measure out a meane' between the fleshly death of Mordant and the self-accusing death of Amavia (II i 58). Because it is used in the geometrical construction of the mean proportional, the square is a symbol for the virtue by which Guyon will continually make the moral construction of the golden mean. The castles of Medina and Alma, however, are both founded on the same mathematical principle, and the set-square is a mason's instrument; so that from one point of view all the closely related architectural and geometrical images in the Book can be regarded as extensions of the emblem.[3] The bridle, a commoner emblem of temperance, is equally unobtrusive. Guyon has a horse with 'golden sell'[4] (II ii 11) called Brigador (v iii 34) – a name which means Golden Bridle (*briglia*

---

1 Achille Bocchi, *Symbolicarum quaestionum libri quinque*, Bologna, 1574, Embl. CXLIV, p. 145, in which the *norma temperantiae* is handed to a prince, is particularly apt as illustration.

2 square

3 Mean proportionals were actually used in Renaissance architecture: see R. W. Wittkower, *Architectural Principles in the Age of Humanism*, 1949, Pt IV, 'The Problem of Harmonic Proportion in Architecture'.

4 saddle: itself emblematic of authority, responsibility and office.

d'oro).[1] And this emblem, too, is functional; for it is Braggadocchio's theft of Brigador that precipitates Guyon into the pedestrian adventures that follow - which is to say, through the ambition of Braggadocchio the Platonic horse of man's desires ceases to be bridled by temperance.[2] I shall be solely concerned here, however, with a third emblem of temperance, which is perhaps the commonest of all - the pouring of water into wine.[3] This emblem makes the least obvious appearance, but only because it is developed on a scale we do not expect; it is hidden, only because most deeply structural.

The very first extended image in the Book is one of water: the nymph's fountain. This fountain of tears from the eyes of a petrified nymph not only occasions Mordant's death, but proves mysteriously immiscible with the blood of Amavia on Ruddymane's hands. The obscurity here, as so often in Spenser, is the result of compression: he has fused two emblematic fountains which apart would have been less difficult, if less original. We find them partly disengaged, as it happens, in a well-known emblem by Herman Hugo. Hugo portrays repentance as a seated female figure - Anima, the human soul - with a stream of tears issuing from her eyes and hair, as she faces a fountain in the form of a petrified nymph, from whose head and outstretched hands water flows into a large pool.[1] This is a visual rendering of Jeremiah ix, 1: 'Oh that my head were waters, and mine eyes a fountain of tears.' For epigram, Hugo gives Anima's prayer to be

1 Yet Warton thought it merely a pompous name 'on the affectation so common in books of chivalry'. For the bridle emblem see Ripa, *Iconologia*, Padua, 1611, pp. 508 f.; and É. Mâle, *L'Art religieux de la fin du Moyen Âge*, Paris, 1925, pp. 313 ff. and figs. 168, 173, 175.

2 At II iv 2 the 'rightfull owner' is described as able to 'menage . . . his pride'; at xii 53 we find him 'Bridling his will'. Cf. Rinaldo's stolen horse, which Harington interprets as 'fervent appetite' (Notes to *Orlando Furioso*, Bks I and II). On the horse as symbol for the wilful passions, see Valeriano, *Hieroglyphica*, Lyons, 1611, IV xx–xxiii; as a special attribute of *superbia* in medieval graphic art, A. Katzenellenbogen, *Allegories of the Virtues and Vices in Medieval Art*, 1939, pp. 10, 79, and fig. 8a.

3 For numerous examples of this emblem, see Mâle, pp. 321–3; Katzenellenbogen, pp. 55 f. *et passim*; and R. van Marle, *Iconographie de l'art profane*, The Hague, 1932, figs. 16, 22, etc.

metamorphosed into a fountain, like Acis, Biblis and Achelous; all of them mythological figures who, like Spenser's nymph, became rivers. (This allusion is reflected in the engraving by Boetius a Bolswert: the iconography of his petrified nymph, not to speak of the river-god in the background, is obviously influenced by illustrations of the *Metamorphoses*.) The streams of water from the nymph's outstretched hands, however, are neither from Jeremiah nor, solely, from the tradition of Ovidian illustration. They belong to another symbolic fountain, the Fountain of Life, as a glance at a later emblem of Hugo's will show (III xli). In it, Christ-Eros is a fountain, with spouts issuing from his outstretched hands, side and feet, and falling into a pool, the bath of salvation. The Fountain of Life – originally an expression of the cult of the Precious Blood – was a very popular motif in late medieval art; in the Reformation it persisted, though associated then with baptism rather than with the mass.[2] However disguised mythologically (as in the later period it often was), it would be readily recognized, in the briefest allusion, by a contemporary reader. Thus Spenser's fountain, to which Mordant came when Amavia reclaimed him, is an extraordinarily complex symbol of the believer's identity with Christ; serving both as fountain of repentance and laver of regeneration, as *fons lachrymarum* and *balnea salutis*.

Closer examination would show that the early cantos form an allegory of baptismal regeneration. The rock of the fountain alludes to the 'spiritual rock', from whom flows the water of baptism (1 Corinthians x, 2–4). Mordant (the 'outer man') and Amavia (the 'inner man') of the old Adam die and are buried by the fountain, because baptism involves a sacramental death and burial with Christ (Romans vi, 3–4). The Edward VI Form for Private Baptism contained a prayer 'that the old Adam in them that shall be baptized in this fountain, may be so buried, that the new man may be raised up again'. As for Guyon's new man, he is present too, in the shape of the laughing baby,

---

1 *Pia desideria*, Antwerp, 1624, I viii, pp. 59–64; illustrated in M. Praz, *Studies in Seventeenth-Century Imagery*, i, 1939, p. 133 (fig. 56).

2 See Mâle, pp. 110–18, and, for the earlier history of the motif, P. A. Underwood, 'The Fountain of Life in Manuscripts of the Gospels', *Dumbarton Oaks Papers*, vol. 5, 1950, pp. 43–138. The motif seems to have been introduced into emblem literature by Georgette de Montenay, in her *Emblemes ou devises chrestiennes*, Lyons, 1571, Embl. III, illus. Praz (fig. 9) from a later edn.

Ruddymane. His 'guilty hands' are baptized simultaneously with Guyon's own; but even the water of life will not wash out the bloody stains, which derive ultimately (ii 4) from the poison of Acrasia (concupiscence). As the Ninth of the Thirty-Nine Articles warned, concupiscence, the cause of the death of the old Adam, is not effaced by baptism. Only the long process of mortification of the flesh – with which Book II deals – can do anything to arrest it. Some theologians, indeed, among them Calvin, held out little hope of concupiscence ever being eradicated in this life. 'This corruption,' he says, 'never ceases in us, but constantly produces new fruits . . . just as . . . a fountain is ever pouring out water' (*Inst.*, IV xv 11, tr. Beveridge).

And this is how Spenser renders it, substantializing the traditional metaphor in the 'Infinit streames' of the fountain of Acrasia. With its erotic sculpture – profane Eroses bathing in the 'liquid ioyes' of love or playing 'wanton toyes' (xii 60) – this fountain is so disturbingly matched against the earlier one that recollection is enforced. Guyon has bathed in tears under the streaming body of Christ; will he, then, bathe in the 'ample lauer' of Acrasia's fountain, under the ivy of Bacchus, whose 'lasciuious armes', creeping into the water, seem 'for wantones to weepe', in blasphemous parody alike of crucifixion and piety?[1] In grasping this opposition, Spenser's first readers would be assisted by their familiarity with the work he was emulating, Trissino's *L'Italia Liberata da Gotti*.[2] In Trissino the two fountains are more closely juxtaposed (IV 873 and V 152), their symbolism less complex. But in Spenser's Book II the whole action flows between the fountain of life and the fountain of death, which set, as it were, its alternative extremes. The contrast involves a paradox: those who drink Acrasia's fountain seem alive, but are virtually dead – reduced, like Cymochles (v 35), to a shade; while those who drink the nymph's fountain die, but only to rise to a new life.

This almost symmetrical opposition is far from being the only one of its kind; contrasted images of water are, indeed, the Book's leitmotive. Thus the dead lake of idleness is set against the lake of grace

1 xii 61. On Fountains of Love and of Youth, and their connexions with the Fountain of Life, see van Marle; also D. J. H. Ross in *J.W.I.*, vol. II (1948), pp. 126-8.

2 Spenser's use of Trissino has been noticed by C. W. Lemmi, 'The Influence of Trissino on the *Faerie Queene*', *P.Q.*, vol. 7 (1928), pp. 220-23.

which swallows up the deathly Maleger in its life. Pyrocles is hotter than 'damned ghoste' in Phlegethon (vi 50), a burning river answered by the nymph's *cold* fountain (ii 9). Equally opposed, this time to its purity (ii 9), is the black river Cocytus, those 'sad waues, which direfull deadly stanke' under the Cave of Mammon.[1] (The burning and the filthy rivers correspond to the two modes of corruption – ireful and appetitive, strong and weak – a dichotomy which runs throughout the Book.) Such contrasts, between good and bad fountains, rivers, lakes, not to speak of wands, nets, boats, pilots, etc., are no doubt in part a device of formal arrangement, in part expressions of the am-bivalence of a natural order calling for constant discrimination. They may, however, carry the further implication that two entire ways of life, two complete mental landscapes, are being presented to our choice.

The Book has also its images of wine. Repeatedly the temptation of the Bower of Bliss is presented as a wine-cup, or is associated with symbols of Bacchus. This is a deliberate emphasis, and one that is not found in Spenser's models, Tasso's Bower of Armida or Trissino's Garden of Acratia.[2] First there is the 'mighty Mazer bowle of wine' of evil Genius; then the golden cup of Excess, with juice pressed from intoxicating grapes; and lastly the cup of Acrasia, the ample laver of her fountain, beneath the ivy of Bacchus. Acrasia's cup makes her lovers animals in the end; but for a time they become embodiments of the god Bacchus himself. Thus Mordant is actually called Bacchus in Acrasia's curse (i 55); while Verdant, as his name suggests, enjoys that green age of youth which was the perpetual condition of the god.[3]

1 See vii 57. Such pairs of contrasted rivers were traditional: Bersuire contrasts the hot Egyptian fountain of avarice and worldly pleasure ('non est refrigeratiua, sed potius inflammatiua') with the waters of compassion and piety (*Dict.*, Pt I, under *aqua*). Landino, the Neoplatonist, interprets the four rivers of Hell as the course of sin, flowing from man's concupiscence – 'a concupiscentia nostra veluti a fonte manat aqua' (*Alleg. in Aen.*, Virgil, *Opera*, Basel, 1596, pp. 3038, 3044). But Spenser works in yet another relevant emblem. When the burning Pyrochles leaps into Idle Lake (II vi 41-51), he effects a mixture of fire and water that enacts a familiar emblem of Discord (e.g. Valeriano, XLVI xxix).

2 Trissino has vines, but no cups of wine.

3 For Bacchus as *semper iuvenis* and *puer aeternus*, see Conti, *Mytholog.*, v xiii, and Alciati, *Emblemata cum comm. ampliss.*, Padua, 1621, p. 140a, on Embl. xxv, 'In statuam Bacchi'.

Into contact with these Bacchic images comes, at the moment of the mission's fulfilment, the principal water-image, Guyon. For the name Guyon derives from one of the four rivers of Paradise (Genesis ii, 10–14). These rivers were from patristic times identified with the four cardinal virtues, Pison usually being prudence, Tigris fortitude, Euphrates justice, and Gihon (Geon, Gaeon, Gyon, etc.) temperance. The Neoplatonist Philo probably invented the allegory; but it was St Ambrose who developed it christologically. In St Ambrose's interpretation, the single river from which the four river-virtues spring is Christ, the fountain of eternal life.[1] The symbol was a familiar one in the Renaissance. To cite well-used reference works: Bersuire (*Comm. in Gen.*, ii, in *Reductorium morale*) traces the rivers back to the fountain of repentance that irrigates a righteous man's conscience; while Valeriano (*Hieroglyph.*, XXI xiv) follows St Ambrose and Philo, explaining that the Gaeon (Nile) signifies temperance because it washes Egypt (i.e. enticing pleasure) and Ethiopia, a land stained, like the human body, with a dark infection: 'it purges the vile body, and quenches the ardour of lust.'

The purpose of the four rivers allegory was to symbolize in a vivid way the absolute dependence of the virtues upon their source, the water of life. The same idea was expressed by a motif in late medieval graphic art, which associated human personifications of the virtues with the Fountain of Life. A Bellegambe painting at Lille, for example, depicts the faithful, assisted by female figures (the virtues), climbing into a large laver beneath the crucified Christ: signifying that men can only achieve virtues after bathing in the blood of salvation, each effusion of which washes out one deadly sin.[2] In a similar manner, and with similar meaning, Guyon the virtue of temperance helps Ruddymane to wash in the Fountain of Life.

Since Guyon's entry into the Bower of Bliss brings images of water and wine together, the missing emblem of temperance has been found. It remains to discover what symbolic force it exerts. Traditionally,

1 *De parad.*, iii. For further details about the history of this allegorization, see Underwood, pp. 47–49; also my note 'The River Guyon', *M.L.N.*, vol. 75 (1960), pp. 289–92.

2 See Mâle, p. 115 and fig. 62; it should be noted that the bath in this painting is an erotic bath, shared with the object of desire.

temperance's pouring of water into wine had meant dilution: moderation in the indulgence of a burning desire. Such is the interpretation in Claude Mignault's Commentary on Alciati; somewhat disappointingly, he explains that when the *Greek Anthology* says that Bacchus delights to link with three nymphs, it only means that wine should be mixed with three parts water: unmixed, it causes fury and insanity. He quotes Plato's advice that 'the drunken god should be tempered with sober nymphs' (Alciati, 143b, 144b, and 146a). Sometimes, however, the two vessels of temperance carried another significance. Ripa tells us that temperance is portrayed with two vessels, one tilted into the other, 'because of the similarity between a mixture of two liquids, and that of two contrary extremes' (*Iconologia*, p. 508). The conception of temperance as the mixture or integration of extremes, as distinct from their avoidance, is clearly expressed in the triads of the Castle of Medina. But the mixture emblem is also worked up into a characteristic piece of poetic theology, more deeply hidden, which underlies the Bower of Bliss temptations, as well as Acrasia's curse upon Mordant.

Spenser seems to have taken a hint from Bersuire's allegorization of an account in Solinus of the marvellous river Diana, near Camerina. According to Solinus, if anyone of unchaste habits draws water from the Diana, it will not mix with the wine in his body (*Polyhistor*, xi). Bersuire takes this to mean that the unchastity of the drinker will be revealed. By water, he says,

can be understood doctrine – especially by the water of the Diana, a name which means 'manifest' [*clara*]. But by wine can be understood the human will; for water (doctrine) cools, but the human will burns with desire. Therefore the water of good doctrine is applied to the wine of ardent will, so that the appetite may be tempered (*Reductorium morale*, VIII iii 33).

By a common and obvious symbolism, intoxication and the consequent heating of the blood has throughout Christian literature been an image of sin. Thus, in Burnet's *Exposition of the Thirty-Nine Articles*, an extended speculation about how original sin altered the human constitution imagines the pathological effect as an inflammation of the blood (on Art. IX). More metaphysically, Neoplatonic writers used the intoxicating draught of Bacchus as a myth to describe the immersion of the mind in matter at birth, when 'the new drink of matter's impetuous flood' intoxicated the soul and brought oblivion. Augustinian theology, which took over the myth, also regarded the soul as overcome at birth; not, however, by matter, but by its failure to dominate the body's original sin, concupiscence.[1] Thus it is concupiscence (Acrasia) whose Bacchic draught brings Mordant such oblivion that he forgets Amavia. And having drunk the wine of wilfulness, he is confronted with his unfaithfulness by waters of doctrine from a fountain of Diana (revelation), so that he knows himself mortally guilty.

Since passions have the darkness of a Bacchic intoxication, the accomplishment of temperance must consist in remaining lucid amidst them, until their sources are understood. This is expressed allegorically by Guyon's refusal to bathe at the Bower of Bliss. Carrying with him on his course water from Diana's fountain, he enters the sphere of the natural, and *resists immersion in it*. For the temptation of the Bower would be underestimated if, with Bowra, we regarded it as 'sexual irregularity'.[2] It is nothing less than the primary temptation to relinquish the mind's dominion and succumb in animal wilfulness to the intoxication of the natural and the material: to succumb, that is, to concupiscence, 'the mind of the flesh', by wallowing in the desires of the heart. Nevertheless, the Bower is not simply to be avoided; to the passionate heart – the fountain of the will – Guyon must bring the water of doctrine and grace.[3] This allegory of a human conduit between fountains was not entirely novel. In Trissino's *L'Italia Liberata*, water is carried in vessels from a fountain made by God from Virtue's tears,

---

1 See Aquinas, *Disp.* IV *De malo*, I, on the soul's contraction of original sin at its infusion. The Platonic myth can be traced from the *Phaedo* through Plotinus (*Enn.*, IV iii 2), Porphyry (*De antr. nymph.*, i 88), and Macrobius (*In somn. Scip.*, I xii) to Renaissance mythographers like Valeriano (*Collectanea*, II ix).

2 Lemmi, who notices much of the Bacchic imagery (*M.L.N.*, vol. 50 (1935), pp. 163–4, and *P.Q.*, vol. 8 (1929), pp. 276–7), sees some of the symbolism, but makes it too narrowly sexual, treating Bacchus as the 'masculine principle' and Mordant as 'oversexed'.

3 For the heart as the *fons voluntatis*, see Valeriano, XVIII xiii, 'Concupiscentia'. N. S. Brooke, 'C. S. Lewis and Spenser', *Cambridge Journal*, vol. 2 (1949), p. 430, noticed that the fountain of Acrasia is the heart, but failed to make the connexion with the will.

and is poured in literal fact into Acratia's fountain of concupiscence.[1] The difference, however, between this allegory and Spenser's is significant. Whereas Trissino automatically overcomes each obstacle by the same device, sprinkling with holy water, Spenser attempts to render the process of regeneration in greater detail, by the introduction of images with assignable psychological meaning, such as the Palmer's staff of concord and net of formal analysis. Characteristically, Trissino calls the water *acqua del sanajo*, but Spenser allows the theological meaning to remain implicit.

The symmetry of Book II now emerges, as we see Guyon on a massive scale bringing together, as temperance should, two vessels. He lives in no exclusively moral, natural world, as some critics have maintained; but in the full tension between spirit and rebellious flesh, between Fidelia's cup and Acrasia's.

Harry Berger Jr

'A Secret Discipline: *The Faerie Queene*, Book VI', in William Nelson (ed.), *Form and Convention in the Poetry of Edmund Spenser*   1961

'Only skilled artists should draw from living bodies, because in most cases these lack grace and good shape'

TINTORETTO,
recorded by Ridolfi

. . . we are told Tintoretto transmuted the gamin divers of the Venetian canals into the angels of his painting. . . . the conquest, in form, of fear and disgust means such a sublimation that the world which once provoked the fear and disgust may now be totally loved in the fullness of contemplation. . . . that gazing . . . is, as Yeats puts it,

1 VI and v. Cf. also Goltzius's engraving 'Satisfactio Christi' (B. 67), where the Fountain of Life pours directly into a human heart opened like a box to receive it.

> . . . our secret discipline
> Wherein the gazing soul doubles her might.
>
> The might is there for the moment when the soul lifts her head.
>
> R. P. WARREN

The Hellenistic scheme for the divisions of the literary treatise – *poesis*, *poema*, *poeta* – might be put to rhetorical use as an approach to the dominant movement evident in Spenser's *Faerie Queene*. *Poesis* adumbrates subject matter, what the poem is about; *poema* refers to questions of form, manner, style, therefore to the imagination in its act of rendering subject matter; *poeta* names the category in which the poet and his conditions are discussed. The increasingly reflexive emphasis articulated by this simple scheme may be transferred to *The Faerie Queene* in the following manner:

1. Books I and II are self-contained, coherent narratives which focus quite clearly on the respective quests of Red Cross and Guyon. The allegorical dimension of each book may be shown to have its main purpose in illuminating the character and quest of the fictional hero – the holiness (wholeness) of Red Cross and the temperance of Guyon.[1]

2. If in the first two books our attention is directed to the nominal subjects, Books III and IV are presented so as to make us more aware of the act of rendering, the behavior of the poetic mind. In meandering through the places of the classical and courtly landscapes, the romance of Britomart explores both the mythopoetic and the erotic imaginations. The magnificent climaxes of IV x and IV xi reveal poetic activity in its most representative aspect, drawing the forms of the mind from oceanic chaos, creating its own symbolic Love and Nature.

3. Books V and VI, though strikingly different from each other, are both unfolded within the ambience of the poet's contemporary world. They reflect not merely the process of imagination as such, but the problems of the Renaissance poet trying to make sense of the world around him, trying also to continue his interior journey through Faerie amid distractions which make this imaginative quest ever more difficult.

The subject of this essay will be the culmination of this development

1 I have discussed this aspect of Book II at length in *The Allegorical Temper*, Yale U.P., 1957.

in the sixth book. Book VI is not, of course, Spenser's final word, but the limits of the topic do not extend to the *Mutabilitie Cantos*. The essential problem confronting Spenser in the third phase is defined in the proem to Book V: how to re-form poetically the corrupt spectacle of modern life in the ideal images of antiquity. The poet sees that the world around him is out of joint, and he feels that if he would discharge his obligation as man and citizen he must try to set it right. Since the actuality perceived offers no hints of order, no models of the reality desired, the poetic mind must confer upon the world its own mythic forms. Spenser's antique forms are those which he has created in his great poem. The life of his imagination is compacted into the lives of Artegal, Britomart, and the other creatures of Faerie. They have their own problems and passions and destinies, they impose their own claims on their creator. Although they are make-believe – or precisely *because* they are make-believe – they are more real to the poet than any of the fragmented forms he sees in the world outside his mind. And so, if he is going to make his creatures express that very different world, he will have to jeopardize their independence. Justice, as he remarks in the tenth canto, 'Oft spilles the principall, to save the part'. And the same holds true for an allegory of justice: the 'principall' is the concrete world of adventure, the 'part' the allegorical or exemplary meaning. But this is not merely a problem facing the poet: he makes it his theme – no doubt, if Josephine Bennett's chronology is right, his revision of Book V was governed by this reflexive awareness. The body of the poem is always threatened with the fate of Munera, the Lady Meed figure in Canto ii. Munera has fair locks and a slender waist, but she also has gold hands and silver feet. Talus nails up her symbolic extremities and throws the rest of her in the river. Though Artegal is momentarily moved by her femininity, he does not interfere. The allegory of justice requires that when a particular episode is over, its apposite meaning be nailed up on the wall, and its remaining details discarded.

Book VI should be understood as the logical result of these developments. It is at once an attempt to cope with justice at the personal and social levels, and to give freer play to the stylistic reflexes of the poet's imagination. In accordance with these needs, the chivalric idiom must be more emblematic, the view of actuality more oblique. To move from justice to courtesy means to turn away from the direct and rigorous moral confrontation of Book v toward the more mannered and esthetic perspective of Book vi. This accords with one of the poem's compositional rhythms: Books i, iii, and v are mainly British books because they are, in different ways, approaches to the real or the actual – as theological, as natural, as social. But Books ii, iv, and vi seem to involve corresponding withdrawals into Faerie. Book v presents the decay of antique norms, and the threatened subjection of Spenser's antique forms, before the darkness of the present. Book vi retreats from the plains, mountains and rocky coast of Book v into the rich wood of Faerie forms and motifs.

Space does not allow a close inquiry into the effects of the transition on the sixth book. But a brief listing of its main features may suggest something of its quality. There is, for example, a deliberate casualness in Spenser's treatment of narrative and character. After the first canto almost every episode is left unresolved: the poet breaks off an incident promising further installments which never materialize; or he presents a situation whose very nature is inconclusive, as in the case of Mirabella (vi viii 17–18, 22, 29–30); or he conclusively ends an episode before our narrative expectations have been fulfilled, as with Priscilla, Serena and Pastorella. This effect is impressed on us by the heavily stressed transition from one story to another. At times he introduces details and motifs of romance which are left undeveloped, and made to flaunt their irrelevance, as in the story told by Matilda to Calepine (vi iv 29–33).

The characters are all flat and typical, and it is often hard to keep them straight. This is made worse by a similarity in names and situations: the same *kinds* of situation recur again and again, and the poet merely substitutes one set of figures for another. There is, however, a pattern in the substitutions, for the second group is always worse or more ineffective than the first – we move from Crudor to Turpine, from Calidore to Calepine, from the hermit to Melibee, from the noble savage to the cannibals to the bandits. As a result, we are aware of a progressive flawing in the romance world. Related to this pattern are the wounds inflicted by the blatant beast, which grow steadily worse and do not respond to physical treatment (vi iv 16; v 31, 39; vi 1–15). Physical action, in general, is played down. The problems posed by courtesy and slander pertain to the sting infixed in the name, not in the body. The physical action demanded by the chivalric idiom is revealed as inadequate – both in its narrative and its symbolic functions.

Though variety is stressed by the transitions and large number of episodes, the poet continually returns to a small number of motifs. There are the motifs of the nursery, the gifts of nature, the foundling; the motif of withdrawal and return, or of retirement; the motif of primitivism, related to the nursery theme and diversely embodied in the savage, the cannibals, and the shepherds. There is the motif of the center and the ring which appears in three progressively higher and more symbolic stages: Serena at the raised altar surrounded by cannibals; Pastorella on a hill surrounded by swains; and the unnamed figure on Mount Acidale surrounded by dancing graces. The most frequently repeated motif is, significantly enough, that of a character surprised in a moment of diversion. Such moments are all perfectly natural or necessary – love, sleep, hunting, or merely a walk in the woods. These are the small but precious joys of everyday life, and they are not the ordinary subjects of the epic world. Yet to these moments the poet adds many touches which might be called homely or realistic – the care of babies, the adjustment of harness and pasturing of mounts, the gathering of food and other agricultural details. This realistic texture keeps the actual world always before us, even in the heart of Faerie. Precisely here, where we feel most secure, where we momentarily turn our backs on the outside world, the danger is greatest. For the beast of slander is no chivalric figure. The hermit, who knows this, gives hard counsel to Timias and Serena: 'Abstaine from pleasure, and restraine your will, | Subdue desire, and bridle loose delight, | Vse scanted diet, and forbeare your fill, | Shun secresie, and talke in open sight' (vi 14). In other words, 'Keep your eye always on the treacherous world around you; don't withdraw, don't relax, for a single moment.'

The result of these features is curiously ambivalent. The poet is bemused, a little bewildered, by the rich variety of Faerie, its many paths, the lure of so many joys: the opening stanzas of the proem and the final stanza of the sixth book together suggest that he is like all the lovers in the woods, or Timias with Belphoebe, or Arthur distracted by thoughts of Gloriana (vii 6). At the same time, the hermit's advice embodies an element of awareness in the poet which is responsible for the stylistic traits just described. The contrivance of the narrative, the inconclusiveness of the adventures, the gradual flawing of the romance world, the failure of chivalric action – these dramatize the claims imposed by actuality on the life of imagination. They also reveal the poet's awareness that the problems of life cannot be solved by poetry, cannot even be adequately represented in the simplified forms of Faerie. J. C. Maxwell has remarked that Spenser's handling of certain episodes 'betrays a mind not fully engaged by what it is doing.'[1] This is meant as criticism, but it is likely that Spenser intended it as a poetic effect: he *shows* poetry facing the actual world to cope with the difficult social problems of slander and courtesy, but he *knows* poetry's true work and pleasure require detachment rather than involvement. Something of this attitude is written into his curious presentation of the blatant beast.

The beast is an emblem or symbol which is clearly distinguished from the thing symbolized, so that the complex relations of slander and courtesy are reduced to an artificial and ideographic fable. Calidore thinks he is chasing some sort of animal possessed of two unfriendly habits: it bites and it reviles. The first is a shorthand version of the effects of the second, and it permits the evil to be expressed in physical terms so that chivalric action is possible. This is a radically reduced image of the social dangers disclosed toward the end of Book v, and of a profound spiritual evil with which Spenser was preoccupied throughout his career. The blatant beast, as I have suggested elsewhere[2] embodies the social expression of the malice produced by despair and self-hatred – the despair of the have-not who hungers after the good of others, who sees himself deprived of place and function, totally dependent on the world outside him, stripped of any 'daily beauty of his life'. The words of Slander in Book IV, of Envy, Detraction and the 'raskall many' in Book v are uttered to alleviate inward pain rather than to express meanings; their words become a form of rending, a spiritual cannibalism whose perverse and irrational music is aimed at the nerves and the affections:

Her words were not, as common words are ment,

1 'The Truancy of Calidore', in *That Soueraine Light*, ed. W. R. Mueller and D. C. Allen, 1952, p. 68.
2 In the early version of this paper, 'The Prospect of Imagination', *Studies in English Literature*, vol. I, 1961, pp. 106–7.

T'expresse the meaning of the inward mind,
But noysome[1] breath, and poysnous spirit sent
From inward parts, with cancred malice lind,
And breathed forth with blast of bitter wind;
Which passing through the eares, would pierce the hart,
And wound the soule it selfe with griefe unkind:
For like the stings of Aspes, that kill with smart,
Her spightfull words did pricke, and wound the inner part.

(IV viii 26)

The emblematic descriptions of the blatant beast (i 7–9, vi 9–12, xii 26–8) adumbrate this evil and suggest the rich complexity of meaning packed into the image. The bite then brings all this to bear on a character in such a way as to compare the peculiarly simplified existence of Faerie creatures with the difficulties of actual victims. Since slander in real life is not conveniently gathered together into the form of a single monster, and since – as the hermit points out (vi 6–7, 13–14) – the sting infixed in the name is not susceptible of physical remedies, Calidore's pursuit and conquest can hardly be anything but wish fulfillment.

This is in fact the way the final battle is presented: the affair is purely literal, and the beast is diminished not only from an emblem to an unsymbolic animal, but also from a fearful monster to little more than a muzzled cur. Thus, after a terrifying prebattle bristle in which it bares a jaw crammed with significance (xii 26–8), it responds to Calidore's attack by 'rearing vp his former feete on hight' and ramping 'vpon him with his rauenous pawes' (xii 29). As Spenser cuts the contest down to size, hero and enemy are compared to a butcher and bull in the abattoir (xii 30), and the beast then behaves like an angry girl: 'almost mad for fell despight.[2] | He grind, hee bit, he scratcht, he venim threw' (xii 31). Compared to this, the epic similes look clearly oversized and are deliberately misapplied to stress disparity rather than likeness (xii 32, 35). While the Hydra's thousand heads increase in stanza 32, the tongues of the waning beast diminish from a thousand (i 9, xii 27) to the hundred he originally owned when he offered Artegal a glancing threat (v xii 41, VI xii 33). Finally, Calidore applies

1 harmful, noxious
2 savage anger

a muzzle and a 'great long chaine' and draws him trembling 'like a fearefull dog' through Faerie. The conclusion of the quest has nothing to do with slander, everything to do with an Elfin hero's dream: it is a ticker-tape parade through Faerie, whose crowds 'much admyr'd the Beast, but more admyr'd the Knight' (xii 37) – the most triumphant and ridiculous of all Elfin homecomings, exposed a moment later when the beast roars into the present and threatens the poet. Thus, as an allegorical creature, given a shape and a place in the poem, the complex evils summarized in the term slander can be understood and controlled. But they can only be controlled in the play world created by the mind. What the beast represents is still in the actual world, and not in a simply identifiable form but diffused among the corrupt, weak and bitter spirits of civilization.

The importance of courtesy is dialectically illuminated by this danger. Maxwell has indicated the allegorical irrelevance of the beast's relationship to its victims,[1] and this irrelevance constitutes its meaning: attacks of slander are not made on the evil but on the virtuous, otherwise they would not be slander. Since the beast represents nothing whatsoever in the souls of its victims, its forays appear as sudden and inexplicable to us as they do to the sufferers. The armor of courtesy consists of 'outward shows' which fulfill rather than deceptively conceal 'inward thoughts'. It is not simply *a* virtue, not merely an ornamental polish distinguishing gentry from boors, but a technique of survival in a difficult world; courtesy makes virtue and virtuous behavior possible, maintains trust between men, keeps open the lines of civilized communication. Actuality, with its dangers, requires a movement out from the virtuous center to the circumference of the self where others are met. But – and this is the trouble for the poet who must exercise this technique even in poetry – such a movement diametrically opposes the poet's tendency to journey inward toward the mind's center, toward the source of his ravishing gift.

Thus the apparent inattention noted by Maxwell seems deliberate, and springs from a conflict which lies at the heart of Spenser's work. On the one hand, poetry is his supreme pleasure; on the other hand he has to survive; especially if he is a professional dependent on patronage, his delight must be tempered to his needs and those of others. Circumstances force the poet as man to adapt his poetry to the actual

1 'The Truancy of Calidore', pp. 68–9.

environment. But the man as poet is concerned with his second nature, the world within the poem, a world of which he is creator and legis- lator. If poetry is play, it is deadly serious play, a way of life in which imaginary experience means more than actuality – Spenser is thoroughly Neoplatonist in his belief that the soul can turn inward and find a second world more perfect and real than the first. But he is also aware of the mind's limits: in a negative sense, the limits placed *on* the imaginary by the actual; in a more positive sense, the limits *of* the imaginary. For if the muses transport him to an ideal world perfected by wish or perverted by nightmare, will they not reward him with a glimpse of the real? Will they render him defenseless against the threats of the beast, or deny the actual world its own rightful claims on a man's inner life? If they ravish him, are they sirens or something better?

Questions of this sort had been raised by Spenser as early as *The Shepheardes Calender*, and they are raised again in the proem to Book VI. They are implicit in the three modes of pastoral whose names were given, and distinctions blurred, by E.K. – *recreative, moral* and *plaintive* may be understood more literally than his discussion indicates. Re- creative pastoral is a poetry of escape in a holiday world free from care: its swains use the problems of life as excuses for indulging in song; delighting chiefly in rhetoric and the manipulation of *topoi*, they pursue their bent both for its own sake and for its social value as enter- tainment. In Colin's 'April' song of Eliza, for example, the mythic figures are nothing more than names – adjectives rather – applied as ornaments to the Queen. The richness of tradition and meaning which makes one mythic figure distinct from another has been rigorously screened out of the poetry; it appears only in E.K.'s gloss where much of it (e.g. the Three Graces, 'April', 267–74) will remain until April is revisited on Acidale.

The moral eclogues are mainly about the inadequacy of the artless to verbalize or clearly reflect on the problems of the great world – behind these eclogues one feels the force of the Ciceronian common- place about wisdom and eloquence both being necessary to hold civilization together. The moral pastors, who live in the English countryside rather than England's Helicon, lack control of thought and expression, are sadly wanting in the poetic, dialectical and rhetorical disciplines necessary to proper communication. These

271 Harry Berger Jr

eclogues argue the ethical function of poetic skill. The great world *is* corrupt, and this is the problem: someone has to deal with it. Someone needs the knowledge, the shrewdness, the sophistication, the command of expression to cope with the evils and articulate them with clarity. In the great world, knaves seize power by playing roles and practising the arts of persuasion, therefore – since the moral pastor is too simple, perhaps too honest, certainly too lazy – poets are enjoined to fulfill their social obligations: the esthetic pleasure must not be channeled into escape and mere recreation, but placed in the service of the public good.

Thus the recreative and moral modes appear incompatible and incomplete as displayed in the *Calender*: the former turns away from life to poetry, the latter from poetry to a sort of life. The plaintive eclogues are quite simply complaints. They center on Colin's skill and, with the exception of the November eclogue, on his love, though their rhetoric shades the meaning into a variety of other problems. As the title of Spenser's later volume suggests, the term *complaints* comes to cover any sort of frustration or disappointment with actual life and the human condition – 'death, or love, or fortunes wreck' (*Epithalamion*, 8). Colin is a recreative shepherd whose art has been cut short by a love which, since it keeps him from poetry, breaks all pastoral rules. He is unlike the moral pastors not only because he embodies rhetorical culture – his personality is compacted of *topoi* – but also because he was first moved by the joy of poetry; he is unlike the recreative pastors because his problem goes beyond the limits of his poetry. Therefore he provides Spenser with a possible way out of the recreative-moral dilemma. This way has two related characteristics: (1) it involves frustration, withdrawal, and the ideal re-creation of life in imaginary forms; (2) it is committed to literary and cultural commonplaces – the treasures of the muses – as the raw materials of poetic style, the traditional seeds which will germinate in the soil of personal experience. It is the way which, as we know, leads to Mount Acidale.

The proem to Book VI begins with an expression of the recreative impulse, though at a much deeper level than in the earlier work. The first two stanzas, after all, follow the moral and plaintive poetry of Book V:

The waies, through which my weary steps I guyde,

In this delightfull land of Faery,
Are so exceeding spacious and wyde,
And sprinckled with such sweet variety,
Of all that pleasant is to eare or eye,
That I nigh rauisht with rare thoughts delight,
My tedious trauell doe forget thereby;
And when I gin to feele decay of might,
It strength to me supplies, and chears my dulled spright.

Such secret comfort, and such heauenly pleasures,
Ye sacred imps, that on *Parnasso* dwell,
And there the keeping haue of learnings threasures,
Which doe all worldly riches farre excell,
Into the mindes of mortall men doe well,
And goodly fury into them infuse;
Guyde ye my footing, and conduct me well
In these strange waies, where neuer foote did vse,
Ne none can find, but who was taught them by the Muse.

The muses make him forget his tedious 'trauell': not only the labor
of art but perhaps also the straight and difficult path dictated by such a
purpose as the allegory of Justice. They tempt him from the goal, lead
him the long way round, and yet refresh the goal-bound spirit. The
imagination recognizes both the risk and the privilege of so profound
a holiday diversion: it cannot find this ideal place unless the muse
reveals, but it may lose its way in Faerie unless the muse leads it out.
The muses are felt to be an independent and objective power, an
ambiguous *Other* imposing on his will. The poet's problem is the
same as Arthur's when he was lured into a new world by his dream of
Gloriana: he has to find out 'whether dreames delude, or true it were'
(1 ix 14). The presence of the muses within him demands a response of
will: it is man who must put them to the test, whose experience or
experiment will discover and articulate their divinity.

Spenser's response in stanzas 3 and 4 of the proem is an attempt to
keep the muses honest. He asks for moral illumination as well as
pleasure: 'Reuele to me the sacred noursery | Of vertue.' From the
fourth to the sixth stanza he poses then rejects the temptation to withdraw completely from the corrupt world around him, to go straight
to 'vertues seat ... deepe within the mynd, | And not in outward

shows, but inward thoughts defynd.' At the end of the proem he acknowledges a source of virtue at the center of the social order in the person of the divinely appointed Queen: 'Right so from you all goodly vertues well | Into the rest, which round about you ring.' This is the first instance of the geometric motif which will be repeated three times in the poem, and it is the only case in which the dynamic image is discerned in forms that inhabit real nature; the others are Faerie rings discovered or devised 'deepe within the mynd'.

The significance of these two kinds of circle, actual and imaginary, becomes clearer if we recall a familiar element of Plotinian thought utilized by Ficino and other Renaissance Neoplatonists: the notion that when the objective Idea proceeds downward from the World Mind to the World Soul and Nature it may divide into two forms of existence, actual and mental. The Idea may be incarnated in the form of one human being and may exist as a form or concept in the mind of another. The mental form is purer than its incarnate analogue and may be aroused by it – this is the more or less utilitarian function of the beloved in Neoplatonist love psychology. In terms of Book VI, the geometrical symbol represents an objective *harmonia* which God has embodied in the Queen and her order, and the muses have implanted in the poetic imagination. Elizabeth's circle will be transfigured on Mount Acidale; when its full richness and meaning are unfolded it will be understood as one of many embodiments of that single form gathered together through the quest of imagination, through the reversion of the mind from the scattered particulars of experience to the Idea which is their formal source. Thus on Acidale the center is, so to speak, pushed upward so that it is the apex of a spiral or a mountain top. . . .

The episode as a whole circles through three familiar emphases: First, the vision of delight, where the earliest recreation becomes the latest re-creation. Second, the plaintive moment in which the vision is interrupted and Colin again breaks his pipe. Third, the moral emphasis when Colin converts the vision into an emblem. Here, he has replaced E.K.; this would have been unthinkable in the *Calender*, where the amplitude of life and meaning was precisely what that first world of conventions excluded. But now Colin catches up the recreative and plaintive moments into the moral. Love, poetry and morality converge – 'Divine resemblaunce, beauty soueraine rare, |

Firme Chastity' (x 27). All become *eros*, the latest gift and the earliest source. For it was *eros* that led him years ago to fall in love, and moved him to confront the fox and ape, and above all impelled him to play with words, to become a poet long before he could know *why* he was so inclined – *eros* was the true source of even that mindless joy. What began in the realm of the Muses ends in the realm of the Graces. One thinks especially of the 'April' eclogue, the meaning of whose forms remained inert in the gloss taken from dictionaries and handbooks. But one is also reminded of the country lass who denied her love, and one realizes that when the poet's amorous insight finally yields its re-fined Acidalian form, the handmaids of Venus have in effect become muses.

Colin's account does more than explain the vanished dance: it im-ports into Spenser's Acidale the rich iconographic tradition of Venus and the Graces elaborated by the human mind in its long cultural dialectic.[1] He begins, again with the widest perspective: the Graces are daughters of 'sky-ruling Iove' and Eurynome, 'The Oceans daughter' (x 22); effects of cosmic force and fertility, justice and generosity, but in Spenser's variation effects produced only on Acidale in a moment of repose and gratuitous delight. The catalogue of their qualities leads to a new image of the Graces:

> two of them still froward seem'd to bee,
> But one still towards shew'd her selfe afore;
> That good should from vs goe, then come in greater store.
>
> (x 24)

The dance is a diaphanous shimmer of meaning and image, turning and interacting, each modifying the other. The Graces are unfolded from Venus in their ancient and familiar poses, advance concretely before us, display their meanings, then fade into qualities as they are infolded by Colin's beloved: 'Another Grace she well deserues to be, | In whom so many Graces gathered are' (x 27). For a moment the beloved is poised alone in visionary splendor; in the next moment she

1 On the Graces, see E. H. Gombrich, 'Botticelli's Mythologies: a Study in the Neoplatonic Symbolism of his Circle', *Journal of the Warburg and Courtauld Institutes*, vol. 8 (1945), p. 32; André Chastel, *Marsile Ficin et l'art*, Geneva, 1954, pp. 146–7; D. T. Starnes, 'Spenser and the Graces', *P.Q.*, vol. 21 (1942), pp. 268–82; Edgar Wind, *Pagan Mysteries of the Renaissance*, New Haven, 1958; Penguin Books, 1965, passim.

275 Harry Berger Jr

recedes to make room for Gloriana though, with the words 'Sunne of the world', the two Ideas make brief contact. The lyric muse reveals her affinity to the epic muse and the vision gives way to the narrative of Book VI.

In that momentary poise, however, and in the circling dance, the vision resonates with harmonious echoes. We may recall the revelation on the mountain top in Book I, and the other in the Gardens of Adonis; the hundred virgins in the temple of Venus; the image of Amoret surrounded by her garland of virtues. The vision is the solution and resolution of all the problems, all the motifs, suggested in earlier parts of the book: the aristocracy and foundling motifs; the nursery, withdrawal and retirement motifs; the motifs of love, of holiday and diversion, of being caught off guard, turning inward – all these, along with the precious circles, are now revealed as symbols and dim prefigurations of Acidale. And at the center of the ring of Graces is no single creature but a richly complicated knot of all the figures the poet has ever meditated on – Rosalind, Elizabeth, Amoret, Belphoebe, Florimell, Britomart, Venus, Psyche – 'Who can aread, what creature mote she bee'? Unlike Pastorella, she has no name, is beyond names; though she has been in part generated from the fictional domain of names and images in the dance of meanings, she has, so to speak, been sprung from this domain, having been 'enchaced' by his thought distilled from so much 'tedious trauell'. He has not ever taken his eye off that first form, the simple country lass, but whoever she is in herself no longer matters. The form has been refined until the beloved has become love, the hieroglyph of *eros* – not an *other*, but a vision or symbol or concept of whatever it is that draws us toward the other.

In its context and in its form, the vision enacts the Neoplatonic idea that the soul is a foundling, an aristocrat long ignorant of its true source. It confuses its principle with primitive beginnings, with something temporally prior and externally simpler, like savagery or rusticity. The true beginning and principle is neither in time nor in space but always vivid at the center, deep within the mind. Only by turning inward, by self-creation, by tirelessly seeking and wooing and invoking the muses, or *eros*, or what lies behind them all – only thus do we regain our long-lost heritage. By some process akin to anamnesis we withdraw, we retire, we return to the nursery, we close the circle of beginnings and endings, we come finally to that first Idea, that pure grace which has always moved us. And our point of contact with the real is the moving geometric form, the dynamism of thought itself. What is felt as divine is not the vision itself so much as the sense of having been given – the sense of a richness and variety, a copious world of forms and meanings which the mind produces *as if* by its own reflex activity, but really by the grace of God. The divine, the real, are now sought for only in their transfigured forms, and they are found not in the transfiguration but in the activity, the process of transfiguring. So *The Faerie Queene* swings on its great axis from the objective reality of Dante's universe, to which Book I is closest, toward the symbolic form of *Paradise Lost*.

It is important to take into account the presence of Rosalind as a simple country lass and poor handmaid of Gloriana, if one is to do justice to the realistic basis of Spenser's vision. The triumph of imagination is partly measured by the extent to which it has converted frustration, brute fact, the world of first sight and first nature, into a symbolic intuition of the real; the presence of the country lass and the early pastoral testifies to this triumph. But the triumph is also measured by acceptance of what the mind cannot transform, by the awareness of limit which Clarion must learn the hard way. The complete self-sufficiency of the second nature, the total inward mastery of experience – this is no triumph at all, only delusion, if it takes itself seriously. For then it would have nothing to do with the poet *now*, a man still faced by life, fortune, malice, Providence. Thus poetry, having triumphed, must dissolve its triumph again and again to show that it is still engaged in the ongoing process of life where experience is not yet ordered. On Mount Acidale, when the play of mind realizes its vision, the poet dissolves it and moves on. In vision the mind objectifies its desires and intuitions so that it can see and respond; Colin's explanation is the response of the mind to the figure it has made and which it accepts as given. But just as the explanation acknowledges the persistence of the country lass, so the poem returns to the blatant beast and to its own dissolution. Spenser's poetic style is generated from the awareness that the poetic universe must be circumscribed as artifice and play; yet within the circumscribed place the poet must adumbrate the raw, the meaningless, so that we see it in the poem but outside the poetry. The secret discipline of imagination is a double burden, discordant and harmonious: first, its delight in the power and freedom of art; second, the controlled surrender whereby it acknowledges the limits of artifice. For Spenser, who is among the true poets, the vision must be bounded and shaped by the sense that it is not reality; and it must yield to reality at last.

(35-75)

Northrop Frye

from 'The Structure of Imagery in *The Faerie Queene*' (first published 1961), *Fables of Identity* 1963

To demonstrate a unity in *The Faerie Queene*, we have to examine the imagery of the poem rather than its allegory. It is Spenser's habitual technique, developing as it did out of emblematic visions he wrote in his nonage, to start with the image, not the allegorical translation of it, and when he says at the beginning of the final canto of Book II:

> Now gins this goodly frame of Temperance
> Fairely to rise

one feels that the 'frame' is built out of the characters and places that are clearly announced to be what they are, not out of their moral or historical shadows. Spenser prefaces the whole poem with sonnets to possible patrons, telling several of them that they are in the poem somewhere, not specifying where: the implication is that for such readers the allegory is to be read more or less *ad libitum*. Spenser's own language about allegory, 'darke conceit', 'clowdily enwrapped', emphasizes its deliberate vagueness. We know that Belphoebe refers to Elizabeth: therefore, when Timias speaks of 'her, to whom the heauens doe serue and sew'¹ (III v 47), is there, as one edition suggests, a reference to the storm that wrecked the Armada? I cite this only as an example of how subjective an allegorical reader can be. Allegory is not only often uncertain, however, but in the work of one of our greatest allegorical poets it can even be addled, as it is in *Mother Hubberds Tale*, where the fox and the ape argue over which of them is more like a man, and hence more worthy to wear the skin of a lion. In such episodes as the legal decisions of Artegall, too, we can see that

1 follow

Spenser, unlike Milton, is a poet of very limited conceptual powers, and is helpless without some kind of visualization to start him thinking. I am far from urging that we should 'let the allegory go' in reading Spenser, but it is self-evident that the imagery is prior in importance to it. One cannot begin to discuss the allegory without using the imagery, but one could work out an exhaustive analysis of the imagery without ever mentioning the allegory.

Our first step is to find a general structure of imagery in the poem as a whole, and with so public a poet as Spenser we should hardly expect to find this in Spenser's private possession, as we might with Blake or Shelley or Keats. We should be better advised to look for it in the axioms and assumptions which Spenser and his public shared, and which form the basis of its imaginative communication. Perhaps the *Mutabilitie Cantos*, which give us so many clues to the sense of *The Faerie Queene* as a whole, will help us here also.

The action of the *Mutabilitie Cantos* embraces four distinguishable levels of existence. First is that of Mutability herself, the level of death, corruption, and dissolution, which would also be, if this poem were using moral categories, the level of sin. Next comes the world of ordinary experience, the nature of the four elements, over which Mutability is also dominant. Its central symbol is the cycle, the round of days, months and hours which Mutability brings forth as evidence of her supremacy. In the cycle there are two elements: becoming or change, which is certainly Mutability's, and a principle of order or recurrence within which the change occurs. Hence Mutability's evidence is not conclusive, but could just as easily be turned against her. Above our world is upper nature, the stars in their courses, a world still cyclical but immortal and unchanged in essence. This upper world is all that is now left of nature as God originally created it, the state described in the Biblical story of Eden and the Classical myth of the Golden Age. Its regent is Jove, armed with the power which, in a world struggling against chaos and evil, is 'the right hand of justice truly hight'. But Jove, however he may bluster and threaten, has no authority over Mutability; that authority belongs to the goddess Nature, whose viceroy he is. If Mutability could be cast out of the world of ordinary experience, lower and upper nature would be re-united, man would re-enter the Golden Age, and the reign of 'Saturn's son' would be replaced by that of Saturn. Above Nature is the real God, to whom Mutability appeals when she brushes Jove out of her way, who is invoked in the last stanza of the poem, and who appears in the reference to the Transfiguration of Christ like a mirage behind the assembly of lower gods.

Man is born into the third of these worlds, the order of physical nature which is theologically 'fallen' and under the sway of Mutability. But though in this world he is not of it: he really belongs to the upper nature of which he formed part before his fall. The order of physical nature, the world of animals and plants, is morally neutral: man is confronted from his birth with a moral dialectic, and must either sink below it into sin or rise above it into his proper human home. The latter he may reach by the practice of virtue and through education, which includes law, religion, and everything the Elizabethans meant by art. The question whether this 'art' included what we mean by art, poetry, painting, and music, was much debated in Spenser's day, and explains why so much of the criticism of the period took the form of apologetic. As a poet, Spenser believed in the moral reality of poetry and in its effectiveness as an educating agent; as a Puritan, he was sensitive to the abuse and perversion of art which had raised the question of its moral value in the first place, and he shows his sense of the importance of the question in his description of the Bower of Bliss.

Spenser means by 'Faerie' primarily the world of realized human nature. It is an 'antique' world, extending backward to Eden and the Golden Age, and its central figure of Prince Arthur was chosen, Spenser tells us, as 'furthest from the daunger of enuy, and suspition of present time'. It occupies the same space as the ordinary physical world, a fact which makes contemporary allusions possible, but its time sequence is different. It is not timeless: we hear of months or years passing, but time seems curiously foreshortened, as though it followed instead of establishing the rhythm of conscious life. Such foreshortening of time suggests a world of dream and wishfulfilment, like the fairylands of Shakespeare's comedies. But Spenser, with his uneasy political feeling that the price of authority is eternal vigilance, will hardly allow his virtuous characters even to sleep, much less dream, and the drowsy narcotic passages which have so impressed his imitators are associated with spiritual peril. He tells us that sleep is one of the three divisions of the lowest world, the other two being death and hell; and Prince Arthur's long tirade against night (III iv) would be out of proportion if night, like its seasonal counterpart winter, did not symbolize a lower world than Faerie. The vision of Faerie may be the *author's* dream, as the pilgrimage of Christian is presented as a dream of Bunyan, but what the poet dreams of is the strenuous effort, physical, mental and moral, of waking up to one's true humanity.

In the ordinary physical world good and evil are inextricably confused; the use and the abuse of natural energies are hard to distinguish, motives are mixed and behaviour inconsistent. The perspective of Faerie, the achieved quest of virtue, clarifies this view. What we now see is a completed moral dialectic. The mixed-up physical world separates out into a human moral world and a demonic one. In this perspective heroes and villains are purely and simply heroic and villainous; characters are either white or black, for the quest or against it; right always has superior might in the long run, for we are looking at reality from the perspective of man as he was originally made in the image of God, unconfused about the difference between heaven and hell. We can now see that physical nature is a source of energy, but that this energy can run only in either of two opposing directions: toward its own fulfilment or toward its own destruction. Nature says to Mutability: 'For thy decay thou seekst by thy desire' (vii 59), and contrasts her with those who, struggling out of the natural cycle, 'Doe worke their owne perfection so by fate' (vii 58).

Spenser, in Hamlet's language, has no interest in holding the mirror up to nature unless he can thereby show virtue her own feature and scorn her own image. His evil characters are rarely converted to good, and while there is one virtuous character who comes to a bad end, Sir Terpine in Book v, this exception proves the rule, as his fate makes an allegorical point about justice. Sometimes the fiction writer clashes with the moralist in Spenser, though never for long. When Malbecco offers to take Hellenore back from the satyrs, he becomes a figure of some dignity as well as pathos; but Spenser cannot let his dramatic sympathy with Malbecco evolve. Complicated behaviour, mixed motives, or the kind of driving energy of character which makes moral considerations seem less important, as it does in all Shakespeare's heroes, and even in Milton's Satan – none of this could be contained in Spenser's framework.

The Faerie Queene in consequence is necessarily a romance, for romance is the genre of simplified or black and white characterization. The imagery of this romance is organized on two major principles. One is that of the natural cycle, the progression of days and seasons. The other is that of the moral dialectic, in which symbols of virtue are parodied by their vicious or demonic counterparts. Any symbol may be used ambivalently, and may be virtuous or demonic according to its context, an obvious example being the symbolism of gold. Cyclical symbols are subordinated to dialectical ones; in other words the upward turn from darkness to dawn or from winter to spring usually symbolizes the lift in perspective from physical to human nature. Ordinary experience, the morally neutral world of physical nature, never appears as such in *The Faerie Queene*, but its place in Spenser's scheme is symbolized by nymphs and other elemental spirits, or by the satyrs, who may be tamed and awed by the sight of Una or more habitually stimulated by the sight of Hellenore. Satyrane, as his name indicates, is, with several puns intended, a good-natured man, and two of the chief heroes, Red Cross and Artegall, are explicitly said to be natives of this world and not, like Guyon, natives of Faerie. What this means in practice is that their quests include a good deal of historical allegory.

(71–5)

The conception of the four levels of existence and the symbols used to represent it come from Spenser's cultural tradition in general and from the Bible in particular. The Bible, as Spenser read it for his purposes, describes how man originally inhabited his own human world, the Garden of Eden, and fell out of it into the present physical world, which fell with him. By his fall he lost the tree and water of life. Below him is hell, represented on earth by the kingdoms of bondage, Egypt, Babylon and Rome, and symbolized by the serpent of Eden, otherwise Satan, otherwise the huge water-monster called Leviathan or the dragon by the prophets. Man is redeemed by the quest of Christ, who after overcoming the world descended to hell and in three days conquered it too. His descent is usually symbolized in art as walking into the open mouth of a dragon, and when he returns in triumph he carries a banner of a red cross on a white ground, the colours typifying his blood and flesh. At the end of time the dragon of death is finally destroyed, man is restored to Eden, and gets back the water and tree of life. In Christianity these last are symbolized by the two sacraments accepted by the Reformed Church, baptism and the Eucharist.

The quest of the Red Cross knight in Book 1 follows the symbolism of the quest of Christ. He carries the same emblem of a red cross on a white ground; the monster he has to kill is 'that old Dragon' (quatrain to Canto xi; cf. Revelation xii, 9) who is identical with the Biblical Satan, Leviathan and serpent of Eden, and the object of killing him is to restore Una's parents, who are Adam and Eve, to their kingdom of Eden, which includes the entire world, now usurped by the dragon. The tyranny of Egypt, Babylon, and the Roman Empire continues in the tyranny of the Roman Church, and the Book of Revelation, as Spenser read it, prophesies the future ascendancy of that church and its ultimate defeat in its vision of the dragon and Great Whore, the latter identified with his Duessa. St George fights the dragon for three days in the garden of Eden, refreshed by the water and tree of life on the first two days respectively.

But Eden is not heaven: in Spenser, as in Dante, it is rather the summit of purgatory, which St George goes through in the House of Holiness. It is the world of recovered human nature, as it originally was and still can be when sin is removed. St George similarly is not Christ, but only the English people trying to be Christian, and the dragon, while he may be part of Satan, is considerably less Satanic than Archimago or Duessa, who survive the book. No monster, however loathsome, can really be evil: for evil there must be a perversion of intelligence, and Spenser drew his dragon with some appreciation of the fact mentioned in an essay of Valéry, that in poetry the most frightful creatures always have something rather childlike about them:

> So dreadfully he towards him did pas,
> Forelifting vp aloft his speckled brest,
> And often bounding on the brused gras,
> As for great ioyance[1] of his newcome guest.

> (I xi 15)

Hence the theatre of operations in the first book is still a human world. The real heaven appears only in the vision of Jerusalem at the end of the tenth canto and in a few other traces, like the invisible husband of Charissa and the heavenly music heard in the background of the final

1 enjoyment

betrothal. Eden is within the order of nature but it is a new earth turned upward, or sacramentally aligned with a new heaven. The main direction of the imagery is also upward: this upward movement is the theme of the House of Holiness, of the final quest, and of various subordinate themes like the worship of Una by the satyrs.

We have spoken of the principle of symbolic parody, which we meet in all books of *The Faerie Queene*. Virtues are contrasted not only with their vicious opposites, but with vices that have similar names and appearances. Thus the golden mean of temperance is parodied by the golden means provided by Mammon; 'That part of justice, which is equity' in Book v is parodied by the anarchistic equality preached by the giant in the second canto, and so on. As the main theme of Book I is really faith, or spiritual fidelity, the sharpest parody of this sort is between Fidelia, or true faith, and Duessa, who calls herself Fidessa. Fidelia holds a golden cup of wine and water (which in other romance patterns would be the Holy Grail, though Spenser's one reference to the Grail shows that he has no interest in it); Duessa holds the golden cup of the Whore of Babylon. Fidelia's cup also contains a serpent (the redeeming brazen serpent of Moses typifying the Crucifixion); Duessa sits on the dragon of the Apocalypse who is metaphorically the same beast as the serpent of Eden. Fidelia's power to raise the dead is stressed; Duessa raises Sansjoy from the dead by the power of Aesculapius, whose emblem is the serpent. Of all such parodies in the first book the most important for the imagery of the poem as a whole is the parody of the tree and water of life in Eden. These symbols have their demonic counterparts in the paralysed trees of Fradubio and Fraelissa and in the paralysing fountain from which St George drinks in the seventh canto.

Thus the first book shows very clearly what we have called the subordinating of cyclical symbols to dialectical ones: the tree and water of life, originally symbols of the rebirth of spring, are here symbols of resurrection, or a permanent change from a life in physical nature above the animals to life in human nature under God. The main interest of the second book is also dialectical, but in the reverse direction, concerned with human life in the ordinary physical world, and with its separation from the demonic world below. The Bower of Bliss is a parody of Eden, and just as the climax of Book I is St George's three-day battle with the dragon of death, so the narrative climax of Book II is Guyon's three-day endurance in the underworld. It is the climax at least as far as Guyon's heroism is concerned, for it is Arthur who defeats Maleger and it is really the Palmer who catches Acrasia.

We should expect to find in Book II, therefore, many demonic parodies of the symbols in Book I, especially of the tree and water of life and its symbolic relatives. At the beginning we note that Acrasia, like Duessa, has a golden cup of death, filled, like Fidelia's, with wine and water ('Bacchus with the nymph'). There follows Ruddymane, with his bloody hands that cannot be washed. Spenser speaks of Red Cross hands as 'baptised' after he falls back into the well of life, and the Ruddymane incident is partly a reference to original sin, removable only by baptism or bathing in a 'liuing well'. The demonic counterparts of both sacraments appear in the hell scene in the cave of Mammon, in connexion with Pilate and Tantalus. Pilate, forever washing his hands in vain, repeats the Ruddymane image in its demonic context, and Tantalus is the corresponding parody of the Eucharist. These figures are preceded by the description of the golden appletree in the garden of Proserpina and the river Cocytus. Images of trees and water are considerably expanded in the description of the Bower of Bliss.

The fact that the fountain of Diana's nymph refuses to cleanse Ruddymane's hands indicates the rather subordinate role of Diana in Spenser's symbolism. It is clear, if we compare the description of Venus in Book IV with the description of Nature in the *Mutabilitie Cantos*, that Venus represents the whole order of nature, in its higher human as well as its lower physical aspect. What Diana stands for is the resistance to corruption, as symbolized by unchastity, which is the beginning, and of course always an essential part, of moral realization. Hence Diana in Spenser is a little like the law in Milton, which can discover sin but not remove it. In the *Mutabilitie Cantos* the glimpsing of Diana's nakedness by Faunus is parallel, on a small scale, to the rebellion of the lower against the higher nature which is also represented by Mutability's thrusting herself into heaven at the place of Cynthia, who is another form of Diana. Naturally Elizabeth's virginity compelled Spenser to give a high place to Diana and her protégé Belphoebe, but for symbolic as well as political reasons he preferred to make the Faerie Queene a young woman proceeding toward marriage, like Britomart. Meanwhile it is the virginal Faerie Queene whose picture Guyon carries on his shield, Guyon being in his whole moral complex something of a male Diana.

Temperance in Spenser is a rather negative virtue, being the resistance of consciousness to impulsive action which is necessary in order to know whether the action is going up or down in the moral dialectic. Conscious action is real action, Aristotle's proairesis; impulsive action is really pseudo-action, a passion which increasingly becomes passivity. Human life in the physical world has something of the feeling of an army of occupation about it, symbolized by the beleaguered castle of Alma. The House of Alma possesses two things in particular: wealth, in Ruskin's sense of well-being, and beauty, in the sense of correct proportion and ordering of parts. Its chief enemies are 'Beauty, and money', the minions of Acrasia and Mammon, the external or instrumental possessions which the active mind uses and the passive mind thinks of as ends in themselves. Temperance is also good temperament, or the balancing of humours, and Guyon's enemies are mainly humours in the Elizabethan sense, although the humours are usually symbolized by their corresponding elements, as the choleric Pyrochles is associated with fire and the phlegmatic Cymochles with water. The battleground between the active and the passive mind is the area of sensation, the steady rain of impressions and stimuli coming in from the outer world which the active mind organizes and the passive mind merely yields to. Normally the sanguine humour predominates in the active mind; the passive one becomes a victim of melancholy, with its progressive weakening of will and of the power to distinguish reality from illusion. In Spenser's picture of the mind the fancy (Phantastes) is predisposed to melancholy and the influence of 'oblique Saturne'; it is not the seat of the poetic imagination, as it would be in a nineteenth-century Romantic. The title of George Macdonald's *Phantastes*, the author tells us, comes not from Spenser but from Phineas Fletcher, who differs from Spenser in making Phantastes the source of art. Maleger, the leader of the assault on Alma, is a spirit of melancholy, and is sprung from the corresponding element of earth.

Having outlined the dialectical extremes of his imagery, Spenser moves on to consider the order of nature on its two main levels in the remaining books. Temperance steers a middle course between care and carelessness, jealousy and wantonness, miserliness and prodigality, Mammon's cave and Acrasia's bower. Acrasia is a kind of sinister Venus, and her victims, Mordant wallowing in his blood, Cymochles, Verdant, have something of a dead, wasted, or frustrated Adonis about them. Mammon is an old man with a daughter, Philotime. Much of the symbolism of the third book is based on these two archetypes. The first half leads up to the description of the Gardens of Adonis in Canto vi by at least three repetitions of the theme of Venus and Adonis. First we have the tapestry in the Castle Joyeous representing the story, with a longish description attached. Then comes the wounding of Marinell on his 'precious shore' by Brito-mart (surely the most irritable heroine known to romance), where the sacrificial imagery, the laments of the nymphs, the strewing of flowers on the bier are all conventional images of Adonis. Next is Timias, discovered by Belphoebe wounded in the thigh with a boar-spear. Both Belphoebe and Marinell's mother Cymoent have pleasant retreats closely analogous to the Gardens of Adonis. In the second half of the book we have three examples of the old man and young woman relationship: Malbecco and Hellenore, Proteus and Florimell, Busirane and Amoret. All these are evil: there is no idealized version of this theme. The reason is that the idealized version would be the counter-part to the vision of charity in the *Hymn of Heavenly Love*. That is, it would be the vision of the female Sapience sitting in the bosom of the Deity that we meet at the end of the *Hymn to Heavenly Beauty*, and this would take us outside the scope of *The Faerie Queene*, or at any rate of its third book.

The central figure in the third book and the fourth is Venus, flanked on either side by Cupid and Adonis, or what a modern poet would call Eros and Thanatos. Cupid and Venus are gods of natural love, and form, not a demonic parody, but a simple analogy of Christian love, an analogy which is the symbolic basis of the *Fowre Hymnes*. Cupid, like Jesus, is lord of gods and creator of the cosmos, and simultaneously an infant, Venus' relation to him being that of an erotic Madonna, as her relation to Adonis is that of an erotic Pièta. Being androgynous, she brings forth Cupid without male assistance (see *Colin Clouts Come Home Again*, 800 ff.); she loses him and goes in search of him, and he returns in triumph in the great masque at the end as lord of all creation.

The Garden of Adonis, with its Genius and its temperate climate, is so carefully paralleled to the Bower of Bliss that it clearly represents the reality of which the Bower is a mirage. It presents the order of nature as a cyclical process of death and renewal, in itself morally innocent, but still within the realm of Mutability, as the presence of Time shows. Like Eden, it is a paradise: it is nature as nature would be if man could live in his proper human world, the 'antique' Golden Age. It is a world where substance is constant but where 'Forms are variable and decay'; and hence it is closely connected with the theme of metamorphosis, which is the central symbol of divine love as the pagans conceived it.

Such love naturally has its perverted form, represented by the possessive jealousy of Malbecco, Busirane, and Proteus, all of whom enact variants of the myth of Tithonus and Aurora, the aged lover and the struggling dawn. Hellenore escapes into the world of satyrs, a world too 'natural' to be wholly sinful. The torturing of Amoret by Busirane, representing the anguish of jealous love, recurs in various images of bleeding, such as the 'long bloody river' in the tapestry of Cupid. Painful or not, it is love that makes the world go round, that keeps the cycle of nature turning, and it is particularly the love of Marinell and Florimell, whose names suggest water and vegetation, that seems linked to the natural cycle. Florimell is imprisoned under the sea during a kind of symbolic winter in which a 'snowy' Florimell takes her place. Marinell is not cured of his illness until his mother turns from 'watry gods' to the sun, and when he sees Florimell he revives

> As withered weed through cruell winters tine,[1]
>   That feeles the warmth of sunny beames reflection,
>   Liftes vp his head, that did before decline
> And gins to spread his leafe before the faire sunshine.
>
> (IV xii 34)

Book IV is full of images of natural revival, some in very unlikely places, and it comes to a climax with the symbolism of the tree and water of life in their natural context. At the temple of Venus, we are told, 'No tree, that is of count.... But there was planted' (x 22), and the next canto is a tremendous outburst of water. The wedding of the

[1] pain, affliction

Thames and the Medway takes place in Proteus' hall, and Proteus, in
the mythological handbooks, is the spirit of metamorphosis, the liquid
energy of substance driving through endless varieties of form . . .

When we move from friendship, an abstract pattern of human community which only noble spirits can form, to justice, in which the
base and evil must also be included, we return to historical allegory.
Spenser's vision of history (III ix) focuses on the legend of Troy: the
first Troy is recalled by Hellenore and Paridell, and the second, or
Rome, by Duessa, who reappears in Books IV and V. The third is of
course England itself, which will not collapse in adultery or superstition if her leading poet can prevent it. In the prophecy of this third
Troy we meet an image connected with the wedding of the Thames
in Book IV:

> It [sc. London] *Troynouant* is hight, that with the waues
> Of wealthy *Thamis* washed is along,
> Vpon whose stubborne neck, whereat he raues
> With roring rage, and sore him selfe does throng,
> That all men feare to tempt his billowes strong,
> She fastned hath her foot, which standes so hy,
> That it a wonder of the world is song
> In forreine landes, and all which passen by,
> Beholding it from far, do thinke it threates the skye.
>
> (III ix 45)

I quote this poetically licentious description of the Thames because
it is so closely linked with Spenser's conception of justice as the har-
nessing of physical power to conquer physical nature. In its lower
aspects this power is mechanical, symbolized by the 'yron man' Talus,
who must be one of the earliest 'science fiction' or technological
symbols in poetry, and who kills without discrimination for the sake
of discrimination, like a South African policeman. In its higher aspects
where justice becomes equity, or consideration of circumstances, the
central image is this one of the virgin guiding the raging monster.
We meet this image very early in the adventures of Una and the lion
in Book I, and the same symbolic shape reappears in the Gardens of
Adonis, where Venus enjoys Adonis with the boar imprisoned in a
cave underneath. Next comes the training of Artegall (who begins his
career by taming animals) by Astraea, identified with the constellation

Virgo. Next is the vision of Isis, where Osiris and the crocodile correspond to Adonis and the boar earlier, but are here explicitly identified.
Finally we have Mercilla and the lion under her throne, where Spenser
naturally refrains from speculating on the lion's possible identity with
a human lover. It may be the link with London on the Thames that
lends such prominence in Book v to the image of the river washing
away the filth of injustice. At the same time the virgin who dominates
the beast is herself the servant of an invisible male deity, hence the
figure of the female rebel is important in the last two books: Radigund
the Amazon in Book v, who rebels against justice, and Mirabell in
Book vi, who rebels against courtesy. Radigund is associated with the
moon because she parodies Isis, and Isis is associated with the moon
partly because Queen Elizabeth is, by virtue of Raleigh's name for her,
Cynthia.

Just as Book iii deals with the secular and natural counterpart of
love, so Book vi deals with the secular and natural counterpart of
grace. The word grace itself in all its human manifestations is a
thematic word in this book, and when the Graces themselves appear
on Mount Acidale we find ourselves in a world that transcends the
world of Venus:

> Those three to men all gifts of grace do graunt,
> And all, that *Venus* in her selfe doth vaunt,
> Is borrowed of them.
>
> (vi x 15)

The Graces, we are told, were begotten by Jove when he returned
from the wedding of Peleus and Thetis. This wedding is referred to
again in the *Mutabilitie Cantos* as the most festive occasion the gods had
held before the lawsuit of Mutability. For it was at this wedding that
Jove was originally 'confirmed in his imperial see'; the marriage to
Peleus removed the threat to Jove's power coming from the son of
Thetis, a threat the secret of which only Prometheus knew, and which
Prometheus was crucified on a rock for not revealing. Thus the
wedding also led, though Spenser does not tell us this, to the reconcil-
ing of Jove and Prometheus, and it was Prometheus, whose name
traditionally means forethought or wisdom, who, according to Book
ii, was the originator of Elves and Fays – that is, of man's moral and
conscious nature. There are still many demonic symbols in Book vi,

especially the attempt to sacrifice Serena, where the custom of eating the flesh and giving the blood to the priests has obvious overtones of parody. But the centre of symbolic gravity, so to speak, in Book VI is a pastoral Arcadian world, where we seem almost to be entering into the original home of man where, as in the child's world of Dylan Thomas's *Fern Hill*, it was all Adam and maiden. It is no longer the world of Eros; yet the sixth book is the most erotic, in the best sense, of all the books in the poem, full of innocent nakedness and copulation, the surprising of which is so acid a test of courtesy, and with many symbols of the state of innocence and of possible regeneration like the Salvage Man and the recognition scene in which Pastorella is reunited to her parents.

Such a world is a world in which the distinction between art and nature is disappearing because nature is taking on a human form. In the Bower of Bliss the *mixing* of art and nature is what is stressed: on Mount Acidale the art itself is nature, to quote Polixenes again. Yet art, especially poetry, has a central place in the legend of courtesy. Grace in religion implies revelation by the Word, and human grace depends much on good human words. All through the second part of *The Faerie Queene*, slander is portrayed as the worst enemy of the human community: we have Ate and Sclaunder herself in Book IV, Malfont with his tongue nailed to a post in Mercilla's court, as an allegory of what ought to be done to *other* poets; and finally the Blatant Beast, the voice of rumour full of tongues. The dependence of courtesy on reasonable speech is emphasized at every turn, and just as the legend of justice leads us to the figure of the Queen, as set forth in Mercilla, who manifests the order of society, so the legend of courtesy leads us to the figure of the poet himself, who manifests the order of words.

(77–86)

Frank Kermode

from 'Spenser and the Allegorists', *Proceedings of the British Academy*, vol. 48 1962

There is no 'Spenser controversy', Spenser has been 'dislodged' with no fuss at all. Why? What follows hints at one possible answer.

Spenser is a known maker of allegories. If you believe, as many people appear to, that allegory is necessarily superficial, *The Faerie Queene* is dull in so far as it is simple, and a failure in so far as it is difficult. Coleridge, perhaps, first specified that allegory was a mode inferior to 'symbolism', and this is now commonplace. Blake's distinction between Vision and Allegory – which is 'formed by the Daughters of Memory' – was accepted, for instance, by Yeats, who blames Spenser and Bunyan for the unhappy vogue of allegory in England. A German Symbolist friend of his – probably Dauthendey, the man who hated verbs – won Yeats's approval by observing that 'Allegory said things which could be said as well, or better, in another way'.[1] As such views gain ground, Spenser's fortunes wilt; and in our own day we may find a critic of distinction, Professor Yvor Winters, willing to dismiss *The Faerie Queene* in a few derisive words.[2] From Hazlitt reading the poem in 'voluptuous indolence', we progress easily to Winters not reading it at all.

On the other hand, though we tend to associate allegory with grey abstraction, we are all fascinated by what Goethe called 'the green and golden archetype'.[3] There are the archetypes of Miss Bodkin, which are Jungian, and those of Professors Wheelwright and Frye, which are not. There is a general and an increasing interest in the exposure of radical myth-structures in works of literature. But Spenser does not come well out of this. The interpreters of Melville and Hawthorne and Kafka welcome every new subtlety of method; but Spenser seems fated to suffer at best a criticism of reduction, a dubious salvation by archetypes.

It is pointless to discuss criticism which, in the teeth of scholarly evidence, finds Spenser too simple. My concern is with reductive criticism, which works by the abolition of contexts, by the sacrifice of the poem's *presence* to its radical myths and types. These are, of course, to be found in the poem, and at the present moment they confer

1 *A Book of Images* drawn by W. T. Horton and introduced by W. B. Yeats, London, 1898, p. 8. (Partially reprinted in *Ideas of Good and Evil*, 1903, and in *Essays and Introductions*, 1961.)
2 *The Function of Criticism*, 1957, p. 44.
3 Quoted in Philip Wheelwright, *The Burning Fountain*, 1954, p. 89.

prestige; but much damage may be done in the process of isolating them in their primitive glory. *The Faerie Queene* is, after all, an heroic poem, extremely conscious of its peculiar relation to history – to 'now and England'. To reduce it to a 'Biblical quest-romance',[1] as Northrop Frye does, is, however brilliant the work, not to glorify but to impoverish it. The mistake, in short, is 'to be led away into exploring the possible significance the myths used may be thought to possess in themselves, into infinite speculations about their archetypal patterns and analogies, instead of the realized meaning of the work itself'. It is not without interest that the excellent book from which I borrow these words[2] is not about Spenser but about Joyce; whose work, it may be thought, deliberately invites such speculations, whereas Spenser's does not.

Perhaps there will always be enmity between those who believe symbols and archetypes to have value in themselves, and those who think it obvious that the value of a symbol, however much traditional significance it may accrete, is finally determined by its context; much as the meaning of redness in a sign varies from 'hot water' to 'stop!' or 'Manchester United'. For example, the most superficial inquiry into the history of the principal figures of the book of Revelation will reveal that for all their antiquity they alter their meanings with their contexts. Professor E. H. Gombrich has more than once castigated the 'mystical antiquarianism' which treats images as if they were possessed of inalienable meanings. To do so is to abandon a complex civility in favour of a dubious *sapientia veterum*. Now the context in which Spenser's archetypes acquire value is not easy to describe; but I think we may gather something of the importance of the attempt if we can find a group of images used in his own way by Spenser and in a revealingly different way by a modern author. Such are the apocalyptic images used by Spenser in the first book of *The Faerie Queene*; and I shall first speak of the use to which Spenser puts them. Later I shall look at the contexts provided by a well-thought-of twentieth-century writer, D. H. Lawrence.

Spenser would have been happy to call the book of Revelation 'a continued Allegory, or darke conceit'. Like his own poem, it has a

1 *Anatomy of Criticism*, 1957, p. 194.
2 S. L. Goldberg, *The Classical Temper*, 1961, pp. 201–2.

spiritual as well as an historical aspect; for if, according to St Augustine, it is an allegory of the soul's escape from bonds of sin,[1] it is also, by weight of tradition, a prophecy to be fulfilled by events in time. Spenser's first book has intentions closely parallel to these, for it proceeds on the old assumption that the history of mankind is the history of man's soul writ large. Book 1 might fairly be designated a Tudor Apocalypse.

Upton first observed the frequent allusions to Revelation (and Warton, I am sorry to say, was shocked by them). Little was added to the subject until recently, when Mrs J. W. Bennett and Professor J. E. Hankins looked into it again and transformed it. Mrs Bennett[2] noticed that the use made of Revelation by Reform theologians was very relevant to Spenser's purposes; and Mr Hankins brought to bear the patristic commentaries.[3] Certain identifications are now, I suppose, beyond dispute. St George and Arthur share qualities of the Christ of Revelation – a point made vivid by those medieval Apocalypses which show the Knight 'faithful and true' bearing, in his battle with the demonic host, a white shield with a cross *gules*.[4] Una is the 'woman clothed with the sun' of Revelation xii, 1, traditionally identified with the true church, which Tertullian called *integram ... incorruptam virginem*,[5] to be echoed down the centuries to Newton.[6] Another glance at some illuminated Apocalypse that shows the

1 *De Civitate Dei*, xx vii.

2 *The Evolution of 'The Faerie Queene'*, 1942, chap. 9.

3 'Spenser and the Revelation of St John', *Publications of the Modern Language Association of America*, vol. 60 (1945), pp. 364–81.

4 See, for example, M. R. James (ed.), *The Apocalypse in Latin*, MS. 10 in the collection of Dyson Perrins, 1927, plate 81; or the corresponding plate in *L'Apocalypse en Français au XIIIᵉ siècle* (Bib. Nat. fr. 403), ed. L. Delisle et P. Meyer, 1900. According to the influential commentary of Beatus, the horse is the body of Christ, the rider 'Dominus maiestatis ... verbum patris altissimi ... id est, divinitas incarnata' (*Beati in Apocalypsin Libri X*, ed. H. A. Sanders, 1930, p. 591).

5 As quoted by Jewel, *Apologia Ecclesiae Anglicanae*, 1562, pars vi, cap. xvi, div. 1; in *The Works of John Jewel* (Parker Society), 1848, vol. 3, p. 41.

6 Sir Isaac Newton, *Observations upon the Prophecies of Daniel and the Apocalypse of St John*, 1733, p. 279; '*the woman ... clothed with the sun*, before she flies into the wilderness, represents the primitive Church catholick ...'

Woman with her glory of sunshine will help to explain why Spenser, at the climax of the book, speaks of

> The blazing brightnesse of her beauties beame,
> And glorious light of her sunshyny face.
>
> (i xii 23)

Duessa, though she is all doubleness and multiplicity, all departures from a primal integrity, is also the Whore of Babylon; and Spenser's Eighth Canto is perfectly illustrated in medieval illustrations of Revelation xvii, 4.[1] Archimago is associated with Antichrist, a person who does not occur in Revelation, but was early attracted into its ambience from the Epistles of John. According to that source there were many antichrists, and the list of historical characters so named by their enemies must be very long; it is a common error, which Mrs Bennett repeats, that Wycliffe first applied the term to a pope. In any case, the application of the word to the papacy in general is the important one for our purposes; this was the work of Luther.[2] Archimago is antichrist in this sense. He is also the false prophet and the beast from the land. Arthur has traits of the knight *fidelis et verax*, but the first account of him is a development in chivalric terms of the angel in Revelation xviii. He wears the seal of the spouse (Canticles viii, 6) and shares the angel's satisfaction at the catastrophic prospects of Babylon, which is Rome.

Many minor allusions to Revelation I here ignore; the structural resemblances are sufficient to establish the point. When Red Cross deserts Una, Spenser is remembering Revelation ii, 4: 'for thou hast left thy first love'.[3] He means that England deserted the true catholic church. Una lost is the woman clothed with the sun who suffers forty-two months in the wilderness (the primary reference is to the typical

1 The beast she rides on has seven heads, standing for the deadly sins, and ten horns, representing – according to Hugh of St Victor– the violated commandments (Migne, *Patrologia Latina*, cxcvi 799; quoted by M. W. Bloomfield, *The Seven Deadly Sins*, 1952, p. 85).
2 *Preface to the Revelation of St John* (1545); in *Works of Martin Luther*, 1932, vi, pp. 479–88. This is Luther's second Preface to the book; in his first (1522) he had found it 'neither apostolic nor prophetic' (ibid., p. 488). The second Preface had much influence. See E. L. Tuveson, *Millennium and Utopia*, 1949, pp. 24 ff.
3 Hankins (loc. cit.) relates this episode to Cant. viii.

wanderings of the Israelites). The overthrow of the dragon is closely associated with the battle of Christ against Satan, and so with the Passion, the Resurrection, and the Harrowing of Hell.[1] The tree and the water which refresh Red Cross during the three-day battle are from Revelation xxii, and signify the two sacraments of the Reformed Church. The book presented by Red Cross to Arthur, the Babylonian House of Pride, the two Jerusalems – Cleopolis, and the city of Red Cross's vision – are further instances.[2]

Spenser was evidently conscious of iconographic and exegetical traditions; it is part of his method to telescope significations by glancing back at them: thus Red Cross, not only England but a saint imitating Christ, dissolves into the object of his imitation. Nevertheless, it remains clear that Mrs Bennett was right in thinking that his use of apocalyptic material was strongly coloured by recent anti-Romanist versions of Revelation. But her emphasis on extreme Protestantism is itself extreme. The apologists of the English settlement give the whole matter a new Anglican interest; and to leave Foxe and Jewel out of account is to miss what is most important to Spenser. I think it is part of the same mistake that Mrs Bennett discourages attempts to give the allegory a clear historical application. I do not mean that we ought to go back to calling Una Anne Boleyn; only that Scott was near the truth when he argued that the adventures of Red Cross 'bear a peculiar and obvious, though not a uniform, reference to the history of the Church of England'.[3] Not, be it noted, to the events of the English Reformation; but more broadly, so that the destruction of Error suggests to Scott the early Church purging itself of such heresies as Arianism, and the victory over Sansfoy Constantine's defeat of paganism.[4] The only commentator to develop Scott's suggestion was Thomas Keightley almost a century ago; and the Variorum editors report his views without approval.[5]

1 As Hankins (loc. cit.) suggests.
2 Hankins relates the House of Coelia to the Earthly Jerusalem.
3 Quoted in *The Works of Spenser: a Variorum Edition*, ed. E. Greenlaw, C. G. Osgood, F. M. Padelford, and R. Heffner, vol. 1 (1932), p. 450.
4 This last idea is all the more probable in the light of the report that Constantine owed his victory to British troops (Foxe, *Acts and Monuments of the Church*, ed. M. H. Seymour, 1838, p. 76).
5 *Variorum*, vol. 1, pp. 454–5.

I do not agree with Keightley's detailed interpretation; but that
there is in the text of the First Book a body of allusion to the history
of the Church seems to me inescapable, though it requires a detailed
demonstration which this hour will not contain. The poem is
addressed to the 'only supreme governor' of the Church; this title in
itself required historical justification, and so did the claim that English
Christianity was older than the Roman church. In fact all the apologists of the Settlement made the appeal to history as a matter of course.
And whoever agreed that the English was the true primitive catholic
church had to think of her history as beginning, not with the con-
vulsions of Henry VIII's reign, but, as Jewel put it, 'after the first
creation of the world'[1] or, more practically, with the arrival in
England of Joseph of Arimathea. For Christianity came here not from
Rome, but from the East; and Una is descended from kings and queens
whose 'scepters stretcht from East to Westerne shore' (i 5). 'Neither
did the east and the west, nor distance of place, divide the church,'
says Foxe; but 'this catholic unity did not long continue.'[2] Thanks, of
course, to the papacy; and Foxe enables us to recognize in Spenser's
text the features of certain especially guilty popes, who were the
progenitors of Duessa. Her father has the West under his rule, 'And
high hath set his throne, where *Tiberis* doth pas' (ii 22). Rome has
divided the world and exiled the catholic church. Who will restore
and re-establish it? . . .

Miss Frances Yates has connected the revival of chivalry at court
(which is clearly relevant to Spenser's procedures in his poem) with a
rather elaborate emperor-cult of Elizabeth[3]. . . . Miss Yates connects
the image of Elizabeth as Astraea with the return of England to
'Constantinian imperial Christianity'; the Virgin returns to the
Empire, as Virgil prophesied.[4] Thus the Queen, after the example of

1 Ed. cit., vol. 3, p. 49.

2 Foxe, p. 168.

3 'Queen Elizabeth as Astraea', *Journal of the Warburg and Courtauld Institutes*,
vol. 10 (1947), pp. 27–82.

4 Constantine officially recognized this application of *iam redit et Virgo*; see
Harold Mattingly, *Journal of the Warburg and Courtauld Institutes*, vol. 10 (1947),
p. 19. It is worth observing that the Woman of Revelation can be related, in
terms of Johannine astrology, to the zodiacal Virgo (see Austin Farrer, *A Rebirth
of Images*, 1949, pp. 202–3).

her predecessor, had united Church and Empire; and the astrological associations of the Astraea figure were available and ingeniously used for imperial propaganda, as, for example, in *Faerie Queene* V.

Similar cults of Charles V, Henri III, and Henri IV and others, indicate that the political value of this theme had been noticed elsewhere. It is expounded not only by Foxe but in the Preface to Erasmus's paraphrases on the New Testament, both books ordered to be placed in English churches. Elizabeth is not likely to have overlooked the special propriety of the theme to herself. 'Let Virgo come from heaven, the glorious star. . . . Let her reduce the Golden Age again', says a character in *The Misfortunes of Arthur*, prophesying the reign of Elizabeth, though in 1588. It is even possible that the eirenic implications of the myth could have helped to conciliate the remaining English Romanists, much as the historians' proof of the ancient liberties of the English church seems to have contented them, at least before the arrival of the Jesuit missions.[1] However that may be, we must obviously allow for the pressure of such a cult on Spenser's poem. The myth of the queen as Astraean empress is inseparable from the use of apocalyptic figures with historical significations, and itself involves a strong sense that the whole history of the Empire, from Aeneas to Constantine, from Charlemagne to Elizabeth, culminated in the present moment. . . .

Now it must be confessed that Spenser *complies* with the archetypes. If the archetype of the hero insists that he fight a dragon, Spenser obliges. Mircea Eliade, arguing from many instances, calls this 'the conversion of event into myth',[2] part of the means by which 'archaic humanity . . . defended itself . . . against all the novelty and irreversibility of history'.[3] And perhaps all the apocalyptic material I have mentioned could be related to this archaic retreat from event into fantasies of perpetual renewal which defeat the terrors of history, or provide an escape from history into myth. If Spenser sacrifices actuality, contemporaneity, to the archetypes; if, celebrating his Astraea, his *renovatio mundi*, he sinks out of history into sibylline

1 M. Powicke, *The Reformation in England*, 1961, p. 143.
2 *The Myth of the Eternal Return*, trans. W. R. Trask, Bollingen Series, vol. 46 (1954), p. 39.
3 ibid., p. 48.

fantasy; then he deserves all the reductive criticism he gets. But to believe that, one would have to forget the whole effort of imagination and reason which conferred upon archetypes complex interrelated meanings for that poem and for that time. The achievement of Spenser in that heroic First Book is not to have dived into the archetypes, but to have given them a context of Virgilian security – to have used them in the expression of an actual, unique, critical moment of a nation's culture and history. He looks backward only to achieve ways of registering the density of the central situation: the reign of Elizabeth. Iam *redit et Virgo*. He does not convert event into myth, but myth into event. His mood is acceptance; he welcomes history, not seeking to lose his own time in some transhistorical pattern. Such patterns of course exist; but only the unique and present moment can validate them. As to that moment, Apocalypse prophesied and history foreshadowed it; the mind of Europe – not merely that of Virgil and Constantine, Dante and Marsilius, Ariosto and Foxe, but of the people – expected its coming. Spenser celebrates the Elizabethan *renovatio* with something of Virgil's sober exaltation. It is a phase of no temporal cycle but a once-for-all historical event, like the Incarnation itself – however cruel the claims of Mutability and the certainty of suffering in the Last Days.

This acceptance of history – this reduction of dream to providential event – is very remote from the popular chiliasm, which, in Eliade's formula, amounts to a prohibition of history 'through a reintegration of human societies within the horizon of archetypes and their repetition'.[1] One might say that Spenser, like Virgil, celebrates the end of the need for such subterfuge: there will be no *ekpyrosis*, the city is eternal. The consequences are not all gay. At the end of Eliade's book the dilemma is projected as a dialogue between archaic and modern man; the passage bears a striking though unconscious resemblance to the *Mutabilitie* cantos, and ends with a choice between Christianity and despair which echoes Spenser's fragmentary last stanzas. To reject the archetypes is to live in the existential complexity of a hard world.

We have experienced in our own times a tendency for the archetypes and cycles to reassert their attractiveness. . . . In literature, as I have argued elsewhere, it is especially evident that the old patterns recur; Yeats, for example, has his archetypes and cycles, his eschatological

1 *The Myth of the Eternal Return*, p. 153.

fantasies of violence upon horses in the Last Days, his harsh masculine millennium of princes and viziers, his numerological speculations about the year 1927. (The bewilderment he felt, in common with Æ, at the failure of that year to be sufficiently catastrophic has many medieval parallels.) Yeats speaks of his systematized fantasy, in a famous phrase, as an attempt 'to hold in a single thought reality and justice';[1] it is a saying much more relevant to *The Faerie Queene* than to *A Vision*, that headlong flight into archetype and cycle (though it applies to some of the poems). Joyce borrowed his cycles from Mme Blavatsky.[2] Henry Miller testifies to the continuance of these tendencies in the *avant-garde* of our own time.

I remember at this point the character Lebedev in Dostoevsky's *The Idiot*. In his view, the European railway system was a disastrous consequence of the fall of 'the star called Wormwood' (Revelation viii, 11). 'The whole spirit of the last few centuries, taken as a whole, sir, in its scientific and practical application, is perhaps really damned, sir!' But as Lebedev, coming expositor of antichrist, proceeds, the fun dies away. Things, we feel the message coming through, really are falling apart. In *War and Peace*, on the other hand, apocalyptic prophecy is only a whimsical trick of characterization. Now, in the books which pour out to prove that the great English poets were all 'adepts' of the 'tradition', we hear the voice of Lebedev, not that of Tolstoy. And in seminal works of modernist poetry, in *The Waste Land* and *The Cantos*, we find ourselves comfortably close to the archetypes.

This is a position very unfavourable to Spenser. His poem is not a decorated anteroom through which initiates pass on their way to some inner chamber where they will find the archetypes, or Mr Joseph Campbell's 'monomyth'.[3] Professor Frye, acting on his belief that 'myths explain the structural principles behind familiar literary facts',[4] provides a brief and brilliant account of *Faerie Queene* I. There is, I think, little to be said against it, considered as part of his classification

1 *A Vision*, 1961, p. 25.
2 See Clive Hart, *Structure and Motif in Finnegan's Wake*, 1962, especially chap. 2.
3 *The Hero with a Thousand Faces*, 1949; and see E. Honig, *Dark Conceit*, 1960, especially chap. 3.
4 *Anatomy of Criticism*, p. 215.

of the world of literature in terms of a physics of archetype; but in so far as this is all he will say about the work, there is a huge, indeed fatal, reduction of the work's actual complexity, its 'presence'. My objection is very similar to that brought by Miss Helen Gardner against Dr Austin Farrer's archetypal reduction of St Mark's Gospel: she says that it 'evaporates St Mark's sense of what we mean by historical reality'.[1] In Spenser this is equally a sense of the uniqueness of the moment celebrated; it acquires a timeless and unrepeatable quality, and the event transcends the archetype.

In the last part of this paper I will try to sharpen the contrast between Spenser's acceptance of history, and the modern rejection of it in favour of the archetypes, by returning to the themes of Apocalypse and their use by a single eminent modern author who was obsessed by them, namely D. H. Lawrence.

Lawrence's interest in the theme, as he observes in his last book, *Apocalypse*,[2] was lifelong. . . .

As early as 1923 he was saying that the Seals are the sympathetic ganglia and the vials 'the corresponding voluntary ganglia' of which Sagittarius stands for the 'most secret, and the most potent . . . the first and last'.[3] Revelation was, when you got down to the real Mystery ritual, a guide to 'emotional-passional knowledge'.[4] Eventually Lawrence gave the theme full treatment in *Apocalypse*.

Richard Aldington, in his preface to that book, affirms incorrectly that Lawrence really cared little for this kind of thing, but adds, rightly, that like the Etruscans, Revelation offered Lawrence another way of saying something he believed to be of extreme importance, something he had often tried to express before: this was the hostility between modern man and the Cosmos in the Christian era, and especially since the Reformation, when Protestants 'substituted the non-vital universe of force and mechanistic order, and the long slow death of

---

1 *The Limits of Literary Criticism*, 1956, p. 33.
2 1932.
3 *Collected Letters*, pp. 745–6. Lawrence at this stage was more certain of the truth than of the details of the sevenfold system, which he had learnt from the Vedantists. For a clear exposition, see Frederick Carter, *D. H. Lawrence and the Body Mystical*, 1932, pp. 20ff.
4 *Collected Letters*, p. 749.

the human being set in'.[1] So, under the veil of the Christian, power-envying, logic-loving sophistries of the present text, he found a mystery ritual, a *katabasis*, a Magna Mater split by the meddling editors into two: the woman clothed with the sun and the Scarlet Woman (for under the bad dispensation 'the colour of life becomes the colour of abomination').[2] The first half of Revelation is the great text of archaic sense-knowledge, a set of images associated not by logic but by intuition. Some such text he had been seeking from his earliest days; he told Jessie Chambers there would never be another Shakespeare because his was an integrated age, whereas 'Things are split up now'.[3] ...

This aspect of the matter suggests a final confrontation between the first book of *The Faerie Queene* and the only modern work of fiction known to me which also comments upon the state of the nation in terms of Apocalypse. This is *Lady Chatterley's Lover*, first published in 1928, when Lawrence was in the midst of his apocalyptic studies, though only recently made available for mature consideration. It is clear enough that the novel echoes those earlier Cyprianic prophecies of Lawrence about the rottenness and death of England, the world of the new logos, of 'mechanized greed'. 'Our old show will come flop', as Dukes puts it;[4] and Mellors himself, 'There's a bad time coming, boys, there's a bad time coming!'[5] It is equally clear that the famous passage about red trousers means little without reference to Lawrence on apocalyptic red.[6] (Lawrence could hardly be expected to believe that the values of symbols is determined by context, and he believed red to be the life-colour.) What is less obvious – yet it follows from his belief in using symbols that are not only archaic but veiled – is the direct relation between the amorous action of *Lady Chatterley* and Lawrence's exposition of the Opening of the Seals. These seals, he held, were the seven centres or gates of 'dynamic consciousness'. The old Adam dies in seven stages; at the climactic

---

1 *Apocalypse*, p. 54.
2 ibid., p. 175.
3 Quoted in H. T. Moore, *The Intelligent Heart*, 1960, p. 94.
4 Edition of 1960, p. 77.
5 *Lady Chatterley's Lover*, p. 315.
6 ibid., p. 229; *Apocalypse*, p. 175.

seventh he is also reborn.[1] Lawrence develops this idea in terms of initiation ritual: the opening of the last seal is compared to 'a stark flame . . . clothed anew' in Hades.[2] 'Then the final flame-point of the eternal self of a man emerges from hell';[3] and, finally, this moment is related to the emergence of the initiate from the goddess's temple, dazed and ecstatic. 'The cycle of individual initiation is fulfilled. . . . The initiate is dead, and alive again in a new body.'[4] Then there is a silence in heaven.

The seals stand for the ganglia, and this rite represents the 'awakening' of a human body; which, as expert witnesses asserted, is a theme in *Lady Chatterley's Lover*. Lady Chatterley dies into life. Indeed, the parallels between her association with Mellors and the Opening of the Seals are very close. There are seven significant sexual encounters in the novel (the eighth occurs during a brief reunion in London, out of series; there has been a pause in heaven). I am glad to have my counting confirmed by the Warden of All Souls, who also observes that the seventh is 'for his purposes', as it is for mine, 'the significant episode'.[5] For reasons made clear by Warden Sparrow, this encounter is different from its predecessors: 'the reckless, shameless sensuality shook her to her foundations, stripped her to the very last, and made a different woman of her . . . burning the soul to tinder . . . the passion licked round her, consuming, and when the sensual flame of it pressed through her bowels and her breast, she really thought she was dying: yet a poignant, marvellous death'. She has the 'deep organic shame' burnt out, and reaches 'the core of the physical jungle'.[6] The act is anal, Adamite. All this is surely concerned with the seventh seal, the secret, potent Sagittarius, Governor of the organs of Generation, by means of which the sacred fire is stolen.[7] The astrology of this may be, to the eye of the profane, obscure. What is beyond doubt is that the

1 *Apocalypse*, pp. 108–9.
2 ibid., p. 117.
3 ibid., pp. 119–20.
4 ibid., p. 124.
5 'Regina *v*. Penguin Books', *Encounter*, no. 101, February 1962, pp. 35–43.
6 *Lady Chatterley's Lover*, pp. 258–9.
7 Pryse, *Prometheus*, pp. 100–101.

seventh stage of the process represents the mystic descent into Hades.[1]
Connie, like the postulant of the Mysteries, must die in this seventh
stage. She dies into life, is initiated. The Mysteries, we remember,
represented this rebirth by a sexual act. So the modern Dragon, the
dirty-white Dragon of the modern Logos, as Lawrence calls it, which
reduces the human consciousness and nervous system to a condition of
death, is defeated. Connie, whom the vulgar may call a Scarlet
Woman, is really the Woman clothed with the sun.

In one respect, at any rate, Lawrence's method here resembles
Spenser's; for it is surely obvious that although the allegory is a
spiritual allegory, dealing with the regeneration of one woman, it is
also historical, and prophesies, or prays for, the regeneration of
England. England, he explains in *A Propos of Lady Chatterley's Lover*,
knows only bad or 'white' sex, 'the nervous, personal, disintegrative
sort'[2] – the sort, in fact, that Lady Chatterley knew before she met
Mellors. 'We can have no hope of the regeneration of England from
such sort of sex. . . . And the other, the warm blood-sex that establishes
the living and revitalizing connexion between man and woman, how
are we to get that back? I don't know. Yet get it back we must . . .
or we are lost.' And he goes on to speak of this necessary regeneration of
England, the religious restoration of 'the ancient seven-cycle' and so
on.[3] The two ideas – of personal and national rebirth – melt into each
other, in the commentary as in the novel itself. Connie is England
and Mellors is Lawrence's Arthur, emperor of the Last Days.

Quoting a passage from *Apocalypse* on the old familiar theme –
'We are unnaturally resisting our connection with the cosmos, etc.' –
Helen Corke remarks: 'The passage changes into the singular as I read
it.'[4] This is shrewd; and it must count against Lawrence in this

1 Clearly explained by Carter, p. 21 and p. 31 (discussing the physiological
facts).
2 p. 115. One may note that Lawrence's preoccupation with 'bad' sex also
echoes that of the Brethren of the Free Spirit. Lawrence would have understood Fränger's explanation of the man buried upside down to his waist in
Bosch's 'Hell' (*The Millennium of Hieronymus Bosch*, p. 119). The triptych has
many other emblems of sterile or egotistic sexuality, consequence of the
divorce of 'spirit and instinct' which 'causes a withering of the vegetation
forces and an over-development of the brain' (Fränger, p. 101).
3 pp. 116–17.
4 *Lawrence and Apocalypse*, 1933, pp. 127–8.

comparison that his apocalyptic researches and applications are secret, 'isolate' to use a favourite word of his, and very remote from the main goings-on of the world. It is a well-known observation of Mr Eliot's that 'a man does not join himself with the Universe so long as he has anything else to join himself with',[1] and it applies closely to Lawrence. But we must not forget that in some ways, as I suggested earlier, Lawrence simply develops à outrance tendencies of some importance in the literary culture not only of his own time but of ours. He is not alone in that garden of archetypes; not only poets but even as Miss Gardner observed, theologians are to be found there. For example, Dr Farrer treats Revelation[2] very much in the fashion reprehended by Miss Gardner in his study of Mark, and asks us to think of the book as made up of images which 'live the life of images, not of concepts' and obey 'imagery laws', not 'the principles of conceptual system' – such images being 'the stuff of revelation' with which theology and metaphysics meddle in vain; they are sealed within the horizon of archetypes, inaccessible to reason.[3] Such a view certainly seems to entail a total rejection of history, and Lawrence would have found it more to his taste than Archdeacon Charles. Even in *Lady Chatterley*, where it has its place, history becomes part of a private myth. This is despair and flight and unreason; Spenser is hope, acceptance, and intellect.

It is clear, then, that a Lawrentian sacrifice of *presence* to *type* is no way to approach *The Faerie Queene*. Hence we mistakenly assume that the poem is allegorical in the sense of superficial, or, in uprooting the archetypes, we destroy its texture. . . .

The warrior 'faithfull true' means more in Spenser than Lawrence could conceive; and in making of him what he did, Spenser assumed that men can keep their heads above the tide of time, and find in the present moment senses which are enriched, but not absorbed, by the ancient images. We need a better understanding of this sober and confident humanity, of the methods by which Spenser provided contexts in which the archetypes find a present meaning. Such an understanding requires a double effort – we must study the causes of Spenser's exclusion from our serious reading as well as the texts and

---

1 *Selected Essays*, 1932, p. 131.
2 *The Rebirth of Images*, 1949.
3 *The Glass of Vision*, 1948, pp. 45, 51.

contexts of *The Faerie Queene* itself. Since I have used Lawrence as typical of beliefs and attitudes I deplore, I may well end with one sentence in *Apocalypse* which my argument endorses: 'The Apocalypse is still a book to conjure with.'[1] Perhaps the spirit of Spenser will one day consent to be called.

(261–79)

Rosemond Tuve

from *Allegorical Imagery* 1966

[The first selection comes from a chapter on medieval analyses of and treatises on the vices and the virtues.]

It makes a great difference in a poetic treatment of a quest for a virtue if a presupposition exists that it has a famous proper opposite, and it made a great difference to Spenser – though he was not intending to present seven opposing actions against Christianity's seven modes of evil but twelve virtues from Aristotle. When he chose to use out of his varied heritage the errant and contending Knight and the quest-image with its implications, and partly impelled by this, chose also to set over against his figures their famous great opposites (thus further determining the nature of his virtues), and finally, chose the mode of figurative language that asks for allegorical reading, it meant that most of his structure of meanings and means of portrayal were lined out for him.

To be sure, no matter how firm his intention to delineate the Aristotelian virtues, a man of 1580 would find it all but unnatural to depict a quest of a virtue without depicting a conquest or escape from a particular opposing vice, without demonstrating the latter's nature and allowing that in part to define the virtue. This has affected Spenser's design markedly. It has often pressed his selection and his conception of his virtues over in the direction of the set that were truly against the vices. He handles all his inheritances with a proper freedom, and I am not in sympathy with attempts to find the total series of seven sins in *The Faerie Queene*. Yet his Temperance has been pushed toward a virtue more resembling Sobriété with its

1 p. 297.

connexions with a rightly directed love despising the world's lures, by the stress put on Luxury and Avarice as chief embodiments of concupiscentia; it is the *intemperateness* of Acrasia that becomes apparent to Guyon; and psychomachias concerned with temptation to the sin of Lechery come elsewhere, just as in the *Somme le roi*, Lecherye riding on her goat occurs in a later section. The temptations of Red Cross are to Pride, not Luxury. Book I is dominated by the idea of countering Pride; Discordia, every form of Ire, is more investigated in Book IV than the nature of Friendship; and there is a clear attempt to set Luxuria against Castitas in Books III and IV, mingled with the equally common emphasis, but peculiar to Christian tradition, on Chastity seen as related to Fidelity (the pure soul faithful in allegiance to God, to the good, to the right loves, to creatures loved through the creator), only very secondarily related to Virginity, and related to marriage only because of the concern to define love as it exists in a knight who always makes the choice that is not self-indulgent. These extended meanings of luxury, of avarice, of wrath, belong of course to Spenser's predecessors, and were perfectly habitual.

The way in which an opposed vice has affected the *definition* of a virtue being sought is very clear in Book I. The Book has always forced commentators into tight corners, not simply because a virtue of Holiness is out of line, but because Pride in its relation to self-reliance (and even to condescending benevolence) is not vicious to Aristotle and his like, and because the great deliverer Arthur has as his *virtue* that Magnificentia which in its Aristotelian exposition is suspiciously akin to the very vice itself of Book I. This is aggravated by the fact that meanwhile, if we forsake an Aristotelian for a Christian frame of reference, its vice of Pride ought to be the special temptation of a Knight on a quest of Humilitas, rather than one especially in love with Truth.

The radical Christian definition of Pride, kept to the forefront (given the persistence all clichés have by the medieval virtues-and-vices literature), is strictly to the point here. Why is Red Cross's first enemy *Error* not arrogance, his first conquered knight Sans*foy* not Sans-humblesse, and why is Truth, which is seemingly the *goal* of the intellectual virtues, here the special *guide* to Holiness, and that which Holiness' patron must espouse, while Duessa or *falsity* in one form after another is his constant temptation, rather than vainglory? We may profitably recall the exemplum chosen by the *Somme le roi* illuminators to set forth Pride typified: Ahaziah. Now Ahaziah or Occosias was not a vainglorious, proud tyrant; he was a king of Samaria who, having injured himself by falling through a lattice in his upper chamber, sent to Ekron's god Baal-zebub – instead of the prophet of the true God – to know whether he was destined to recover. That was the sin which caused Elijah to declare God's judgement, 'Thou shalt not come down from the bed . . . but shalt surely die.' He is always pictured coming down in no uncertain sense, but actually his miscreance was the 'fall' of Pride, not the one from the lattice.

For the same reason, the first branch of Pride is commonly untrewth – that is Spenser's Sansfoy, the Sarazin, Infidelity. For the same reason, Error with her filthy poison of false books and papers manifestly figures the first mistaken way in which those err and wander who worship falsely by believing in the wrong things. Hence Una says during that first fight (1 i 19), 'Add *faith* vnto your force' (Fortitudo). For the same reason, Hypocrisy, proud Lucifer's quality, plays so large a part, being again a prominent branch of Pride in all the lists. Archimago the shape-shifter (evil is multiple) hates Una, who is single in her nature (Truth's nature) and in her devotion, because she is his exact opposite – one true to the Truth.

The meaning of the word 'truth' which connects it with troth to an allegiance, and makes it include both *veritas* and *fides*, is a very important meaning in incident after incident of Book I. Both sides of Una's trueness are continually played upon. When Red Cross in the second dream 'suspects her *truth*' though as yet 'no'vntruth he knew' (i 53), fidelity not rightness is being spoken of, yet it is 'faire falshood', both as false religion and as duplicity, who steps into Truth's stead (canto ii, prefatory verses). Fradubio, because he was in doubt which to think more beautiful, his frail but true faith or the meretriciously attractive, untrue mistress, saw his true love turn into a wooden, lifeless thing and met both deceptiveness and infidelity in the untrue love; Red Cross learns nothing from seeing the exact parallel to his own situation because he has lost truth through failing to keep troth. The double emphasis on Truth and Faith is indigenous to all treatments which discuss the fundamental spring of the sin of Pride, which is not self-conceit or arrogance or vaingloriousness but the cause of those (all are branches) – an unwillingness to worship the true God, Lucifer's flaw. 'This is the first synne that assaileth Goddes knyt', 'the lioun that al swelweth and biteth', and it is perilous 'for it blyndeth a man that he ne knoweth not hymself, ne seeth not hymself.'[1]

The blindness is certainly being used to define the nature of 'sight'. Pride's special blindness is to man's true nature and limits; as a creature he must first recognize the true God to whom he owes allegiance, and secondly, maintain this allegiance with no trace of rebellion (basic *humilitas*) because he sees God's nature rightly. This understanding of Pride's failure of sight accounts for the stress throughout on darkness: Night and her forces are arrayed against Red Cross, 'old *Aveugles* sonnes' are her nephews Sansfoy and Sansjoy, and the Lucifer-parallel of the rebellion against Jove is recalled; blind Ignaro has the keys to Orgoglio's castle; Corceca's blind heart cannot achieve the first recognition, while her favorite Kirkrapine robs the body of the faithful, replacing right allegiance with idolatrous whoredom. The three brothers can stand by one another loyally enough, but this is not an alleviating characteristic to give them human complexity. This kept faith to wrong instead of right underscores their blind faithlessness as miscreants, the opprobrious term cast at them when Sarazin is not preferred. Yet every sight image is not attached to this concept, and it is just as natural in allegory, which asks us to discriminate between the significant and the casual, that when Una is momentarily blind to the identity of Archimago, unable like Milton's Uriel to see through devilish Hypocrisy, we must refuse to read this as a confusing error made by Truth. Una, too, is a creature, and does not equal Truth but shadows Truth so far as may be; she is not God Himself come down from heaven, the only perfect Truth.

The emphasis on clear sight of the true is accompanied by images showing rather firm faith to it. The 'salvage nation' who can see enough of truth's beauty not to destroy her is neither an idealization nor a condemnation of man's nature, but demonstrates its insufficiency to Una's double discipline 'of *faith* and *veritie*' (I vi 31).

1 *The Book of Vices and Virtues*, ed. W. Nelson Francis, Early English Text Society, No. 217, 1942, pp. 11–12. This work is a fourteenth-century English translation of the *Somme Le Roi* of Lorens d'Orléans, a thirteenth-century Dominican friar. [Ed.].

Spenser plainly means to leave undenied the connexions with lust and brutishness, even in Satyrane's heritage, and the latter's story shows us, without overnervous constant translation into ideas, the reasons why he alone could learn, and be 'plaine, faithfull, true'. Spenser keeps as close as ever in these sections to his theme of the virtue that is against Pride, but the kinds of pride he thinks it is against have helped to define it. It is cunning of him to introduce the humble who are without all trace of Humility by the radical definition of the Book, and distinguish among his miscreants. In apprehending such nuances, it is a disadvantage to see too morally; Book I is so often strictly allegorical, letting moral allegory take its chances.

Yet a hint of these conceptions, rather than an ironbound system of correspondences, is profitable. This comes out apropos of the Lion, whom we have had to take as only too many obfuscating equivalents. Lions 'as Nature' would have astonished any Elizabethan; they are no more Nature than chickens or scholars to those who have not yet identified savage, uncivilized, irrational, ungoverned, with natural. Spenser also avoids the irrelevancies of that famous character, the Grateful Lion. To be sure, he is not ingrata, in the sense which made Ungratefulness one of the branches of Pride (a human sin, man's unkindly [unnatural] resentment at owing service to God, manifest truth; long after the Elizabethans, it was still a cliché that brute creation escaped this diabolical perversion). A reasonable link connects the many references to Christ as Leo, the strong sun in Leo, the Lion upon whom Wrath rides in Spenser as in so many places, Leo as Pride. Spenser's phrasings show that he thinks of how the 'mightie proud' has once more yielded to the 'humble weake' (iii 7), as in the innumerable allegorical pictures of virtues standing upon, exacting submission from, their opposites. The power of truth against princely puissance, its simplicity and divine grounding compelling proud submission, is felt throughout but elsewhere not so specifically depicted. It is the theme all over again, but the different ideas brought in prove how far from repetitious it is; the choice of concretions must be intelligently managed to secure this – though Leo is Pride, we may try to imagine Spenser using him as the devilish apotheosis of the vice pure that he can make of Orgoglio. But the nature of the vice is providing the differentia which define the virtue.

It is notable that we are not given a story of man's temptations to power. Red Cross does not lapse into vainglorious tyranny; he lapses into trusting in his own powers to get on with his quest and know what mistresses to offer his help to. We do not see him captived by Lucifera, for he walks through her court as one who 'Thought all their glorie vaine' and their Princess 'too exceeding prowd' (iv 15); we see him the spoil of Untruth and Untroth, far more basic causes of Pride; and it is therefore that he *takes his armor off*, 'Poured out in loosnesse on the grassy grownd' (vii 7). That he was carelesse was his Pride. Spenser's inclusion of temptations not felt as such by his protagonist, as in the more famous example of Guyon, shows a poet interested less in dramatic struggles than in investigating through actions and images the nature and the definition of a virtue. (Of course, we could be simultaneously reading Spenser's thoughts on the present state of England, declared in the images.) I attribute the inclusiveness not to a moralist's effort to be tidily complete, but to a true pleasure in distinguishing varied motivations, effects, moral nuances, doctrinal profundities. Before Red Cross's almost fatal captivity, there is no warning tale of a psychological temptation to Sloth, and battle against it lost; he fell victim to 'foolish pride' and 'weaknesse' (viii 1) and *their* nature, not his, is exposed to us.

The form taken by proud power is not pride-in-power but usurpation. This is not only stated of Lucifera (iv 12) but made clear before the statements by use of the common figure of Phaeton, a metaphor for presumptuous usurpation of divine prerogative. This theme is never dropped, for it is radical Pride which Spenser shows us. Of course, he shows it finally in the ancient images used for Satan the prime usurper. The greatest temptation scene in the Book, with Despair, is quite fitly that temptation to a misapprehension of the nature of God, denying His mercy, which *veritas-fides* must save him from. These qualities were exactly what Dr Faustus did not have. That Una seizes the knife and pulls her knight back from danger with the words 'thou ... that *chosen* art' (ix 53) is the fundamental Christian answer to *man*, common to all Christian churches, who all conserved the Judaic faith in God's relation to a chosen – if a faithful – people. It is a pitiful diminution of this great scene to use it as proof of Spenser's Calvinism merely because we hear so loudly the echoes of a peculiar use of that universal word.

These later developments in the Book make it the more apparent that what Red Cross receives in the House of Holiness is knowledge of the virtue truly opposing the radical vice of Pride; he also receives that condition of the spirit which would lead him to strengths to piece out his own (as he shows in canto xi). The first of the Seven Gifts, we recall, was Timor Domini – the beginning of Wisdom to which it ultimately could lead, the Sapientia of the beatific vision. The virtue it nourishes is Humility. This radical virtue (for instance the prime virtue of Christ and of the Virgin Mary, and the root in many a diagram) is to be defined in its opposition to radical Pride and has very little to do with self-deprecation; it is what we watch slowly taking shape as we read Book I – a virtue built of clear-sighted realization of man's dependence on and grateful faith in his divine Lord.

I believe Spenser's dependences to have been usually very general ones, his inheritances to have been typically more uncircumscribed than precise, almost never schematic and often unrealized. He certainly realized this one, and chose to send his first Knight in quest of Holiness not Humility. It turns out to be a better name for the special *humilitas* he means. I am sure he thought to avoid some misunderstandings, wanted a chivalric virtue, and knew that the virtue of the First Beatitude, complete contrary to Pride, is the virtue Holiness begins with – recognition of the Truth of the Godhead and a perfect Troth kept in that owed allegiance. The treatises declare this to be the case, but indeed, the matching of names makes little difference. We see that the whole set of awkwardnesses disappears (e.g. Holiness is not a Christian virtue any more than a Greek one, neither it nor Truth is opposite to Pride), when we read the still-accepted double meaning of Truth–Troth, true contrary of fundamental radical Pride.

The demonstration of ways in which the use of an opposing vice has affected the portrayal of a virtue's nature has drawn us some distance from my related statement: that the design of *The Faerie Queene* has been affected by the existence of another famous set of virtues, best known as the contraries of the seven vices. A Spenserian must find some interest in a series of virtues that includes Amitié, Chasteté, Debonnerté and Largesse, when so much difficulty has been made about Friendship, Chastity and Courtesy as truly eminent Aristotelian virtues. The names, I think, had their influence, but the nature of what was signified by the names had much more – their relations, characters, wherein 'virtues', and the like. This point may be conveniently woven in with another: the effect on the structure of treatments of virtues of an element in the Ciceronian and Macrobian traditions which was perhaps strengthened by men's natural desire to find places in each tradition for the other. From the beginning, the character of these two traditions had something to do with the universal medieval habit of dividing virtues, and later vices, into aspects and branches, though many typically medieval reasons kept the habit lively (mnemonic convenience in confession, and in debate, for example).

One large imprecise related point stands out, for causes of such results are bound to be multiple. Spenser in *The Faerie Queene*, in so far as it is a work examining virtues, wrote something comparable to many lesser preceding pieces: a work that exposes the nature of these great abstractions which interested him. He exposes them by opening to us through fictional adventures or great speaking pictures facet after facet, manifestation after manifestation. This is a key to his design – an unclassical structure and one very unlike epic. There are other reasons for his choice, but it suited phenomenally well the presentation of virtues as they were customarily presented.

He does not undertake a vast psychomachia, nor a series of smaller ones, though one result of the definition via opposites is that multitudes of minor incidents each have the motive if not the form of a Prudential psychomachia. Sometimes these great posed oppositions occupy his climactic places – about the middle, and toward the end, of each Book; sometimes they are undynamic images of great antithetical principles, for the hero is not always the principle in action but a learner who thus comprehends what it is. The Mammon and Acrasia and Mutability and dragon cantos present such oppositions; but the Garden of Adonis rather reveals like a vision, while the House of Busirane and Masque of Cupid lay out false love in all its operations and adjuncts ('displayd'), and Venus Temple sets before us all Venus had come to mean, as if resolving the ambiguities were part of our responsibility. The history is in abeyance, the characters all but stand by and wait, poised precariously on some narrative link that is tenuous but important, while we learn what we need in order to understand the story. The existence of a great contrary vice is often the immediate cause of such great imaged expositions, but what gets exposed is the complicated multiform nature of the virtue involved. No mode has ever existed, perhaps, which could match the power of allegory to accomplish such tasks. The intervening parts of Books, so famously episodic in structure, are taken up with interlaced presentations of each of the many faces the virtue and the vice can wear. This, too, is a natural operation of the figure of allegory, but also, since the time of Cicero, it had been the way to go about understanding a cardinal virtue – with no notion at all at first of allegorizing the manifested shapes.

(118–27)

By far the most striking element of structure which Spenser has caught from much attention to romances is the principle of entrelacement. . . . No doubt it is this characteristically 'interrupted' and interwoven structure which is referred to when W. J. B. Owen distinguishes the typical 'Ariostan structure' of Books III and IV of *The Faerie Queene* from the contrasted 'repetitive structure' of Books I and II; Spenser is thought to have failed to accommodate these structures to each other when he conceived the idea of a 'super-epic', in which each Book should be a little epic or miniature *Aeneid*, with its separate hero, as in Books I and II. However, typical romance entrelacement, a thoroughly medieval development though altered by Ariosto for more suspense and variety, seems to me to characterize all Spenser's designs – those of the books written early, and later (though Books III and IV appear as less skilful; they seem to me also, as Mrs Bennett and later writers have taught us, to contain the earliest and most Ariostan writing). The well-organized Books I and II are not little epics with separate heroes, but parts of a whole, connected as the parts of cyclical romances are ordinarily connected, and in fact showing extreme likeness to the way the different quests of the *Queste* are connected. The separate Books exhibit, as units and as parts of the unfinished whole, a romance's kind of coherence. It is unlike, even opposed to, that epic coherence which was most palatable to the eighteenth and nineteenth centuries, and which was all the more attractive to the nineteenth century if the piece got its unity from an epic hero more visibly than from an epic action.

These oppositions actually received most articulate statement in still a different century – Spenser's own. For the modern objections to Spenser's structure are often almost humorously those we hear repeated time and again in the famous quarrel over the structure of Ariosto and later, of Tasso – the structure 'dei romanzi'. It seems to me more likely than not that Spenser's poem, written and published when controversial treatments on one side or the other were coming off the press regularly, constitutes a stand taken on the matter – for of course he blithely adopts a 'romance' structure and in the Letter to Raleigh cites as virtues the very disputed characteristics of the accused genre. Conditions of his life perhaps precluded his following all steps of the quarrel, but after warm squabbles in the '50s, it broke out with voluble fervor sustained right through the '80s. What we know of Spenser's friends, his interests, and his advocacy of Ariosto in the direct form of declared emulation, disposes us to believe him not naïve about contemporary poetics.

Of course, I do not wish to deny the plain fact that Spenser knew and deliberately emulated epic structure and epic conventions. But *The Faerie Queene* stands like a demonstration to prove that it was possible still to avoid the misunderstanding of romance *virtues* which turns up so stubbornly in the theorists nourished on Aristotle and chained to 'his' definitions of unity, of an action, of superiority of epic, and the like. It does not seem possible that Spenser could have emphasized so neatly the 'new' merits pointed to as native to the romance form, praised them on similar principles, and relinquished contradictory 'epic' merits in their favor, if he had been quite unaware that he was taking a well-known stand on a famous question. It is sufficient for our point to recognize in the repeatedly stressed flaws for which Ariosto and romance-writers were belabored those structural flaws with which *Spenser* has been charged, from the 1700s through to the present. The 'flaws' are indeed departures from epic structure, but they are characteristic and deliberately followed principles of romance composition.

The most important complaint is that against a multiple action with multiple actors. The principle of entrelacement deliberately and inextricably attached thereto is condemned as interruption; objectors are quite oblivious to the narrative virtues of this structural device and denigrate it in phrases very reminiscent of modern comments on the structure of medieval romances. 'Variety' as the principle most stressed in defense is not only mentioned (as in the *Letter* and in treatments both by enemies and friends) but enormously developed as a chief literary pleasure, applicable to characters, supplying the place of unity, the major lesson learned by Ariosto from the romances. We seem to meet well-known friends in the condemnatory remarks about episodic structure, digression and the objection that even supposedly important characters do not stand out as 'main' or 'chief'. There is also much discussion of the suspicious importance of marvels in the action, and of their fantastic nature. The great medieval development of the romance form was in French, and it makes an interesting point that whereas some of these eminent critics launched their objections with an eye primarily upon extreme developments of the medieval principles in Ariosto later, Spenser somehow managed to return to more restrained application of some of the heretical conceptions. I believe this was possible because he read widely in the corpus of Arthurian romances, to which he intended a sophisticated contribution, but which developed chiefly in the great high period. It is astonishing to observe how like virtues some of Spenser's presumed lacks or inattentions look if we see how such traits are regarded in theories of *romance* design.

One must distinguish entrelacement from the mere practice, ubiquitous in narrative, of taking one character through a series of actions, then deserting him temporarily – often with the object of introducing suspense – while another character is given primary attention, then returning to the first, and so on. This is a simple device to get around the fact that the medium of words cannot recount events happening simultaneously to different persons living through the same time; though we cannot play on several strings simultaneously, we accept the convention that we can show the polyphonic nature of what we have to tell by juxtaposing separable persons' stories. But events connected by entrelacement are not juxtaposed; they are interlaced, and when we get back to our first character he is not where we left him as we finished his episode, but in the place of psychological state or condition of meaningfulness to which he has been pulled by the events occurring in following episodes written about some one else. Moreover, though the intervening episode will look like a digression from the line previously followed, it will transpire that that line could not go on without something furnished in the seemingly unrelated second line of narrative, the 'digression'. Or, if the digression has rather the character of a flashback or an elaboration or a supplying of background, it will turn out to carry onward some second 'new' theme as well as the first one which needed the background; and from that in turn we digress, or seem to, and then come back, not to precisely what we left but to something we understand differently because of what we have since seen.

All this is, of course, extraordinarily well suited to a narrative organized as a quest, but not all romances making use of such principles of structure are romances of knight-errantry. Moreover, some romance-authors have genius and wit, but some only succeed in showing up the natural weaknesses of their chosen form; late prose romances so abuse this principle that they degenerate into haphazard aggregations of adventures.

Specific analysis of successful use has chiefly touched on the *Lancelot* and the *Mort Artu*; but the *Queste*, which appeared between these in the cycle, exemplifies many of the narrative advantages of this structural habit. We take in quickly the significance of Bohort's rapidly presented dilemmas and choices, because we have accompanied Lancelot slowly in the pain and pathos of his recurrent failures, and with guileless Perceval have learned when to suspect machinations of the same enemy whose disguises bring Bohort to such anguished indecisions. One character's dream may assist us to see through another character's experiences the moral double meanings that are hard for himself to see. Minor characters like Meliant demonstrate motives, or minor incidents (this damsel helped or that castle rescued from siege) may harp upon consequences, which enable us to see that there are implications in the innocent-looking behavior of, say, Gawain, or Hector, or the uninstructed early Lancelot – though the stories are seemingly unrelated. We should never understand the purport of Galahad's actions or take in the quality of his single-minded fidelity, if we did not come to it by way of the several varied and flawed forms of devotion which the other questers exhibit. And in all this I do not mention the intensifying of meanings through their reappearance – never identical, never repeated, but like enough to illuminate some difficult conception that later comes close to showing as the 'theme' (as intervening tales of the searches of the others help us to take in what *is* Galahad's 'achievement of the Grail').

This is not truly a repetitive structure, which we see exemplified, e.g. in the repeated conquests of a Tamburlaine, though the quest-organization in romances or in Spenser makes the not-truly-parallel encounters look repetitive or purely episodic – as it makes the frequent necessary transitions easy and deceptively naïve. It has always been noticed that Spenser looks at his chosen abstraction or virtue through the perspectives of several incidents, as in Book V we look at aspects of Justice and In-Justice or unrighteous tyranny through one after another token incident or fable. We therefore approach with clarified sight the real unveiling, or the climactic joining of the issue if the terms are those of a conflict, near the middle and near the end. This structure also is incorrectly termed episodic or repetitive or parallel, for the subtler effects and advantages here noted as typical of interlaced, not parallel, happenings will be seen to characterize any Book the reader cares to examine closely.

This web-structure has special possibilities of gradually discernible meaning as the woven pattern shows it *is* a pattern and *takes* shape. Hence it was a superbly invented instrument for conveying not only what we called the polyphonic nature of what is happening, but that which interested Spenser supremely, the fact that to human minds what happens 'means' something, is significant. We may seem to digress from the pursuit of Florimell, and flash back to the Merlin's cave episode to know why Britomart is on that road and meets the others; we also experience, however, the way the 'love' we condemned in Castle Joyous in III i, now retroacts to complicate the love that seizes the heroine in III ii, for we perceive likenesses as well as differences. We see that the Florimell-pursuit is going to have meanings which the Artegall-pursuit will clarify, that the genealogical prophecies had been given significance (before we knew we were meeting them) by the British emphases of Book II. No matter which was written first, the Braggadochio-False Florimell section or the Braggadochio-Belphoebe of Book II, the 'patchiness' with which a later-appearing character is just lightly drawn in for an episode in a Book we read first, merely *seems* patchy. For both appearances are needed, in the contexts they are in, to fill out the presentation of the Bad Knight – as he lacks understanding of chaste love, and as he lacks understanding of temperance. The presentation will be properly continued in the episode in Book V where Braggadochio is the Bad Knight since he lacks that virtue which gives 'to each man his own', or in Book IV where he is the Bad Knight incapable of Friendship, a knight sought out and preferred by falsity.

The Marinell of III iv would not be capable of conceiving the love he is later to give Florimell, nor have we quite distinguished it ourselves before it occurs (or is patently missing) in incidents involving others. Florimell must remain in the straits we leave her in in III viii until those happenings occur which bring the characters and the readers through the changes that make us (and Cymoent and Marinell) consent to the marriage in Book IV. The romance convention of *enfances* furnished for Amoret and Belphoebe in III vi throws light backward upon Belphoebe's actions toward Timias and the 'love' therein portrayed (III v 36), just as canto vi also prevents us from suspecting Spenser of oversimplification when we confront sexual love as it is portrayed in the seemingly unrelated episodes of Paridell and Hellenore or the tapestries of Busirane's house.

Meanwhile, while the real principle of unity lies in 'meanings' of happenings, *which inform what happened* and are not separable from the story, the events can be made to happen without pinning all importance upon psychological motivation. In any romance, the story can be easily advanced by such conventions as 'customs' of castles, quarrelsome knights provoking battle, stops for lodging, knights-errant who merely 'meet' adventure, inquiry into lignage[1] and enfances,[2] or climactic meaning concentrated in some other-worldly or symbolic *place*. It is this use of significances as the cohering factor, not the fancifulness of romance, which enables us to move in and out of symbols like the 'real' places they are.

This mode of making separate incidents cohere in a unity is even easier to see in Books where a single hero achieves some aim or learns some great definition. The series of happenings chosen by Spenser is not the sequential series natural to a biography-of-hero principle of organization; we deal with a different structural conception from that which would give us an epic action toward which every event builds, or an epic hero whom every action ultimately exalts. In a 'well-organized' single-hero Book (II), Braggadochio looks like a digression, from the Bloody Babe story or the Medina section. But we are dealing with a design wherein pattern slowly *takes* shape rather than with a design wherein a theme is stated and variants develop it. The Braggadochio episode is neither a digression from Medina nor a continuation of her theme – it is the constant problem presented in a different

1 lineage
2 childhood stories

frame of reference. He is intemperate in every way the Knight may not be and maintain 'chivalry' by definition based on fidelity to good. He is fearful, vainglorious, advises expedient cunning not prudence or wisdom, responds to beauty with lascivious desire rather than love or wonder. In a word, his allegiance is to 'the world', and the climax is his sensuality and his vulgar advice to Belphoebe to go where she can make the most of her charms.

But for the notion that the episode ought to mean Aristotle's middle way between foolhardiness and cowardice and thus attach to Canto ii, we would have noticed that foolhardiness is absent, that the character does not err by excess but by confusing vainglory with fortitude, and shows not wrong balance but wrong aims (just as prodigality is not there to answer to avarice, and as *any* traffic with Acrasia, not *too much* traffic with her, is intemperate). Having brought us to think of aspects of the problem connected with temperance defined as the mean, Spenser half-leaves this conception to illustrate temperance as defined by that element of right allegiance which Christian thought gave to it down through the centuries to Milton's *Comus* (fidelity to 'the right loves' is the emphasis we persistently meet from Augustine onward, preventing the excesses of enslavement to Mammon or to Acrasia).

Similarly the opening up of the nature of Temperance is continued in the Guyon–Furor encounter which happens during this Braggadochio passage. So too does the Squire's Hero-and-Claudio story seem to be a digression from Guyon-and-Furor, just adventitiously attached in that Furor maltreats its teller the Squire; actually, however, it opens Temperance's nature to our view by showing how a faked 'Occasion' roused 'Furor' in the Squire. Thus the supposedly separable episode really enacts the meanings of the very characters it seems to desert capriciously. . . .

But one aesthetic result is outstanding, and makes Spenser's inheritance of structural entrelacement a piece of real good fortune. He did not inherit this as an advantage, but made it one by the all but new turn he gave to the form. We change from character to character but never leave Temperance. We cannot keep straight what happened next to Artegall but we watch each canto add lines to the drawing of a just knight. We find no hero at all to embody it, but we do not misunderstand the nature of Friendship or its opposite; we are

discent with the portrayal of the Courteous Knight, but we find no
objections to raise to the portrayal of Courtesy. We shift rapidly from
incident to incident and place to place, but we pursue steadfastly and
without agitation the question of the nature of Chastity. Especially
this last unit will be seen to adhere carefully to the exposing or opening out of its subject, once we define Chastity with its traditional
Christian overtones of total fidelity, love purified of idolatry, lust and
self-indulgence. Incident after incident and character after character
build up the inquiry into the part played by a right love in man's life –
what draws him to it, its opposites, perversions, faked appearances,
striking examples where it shines out, its relation to 'natural' love and
generation as cosmological principles since it alone is creative and its
great opposites are destructive principles opposed to it in their *direction* which is toward possession and self-aggrandizement, the self-
idolatrous ends of sterile and indulgent lust. It is wanton quarrelsomeness
to point to such observations as evidence that Spenser was interested
first in the ideas, for in the piece itself there is no separating idea from
story (absurd notion); it is we late-comers who phrase these sum-
maries. For a writer with Sidneyan poetics, the medieval structure
which promoted ever-fresh but never repeated 'actions' and thus
allowed these meanings to re-state themselves, was a fortunate gift of
time. . . .

Spenser's usual structure is this complex interweaving of seemingly
unrelated parts that unobtrusively take shape as a pattern. Unity is not
provided by a hero's series of exploits, even when it looks so, nor by a
single mind's development (like an assumed growth of Guyon in Book
II), nor by a conflict. An opposition defined, fought out, concluded in
triumph, is the structure of I xi, but not of Book I, of III xii, but not of
Book III. The sought virtue is the unifying factor in *every* Book. This is
usual enough in romance (the *Lancelot* with its attempt to combine
presentation of the ideal knightly code and the ideal knightly lover is a
complex example); also, Spenser seems to have fallen into it and then
realized that his earliest portions (now embedded in Books III and
IV) really do consider what it is man seeks under the name of 'true
love', and that he had looked at aspect after aspect of a quiddity whose
Christian name was Chastity – for neither Caritas nor Agape, Eros nor
Love, will convey the meanings we are shown. When he then chose
as the design of other Books the seeking and realizing of a virtue, his

fidelity to the romance structure was wise, since it fits his quest-organization and his narrative texture, which are conventional, as well as his allegorical use of them, which is unusual and original. Allegorical reading is very well served by this opportunity to realize, re-realize, and realize again, the full import of something we can only lamely point to by its abstract name.

I think it should be noticed as a by-point whenever chance brings it up, that through this inheritance of a structure that was neither episodic nor articulated like an epic action, Spenser could heighten the presentation of reigning themes to produce actual allegory, and yet evade the problem which teases moderns, whether and when the story is subordinate to the allegory.

I am convinced that this is a nonexistent problem which did not worry Spenser and only makes us misread when it worries us. The reason is much the same as with the point above touching 'happening and interpretation', event and meaning. The story is *read* allegorically. If I am asked to write down the notes which constitute a tune or to write down a tune, the same demand is made of me; 'the Book is Red Cross's story' is the same statement as 'the Book is the discovery of Holiness,' for there exists no man 'Red Cross' whose story would be different if the author did not have the claims of allegorical Holiness modifying his intents. The unifying principle is not the *history* of a particular or an individual; the action is not a biography, a life, but an action. However varied the definitions of allegory, they are at one in raising to an extreme Sidney's remark about poetry, that it deals with things 'in their universal consideration' so that we view abstractions themselves interacting. It was brilliant of Spenser to realize that a structure which weaves a tapestry before us is particularly well suited to allegory, where pattern must steal upon us. He was also supremely successful at this secret conveying of unparaphrasable meaning, and we should not obscure the success by re-writing his stories into their allegories, but resolutely claim whole images with all their depicted feelings as the sole true statements of his allegorical meanings.

(359–70)

Martha Craig

from 'The Secret Wit of Spenser's Language', in Paul J. Alpers (ed.),
Elizabethan Poetry: Modern Essays in Criticism 1967

The language of *The Faerie Queene* to most modern readers seems alien and unaccountable. Spenser seems to have overlooked the expressive possibilities of idiomatic speech revealed so magnificently by Shakespeare and devised an artificial language which, in contrast to the artificialities of Milton's language in *Paradise Lost*, seems less significant and less forceful than the ordinary language it replaces. Many qualities may seem unfortunate, but perhaps the most vitiating are the archaisms and an apparently purposeless distortion of words. Even after careful study, Spenser's archaism seems superficial and specious, consisting more in odd spellings and grammatical forms than in a genuine rejuvenation of obsolete words that are needed because they are particularly meaningful or expressive. And his liberties with language, the coinages and peculiar forms, seem willful and meaningless; alteration of words for the sake of rhyme seems to betray not only lack of resourcefulness but irresponsibility. It is no exaggeration to say that for many readers the language of *The Faerie Queene* is at best merely curious or quaint, at worst hollow and contorted. And this is especially puzzling because the faults seem not only bad but often utterly gratuitous.

The traditional account of Spenser's language provides no reassurance but instead confirms the reader's suspicions. Spenser's diction is said to be 'decorative' and to appeal 'through spontaneity and inherent suggestiveness, independent of source or application.'[1] If so, this has become not a defense but a condemnation. And any other defense of *The Faerie Queene*, of the structure or the allegory, for example, seems ineffectual to the modern reader, for according to his expectations, his implicit hierarchy of literary values, in ignoring the language it presupposes what is primary and most in doubt.

The most influential modern critic of Spenser, C. S. Lewis, suggests that the reader revise these values. Spenser's poetry belongs to an older narrative school in which richness or subtlety of language is not required and would even be inappropriate. It 'has in view an

1 B. E. C. Davis, *Edmund Spenser, A Critical Study*, 1933, p. 155.

audience who have settled down to hear a long story and do not want to savour each line as a separate work of art. Much of *The Faerie Queene* will therefore seem thin or over-obvious if judged by modern standards. The "thickness" or "density" which I have claimed for it does not come from its language."[1] This account will not solve the reader's problem, however, for the language seems to call more than usual attention to itself. The peculiarities of spelling and form, the rare words, and the high degree of formal organization in the Spenserian stanza seem to encourage and even enforce close inspection of the language. If Spenser's language lacks the density of Donne or Shakespeare, it also lacks the seeming transparency of Chaucer. A language merely thin or over-obvious might be more generally acceptable, but to many the language does seem dense, not dense with meaning but slightly muddy or opaque in a way they do not penetrate or understand and yet cannot ignore.

Another account offered by W. L. Renwick explains the language in terms of the linguistic goals of the Renaissance. Spenser is said to have been influenced by the program of the Pleiade which urged the poet to revive archaic words, introduce foreign words, and construct new ones out of the existing vocabulary. The purpose was to enrich the language, ultimately the language as a whole but intermediately the language of poetry.[2] Spenser certainly shares the spirit of the Pleiade and their belief in the creative right and creative power of the poet. But their program does not explain his style very exactly nor justify his style to the modern reader, for it does not show how the language has been truly 'enriched'. The vocabulary of *The Faerie Queene* is in general rather circumscribed compared to that of Spenser's contemporaries. Most of his archaisms consist not in the revival of obsolete words to enrich the language but simply in the substitution of archaic forms for modern ones. Though Spenser does adopt some foreign words and invent some new ones, the liberties he takes consist primarily in special modifications of current words, and even these are not consistent in the poem.[3] Why, for example, should the

1 C. S. Lewis, 'Edmund Spenser, 1552–99', *Studies in Medieval and Renaissance Literature*, 1966, p. 143.
2 W. L. Renwick, *Edmund Spenser, An Essay on Renaissance Poetry*, 1925.
3 Bruce R. McElderry Jr, 'Archaism and Innovation in Spenser's Poetic Diction', *P.M.L.A.*, vol. 47 (1932), pp. 144–70, concludes that the number of

text of the proem to Book I read 'scryne' instead of 'shrine' as it does in the proem to Book III?

The qualities of style that seem puzzling may be accounted for more adequately if, in place of the specific recommendations of the Pleiade, we consult a more fundamental view of language and reality which the recommendations of the Pleiade only in part represent, that is, the Platonic or 'Platonistic' view. A useful document to study in this connexion is Plato's *Cratylus*, useful because as an abstract exposition of the fundamental view, it makes the view explicit.

The *Cratylus* is cited prominently by two of Spenser's mentors in their works on language, and references to the dialogue elsewhere during the Renaissance suggest that Plato's discussion had a certain vogue.[1] Spenser must surely have been aware of it and the view of language it presents. The specific question of influence is not primary to an understanding of his poem, however. The dialogue is important to the modern reader as a rationale to account for Spenser's linguistic impulses and to disclose the attitude toward language which *The Faerie Queene* presupposes.

1 Richard Mulcaster, Spenser's master at the Merchant Taylors' School, cites the *Cratylus* in the peroration to the first part of his *Elementarie*, 1582, proving the existence and importance of 'right names' (ed. E. T. Campagnac, 1925, p. 188), and Richard Wills, commonly regarded as the Willye of Spenser's *Shepheardes Calender*, in his *De Re Poetica*, 1573, gives a nearly verbatim rendering of a passage from Marsilio Ficino's introduction to the dialogue for his Latin edition of Plato (*De Re Poetica*, ed. A. D. S. Fowler, Oxford, Luttrell Society, 1958, p. 73). Interest in the *Cratylus* during the Renaissance seems to have been spurred by Peter Ramus (Pierre de la Ramée). He first cites the *Cratylus* in his *Dialecticae Institutiones* (Paris, 1543). The reference is dropped from the text of the famous *Dialecticae Libri Duo* (Paris, 1556) but returns and is greatly elaborated in the commentaries of Ramus' editors, in the edition of Beurhusius, for example, printed at London in 1581, or in Abraham Fraunce, *Lawiers Logike*, 1588.

archaisms and innovations in Spenser's poetry has been greatly over-estimated. Yet the list according to McElderry's criteria, in turn, tends to be too inclusive: he regards 'keen' in the sense of 'sharp' as an archaism, for example (p. 151). What strikes the reader most vividly about McElderry's list is the number of terms that seem to be simple substitutions for terms current in Spenser's day: 'allege' for 'allay', 'blend' for 'blind', 'eath' for 'easy', 'forthy' for 'therefore'. Other terms, like 'yfere' for 'together', are more formally distinct, yet they still do not seem needed to fill a gap in the Elizabethan vocabulary. There are very few archaisms and innovations with sufficiently distinctive connotation to 'enrich the language' as the modern reader understands that phrase.

In the *Cratylus* Socrates sets forth the view that words must be not merely conventional and arbitrary, as many believe, but in fact 'correct' and 'true'. For if there is such a thing as reality and knowledge of it, our statements must be about reality, and they must be true to it. And if statements as a whole are to be true, the parts, that is, the words of which they are composed, must be true as well. Or, on the analogy of a craft like weaving or cutting, speaking is an action performed for a certain purpose and must be done not according to our own opinion or arbitrary whim but according to nature. We must have the proper instrument correctly suited to the task. In the craft of weaving, the instrument is the shuttle used to separate the web. In the craft of speaking, the instrument is the word.

The instruments of a craft are originally made by someone; so words, too, must have been constructed by an original law-giver or name-maker. An instrument that is good must be constructed according to an ideal. The one who judges whether this has been done successfully, who superintends, is the one who uses the instrument; the carpenter judges the awl. In the case of words the one who judges is the one who knows how to ask and answer questions, who knows how to use words, that is, the dialectician.

What, then, is the principle of 'correctness' in words? Socrates says that he does not have the money for a course with the Sophists, so he suggests that the poets be consulted instead. For the modern student of Plato, this advice is tinged with irony, but the Renaissance Platonist, who took at face value the description of poetic inspiration in the *Ion*, Marsilio Ficino, for example, accepts and even approves of the appeal to the poets.

After thus carefully inquiring from whom the correctness of
names, that is, the proper principle by which they are constituted,
is to be learned, he mocks the Sophists, and he leads us
rather to the poets, not just any of them but the divine ones,
as if they had received the true names of things from the gods,
among whom are the true names.[1]

In a similar spirit, the Ramist logic acknowledged no fundamental distinction between dialectic and poetry.[2] In respect to words as well

1 Marsilio Ficino, 'In Cratylum', *Opera Omnia*, Torino, 1959 (a reproduction of the *Opera Omnia*, Basilea, 1576), II, i, p. 1311, translated by the author.
2 Abraham Fraunce, for example, makes this clear in *Lawiers Logike*, I, i, p. 4.

as ideas, the poet ideally is a dialectician; he has divinely inspired insight into the truth.

If we consult the poet Homer, we discover that correctness of words consists in revealing the nature of the things named. Words reveal reality through their etymologies. The composition of 'Agamemnon', for example, shows that he is admirable (*agastos*) for enduring (*menein*); the derivation of 'Atreus' shows that he is the destructive one (*atēros*). Words contain within them little self-explanatory statements. The subject of the statement is the word itself, the predicate is the elemental word or words from which it is made, what we would call the morphemes. Words are 'true' because they imply a true statement.

The Ramists on these grounds even introduced etymologizing into logic. Words are a form of argument because the 'notation' or etymology of the word bears some logical relation to the 'notion' of the thing. 'A woman is a woe man because shee worketh a man woe.'[1] As the Ramist discussion reveals, the 'etymology' here is not necessarily the grammatical one, for this may not furnish a second term: we can not make a significant statement out of 'argument' from 'argue'. The etymology required is the 'logical' one which 'explains the cause why this name is imposed for this thing.'[2] That is, the 'etymology' or 'true word' is not historically true but philosophically true, and it is not the function of the grammarian but the dialectician to interpret words. Often philosophically true turns out to be what we would simply call 'fanciful', but neither Plato nor the Renaissance Platonists had any definite standard for distinguishing the two nor any desire to do so.

The names of Spenser's characters are clearly philosophic and true, for they reveal the nature of the one named through the etymology. The heroes' names, like the names of Homer's heroes, are 'composed according to a certain allegorical rationale', as Ficino would say. Belphoebe is the 'beautiful, pure one', Artegall is the 'art of justice'. As a poet-dialectician Spenser also interprets given words truly and philosophically through etymology. 'Magnificence' is not properly conspicuous consumption but 'doing great deeds' as the etymology shows.

1 Fraunce, I, xii, p. 57.
2 Fraunce, I, xii, p. 51.

When a suitable etymology is not apparent in the current form of a word, Socrates looks to its archaic form or other archaic words to see if they are more suggestive, for if language has been handed down from some original name-maker, words may have been corrupted in the course of time. If so, the early form should be the right one (*Cratylus* 418-19). Through his theory of language Plato in fact acts out the etymology of 'etymology': the true explanation of words is in their origin. The original name-maker in Plato is really a metaphor for whatever principle of order and reason there may be in language. The search for older forms is a search for the true forms that are ideally expressive.

Plato's etymologizing expedient explains the sort of archaizing Spenser does in *The Faerie Queene*. Through archaism Spenser carries out the basic Platonic metaphor of the poem, the metaphor of the antique world, a time in the past when the world was more rational and comprehensible, an ideal time, 'ideal' not because there was no evil or difference, but because evil and difference could be more readily perceived and understood. The purpose of his archaisms is not primarily to enlarge his vocabulary, the concern of the Pleiade, but to make it more flexible and expressive. The archaic forms and form words, '-en' endings, 'y-' prefixes, and expressions like 'ywis' act as a sort of solvent of language, dissolving ordinary patterns and the reader's usual expectation. With archaism established as a mode of diction, Spenser is free to pick out archaic forms that are more suggestive of philosophic meaning.

The state of the language in the sixteenth century made such usage more possible and more likely than it would be now. No fixed standard of spelling and syntax had been established. There was less pattern or expectation to overcome, and the writer was free to choose among many forms available. Spenser simply exercised this freedom more widely than other writers of the time by reviving forms that were obsolete or obsolescent. Because there was no fixed standard, the sixteenth-century reader always needed to be more resourceful and interpretive than we. It might not be obvious or indisputable even what word was before him. He would always examine word forms more carefully than we and so would be more apt to see their 'etymological' nature, the meaningful affinities which they suggest.

As the analysis of words in the *Cratylus* progresses, it soon becomes clear that even the aid of archaism does not yield a perfect language. The given language is clearly deficient; it is not an adequate or reliable source of truth. But for that very reason language should be improved. Words are only approximations, but as such, they can be perfected. Numbers, because they are images simply of quantities, can not be; if we change II to III, we do not refer to the same number better, we refer to another number. But if we change 'demon' to 'daemon', we improve the word and make it more revealing by showing more clearly the identity of spirit and intelligence.

The poet's alterations are an effort to correct language according to his vision or insight so that it reveals reality more adequately. Forms and spellings are improved in order to disclose the etymological rationale of the word. Slight alterations in sound or spelling are admitted so that connexions in meaning may be clearer. Rhyme words are spelled the same, not only implying connexion in sound but encouraging comparison of meaning. Portmanteau words are devised to cover complex notions.

The lack of 'realism', the uncolloquial, unidiomatic character of the language ultimately follows from Spenser's philosophic realism, his belief that truth is not found in the everyday or in immediate surroundings, the 'world of appearances', but in a realm of ideas that are only partially and imperfectly reflected in the everyday world. Ordinary language is not adequate to this world of fuller insight. So Spenser's major heroes are not personifications of common terms, like most of the characters in medieval allegory, but of words he has invented. He writes not of 'chastity' but of 'Belphoebe', a perfected insight into chastity, not of 'courtesy' but 'Calidore', a concept something like courtesy but refined and redefined.[1] It is the same basic impulse at work which occasions the form 'scryne' to suggest that the shrine the poet seeks in his invocation is, according to the Latin root of the word, a *scrinium* or box of papers where the secret wisdom of the sacred muse may be found.

What the modern reader or the lexicographer sees as a distortion

---

1 It requires the whole of Book VI to reveal all the implications of 'Calidore', derived from Greek *kalos*, beauty, and *dōron*, gift. The most important aspect of Spenser's meaning is symbolized by the Graces on Mount Acidale who present their gift of beauty to the poet Colin Clout not when he wills but as they will, graciously. Courtesy like grace is a gift which the receiver in turn gives.

of language is in fact an impulse to perfect it. Like the action as a whole, individual words are allegorical; they contain hidden meaning or implied metaphors. It has frequently been said that Spenser's language suits the poem – a fancy language for a fanciful world. This should at least be supplemented: a more fully significant language for a more fully significant world.

No word even so perfected is ever quite adequate to the idea, however, for words according to Plato are ultimately a kind of image. An image can never be a perfect reproduction, for if it were, it would not be an image at all but the very thing; it would be not the word 'horse' but the real horse itself. Such inevitable inadequacy of language might, it seems, lead to despair of ever successfully expressing the truth. In the *Seventh Epistle* Plato vehemently disavows a pupil precisely for trying to state first principles, ultimate realities, explicitly. Yet truth can be reached. It is reached through indirection, through the use of three separate but mutually complementary instruments: the word, the definition, and the image. Each of these suggests different aspects of the truth. By the continual, energetic comparison of the three, the soul rises to a comprehension of the thing itself. The three are constantly rubbed together, so to speak, and the friction ignites and illuminates the soul.

In poetry the definition is dramatized either literally or symbolically by the action. The meaning of 'Agamemnon' in the view of classical and Renaissance commentators, is implicit in the etymology, but it is fully disclosed only in the action of the *Iliad*. The reader discovers the meaning of the name by analysing the action of the poem. Homer, with the aid of divine inspiration, originally discovered the proper name, or the true meaning of the given name, by analysing the conduct of his character in life. Since the heroes of *The Faerie Queene* are not types but concepts and universals, their proper names must be discovered in the conduct of life as a whole. The author, if a true poet-dialectician, was inspired to direct intuition of the concept, only adumbrated in life. He then invented the proper name, a personification, and a symbolic action through which it is fully revealed.

The action of Spenser's heroes in *The Faerie Queene* continually unfolds an 'etymological' rationale, the secret wit of reality which his language is devised to disclose. Nothing, therefore, could be more misleading than the opinion that Spenser's language is negligible in our reading of the poem. In fact 'etymological' associations of language are a constant guide to the implicit meaning of the poem and form the very principle of its organization. From the beginning, the poem evolves according to such a rationale: for example, in the action of Book I, a *hero* inspired by *eros* (these terms are explicitly connected in the *Cratylus*, 398 D and make up a traditional 'etymology') rides forth as a knight *errant*. His first adventure as a knight errant is, naturally, an encounter with Errour: he defeats her but then proceeds to err through eros, the misplaced affections of his 'heroicke' heart.[1] So misled, he goes to the house of Pride from which he emerges safely, only to err again in the *arrogance* of Orgoglio, the presumptuous spirit, the *airs* of man. He is then redeemed from Orgoglio by *Arthur*, the *ardor* and the *art* or efficacy of grace. Yet again he almost errs in *despair* before he is led to the house of Holiness by *Una* where he is restored to *wholeness* and the whole of *holiness* is symbolically revealed. The action thus proceeds by a series of etymological puns, yet their presence is frequently unobtrusive; the wit appears to us as a secret wit. . . .

With the killing of Errour the knight's first encounter is complete. He proves that he is not in this sense an errant knight: he is not subject to a form of error which, as the language re-asserts again and again, can be made 'plaine'. He proves worthy of the 'Armorie' which first won his heroic heart.

The action then proceeds to show that the knight is 'errant', however, in another sense made fully clear when the word is at last used in Fradubio's speech: he is subject to Duessa or duplicity. 'The author then (said he) of all my smarts, | Is one *Duessa* a false sorceresse, | That many errant knights hath brought to wretchednesse' (I ii 34). '*Duessa*' is, of course, associated with *duo*, two to suggest her doubleness or deceit but also with Greek *dus*-, bad, ill and *duē*, misery to suggest the wretchedness she brings.

The Red Cross Knight is parted from Una, the one truth, by Archimago, the arch magician, and can be because '*Archimago*' in his 'Hermitage' is the architect of images, of delusive likenesses. Archi-

1 The 'heroicke' spirit is an erotic one, Amor and Mars natural companions, as the ambiguity of 'courage' and 'heart' in the poem confirms. This idea is first suggested in the Proem to Book I but is most explicitly elaborated in the defense of love in the Proem to Book IV.

mago sends to '*Morpheus*', the former or fashioner, for a 'diverse' or, etymologically, misleading dream, subtler and more seductive than the 'diverse doubt' of Errour because the threat then made 'plaine' now becomes an ambiguous 'plaint'. The 'doubtfull words' of the dream-lady make the 'redoubted knight | Suspect her truth' (1 i 53). Yet 'since no'vntruth he knew', he is not seduced but interprets her appeal in an honorable way. Sheer ambiguity can not destroy him because if the evil is truly ambiguous, the interpreter must ascertain or supply it, and the knight as 'redoubted', reverent as well as revered, has no such evil in him to supply. Archimago must create a definite false illusion of Una as unfaithful which exploits the knight's virtue, his love of her. Una and the Red Cross are thus divided into 'double parts' or separated through duplicity and Una left 'wandring', the end of Archimago's 'drift', leaving the Red Cross to Duessa's wiles.

The nature of the Red Cross Knight's susceptibility is then further dramatized by the difference between Duessa and Sans Foy. The Red Cross defeats Sans Foy; it is not a complete loss of faith on his part which is leading him astray. But he errs, he falls prey to Duessa as Fidessa, a superficially perfect semblance of faith, through his impulse to love, the 'heroicke' character of his stout heart. His love for Duessa is certainly a crude bedazzlement revealed in the way he looks her up and down, and in respect to him she is '*Fidessa*' or little faith, but it is significant that his faith is not lost primarily but misplaced: he always believes but he may misbelieve.

The analysis of error which began in the 'wandring wood' is completed in the encounter with Fradubio, metamorphosed into a tree or an instance of error in its more refined and significant sense. In the symbolic plant the meaning of the action which began with the earlier 'plaints' is 'plast in open plaines' (1 ii 32, 33) and made explicit. Fradubio like the Red Cross was overcome not by doubt *per se* but by guile, the guile to which doubt as an indeterminate state of mind makes him prey. When he tried to judge between his lady and Duessa, 'the doubtfull ballaunce' swayed equally; doubt itself determines in no way. So Duessa intervened with an act of misrepresentation, obscuring his lady in a fog. Fradubio suggests *dubius*, doubting, and reflects its dangers; more specifically, though, he is the victim of 'fraud' (1 iv 1), the active evil to which the uncommitted state of doubt makes him vulnerable.

The Red Cross Knight misled by Archimago's Duessa next appears at the house of Pride, implicitly the palace of hypocrisy, as playfully derived from *Hyper chrysos*, covered over with gold.[1]

> A stately Pallace built of squared bricke,
> Which cunningly was without morter laid,
> Whose wals were high, but nothing strong, nor thick,
> And golden foile all ouer them displaid,
> That purest skye with brightnesse they dismaid.
>
> (I iv 4)

It is a house, as the *Bible* suggests, not on the strait but the broad way and built on sand, but it is 'painted cunningly'. The porter *'Malvenu'*, a parody of *bienvenu* or welcome, greets them, prefiguring the evil that will come. Then *'Lucifera'* appears, the bringer of light who like Phaeton proudly burns and bedazzles with light intended 'fairely for to shyne' or *phaēthōn* (I iv 9).

In the pageant of the Seven Deadly Sins which follows Spenser's wit is comically farfetched in keeping with the gaudy cartoon quality of the parade. The first sin *'Idlenesse'*, dressed like a monk in 'habit blacke, and amis[2] thin', which may by some extravagant puns suggest the poet's condemnation, carries his 'Portesse', but unfortunately the prayer book is only a 'portesse' only carried and rarely read. Certainly the 'wayne' is poorly led with such a vacuous and inattentive fellow guiding its 'way'. Idlenesse 'esloynes'[3] himself and challenges 'essoyne'[4] 'from worldly cares' (*soins* in French); the legal terms suggest his Jesuitical invocation of the letter of the law to free him ironically for 'lawlesse riotise'[5] (I iv 19, 20).

Gluttony follows with the long fine neck of a crane; 'gluttony' in Latin is derived from *glutire*, to swallow. He is depicted as Silenus the satyr (*satur*, full); his drunken 'corse'[6] reflects the course he leads. Lechery, who appears on the traditional goat, *caper*, is true to that

---

1 Fraunce, I, xii, p. 57, derives 'Hypocrisis, of *hypo*' (for *hyper* it seems), 'which is over, and *chrysos*, gold, because hypocrites bee cloaked with a golden shew overcast'. He regards this as a 'monkish' and ignorant definition, however, and gives the proper one as *hypokrinomai*, to dissemble.
2 hood, cape
3 withdraws
4 exemption
5 riotous life, extravagance
6 body

depiction, capricious; his 'whally' eyes, white or wall eyes, are the goat's eye or *oeil de chèvre* in French.[1]

Envy is presented primarily as a vile mouth, stressed by the rare form 'chaw' for jaw to reiterate his endless malicious and mordant backbiting. His gown of satin as 'discolourd say'[2] seems to pun on the vicious things he says; the snake he carries in his bosom 'impl-yes'[3] his mortal sting. Envy's gown 'ypainted full of eyes' reflects the root meaning of envy in Latin, *invidia*, the evil eye. He eyes all with hatred but particularly looks at his percursor 'Couetyse' or avarice with covet eyes, reflecting their close connexion.

Wrath is depicted through associations in English as rash or rathe; his is a '*hasty* rage'. And when Satan tries to drive this 'laesie teme' of evils, Idleness is called '*Slowth*', spelled as if derived from 'slow'.

(447–57)

The Red Cross is redeemed from the wrath of Orgoglio by Arthur, symbol of the ardor and art of God's grace. Arthur represents not the magnanimity of God, his potentiality or etymologically his great spirit, but his magnificence, his actuality or etymologically his doing great deeds. Arthur's image and genealogy are resplendent with the glory of such greatness. He appears with a headpiece like an almond tree on the top of 'greene *Selinis*'; '*Selinis*' in Greek resembles *selinon*, the plant from which the chaplets of victors in the ancient games were made; Virgil calls it 'palmosa Selinus' (*Aeneid* III 705).

A comparison of Spenser's image of Arthur with Marlowe's adaptation in *Tamburlaine* reveals how carefully Spenser's language maintains the suggestions of the almond tree and transfers them to his hero.

> Vpon the top of all his *loftie crest*,
> A bunch of haires discolourd diuersly,
> With sprincled pearle, and gold full richly drest,
> Did shake, and seem'd to daunce for iollity,
> Like to an Almond tree ymounted hye
> On top of greene *Selinis* all alone,
> With blossomes braue bedecked daintily;

1 Randle Cotgrave, *A Dictionarie of the French and English Tongues*, 1611.
2 fine textured cloth
3 enfolds

Whose tender *locks* do tremble euery one
At euery little *breath*, that vnder heauen is *blowne*.

(I vii 32)

I'll ride in golden armour like the sun;
And in my *helm* a triple *plume* shall spring,
Spangled with diamonds, dancing in the air,
To note me emperor of the three-fold world;
Like to an almond tree ymounted high
Upon the lofty and celestial mount
Of ever green Selinis, quaintly decked
With bloom more white than Herycina's brows,
Whose tender *blossoms* tremble every one
At every little breath that thorough heaven is blown.

Tamburlaine 4092–4101
(Pt 2, IV iii 115–24)

In both passages there is a personification; the hero is compared to the personified almond tree. But in Marlowe the personification is incidental while in Spenser it is so radical and persistent that the language seems continuously symbolic of the hero. Instead of 'helm' Spenser uses 'crest' which suggests not only the plume on the helmet but an identifying insignia, as if the crest were Arthur's sign; 'crest' also suggests the summit of a mountain, anticipating the comparison and so suggesting that the almond on Selinis is the sign. Yet because this is merely suggested the tree on the mountain remains natural, free, and alive.

Applied to the ambivalent 'crest', Spenser's 'loftie' exercises more of its ethical implication than in the Marlowe passage when applied to the more literal 'mount'. 'Haires' in place of 'plume' helps to personify the crest; 'drest' applies more readily than 'spangled' to a person in the sense clothed, to hair in the sense combed, and to the plume in the sense adorned. The line could even be a description of the person instead of the plume. The phrase 'for iollity' makes sure that 'daunce' keeps its literal as well as its transferred meaning, while in Marlowe's phrase 'dancing in the air' the personification is almost dead. Even 'daintily' with its association of gentleness seems more human than Marlowe's 'quaintly'.

The suggestions are further carried out by the term 'braue' which in contrast to the phrase 'more white than Herycina's brows', suggests the courage as well as the esthetic splendor of the glory implied. 'Locks' instead of 'blossoms' suggests tufts of hair as well as foliage, maintaining the personification and implying that Arthur himself as the succourer trembles in sympathy at every breath blown. The idea is not clearly controlled in Marlowe's lines; it would certainly be inappropriate for Tamburlaine, yet without it this part of the comparison seems pointless. In Spenser's stanza there is even a slight metaphoric play in the phrase 'all alone' between 'by itself' and 'the only one' which underlines Arthur's pre-eminence and makes an obtrusive explicating phrase like Marlowe's 'to note me emperor of the threefold world' totally unnecessary. We notice, incidentally, that Spenser's Selinis is not 'celestial', and his almond tree trembles at every breath blown 'vnder' not 'thorough' heaven. Though the almond tree is 'ymounted hye' on the mount, it is in this world. Arthur is the highest man and one alone, God's vice-regent, but he is not God.

(459–60)

Spenser's secret wit suggests not only the moral implication of the action but political and social instances which substantiate and exemplify. A most vivid instance occurs in Guyon's encounter with Phaedria, Book II, canto vi; a series of puns associates her with Italy and the Italian way of life during the Renaissance. Phaedria's boat is called a 'little Gondelay'(4) and a 'little frigot'(7). Both terms had been introduced into English not long before from the Italian. With his use of them in the Phaedria passage Spenser seems to be punning in Italian: 'gondola' suggests the Italian term *gongolare*, 'to laugh till ones heart be sore or shoulders ake, to shuckle and be full of joy, or excessive gladnesse'; 'frigot' suggests *frigotare*, 'to shuckle, to shrug, or strut for overjoy'. These puns are reinforced by the epithets of her 'shallow ship'(5), 'painted bote'(4) (false good), and 'flit barke'(20) (meaning airy, insubstantial, as well as swift). The puns become an allusion to Italy through the meaning of 'gondola' which Florio defines as 'a little boat or whirry used no where but a bout and in Venice.'[1]

1 John Florio, *Queen Anna's New World of Words*, 1611. (Not included in *A Worlde of Wordes*, 1598.)

Other references suggest the allusion. In repudiating war, Phaedria refers to the kind of skirmishes she prefers as 'scarmoges'(34). This spelling instead of the usual 'skirmish' (IV ix 20) associates the term with Italian *scaramuccia*, the name of Harlequin's companion with his buffoonish battles in the Italian farce. Phaedria locates her world 'In this wide Inland sea, that hight by name | *The Idle lake*'(10); 'Inland sea' is a translation of 'Mediterranean'; the '*Idle lake*' is apparently the Adriatic, which Spenser associates with *adraneia*, inactivity. She lives on an idyllic island suggesting Venice, to the Renaissance Englishman the very land of Venus. The 1590 edition of *The Faerie Queene* even carried a proverbial allusion to the pope: 'Sometimes she sung, as loud as lark in aire, | Sometimes she laught, as merry as Pope Ione.' The song she sings is the magnificent perversion of the Biblical 'Behold the lilies of the field, they toil not neither do they spin'.

Through such puns the Phaedria incident forms an elaborate commentary on the Italian way of life during the Renaissance and a criticism of the young Englishman's practice of sowing his wild oats there and affecting the Italianate style. Spenser finds reflected in Italy the prototype of inane mirth and shallow epicureanism; in the virtual enclosure of the Mediterranean Sea he finds a symbol of stagnation and idleness.

Phaedria entertains her companions with stories like those of the joke-books, the thesauri of merry tales which flourished in the period, many from Italy, offering crude tales without any formal elegance: '. . . And greatly ioyed merry tales to faine, | Of which a store-house did with her remaine, | Yet seemed, nothing well they her became; | For all her words she drownd with laughter vaine, | And wanted grace in vtt'ring of the same . . .' (II vi 6). Part of Spenser's ambition to 'overgo' Ariosto was a desire to prevent the epic from descending to this level.

In the Bower of Bliss Spenser continues such allusions but also turns to the goals of the Elizabethan Merchant Adventurers, the ports they sought in ships like the 'Delight', the 'Desire', and the 'Castle of Comfort' as they sailed for the expected sweet life of the West Indies. The 'wandring Islands' recall Cuba and La Dominica, called the wandering islands because they wandered all over the map in Spain and Portugal's dispute over their location and thus ownership. 'Verdant' may recall Cape Verde; the Bower of Bliss itself suggests

Deseado or Port Desire and more generally Florida. It is 'goodly beautifide | With all the ornaments of *Floraes* pride, | Wherewith her mother Art, as halfe in scorne | Of niggard Nature ... | Did decke her' (II xii 50). The art that Spenser refers to would include the art of the voyagers in their hyperbolic accounts which 'too lavishly adorne' with wealth and fertility the nature they actually encountered.

The journey to the Bower of Bliss reveals the financial disasters which resulted from adventuring in the hope of perfect pleasure. The most vivid depiction is in '*The Rocke of* vile *Reproch*', a dramatization of bankruptcy as the bank on which men break. The rock hovers over its potential victims 'Threatning it selfe on them to ruinate'; one sees on its 'sharpe clifts the ribs of vessels broke' and the 'carkasses exanimate[1] | Of such, as hauing all their substance spent | In wanton ioyes, and lustes intemperate, | Did afterwards make shipwracke violent, | Both of their life, and fame for euer fowly blent' (II xii 7). The greedy 'Cormoyrants' or moneylenders and 'birds of rauenous race' wait there for the 'spoyle of wretches', that is, their ruin and so the confiscation of their goods 'After lost credite and consumed thrift, | At last them driuen hath to this despairefull drift' (II xii 8). 'Credit' had just recently acquired its specifically commercial sense in addition to the more general moral one, and 'thrift', too, contains a comparable ambiguity. '*The Rocke of* vile *Reproch*' is the counterpart of Homer's Scylla, etymologized to *skyleuein*, to strip, to spoil. The Gulf of Greediness opposite corresponds to Charybdis (*charis hybris*) which Cicero, for example, uses as a metaphor for prodigality in attacking Antony (*Phillipics*, II xxvii 67).

'The *wandring Islands*', the counterpart of Homer's Wandering Rocks, in respect to the commercial and social world etymologically suggest the vagabonds and vagrants, travesties of the knight errant, whose devices Robert Greene was soon to expose. Pictured as '*wandring Islands*' 'seeming now and than,' like the classical Delos (II xii, II 13), which Spenser etymologizes traditionally to *dēlos*, apparent because the islands simply appeared out of nowhere, their seemingly fair and fruitful grounds are seductive but unsure. When Phaedria re-appears on a 'wandring Island' with her little boat beside her, the boat is called a 'skippet' (I xii 14) meaning basket, a nonce usage by Spenser here (*N.E.D.*), suggesting perhaps the baudy baskets exposed by Greene's

1 lifeless

precursor Thomas Harman in his *A Caveat or Warening for Common Cursetors, Vulgarely Called Vagabones* (chapter xvi). The basket was a device of Elizabethan prostitutes who first presented themselves as pedlars of notions before they exposed their baudy purposes. Certainly Phaedria at her reappearance is more crudely and clearly just such a wayside prostitute. Spenser's term 'skippet' resembling 'skipper' and 'skiff' accommodates her very nicely to the maritime setting and resembling 'skip' implies the frivolity and the insecurity of her mode of travel, her way of life.

It may even seem as if Spenser in calling Acrasia's victim '*Verdant*' was alluding to Greene himself whose demise he thereby predicts and attempts to prevent. Greene at any rate gained a witty benefit from his degradation by moralizing on himself with such a pun in the last stanza of his poem of repentance: 'My wretched end may warn *Greene springing youth* | To use delights, as toyes that will deceive | And scorne the world before the world them leaves: | For all worlds trust, is ruine without ruth.'[1]

But the development which emerges most strongly moves in the direction of amplifying symbolic implication rather than pursuing social allusions in detail. Like '*Mordant*' (or '*Mortdant*' II i 49) his counterpart, '*Verdant*', the flourishing young man whose spirit Acrasia 'depastures' (II xii 73),[2] must receive what he gives, though in his case the outcome is happily reversed. Acrasia with her curse enacting '*Mortdant*' gives 'death to him that death does giue' (II i 55); the Palmer, through his 'counsel sage' enacting '*Verdant*' gives truth to him that truth does give or instructs the victim in the true harm of Acrasia which he depicts and so frees him from her.

The language of the voyage projects a world of the moral imagination above the social scene to which it simply dips in specific allusion with an occasional detail of incident, image, or term. The sea-beasts encountered by Guyon and the Palmer are not the conies and quail of the Elizabethan underworld or their sea counterparts, nor even sea-lions and sea-foxes but the most fantastic monsters imaginable. The catalogue begins by literary allusion: a battle with the 'many headed

1 Greene ends with a very practical moral: 'Then blest are they that like the toyling Ant,| Provide in time gainst winters wofull want,' *Groats-worth of Witte, Bought with a Million of Repentance*, 1592, the end.
2 consumes, feeds on

hydra' is Plato's symbol in Book IV of the *Republic* (426 e) for the futility of attempting to legislate the end of fraud instead of converting the spirit of man, since without such a change of spirit new forms of fraud like the heads of a hydra will continually spring forth. The scolopendra, it was thought, 'feeling himselfe taken with a hooke, casteth out his bowels, untill he hath unloosed the hooke, and then swalloweth them up againe,'[1] which perhaps resembles certain specific devices of the sharper. But what the chosen epithets depict is images of evil monstrously general. The hazards of the course are immense and indefinable except as threat, the 'Ziffius' or swordfish, for example, and its consequence, the morse, which Spenser derives from the Latin *mors* to mean death.

This is the advantage of Spenser's secret wit. He may suggest implications at every possible level of experience without disrupting the symbolic unity and continuity of the moral world. The operation of his style was perfectly described by Spenser's first critic, Kenelm Digby, in a letter of appreciation addressed to Henry May, 1638 [quoted above, pp. 57–60].

The Faerie Queene has disappointed the modern reader, for in an age that admires the difficult and complex it seems 'familiar and easy'. But, as Kenelm Digby testifies, it offers 'rare and wonderful conceptions' to the attentive reader who does not let them slide by. To discover their fullness the reader must heed the language closely, however. The language must be savored for the cunning within its gentleness and ease.

(463–72)

Paul J. Alpers

from *The Poetry of 'The Faerie Queene'* 1967

'Literally . . . a poem's narrative is its rhythm or movement of words,' Northrop Frye has remarked. But 'when we think of a poem's narrative as a description of events, we no longer think of the narrative as literally embracing every word and letter. We think rather of a sequence of gross events, of the obvious and externally striking elements

1 Bollakar, *English Expositor*, 1616, quoted in the *N.E.D.* This idea is traditional from Aristotle, *History of Animals*, 519.19.

in the word-order.'[1] In Frye's terms, the argument of the last chapter is that we have forsaken the literal narration of *The Faerie Queene*, the continuous flow of words, for a kind of narration that is really not there. But if Spenser's narration is not a descriptive fiction, if *The Faerie Queene* is not a world, of what does its surface consist? The 'gross events' of *The Faerie Queene* are verbal phenomena – lines and stanzas of poetry. Their constituent elements are verbal formulas, not observed details in a putative world. Spenser's stanzas are frankly arrangements of words, and do not purport to imitate or create a reality external to the speaker. What is striking, of course, is that Spenser's words are prompted by and derive from narrative materials. We have so far equated 'narrative materials' and 'fiction', but we should now recognize the difference between them. Tasso, speaking of the poet's materials, observes: 'Before this has been subjected to the artifice of epic, it is called matter. After it has been disposed and treated by the poet, and clothed with eloquence, it forms the fable, which is no longer matter, but the form and soul of the poem.'[2] Precisely what interests us in *The Faerie Queene* is the fact that Spenser transforms his narrative materials not into parts of a fiction, but into stanzas of poetry, arrangements of words.

(36)

Narrative materials are not the same as a poetic fiction, but are literally materials – capable of being turned into more than one kind of poetic narration. Nothing illustrates this more strikingly than a comparison of the story of Phedon (*Faerie Queene*, II iv 17–36) with its source in *Orlando Furioso*, the story of Ariodante and Ginevra (IV 51–vi 16). The most familiar form of the story is the main plot of *Much Ado about Nothing*. In Ariosto's version, it begins when Rinaldo lands in Scotland and is told about the impending death of Ginevra, the daughter of the king. She has been accused of being unchaste, and according to an ancient law she will be killed unless her accuser is challenged and defeated in battle within a month of the accusation. Rinaldo immediately sets out for the Scottish court, and on his journey he rescues a lady from two villains who are about to murder her. The lady turns out to be Dalinda, Ginevra's lady-in-waiting, and as they travel she tells Rinaldo the story of her mistress. Ginevra was loved by the Ital-

1 *Anatomy of Criticism*, Princeton, 1957, pp. 78–9.
2 Torquato Tasso, *Prose diverse*, ed. Cesare Guasti, Florence, 1875, vol. 1, p. 126.

ian knight Ariodante and loved him in return; since he was a favorite of the king, there seemed no impediment to their marriage. But the jealous Polinesso, the Duke of Albany, tells Ariodante that he is Ginevra's lover, and that a few nights hence Ariodante can see her let him into her bedchamber. Polinesso is in fact the lover of Dalinda, who loves him so much that she does not question his request that she dress for this night in her mistress' clothes. Their meeting place is a bedchamber of Ginevra's which they use because it overlooks an uninhabited area of the city; no one can see a man climbing up to the balcony of this room. Polinesso tells Ariodante to hide in a ruined dwelling directly opposite the balcony. Ariodante agrees, but fearful that Polinesso may be planning simply to ambush him, he brings along his brother, Lurcanio. If Polinesso's story is true, Ariodante does not want Lurcanio to see Ginevra's shame, so he tells him to stay at a distance and only to come if he hears Ariodante call. But driven both by concern and by natural curiosity, Lurcanio comes much closer and is thus able, first to see Polinesso (whom he does not recognize) climb the rope let down to him by Dalinda dressed as Ginevra, and, second, to stop Ariodante from killing himself on the spot. Ariodante promises to calm himself, but leaves the court secretly the next morning. Nothing is heard of him for eight days until a traveler stops at the court to tell that he has seen Ariodante throw himself from a cliff into the sea. Lurcanio is so enraged at Ginevra for causing his brother's death that he accuses her, despite his knowledge that the king and the people will turn their favor towards him into hatred. No one is willing to challenge Lurcanio, partly because he is so powerful a warrior, partly because he is an honorable man, and it is assumed that he would not swear to anything that was not true. The king, meanwhile, proposes to conduct his own investigation and to begin with his daughter's chambermaids. Dalinda, fearful that she and Polinesso will be undone, appeals to Polinesso for help. He promises to have her taken in safety to one of his castles, but he secretly plans to have her escorts kill her, and she is at the point of death when Rinaldo hears her screams and rescues her.

Perhaps the intricacy of this summary will indicate the degree to which Ariosto devotes his attention to external dramatic action. This becomes clear when we consider how important seeing is in the episode. The central deception, of course, is visual, and Ariodante's cryptic message to Ginevra is that 'the whole cause of his harsh and sad fate was that he had seen too much' (v 60, cf. 58). But more important is the fact that seeing is regarded as the essential means of human knowledge. Ariodante insists on seeing before he believes (v 41). He tells the traveler to make his fate 'manifesto' to Ginevra, and the traveler provides a visual description of Ariodante's leap from the cliff (v 57, 59). Words like *manifestar*, *rivelar*, and *mostrar* occur throughout the episode, and reach their climax in the trial by battle, the point of which is to render a moral decision in full public view. Thus Rinaldo, saying 'Now we shall see the outcome' (v 86), offers to prove the truth of his story by fighting Polinesso, and the king and the people watching the battle 'all hope that God will make plain that unjustly she was called unchaste' (v 87). In a context in which seeing is believing, Polinesso's trick is poetically and dramatically of a piece with the rest of the episode, and not bizarrely magnified in importance, like the 'ocular proof' of the handkerchief in *Othello*. Even mental experiences that do not involve visual experience are spoken of as if they did. Dalinda says that she was so blind with love that she could not see the 'thousand sure signs' that Polinesso did not love her (v 11), and that Polinesso's proposal to dress her as Ginevra 'was only too plain a fraud' (v 26). Dalinda's fine scorn for Polinesso and herself characteristically finds expression in exclamations beginning 'Vedi', 'See', and that word, with its mocking tone and its reminder that everything really is obvious, contains much of the ironic force of the episode. Here is Dalinda's comment on Polinesso's revealing, a few days after he becomes her lover, that he is a suitor for Ginevra's hand:

See if he had become arrogant toward me, if he had taken to himself empire over my heart, for to me he revealed this new love and did not blush to ask my aid (v 12).

Dalinda begins with anger at Polinesso, but in the second line, which describes a natural phenomenon of love, she is mocking herself. Similarly at the end of her narration, her indignation turns into a sense that the joke was on her:

You have heard, Sir, with how many deeds I made Polinesso sure of my love, and you see plainly whether by such causes he was bound to hold me dear or not. Now hear of the recompense I received; see the great reward for my great merit; see whether, because she loves much, a woman can hope to be loved always (v 72).

And the last line of her narration is, 'Ve' come Amor ben chi lui segue, tratta!' – 'See how Love treats even those who follow him' (v 74).

The ironic force of Dalinda's 'Vedi' depends on our feeling that what she asks us to see is perfectly clear and obvious. And it is precisely the clarity of dramatic events that produces the particular wit and sadness of the episode. The complexities of love are expressed not by any single action or character, but by the way in which the characters' various desires, purposes, and actions – each of them lucid and easy to account for – become entangled with each other.

(54–7)

The nature of Spenser's use of these materials can be seen in the first two stanzas of Phedon's narration:

> It was a faithlesse Squire, that was the sourse
> Of all my sorrow, and of these sad teares,
> With whom from tender dug of commune nourse,
> Attonce[1] I was vpbrought, and eft[2] when yeares
> More rype vs reason lent to chose our Peares,
> Our selues in league of vowed loue we knit:
> In which we long time without gealous feares,
> Or faultie thoughts continewd, as was fit;
> And for my part I vow, dissembled not a whit.

> It was my fortune commune to that age,
> To loue a Ladie faire of great degree,
> The which was borne of noble parentage,
> And set in highest seat of dignitee,
> Yet seemd no lesse to loue, then loued to bee:
> Long I her seru'd, and found her faithfull still,
> Ne euer thing could cause vs disagree:
> Loue that two harts makes one, makes eke[3] one will:
> Each stroue to please, and others pleasure to fulfill.

(II iv 18–19)

1 together   2 afterwards   3 also

Where Ariosto gives us dramatic characters, each separate from the others, pursuing his own desires, and caught up in his own schemes and thoughts, Spenser produces images and formulas that express complete unity. Instead of showing the behavior of two people to each other, he describes feelings or purposes they share. In these stanzas it is quite literally true that 'Loue that two harts makes one, makes eke one will.'

Our sense of dealing with a single mind, rather than with three different characters, is brought out in the next stanza, which draws the third leg of the triangle:

My friend, hight *Philemon*, I did partake[1]
Of all my loue and all my priuitie;
Who greatly ioyous seemed for my sake,
And gratious to that Ladie, as to mee,
Ne euer wight, that mote so welcome bee,
As he to her, withouten blot or blame,
Ne euer thing, that she could thinke or see,
But vnto him she would impart the same:
O wretched man, that would abuse so gentle Dame.

(II iv 20)

Naming a character ordinarily gives him a separate identity, but Philemon means simply 'my friend', and he is very much the sharer 'of all my loue and all my priuitie.' The stanza describes dramatic behavior, but it seems like that of a lover to his lady. The final exclamation is one that would be made about a lover, and it has hardly any connexion with the narrative action. It is Phedon who is abused by Philemon, who can be said to abuse Claribella only in the sense that he speaks injuriously of her. Even if this meaning of the word were available to Spenser,[2] we do not limit ourselves to it as we read the line. The resonance of 'abuse' comes from its participation in a formulaic exclamation, and not from the way it corresponds to dramatic action.

Even when Philemon deceives Phedon, dramatic personages and events are drawn together into the phenomena of a single mind. At first Philemon says only that he has heard that Claribella

Had both distaind her honorable blood,
And eke the faith, which she to me did bynd;

1 make a sharer of
2 O.E.D. (sense 7) cites *Othello* v i 123 as the first use in this sense.

And therfore wisht me stay, till I more truth should fynd.

(II iv 22)

The brevity of Philemon's revelation is in key with his recommendation of caution. But the next stanza produces a sudden increase in emotional intensity by means of an initial formula that takes us directly into the feelings of the jealous lover:

> The gnawing anguish and sharpe gelosy,
> Which his sad speech infixed in my brest,
> Ranckled so sore, and festred inwardly,
> That my engreeued mind could find no rest,
> Till that the truth thereof I did outwrest,
> And him besought by that same sacred band
> Betwixt vs both, to counsell me the best.
> He then with solemne oath and plighted hand
Assur'd, ere long the truth to let me vnderstand.

(II iv 23)

This stanza and a half provides a brief outline of one of the important movements in *Othello* – the friend's casual insinuation produces passionate suffering on the part of the hero, who then binds his friend to him in a pact of heroic resolve. The effect of this movement in Spenser's stanzas can best be seen by following the word 'truth'. When Philemon 'wisht me stay, till I more truth should fynd', the word referred to knowledge of external facts. By the middle of this stanza the truth seems to be something that will be produced from the efforts of Phedon's own mind. Hence Philemon's final assurance 'the truth to let me vnderstand' is not simply the office of an external agent. As in *Othello*, the friend's role is produced by the energies of the hero's own mind, and the false friend becomes inextricably part of him. We are not surprised, then, at the way Spenser renders Philemon's fulfilling his promise:

> Ere long with like againe he boorded[1] mee,
> Saying, he now had boulted[2] all the floure,
> And that it was a groome of base degree,
> Which of my loue was partner Paramoure:
> Who vsed in a darkesome inner bowre
> Her oft to meet: which better to approue,

[1] accosted   [2] sifted

He promised to bring me at that howre,
  When I should see, that would me nearer moue,
And driue me to withdraw my blind abused loue.

(II iv 24)

This is the very opposite of Polinesso's offer to Ariodante of ocular
proof. What Phedon will see is 'that would me nearer moue'. The
physical details that support this phrase do not constitute a dramatic
depiction of Claribella's misbehavior, but appear as a series of formulas, each of which suggests a disturbing quality of feeling. From the
coarse heartiness of 'boulted all the floure', we go to the social low-
ness of the groom, then to the suggestion of courtly sexuality in 'part-
ner Paramoure', and finally to the 'darkesome inner bowre' at the
center of the stanza. In the final phrase we are not conscious of what
Phedon has been blind to or what he has been abused by. 'Blind
abused loue' has an absolute force and directly suggests the power
and confusion of Phedon's feelings.

The difference between Ariosto's and Spenser's poetic realizations
of this story is evident, as one would expect, in their handling of the
hero's deception by the maid disguised as her mistress. Ariosto gives
a full description of Dalinda in Ginevra's clothes and a clear explanation of why Ariodante and Lurcanio would have been fooled by her
appearance (v 47–9). By contrast, here is Spenser's rendering of the
scene:

Eftsoones he came vnto th'appointed place,
  And with him brought *Pryene*, rich arayd,
  In *Claribellaes* clothes. Her proper face
I not descerned in that darkesome shade,
But weend it was my loue, with whom he playd.
  Ah God, what horrour and tormenting griefe
  My hart, my hands, mine eyes, and all assayd?
Me liefer were[1] ten thousand deathes priefe,[2]
Then wound of gealous worme, and shame of such repriefe.[3]

(II iv 28)

'But weend it was my loue, with whom he playd' seems a product not

1 I would have preferred
2 experience
3 reproach, reproof

of visual deception, but of the jealous lover's imagination. The preceding line and a half render the viewer's attempt to see, rather than the sight imposed on him, and the psychological energy that explodes in the second half of the stanza comes from the formulas that have been developed over the past several stanzas – 'rich arayd', which draws on the erotic glamor of Philemon's speech to Pryene (II iv 25–6), and 'that darkesome shade'.

Whereas in Ariosto's episode we are observers of a comedy and feel closest to Rinaldo and to Dalinda as she looks back over what happened, in Spenser we are made to feel the change in Phedon from trust and love to the torments of jealousy. But in what sense, then, is Spenser not simply dramatizing the experiences of the jealous lover; why do we say that he turns Ariosto's materials into lines and stanzas of poetry? When we look at the verse of the episode, we do not feel, as we do with Dalinda's self-mockery, that it expresses Phedon's dramatic presence as either hero or narrator. Richness of meaning is no more based on the fictional complexity of Phedon's feelings than it was based on narrative realities in 'O wretched man, that would abuse so gentle Dame'. Rather, poetic significance is constantly a function of the meanings inherent in formulaic lines of verse. The distinction we are making is apparent in the stanza preceding the one just quoted:

> The whiles to me the treachour did remoue
> His craftie engin, and as he had sayd,
> Me leading, in a secret corner layd,
> The sad spectatour of my Tragedie;
> Where left, he went, and his owne false part playd,
> Disguised like that groome of base degree,
> Whom he had feignd th'abuser of my loue to bee.
>
> (II iv 27)

'The sad spectatour of my Tragedie' could serve as the motto of the whole episode. The paradox of one person being both spectator and actor (for 'my Tragedie' means 'the tragedy of which I am the hero') awakens our recognition of the way in which Spenser, throughout the episode, has turned the external events that victimize Phedon into the active projections of his own mind. Especially after the inwardness of 'in a secret corner layd', we see the 'tragedy' as part of a complex psychological phenomenon – the mind feeling that it is about to do something dreadful and being helpless to stop itself. But Phedon himself – if indeed we feel his presence as the dramatized narrator – is not aware of the meanings that make this so resonant a line. To him 'my Tragedie' refers to an external event, and can only mean 'the (staged) action that was catastrophic to me'.

In the three concluding lines, on the other hand, fictional reference is exceptionally clear. The result is that the meaning of each line is impoverished, even though each contains a formula that Spenser has been at pains to establish and develop earlier in the episode. As we have already seen, 'abuse' is a crucial word in two earlier alexandrines; 'his owne false part' should draw support from several earlier phrases ('It was a faithlesse Squire', stanza 18; 'my falser friend', stanza 21; 'This gracelesse man for furtherance of his guile', stanza 25), and we have already seen how effective 'groome of base degree' (stanza 24) is as a poetic formula. But 'his owne false part playd' so unequivocally indicates an action here, especially when we see that it is part of a theatrical metaphor, and 'that groome of base degree' so directly points to a specific person, that we are unable to see in them anything but a fiction. What we miss is the way in which such formulas usually convey qualities of feeling – compare, earlier in the stanza, the way 'treachour' and 'His craftie engin' support 'in a secret corner layd'. In the final line, 'th'abuser of my loue' so clearly refers to the groom that other meanings do not come into play, and there is none of the resonance that we would have expected the phrase to have at this point.

Dramatic clarity robs Spenser's formulaic lines of the kind of potency that we find in the final, and most brilliant, passage of the episode. Phedon, 'chawing vengeance all the way', slays Claribella, but his vengeance turns to grief when Pryene confesses:

> Which when I heard, with horrible affright
> And hellish fury all enragd, I sought
> Vpon my selfe that vengeable despight[1]
> To punish: yet it better first I thought,
> To wreake my wrath on him, that first it wrought.
> To *Philemon*, false faytour[2] *Philemon*
> I cast[3] to pay, that I so dearely bought;

1 wrong, malice   2 villain, impostor   3 resolved

> Of deadly drugs I gaue him drinke anon,
> And washt away his guilt with guiltie potion.
> (II iv 30)

The first four lines are perfectly straightforward, and the run-on lines suggest genuine narrative movement. But 'To wreake my wrath on him, that first it wrought' is emphatically formulaic and sets the pattern for the rest of the stanza. Phedon means it simply as a circumlocution for Philemon, but in the most literal sense the person who first wrought wrath is the wrathful person himself. The line thus turns Phedon's proposed act of suicide into a moral formula, and with its tautology supported by alliteration, it brings out something important in the nature of wrath – its self-proliferation. The ideas of justice in the last four lines produce formulas that invert the earlier formulas of friendship, and that indicate, as much as they did, that Philemon and his crime are inseparable from Phedon's mind. The reciprocity of 'I cast to pay, that I so dearely bought' is not like that of 'an eye for an eye', because there is nothing external or measurable to exchange. Spenser's formula, with its unclear fictional references, expresses not the settling of a finite account, but the continual toll taken by a criminal passion – a point explicitly made by the rhetorical and moral reciprocity of the last line.

The matching of 'guilt' with 'guiltie potion' not only makes an analytic moral point. It also renders a quality of experience that is fully expressed in the next stanza:

> Thus heaping crime on crime, and griefe on griefe,
> To losse of loue adioyning losse of frend,
> I meant to purge both with a third mischiefe,
> And in my woes beginner it to end:
> That was *Pryene*; she did first offend,
> She last should smart: with which cruell intent,
> When I at her my murdrous blade did bend,
> She fled away with ghastly dreriment,[1]
> And I pursewing my fell[2] purpose, after went.
> (II iv 31)

1 grief, sorrow
2 fierce, savage

The first two lines – like 'guilt with guiltie potion' – heap words on words and render a sense of accumulating anguish. The climax and resolution of these griefs does not, however, take the form of the fiction that seems to be indicated by lines 3 and 4. 'In my woes beginner it to end' does not, as the reader thinks it must, refer to Phedon's suicide. It is of course quite implausible as a fictional reference to Pryene, made by Phedon in the role of dramatized narrator. The plausibility and poetic truth of the line lie in the way its meanings recoil on Phedon in the second half of the stanza. He cannot bring his woes to an end, but they do indeed end where they began – in himself. The outgoing energy that is expressed by 'That was *Pryene*', 'cruell intent', and 'my murdrous blade did bend' finds no object and manifests itself not in an action, but in the anguished feeling that has become the whole story of this episode. Phedon is literally pursuing not another character, but 'my fell purpose'. In the next stanza, the internal psychological action becomes an event in the poem:

> Feare gaue her wings, and rage enforst my flight;
> Through woods and plaines so long I did her chace,
> Till this mad man, whom your victorious might
> Hath now fast bound, me met in middle space,
> As I her, so he me pursewd apace,
> And shortly ouertooke: I, breathing yre,
> Sore chauffed[1] at my stay[2] in such a cace,
> And with my heat kindled his cruell fyre;
> Which kindled once, his mother did more rage inspyre.

(II iv 32)

Before Furor arrives, Phedon's feelings are described with personifications, and one might expect Furor's intervention simply to act out 'rage enforst my flight'. But the energies that are registered in almost every line manifest themselves most drastically not in the actions of Furor, but in Phedon's anger itself. Just at the point that Phedon is possessed by a passion, Spenser makes it explicit that this is a human reality, not simply a convention of allegorical narrative. 'Breathing yre' could not be an event in an allegorical fiction; it is a locution that directly renders wrathful feeling. It is Phedon who gives life to his captors – 'And with my heat kindled his cruell fyre' – and in the next

1 angered 2 restraint

stanza his story ends, not with the personifications of Furor and Occasion, but with the passions of grief and fury:

> Betwixt them both, they haue me doen to dye,[1]
> Through wounds, and strokes, and stubborne handeling,
> That death were better, then such agony,
> As griefe and furie vnto me did bring;
> Of which in me yet stickes the mortall sting,
> That during life will neuer be appeasd.
> When he thus ended had his sorrowing,
> Said *Guyon*, Squire, sore haue ye beene diseasd;
> But all your hurts may soone through temperance be easd.
>
> (II iv 33)

The 'mortall sting' that sticks in Phedon has been made to seem so
relentless and ineradicable, that one is rather surprised at the offer of
relief held out by Guyon. The question is whether any human act can
ease the kind of anguish Phedon has undergone. This seems to be a
moment when Spenser allows simple moral categories to take over the
complex realities rendered in his verse. But there is nothing in the
Palmer's first words to suggest that he fails to understand the psychological reality that has been presented:

> Then gan the Palmer thus, Most wretched man,
> That to affections does the bridle lend;
> In their beginning they are weake and wan,
> But soone through suff'rance grow to fearefull end;
> Whiles they are weake betimes with them contend:
> For when they once to perfect strength do grow,
> Strong warres they make, and cruell battry bend
> Gainst fort of Reason, it to ouerthrow:
> Wrath, gelosie, griefe, loue this Squire haue layd thus low.
>
> (II iv 34)

'To affections does the bridle lend' may be a commonplace image,
but it perfectly brings out both sides of Phedon's tragedy – that he let
himself be carried away, there was some fault of will, and yet the
affections have an independent energy of their own. The word
'suff'rance' embraces the same double idea of moral permission and

[1] put to death

helplessness. The Palmer's moralizing is genuinely impressive, because it is based on his recognition of the power of the internal forces with which man must deal. Though we are told to deal with passions while they are weak, our 'contending' with them is made to seem inherently like heroic struggle. The Palmer does not appeal to the 'fort of Reason' until it emerges from the verse as the proper object, so to speak, of the affections' 'strong warres' and 'cruell battry'.

When we stop and think about it, it is surprising that the Palmer speaks only of psychological struggles and says not a word about the murders Phedon committed. But in fact we have to stop and step back from the verse to realize this, because the transformation of actual crimes into psychological disasters has occurred some stanzas before. In Ariosto, the death of Ginevra would have made the episode an irredeemable tragedy. But when Phedon says, 'Of which in me yet stickes the mortall sting, | That during life will neuer be appeasd,' he refers to the passions of grief and fury, and not to what he has done. One could hardly hope for anything more thoroughgoing by way of transforming narrative materials. The effect in the poetry is that Spenser can give a more severe and fearful rendering of the passions than Ariosto does, and at the same time can hold out the possibility of averting disaster by an act of temperance. This occurs in the next stanza of the Palmer's speech:

> Wrath, gealosie, griefe, loue do thus expell:
> Wrath is a fire, and gealosie a weede,
> Griefe is a flood, and loue a monster fell;
> The fire of sparkes, the weede of little seede,
> The flood of drops, the Monster filth did breede:
> But sparks, seed, drops, and filth do thus delay;
> The sparks soone quench, the springing seed outweed,
> The drops dry vp, and filth wipe cleane away:
> So shall wrath, gealosie, griefe, loue dye and decay.

(II iv 35)

After the first line, one perhaps expects an instruction to perform some external or psychological action – for example, 'Whiles they are weake betimes with them contend.' Instead this stanza takes the basic idea of catching the passions when they are weak, and by putting it into a special schematic form, directly creates a psychological action.

The basic device of the stanza is simply the continual transferring of
attention to new sets of terms. The four terms listed in line 1 are metaphorically equated with four new terms, which then become the
realities with which the stanza is concerned. They in turn generate four
new terms and the process is repeated. As we follow this process, the
passions and their awesome metaphoric equivalents turn into their
small beginnings; hence in lines 7 and 8, temperance becomes an easy
and even natural process, and the imperative 'expell' in the first line
turns into the declarative 'dye and decay' in the last. Only then does
Guyon, in the last stanza of the episode, give real instructions to Phedon:

> Vnlucky Squire (said *Guyon*) sith thou hast
> Falne into mischiefe through intemperaunce,
> Henceforth take heede of that thou now hast past,
> And guide thy wayes with warie gouernaunce,
> Least worse betide thee by some later chaunce.
> But read how art thou nam'd, and of what kin.
> *Phedon* I hight (quoth he) and do aduaunce
> Mine auncestry from famous *Coradin*,
> Who first to rayse our house to honour did begin.
>
> (II iv 36)

By being purged of the passions that so dreadfully transformed him,
Phedon becomes a man again, and the sign of his restored humanity
is his being named for the first time. It is a wonderful gesture with
which to conclude the episode. But considering our interests in this
chapter, what should most arouse our wonder is the way the easing of
Phedon's hurts was accomplished. Nothing, of course, has happened
to him dramatically. It is the reader's mind which, simply by following
the devices of the next to last stanza, enacts the process of being
purged of passion. The climax of the episode is not an action at all,
but a rhetorical scheme, a formal arrangement of words – precisely a
stanza of poetry, and nothing else.

(59–69)

Roger Sale

from *Reading Spenser*   1968

We may not, as we read, think of each book [of *The Faerie Queene*] as
a unit, but because each book introduces us to a new set of characters,
beginning to read each book gives a new sense of starting out. The
subject – human life in the universe – does not change, but the emphasis
does. This means that there must be something tentative about our
reading in the early cantos of each book. We know we are being told
all we need to know at every moment, but none the less, if Spenser's
vision did not become clearer as we read, there would be no point in
our going on. For instance, the first two books have their comic moments, but nothing on the scale of Britomart's scenes with Glauce.
We may, coming on these, even after the comic moments in Canto i,
feel we are not reading rightly if we find them amusing. Or, to take a
smaller example, when Arthur and Guyon set off after Florimell in
Canto i, Spenser pauses to praise the constant mind of Britomart, who
does not give chase. It is fair to ask if this implies criticism of Arthur
and Guyon. Or, in the instance with which we began, we may not
know how much weight to give Merlin's trancing vision of the future
beyond Elizabeth. We 'see' what is 'there', but often we may not
know what to make of what is seen. Probably the only decent reply to
this puzzlement is to say that if the matter is important Spenser will
make it important by folding it into the fabric of his vision in what
follows. As we read, if we cannot tell how strongly we are to interpret something, the best thing to do is to read on. If this is so, then the
comic scenes do matter because there is a whole string of them, and
each one makes it clearer that the fires, pains, and confusions of love do
not, or do not yet, cause Spenser the alarm they seem to cause the
characters themselves. At first sight we can say that loving and wanting
are comic to the extent that they blind or debilitate. But, on the
same score, Spenser's praise of Britomart does not imply strong criticism of Arthur or Guyon, and Merlin's trance is not as important as
Merlin's whole 'placing' of Britomart's predicament by means of
historical vision.

Coming out on the other side of that vision we find that the
comedy has been lost. Britomart sets out after the man whose face

appeared in the glass and we return to Faerie Land where Britomart takes leave of the Red Cross Knight. Nothing has happened to them since we left them in the middle of Canto ii, but the intervening flashback has happened to us. We now have a double vision of Britomart. On the one hand, because of Merlin's prophecy, she is a champion, a shining image, and so Spenser praises her:

> Yet these, and all that else had puissaunce,[1]
> Cannot with noble *Britomart* compare,
> Aswell for glory of great valiaunce,
> As for pure chastitie and vertue rare,
> That all her goodly deeds do well declare.
> Well worthy stock, from which the branches sprong,
> That in late yeares so faire a blossome bare,
> As thee, O Queene, the matter of my song,
> Whose lignage[2] from this Lady I deriue along.
>
> (III iv 3)

But that image of power, chastity, virtue, and historical triumph cannot change the 'facts' of Britomart's condition, and so we come back to the lovesick girl, pathetic now and unprotected, as it were, by the confidence of Spenser's earlier comedy:

> And the deepe wound more deepe engord her hart,
> That nought but death her dolour mote depart.
> So forth she rode without repose or rest,
> Searching all lands and each remotest part,
> Following the guidaunce of her blinded guest,
> Till that to the sea-coast at length she her addrest.
>
> (III iv 6)

Because to the girl Spenser's image of her glory is only a daydream, as she comes to the coast, guided by Cupid her 'guest', it is not to knightly heroism or to the future that she turns, but to her sickness and loneliness:

> Huge sea of sorrow, and tempestuous griefe,
> Wherein my feeble barke is tossed long,

1 power
2 lineage

> Far from the hoped hauen of reliefe,
> Why do thy cruell billowes beat so strong ...
>
> (III iv 8)

But the answer that comes to her is Marinell, and what happens next is both heroic and destructive. Britomart is both immensely powerful and a pathetic victim, so that the double vision at the opening of the canto is easily and marvelously made one. As Marinell approaches:

> Her dolour soone she ceast, and on her dight[1]
> Her Helmet, to her Courser mounting light:
> Her former sorrow into suddein wrath,
> Both coosen passions of distroubled spright,
> Conuerting, forth she beates the dustie path;
> Loue and despight[2] attonce her courage kindled hath.
>
> (III iv 12)

On the one hand Britomart is large and powerful as she converts her sorrow into wrath and beats the dusty path. On the other hand she is helpless as love and malice kindle 'her' courage. We cannot say, then, who is responsible for what, exactly; Britomart acts, but love and 'despight' act on her. The result is courage, but of a kind that can only act blindly:

> As when a foggy mist hath ouercast
> The face of heauen, and the cleare aire engrost,
> The world in darkenesse dwels, till that at last
> The watry Southwinde from the seabord cost
> Vpblowing, doth disperse the vapour lo'st,[3]
> And poures it selfe forth in a stormy showre;
> So the faire *Britomart* hauing disclo'st[4]
> Her clowdy care into a wrathfull stowre,
> The mist of griefe dissolu'd, did into vengeance powre.
>
> (III iv 13)

On the one hand Britomart is superb and large, able to do as the

1 placed
2 anger
3 released, set free
4 revealed

heavens do. They feel the wind from the south and 'disperse the vapour lo'st', and she sees Marinell come and 'disclo'st | Her clowdy care into a wrathfull stowre'. On the other hand her power is only the tool of vengeance, and as she is a victim of love and malice, so into such a victim she turns Marinell. It would be a scary moment indeed were it not also so grand.

The knight threatens her and she pushes him aside:

> She shortly thus; Fly they, that need to fly;
> Words fearen babes. I meane not thee entreat
> To passe; but maugre[1] thee will passe or dy ...
> (III iv 15)

The knight rushes at her, but of course he has no chance; after two blows 'He tombled on an heape, and wallowd in his gore.' She rides on, gazing at the gold and pearls on the strond: 'But them despised all; for all was in her powre.' That line indicates praise for Britomart's being above earthly wealth, but it indicates also the cruel, haughty air that Britomart's lost and frustrating love has brought her to. The 'all' that is in her power is too much for her to bear. Thus, grand, heroic, lost, bitter, cruel, a victim but no longer a comic figure, Britomart leaves the poem and does not return until the ninth canto.

At this point Spenser turns to Marinell and Cymoent. Marinell is generically a type of the reluctant bachelor, mythically and mythologically a type of Achilles and a creature of the sea. But here, in Canto iv, what we see is quite different. The parallels are all with Britomart; both are victims, not of love but of destiny. As a character he is almost impossible to assemble. He appears before Britomart as a 'mightie man at armes', an achiever of 'great aduentures'. But then his name and parentage suggest something different: the famous earthly Dumarin was his father, and his mother is Cymoent, daughter of the sea god Nereus (thus the connexion with Achilles); his occupation is protector of the riches of the sea. All this suggests a quasi-mythic relation with the sea. Then again he has a third 'role', his destiny as told to Cymoent by Proteus, and this is only partly connected with the other two. In the story he is wounded, on the one hand, because of his and his mother's interpretation of Proteus' prophecy. Cymoent warns him every day

[1] in spite of

not to entertain the love of women; he does not, and yet he falls. But on the other hand he is wounded because Britomart, at the moment he arrives, is ready to turn her sorrow into wrath. Spenser is quite clear on this point: 'But ah, who can deceiue his destiny, | Or weene[1] by warning to auoyd his fate?' (III iv 27). This is what Marinell is doing here, in Canto iv; two knights collide, one deluded by a prophecy and the other uncured by a prophecy. Destiny rules, as it ruled Adonis, Malecasta and Britomart, in incomprehensible and often ruthlessly careless ways. More than anything else, Marinell, Britomart and Cymoent seem simply lost. Cymoent's lament after she discovers her wounded son, though on a different subject from Britomart's lament at the beginning of the canto, is equally the complaint of one buffeted by an unavoidable fate:

O what auailes it of immortall seed
To beene ybred and neuer borne to die?

(III iv 38)

This 'says' almost the opposite of what Britomart says earlier, but the two sound very much alike:

O do thy cruell wrath and spightfull wrong
At length allay, and stint[2] thy stormy strife,
Which in these troubled bowels raignes, and rageth rife.

(III iv 8)

To Britomart the pain of love leads to a plea for respite, while to Cymoent the pain of loss leads to a longing for an impossible death.

Marinell here, then, is one of a group of victims, and noting this fact shows how reading in sequence places a different emphasis from any derived from treating the story of Marinell as though the bits and pieces describing him over the course of three books were meant to be put together, as in a biography. Granted that there are hints here of a different, mythological function for Marinell, granted that he is tantalizing no matter how he is considered because he seems to demand a place in our sense of the poem larger than the few stanzas devoted to him here and there would suggest. We can grant this because later he will belong with the obviously important Florimell. But that is later, and here Florimell has not been introduced as part of his story. The

1 think   2 cease

Marinell that is important is the crowning figure of the end of Book
IV, not this further instance of a victim wandering and desperate
because tied to self. If we continue to read the poem as it comes,
Marinell's symbolic function will become clear in due time. Certainly
if we tried to find the magnificent Marinell that 'gins to spread his
leafe before the faire sunshine' (IV xii 34) in the cloudy knight on the
strond, we would be insisting on making the poem give back what
we gave to it.

A fit sequel to this episode is the splitting up of Guyon, Timias, and
Arthur, and Arthur's scene with the Night. For here, as part of a story
that has no narrative connexion to those of either Britomart or
Cymoent, we encounter a third complaint against large and obdurate
forces. Arthur chases Florimell all day but loses sight of her as night
falls, and the prince lies down to sleep: 'The cold earth was his couch,
the hard steele his pillow':

> But gentle Sleepe enuyde him any rest;
> In stead thereof sad sorrow, and disdaine
> Of his hard hap did vexe his noble brest,
> And thousand fancies bet[1] his idle braine . . .
>
> (III iv 54)

To a reader reading along and not finding anything very remarkable,
the first line above may not seem extraordinary, and certainly one can
find many instances in *The Faerie Queene* where Spenser has something
happen like what happens here. That sleep is gentle is hardly a surprise, but that gentle sleep should envy perhaps is. There is nothing
gentle about what sleep is doing to Arthur here: because it envies
Arthur any rest, sorrow and disdain vex his breast. The adjective has
nothing to do with the particular activity of the noun it modifies;
sleep is gentle, we know, because it refreshes, relaxes, and quiets the
sleeper, but here it is envious. The epithet is not idly used, for the
whole point is that sleep would be gentle if it did not envy, but
because it does, a thousand fancies beat Arthur's brain and make it
idle. In such a world it is perfectly appropriate that Arthur should
blame the night for what has happened. There is perhaps no more
'point' to Arthur's complaint than there is to Britomart's or Cymoent's,
but that we are moving on none the less becomes clear after the complaint is over:

1 beat

> Thus did the Prince that wearie night outweare,
> In restlesse anguish and vnquiet paine:
> And earely, ere the morrow did vpreare
> His deawy head out of the *Ocean* maine,
> He vp arose, as halfe in great disdaine,
> And clombe vnto his steed. So forth he went,
> With heauie looke and lumpish pace, that plaine
> In him bewraid[1] great grudge and maltalent:[2]
> His steed eke seem'd t'apply his steps to his intent.

(III iv 61)

If we tried to paraphrase this stanza we might then be able to see how much is here that we would have to leave out. 'The night passed and before dawn Arthur arose, half disdainful but born down by the loss of Florimell.' We could, of course, give a closer paraphrase than that. But it could hardly do justice in any event to 'Thus did the Prince that wearie night outweare.' In one sense it is Arthur who is weary and worn out; the preceding stanzas of lament have shown this. But the sentence says he wore out the night and made it weary, and, if this seems like nonsense, we need look no further than three lines down to see that it is not. For Arthur 'vp arose, as halfe in great disdaine', and we see that though the night has worn out Arthur so that he proceeds 'With heauie looke and lumpish pace', it is also true that he has worn out the night and is 'halfe in great disdaine' of it. Arthur's lament becomes something both self-defeating because it wears him out and heroic because it wears out the night. The forces outside Arthur have done their worst, and they have done much. But in his lament he becomes heroic because he has done all that can be done to combat an eternal foe that brings with it 'The drearie image of sad death' (III iv 57). He has not won, for night will return and once again will hide 'traiterous intent, | Abhorred bloudshed, and vile felony' (58). But night has not won either, for even before the morrow uprears his dewy head, Arthur too rises to seek and to rescue for another day. Of course Arthur need be aware of none of this; his stoic heroism implies no conscious effort.

So the three major episodes in canto iv fall into sequential place and

1 revealed
2 malevolence

show us that what we are concerned with is not an ideal of chastity but with the attempts of mortals to act in a world far beyond their power to control or understand. It is a world without enemies; the struggles with paynim knights and with allegorical monsters of the first two Books have been replaced by shadowy encounters that first are comic, then pathetic, and then, for a moment, heroic. Adonis and Malecasta are victims, so too in her totally comic way, is Glauce, and of course so are the figures that dominate this canto. In order to create this world Spenser could not use large and clearly allegorical pageants. Rather, the allegory, if it can be so called, takes place in the sudden appearance of sprite-like figures like 'gentle Sleepe', or the 'Love and despight' that kindled Britomart's courage, or 'the black vele of guilty night' behind which Malecasta steals up on Britomart. The forces at work in the world to confuse and defeat are all named with abstractions, and in that sense they are like the obvious allegorical constructions, but all are hidden and unknown in their effects and actions.

Having paused thus long to summarize, we might make at least a preliminary comment on the qualities of Spenser's verse. Canto iv is a good one to discuss precisely because it contains none of the large set-pieces which are usually cited as evidence of Spenser's excellence as a poet. Anyone who has read this far in the poem knows that often Spenser does not 'write very well', and F. W. Bateson once said that anyone who could cheerfully concede this could not really go on to claim greatness for The Faerie Queene.[1] Examples of sloppy writing are not hard to find:

> His vncouth shield and straunge armes her dismayd,
> Whose like in Faery lond were seldome seene,
> That fast she from him fled, no lesse affrayd,
> Then of wilde beastes if she had chased beene . . .
>
> (III iv 51)

This surely has more faults than it does lines. Each clause has a quite unnecessary and awkward inversion, and the last line – 'Then of wilde beastes if she had chased beene' – borders on total incompetence. The diction has its share of clichés – 'seldome seene', 'fast . . . fled', 'wilde beastes' – and the rest is not far above that level. Perhaps the only fact

1 Essays in Criticism, 1953, vol. 2, pp. 6–7.

worth noting is the 'vncouth shield and straunge armes' that have taken the place of the 'mightie shild' and 'blade all burning bright' that Arthur has worn previously.

Now compare these lines with some three stanzas earlier:

> So beene they three three sundry wayes ybent.
> But fairest fortune to the Prince befell,
> Whose chaunce it was, that soone he did repent,
> To take that way, in which that Damozell
> Was fled afore, affraid of him, as feend of hell.

(III iv 47)

The first three lines here are also clogged with inversions that seem more the result of Spenser's need for a rhyme than of any desire to stress the verbs. The diction and meter are as flat and unremarkable as in the first passage. But here something is really happening. On the one hand, finding the path on which Florimell is flying is the Prince's 'fairest fortune'; on the other, having found the right way, 'soone he did repent'. Here 'repent' seems to mean only 'feel sad', and Arthur soon 'repents' because Florimell will not stop at his call and soon night comes. Yet, of the three, Arthur has the 'fairest fortune'. His is the luck of one who really is chasing beauty; Spenser is not praising Arthur here, but he is insisting that no matter what Arthur himself feels, his fortune is fairer than Guyon's or Timias'. There is something intrinsically fair in the chase regardless of the feelings it causes or the success of the venture. Spenser stands over Arthur and shows the values that Arthur himself, because of his consciousness of his sadness and failure, cannot know.

As phrases 'fairest fortune' and 'soone he did repent' are as flat and uninteresting as any in the poem, but their juxtaposition makes them momentarily quite different. It is almost always by means of such effects that Spenser makes himself clear, and what he makes clear is seldom a simple matter. Few readers would pay attention to this juxtaposition without forewarning, but what it seeks to express, after all, is what the whole Canto has been saying in different ways, and it is by means of the gradual accumulation of such things that Spenser gains his 'meaning'. In a poem of such even tones, Spenser has no way of giving one stanza or episode much weight over another, and so he indicates almost silently what his world is like at the level of word and phrase in most of the stanzas. The slow movement of the poem is reflected in the slow movement of the stanzaic form, and any effort to break into the even flow would probably fail because the form would make it simply seem feverish or sluggish. Spenser's few apostrophes are allowed to dwindle away in their force before one stanza is over, and stand not as guideposts to the 'meaning' but as momentary responses to the immediate situation. Whatever sense of Faerie Land we have, therefore, is almost bound to be the result of Spenser's successful working with the same materials that he in other places uses mechanically. We can see it as great or even good poetry only after we see what it is doing.

Perhaps we should not say that the verse is only functional, but what is good, measured by the standards of other long poems like *Paradise Lost* and *The Prelude*, is also usually flat. Both Milton's and Wordsworth's poems, though much shorter than *The Faerie Queene*, have many more memorable lines. But the fact that the poetry is often embarrassing to read aloud need not be a definitive judgement. We must read him slowly, not relaxing our sense of what good poetry should be, judging individual passages as well as the whole, but also trying to see if and how passages contribute to the whole. This is why our best terms of praise for his poetry often are 'accurate' and 'precise'. When he is good he is simply being very clear about mysterious matters; he is precise in showing us what Arthur does and does not know, and so, in one more way, he is being precise about Faerie Land. The effect has to be cumulative because there is no other way; no single passage can give the same brooding and wondering quality that long stretches and the whole poem give.

So, as a preliminary judgement, let us say that Canto iv has no great things in it, nothing that would seem remarkable to anyone who has not read at least the first three cantos of Book iii. We will come later to passages more clearly great than anything here, but we cannot read the poem just for these because they, like everything else, take on their particular coloration from what precedes them. In coming to terms with the more ordinary stuff of the poem we face the major difficulties most unsympathetic readers have, and for now we can say that for most of the poem Spenser claims no more for his verse than that it does its job, and that its job is to show the bases of his certainty about a world in which the characters may be lost but in which Spenser knows what life really is. What life 'really is', furthermore, is only tangentially related to the large abstract nouns like 'Chastity' which nominally outline his poem. Here life 'really is' being lost or being made a victim, finding the path between self and committed goals beset with obscurities and obstacles. As yet in the poem no one has been able to move outside himself and towards the goal without an act of violence.

In Canto v more is possible. At the beginning the dwarf Dony appears, and we have, after a canto of laments and unseen encounters, a conversation. Dony identifies the fleeting maid as Florimell and Marinell as her love. Here Marinell's commitment against women is seen as something more purposeful than it did a canto earlier, for here he is refusing a particular girl and not, as before, simply being unaware of the unknowable fact that Britomart is a girl. Arthur vows never to forsake Dony or the chase for Florimell, thinks for a moment of his squire Timias, and suddenly Spenser is focusing on Timias and his fight with the brothers of the forester who had been (but is no longer) chasing Florimell. The battle is rather standard, but at its conclusion we have moved another step towards a new sense of possibility:

> So mischief fel vpon the meaners crowne;
> They three be dead with shame, the Squire liues with renowne.
>
> (III v 25)

The 'shame' and the 'renowne' are not really public, and are only values intrinsic to the battle itself, but Timias' 'renowne' does indeed move us into a social world. The first to 'know' Timias' bravery is Spenser himself:

> Now God thee keepe, thou gentlest Squire aliue,
> Els shall thy louing Lord thee see no more,
> But both of comfort him thou shalt depriue,
> And eke thy selfe of honour, which thou didst atchiue.
>
> (III v 26)

Spenser breaks in so seldom that when he does, even mildly as here, the effect insists that a moment not pass unnoticed. What we need to be told here, simply, is that Timias, filled though he has been with wrath and vengeance, is none the less the 'gentlest Squire aliue', one capable of comforting his long departed lord simply by staying alive. On the one hand the victim has become more frail than Arthur or Britomart were earlier, but on the other hand frailty is itself a kind of pathetic virtue, so that living itself becomes a source of honor.

For one in such condition Providence extends relief, and the woods suddenly become those in which Belphoebe hunts:

> Shortly she came, whereas that woefull Squire
> With bloud deformed, lay in deadly swownd:
> In whose faire eyes, like lamps of quenched fire,
> The Christall humour stood congealed rownd;
> His locks, like faded leaues fallen to grownd,
> Knotted with bloud, in bounches rudely ran,
> And his sweete lips, on which before that stownd[1]
> The bud of youth to blossome faire began,
> Spoild of their rosie red, were woxen pale and wan.
>
> (III v 29)

There has been nothing quite like this earlier in Book III. The victims Malecasta, Britomart, Marinell, Cymoent, and Arthur, have been simply pale, poisoned, disagreeable, complaining. Here we are not told that he 'wallowd in his gore', but that the blood knotted his hair into bunches of falling leaves, not only that his lips were pale, but that they had had on them the bud of blossoming youth. The victim is seen; providentially, Timias is not alone. Cymoent presumes Marinell is dead and laments, but Belphoebe is filled with soft passion and, in a beautiful locution, 'She cast to comfort him with busie paine' (III v 31). The huntress feels 'the point of pitty' and, pained herself, makes busy to comfort him. Given the lonely pain that has been modified hitherto only by the helpless ministrations of Glauce and the 'irrelevant' vision of Merlin, this is a moment of great achievement, and Spenser celebrates it quietly:

> His double folded necke she reard vpright,
> And rubd his temples, and each trembling vaine;
> His mayled habericon[2] she did vndight,[3]
> And from his head his heauy burganet[4] did light.[5]
>
> (III v 31)

---

1 assault   2 sleeveless coat of mail   3 took off
4 steel cap   5 remove

The wound cannot be simply healed, but the burden can be lightened;
she dresses his wound and slowly he regains consciousness:

> He vp gan lift toward the azure skies,
> From whence descend all hopelesse[1] remedies:
> Therewith he sigh'd, and turning him aside,
> The goodly Mayd full of diuinities,
> And gifts of heauenly grace he by him spide,
> Her bow and gilden quiuer lying him beside.
>
> (III v 34)

Because the gift of nursing is divine, Timias makes the mistake
made by many readers and assumes that what he sees is also divine:

> Mercy deare Lord (said he) what grace is this,
> That thou hast shewed to me sinfull wight,
> To send thine Angell from her bowre of blis,
> To comfort me in my distressed plight?
>
> (III v 35)

We know already that 'Prouidence' 'doth for wretched mens reliefe
make way', but it is no angel who gives the relief:

> Thereat she blushing said, Ah gentle Squire,
> Nor Goddesse I, nor Angell, but the Mayd,
> And daughter of a woody Nymphe, desire
> No seruice, but thy safety and ayd;
> Which if thou gaine, I shalbe well apayd.
> We mortall wights whose liues and fortunes bee
> To commun accidents still open layd,
> Are bound with commun bond of frailtee,
> To succour wretched wights, whom we captiued see.
>
> (III v 36)

It does not matter at all that Belphoebe, in one sense, does not know
who she is. The lady here is only analogous to the goddess that con-
fronts Trompart in Book II, and were she in fact divine that poignancy
would be dissipated. Here we see the 'commun bond'. Belphoebe is
'like' the Belphoebe of Book II, 'like' Queen Elizabeth, even 'like' a

[1] unhoped for

personified image of virginal chastity. But here she is a ministering maid asserting the need of mortals to give succor and to stop the victim from being 'captive' – and in the context we have here, 'captive' means only 'alone'. Over and over in the succeeding stanzas it is not chastity or grace or regality that Spenser shows us, but human tenderness:

> Where when they saw that goodly boy, with blood
> Defowled, and their Lady dresse his wownd,
> They wondred much, and shortly vnderstood,
> How him in deadly case[1] their Lady fownd,
> And reskewed out of the heauy stownd.[2]
>
> (III v 38)

But we do not escape the pain, for if the common bond of frailty can be renewed, so too can the pain of love:

> O foolish Physick, and vnfruitfull paine,
> That heales vp one and makes another wound:
> She his hurt thigh to him recur'd[3] againe,
> But hurt his hart, the which before was sound . . .
>
> (III v 42)

At this point the scene ends and Spenser shows us two emblems of human fidelity, one shining and the other painful, as salves and alternatives to the lovesickness and frailty that are so clearly the common lot. The scene ends because the two emblems are not compatible in the narrative. First we have Timias' response to his wounding, the lyric choice to love his saviour silently and fatally:

> What can I lesse do, then her loue therefore,
> Sith I her dew reward cannot restore?
> Dye rather, dye, and dying do her serue,
> Dying her serue, and liuing her adore . . .
>
> (III v 46)

Such resolution does not in the least diminish the poison or the pain of

---

1 plight
2 peril, trouble
3 restored, recovered

impossible love ('Yet still he wasted, as the snow congealed'), but it does turn the plaintive loneliness of Britomart, Cymoent and Arthur into a kind of heroic virtue. Britomart asks that the pain cease because she seeks to avoid the implications of what has happened to her. But Timias accepts his fate and transforms the pain and the dying into a living service to his love.

Spenser then says that Belphoebe knows nothing of Timias' vow. When he adds that she 'did enuy' Timias the 'soueraigne salue' of her love, Spenser dissolves the narrative in order to praise virginity; she can hardly begrudge Timias what she does not even know he wants. But he has not dissolved the slowly forming bonds of the terms he has been using. The cordials Belphoebe used to heal Timias' wounds were herbs, panachaea and polygony. When Timias is rescued he is laid in a glade of myrtle and laurel, and his wound is dressed in salves. As the thigh heals the heart is wounded, but the cordials and salves are there too, and 'sweet'. Here Spenser makes Belphoebe's gift of love, which she denies him, something that does not wound or burn: 'that soueraigne salue'. But right in this stanza Spenser begins to move away from the immediate situation:

> But that sweet Cordiall, which can restore
> A loue-sick hart, she did to him enuy;[1]
> To him, and to all th' vnworthy world forlore
> She did enuy that soueraigne salue, in secret store.

(III v 50)

That the worthy Timias should suddenly be part of an 'vnworthy world' is not and cannot be a slight to him; the clause is there to define Belphoebe's virginity. It is not a grand or triumphant thing, not an asserted or militant chastity, nor is it virginity achieved by simple, prudent avoidance of the dart of love. Belphoebe's chastity is natural, and Spenser beautifully transforms her into an emblematic flower:

> That dainty Rose, the daughter of her Morne,
> More deare than life she tendered, whose flowre
> The girlond of her honour did adorne:
> Ne suffred she the Middayes scorching powre,
> Ne the sharp Northerne wind thereon to showre,
> But lapped[2] vp her silken leaues most chaire,[3]

1 grudge   2 folded   3 dear

When so the froward[1] skye began to lowre:
  But soone as calmed was the Christall aire,
She did it faire dispred,[2] and let to florish faire.

(III v 51)

At the beginning of the stanza Belphoebe and the rose are separate –
'More deare then life she tendered' – but then Belphoebe assumes the
powers of nature over the rose, folding it against sun and wind,
spreading it in 'the Christall aire'. There is nothing coy about lady or
flower, nothing anatomical about the images, yet what is conveyed is
a sense that what the rose does is a sexual activity natural to it. The
rose, the daughter of Belphoebe's morn, must be nourished, nurtured,
cherished, and if it is, we learn in the next stanza, it 'beareth fruit of
honour and all chast desire':

Faire ympes of beautie, whose bright shining beames
Adorne the world with like to heauenly light,
And to your willes both royalties and Realmes
Subdew, through conquest of your wondrous might,
With this faire flowre your goodly girlonds dight,[3]
Of chastity and vertue virginall,
That shall embellish more your beautie bright,
And crowne your heades with heauenly coronall,
Such as the Angels weare before Gods tribunall.

(III v 53)

Strictly speaking this is incompatible with all that has preceded.
Here women are not victims of a vision of love like Britomart, or of
lustful men like Florimell, but are subduers of the masters of the
world. It is thus imagined possible to live above what had been the
human lot – crowned by heaven, an angel before God's tribunal. Just
as the meeting of Timias and Belphoebe celebrates the acknowledgement of frailty, so this emblematic rendering of Belphoebe celebrates
a natural possibility above such frailty. Mortals can wear their flesh like
garlands as much as they can allow their flesh to victimize them with
pain and shame. Of course this wearing is not possible or desirable for
all – that goes without saying. Of course there is our by now distant

1 perverse
2 spread out
3 adorn

emblem of the fruitful love of Britomart and Artegall which had as its
key verb not 'embellish', but 'branch'. But that was prophecy and
this is human possibility so rare and lovely that it transforms Timias'
pain into heroic stoicism and itself touches the divine. We are indeed
ready for the splendors of the next canto.

Having moved from the aimless and destructive 'meetings' in the
fourth canto to the painful but moving meeting of Timias and
Belphoebe, having then moved from the mortal Belphoebe to a
quasi-divine image of her virtue, Spenser makes the next step – into
the mythic – easily. Here is the story of the conception of Marinell in
Canto iv:

> The famous *Dumarin*; who on a day
> Finding the Nymph a sleepe in secret wheare,[1]
> As he by chaunce did wander that same way,
> Was taken with her loue, and by her closely lay.
>
> (III iv 19)

It is difficult to imagine anything less joyous: Cymoent lay asleep,
Dumarin happened by, he lay with her. But here, at the beginning of
Canto vi, is another nymph lying asleep, this time Chrysogonee:

> Vpon the grassie ground her selfe she layd
> To sleepe, the whiles a gentle slombring swowne
> Vpon her fell all naked bare displayed;
> The sunne-beames bright vpon her body playd,
> Being through former bathing mollifide,[2]
> And pierst into her wombe, where they embayd[3]
> With so sweet sence and secret power vnspide,
> That in her pregnant flesh they shortly fructifide.
>
> (III vi 7)

We can see from this both how far we have come and how completely the place an event comes in the poem dictates Spenser's
rendering of it. In each tale a sleeping nymph, but in one the meeting
resembles that of Britomart and Marinell, while in the other we meet
'Great father he of generation'.

(75–97)

1 place   2 softened   3 suffused

Acknowledgements

For permission to use copyright material acknowledgement is made to the following:

For the extract from Walter Raleigh, *Milton*, to Edward Arnold (Publishers) Ltd and the Lyall Book Depot, India; for the extract from W. B. Yeats' Introduction to *Poems of Spenser* to Mr M. Yeats, Macmillan & Co. Ltd and the Macmillan Company of New York; for the extract from William Empson, *Seven Types of Ambiguity*, to Chatto & Windus Ltd, the author and New Directions Publishing Corporation; for the extract from C. S. Lewis, *The Allegory of Love*, to The Clarendon Press, Oxford; for the extract from D. A. Traversi's article to the editors of *Scrutiny*, the author and Cambridge University Press; for the extract from G. Wilson Knight, *Poets of Action*, to Methuen & Co. Ltd; for the extract from Hallett Smith, *Elizabethan Poetry*, to the President and Fellows of Harvard College; for the extract from C. S. Lewis, *English Literature in the Sixteenth Century*, to The Clarendon Press, Oxford; for the extract from Yvor Winters, *The Function of Criticism*, to Routledge & Kegan Paul Ltd and The Swallow Press Inc.; for the article by Alastair Fowler from *Review of English Studies* to the author and The Clarendon Press, Oxford; for the extract from Harry Berger Jr, *Form and Convention in the Poetry of Spenser*, ed. William Nelson, to Columbia University Press and the author; for the extract from Northrop Frye, *Fables of Identity*, to the University of Toronto Press and the author; for the lecture by Frank Kermode to The British Academy; for the extract from Rosemond Tuve, *Allegorical Imagery*, to Princeton University Press; for the extract from Martha Craig's article from *Elizabethan Poetry: Modern Essays in Criticism*, ed. Paul J. Alpers, to Oxford University Press Inc.; for the extract from Paul J. Alpers, *The Poetry of 'The Faerie Queene'*, to Princeton University Press; for the extract from Roger Sale, *Reading Spenser*, to Random House Inc. and the author.

Select Bibliography

Editions

Edwin A. Greenlaw, F. M. Padelford, C. G. Osgood *et al.* (eds.), *The Works of Edmund Spenser: A Variorum Edition*, 10 vols., John Hopkins University Press and Oxford University Press, 1932–49.

J. C. Smith (ed.), *Spenser's Faerie Queene*, 2 vols., Oxford University Press, 1909.

Ernest de Selincourt (ed.), *Spenser's Minor Poems*, Oxford University Press, 1910.

The texts from these two editions are reprinted in one volume, with glossary, as *The Poetical Works of Edmund Spenser*, Oxford University Press, 1912.

W. L. Renwick (ed.), *Complaints*, Scholartis Press, 1928.

W. L. Renwick (ed.), *Daphnaida and Other Poems*, Scholartis Press 1929.

W. L. Renwick (ed.), *The Shepherd's Calendar*, Scholartis Press, 1929.

Note: There is unfortunately no inexpensive edition of *The Faerie Queene* with a text that is both reliable and readable.

Bibliographies and Reference Works

Dorothy Atkinson, *Edmund Spenser: A Bibliographical Supplement*, John Hopkins University Press, 1937.

Frederic Ives Carpenter, *A Reference Guide to Edmund Spenser*, 1923; reprinted by Peter Smith, 1950.

Francis R. Johnson, *A Critical Bibliography of the Works of Edmund Spenser Printed before 1700*, 1933; reprinted in facsimile by Dawsons, 1967.

Henry Gibbons Lotspeich, *Classical Mythology in the Poetry of Edmund Spenser*, Princeton University Press, 1932; reprinted by Gordian Press and Octagon Books Inc., 1965.

Waldo F. McNeir and Foster Provost, *Annotated Bibliography of Edmund Spenser, 1937–1960*, Duquesne University Press, 1962.

Charles G. Osgood, *A Concordance to the Poems of Edmund Spenser*, 1915; reprinted by Peter Smith, 1963.

Charles H. Whitman, *A Subject-Index to the Poems of Edmund Spenser*, Russell & Russell, 1918.

Biography

Alexander C. Judson, *The Life of Edmund Spenser*, Johns Hopkins University Press, 1945.

Criticism

Paul J. Alpers (ed.), *Elizabethan Poetry: Modern Essays in Criticism*, Oxford University Press, 1967 (includes selections from the work, cited below, of Roche, Sale, Tuve and Woodhouse).

Paul J. Alpers, 'How to Read *The Faerie Queene*', *Essays in Criticism*, vol. 18, 1968, pp. 429–43.

Paul J. Alpers, *The Poetry of 'The Faerie Queene'*, Princeton University Press, 1967.

Josephine Waters Bennett, *The Evolution of 'The Faerie Queen'*, University of Chicago Press, 1942; reprinted 1960.

Harry Berger Jr, *The Allegorical Temper: Vision and Reality in Book II of Spenser's 'Faerie Queene'*, Yale University Press, 1957.

Martha Craig, 'The Secret Wit of Spenser's Language', in Paul J. Alpers (ed.), *Elizabethan Poetry: Modern Essays in Criticism*, Oxford University Press, 1967.

Robert Ellrodt, *Neoplatonism in the Poetry of Spenser*, Geneva: E. Droz, 1960.

William Empson, *Seven Types of Ambiguity*, first published 1930; second revised edition, Chatto & Windus and New Directions, 1947; reprinted by Penguin Books, 1953.

Angus Fletcher, *Allegory: The Theory of a Symbolic Mode*, Cornell University Press, 1964.

Alastair Fowler, 'Emblems of Temperance in *The Faerie Queene*, Book II', *Review of English Studies*, n.s. vol. 11, 1960, pp. 143–9.

Alastair Fowler, 'The Image of Mortality: *The Faerie Queene*, II i–ii', *Huntington Library Quarterly*, vol. 24, 1961, pp. 91–110.

Alastair Fowler, 'A New Critic on Spenser', *Essays in Criticism*, vol. 10, 1960, pp. 334–41. (A review of Berger's *Allegorical Temper*. The discussion it provoked will be found in *Essays in Criticism*, vol. 11, 1961, pp. 233–8, 480–81; and vol. 12, 1962, pp. 227–9.)

Alastair Fowler, *Spenser and the Numbers of Time*, Barnes & Noble and Routledge & Kegan Paul, 1964.

Northrop Frye, 'The Structure of Imagery in *The Faerie Queene*', *University of Toronto Quarterly*, vol. 30, 1960–61, pp. 109–27; reprinted in *Fables of Identity*, Harcourt, Brace, 1963, pp. 69–87.

Thomas M. Greene, 'Spenser and the Epithalamic Convention', *Comparative Literature*, vol. 9, 1957, pp. 215–28.

Edwin A. Greenlaw, *Studies in Spenser's Historical Allegory*, Johns Hopkins Press, 1932.

A. C. Hamilton, 'The Argument of Spenser's *Shepheardes Calender*', *Journal of English Literary History*, vol. 23, 1956, pp. 171–82.

A. C. Hamilton, *The Structure of Allegory in 'The Faerie Queene'*, Oxford University Press, 1961.

A. Kent Hieatt, *Short Time's Endless Monument: The Symbolism of the Numbers in Edmund Spenser's 'Epithalamion'*, Columbia University Press, 1960.

Graham Hough, *A Preface to 'The Faerie Queene'*, Duckworth and Norton, 1962.

Merritt Y. Hughes, 'Spenser's Acrasia and the Circe of the Renaissance', *Journal of the History of Ideas*, vol. 4, 1943, pp. 381–99.

Frank Kermode, 'The Cave of Mammon', in *Elizabethan Poetry* (Stratford-upon-Avon Studies 2), ed. J. R. Brown and B. Harris, 1960, pp. 151–73.

Frank Kermode, '*The Faerie Queene*, I and V', *Bulletin of the John Rylands Library*, vol. 47, 1964, pp. 123–50.

Frank Kermode, 'Spenser and the Allegorists', *Proceedings of the British Academy*, vol. 48, 1962, pp. 261–79.

G. Wilson Knight, 'The Spenserian Fluidity', *The Burning Oracle*, 1939, reprinted as *Poets of Action*, Methuen, 1968, pp. 3–16.

C. S. Lewis, *The Allegory of Love*, Oxford University Press, 1936.

C. S. Lewis, *English Literature in the Sixteenth Century*, Oxford University Press, 1954.

C. S. Lewis, *Spenser's Images of Life*, ed. A. Fowler, Cambridge University Press, 1967.

William Nelson (ed.), *Form and Convention in the Poetry of Edmund Spenser: Selected Papers from the English Institute*, Columbia University Press, 1961.

William Nelson, *The Poetry of Edmund Spenser*, Columbia University Press, 1963.

W. L. Renwick, *Edmund Spenser: An Essay on Renaissance Poetry*, St Martin's Press, 1925; reprinted by Methuen and Random House, 1965.

Thomas P. Roche Jr, *The Kindly Flame: A Study of the Third and Fourth Books of Spenser's 'Faerie Queene'*, Princeton University Press, 1964.

Roger Sale, *Reading Spenser: An Introduction to 'The Faerie Queene'*, Random House, 1968.

Hallett Smith, *Elizabethan Poetry: A Study in Conventions, Meaning, and Expression*, Harvard University Press, 1952.

Leo Spitzer, 'Spenser, *Shepheardes Calender, March*, ll. 61–114, and the Variorum Edition', *Studies in Philology*, vol. 47, 1950, pp. 494–505.

John Thompson, *The Founding of English Metre*, Columbia University Press, 1961 (chapter on *The Shepheardes Calender*).

D. A. Traversi, 'Revaluation: "The Vision of Piers Plowman"', *Scrutiny*, vol. 5, 1936, pp. 276–91; reprinted in F. R. Leavis (ed.), *A Selection from Scrutiny*, Cambridge University Press, 1968, vol. 2, pp. 227–40.

Rosemond Tuve, *Allegorical Imagery*, Princeton University Press, 1966.

Rosemond Tuve, *Elizabethan and Metaphysical Imagery*, University of Chicago Press, 1947.

Rosemond Tuve, '"Spenserus"', in M. MacLure and F. W. Watt (eds.), *Essays in English Literature from the Renaissance to the Victorian Age: Presented to A. S. P. Woodhouse*, University of Toronto Press, 1964, pp. 3–25 (on *The Ruins of Time*).

W. B. C. Watkins, *Shakespeare and Spenser*, Princeton University Press, 1950.

A. S. P. Woodhouse, 'Nature and Grace in *The Faerie Queene*', *Journal of English Literary History*, vol. 16, 1949, pp. 194–228; reprinted in Paul J. Alpers (ed.), *Elizabethan Poetry: Modern Essays in Criticism*, Oxford University Press, 1967.

Index

Extracts included in this anthology are indicated by bold page references.

the essay 'Of Poetry' (1690), in *Critical Essays of the Seventeenth Century*,
   ed. J. E. Spingarn (Bloomington, Indiana, 1957), Vol. III, p. 99 64, 87, 89
Tennyson, Alfred, Lord (1809–92) 70, 221
Terence (Publius Terentius Afer) (?195–159 B.C.) Roman comic dramatist 37
Theocritus (*c.* 310–250 B.C.) The father of pastoral poetry, most of whose
idylls (not all of which are bucolic) are written in literary Doric 30, 38–9,
75–6
Thirty-Nine Articles The officially established articles of faith of the
Church of England 257
Thomas, Dylan (1914–53) 290
Thomas à Kempis (1380–1471) Author of the immensely popular
devotional manual, *The Imitation of Christ* 173
Thomson, James (1700–48)
   Castle of Indolence 114
Three Proper and Witty Familiar Letters 35–7
Tintoretto, Jacopo (1518–94) Venetian painter. His biography by Carlo
Ridolfi (1642) was incorporated in the latter's collection of biographies of
Venetian artists (1648) 262
Titus Calpurnius ◊ **Calpurnius**
Tityrus Traditionally considered Virgil's pastoral pseudonym, because in
Eclogue 1, Tityrus is the shepherd whose farm is saved by the quasi-divine
youth (i.e. Augustus) in Rome 26, 33, 234–5, 238
Tolstoy, Leo (1828–1910) 299
Topoi Rhetorical or poetic commonplaces 270–71
Traversi, D. A. 181, 185, **212–22**
Trissino, Gian Giorgio (1478–1550) 257–8, 261–2
Tully ◊ **Cicero**
Turner, J. M. W. (1775–1851) English painter of romantic landscapes, in
whose defence Ruskin wrote *Modern Painters* (1843) 176
Tuscan The dialect of Tuscany (chief city, Florence), in which Dante wrote
The Divine Comedy; became the standard literary language of Italy 59
Tuscany 58 ◊ **Tuscan**
Tuve, Rosemond (1903–64) 19, 181–7, **305–21**

Ulysses 41, 83, 157
Upton, John (1707–60) His edition of *Faerie Queene* (1758) is the first with
full and scholarly annotation 64, 117, 293

Vaenius, Otho (Otto van Veen) (*c.* 1560–*c.* 1629) Dutch artist, teacher of
Rubens, illustrator of several emblem books 99
Valeriano, Pierio (1477–1558) Italian scholar, whose *Hieroglyphica* is an
encyclopedia of arcane symbols 255n, 258n, 259, 261n
Valéry, Paul (1871–1945) French poet, essayist and critic 282
Valla, Lorenzo (*c.* 1406–57) Italian humanist 27
Vekke The name of the beloved's duenna in the Middle English translation
of the *Roman de la Rose* 206